O-umajirushi

A 17th-Century Compendium of Samurai Heraldry

Translated and Annotated by Xavid "Kihō" Pretzer

The Academy of the Four Directions
Cambridge, MA

First Edition

Scanned images of *O-umajirushi* are courtesy of the National Diet Library of Japan. These images may also be viewed on the National Diet Library website at: `http://dl.ndl.go.jp/info:ndljp/pid/1288484?__lang=en`.

Publisher's Cataloging-in-Publication Data

Pretzer, Xavid "Kihō"
    O-umajirushi : a 17th-century compendium of samurai heraldry / translated and
        annotated by Xavid "Kihō" Pretzer
      p. cm.
    ISBN 978-0-692-37740-6

    1. Heraldry—Japan
    2. Samurai—History
    3. Printing—Japan—History
    4. Japan—History—Tokugawa period, 1600–1868—Sources
    I. Title

    CR2552 .P7 2015
    929.60952
    Library of Congress Control Number: 2015932214

Main body text is typeset in Linux Libertine.
Japanese text is typeset in Hanazono Minchō (花園明朝).
Supplemental glyphs from GlyphWiki: `http://en.glyphwiki.org/` and Koin Hentaigana Gaiji Minchō (Koin変体仮名外字明朝): `http://www10.plala.or.jp/koin/koinhentaigana.html`
Typeset using the X⅃ᴇTᴇX typesetting system. Special thanks to Bruno Le Floch, whose code for reversing page order for part of a document was very helpful.

Contents

Acknowledgements

This book wouldn't be possible without all my Kickstarter backers. Thanks for all your support! It's been a crazy ride.

Thanks to Sarah Tuttle, Barbara Fleming, Susanna Pretzer, and James Pretzer for editing and feedback.

Thanks to Eric Obershaw of `http://www.jcastle.info/`, who kindly provided a variety of pictures from Japanese castles and quarries used in this book.

Thanks to Daniel Joseph for assistance with Classical Japanese translation.

Thanks to the National Diet Library of Japan, the Ōsaka Castle Museum, the Metropolitan Museum of Art, the Schøyen Collection, and other institutions that provided imaged for this book.

Thanks to Google Books and HaithiTrust whose book search services were invaluable in the research for this book.

A print from 1857 depicting the mid-16th-century Battle of Kawanakajima.
Library of Congress

Using this Book

This book is divided into four parts.

The first part, which immediately follows, is *O-umajirushi* **in Context**. It discusses the historic and literary context in which the book was created. It uses a blue thumb index tab (on the page edge) and is numbered with lowercase Roman numerals.

The second part is **About Mon**, which digs deeper into mon, the crests that feature heavily in Japanese heraldry. It continues on from *O-umajirushi* **in Context** with a blue thumb index tab and Roman numerals.

The third part, *O-umajirushi*: **Annotated Translation**, presents images of the original manuscript with accompanying translations, bibliographic notes, and supplemental information. To maintain the format of the original work, it is presented in right-to-left order. Thus, it starts near the back of the book and ends immediately after **About Mon**. To read it, turn to the end of the portion of the book with a red thumb index tab. Its page numbers use ordinary Arabic numerals. For an explanation of how to read the translation and annotations, see "Using this Translation" on page xxii.

Finally, at the end of the book there are appendices, an index, and other reference materials. This portion uses a yellow thumb index tab and is numbered with numbers prefixed with the letter 'B' (for "back matter").

For citations, this book uses numbers in superscript square brackets. These numbers refer to the corresponding entry in the Bibliography on page B19.

Images from historical books have a bibliography citation indicating source. Other images have a credit included in the caption. Detailed information on artifacts from museums can be found in the Included Images section on page B23. In some cases, I use images licensed under Creative Commons licenses. For those images, the license in abbreviated form is given in the caption, and more details are available in the Included Images section.

For updates and errata, please visit `http://o-umajirushi.xavid.us/`.

An 1854 screen depicting the Battle of Sekigahara, which happened in 1600, based on a 1620s screen. Banners are used extensively on the battlefield.
The Town of Sekigahara Archive of History and Cultural Anthropology

Another folding screen showing the Battle of Sekigahara, also painted in the 19th century, showing a different view of the battle.
The City of Gifu Museum of History

O-umajirushi in Context

As samurai families rose and fell during the constant battles of Sengoku period (1467–1590) Japan, the system of heraldry for identifying individuals became increasingly complex and varied. *O-umajirushi* (御馬印) is a groundbreaking compendium, first published circa 1624–1644, that records the heraldry of the time in great detail. It showcases the banners and other identifying heraldic devices used by the commanders in the recently-concluded century of conflict and the samurai who ruled the various domains at the time, giving heraldry for 170 samurai in all.[36] It is the earliest known collection of Japanese heraldry printed in color, and also a pioneering work in multicolor Japanese woodblock printing, being the first known work of Japanese origin to combine multiple blocks of different colors to form a single image.[8, p. 22] By establishing this technique, it formed the seed for the full-color prints that would become widespread in the 18th century.

Historical Context

O-umajirushi was published at a pivotal point in Japanese history. The Tokugawa clan had just taken control over all Japan, with the last major opposition defeated in the Siege of Ōsaka in 1615. The preceding decades of conflict in and following the Sengoku period (1467–1590) had brought major upheaval to the social structures of Japan.

Upon seizing effective control of Japan in the Battle of Sekigahara, Tokugawa Ieyasu was eager to reward his supporters and restrict the power of those who had opposed him. He redistributed the various feudal domains, creating a new set of *daimyō* (大名, literally "great name"), hereditary feudal lords who ruled particular territories. This established the structure of Japan for the following two and a half centuries of peace under Tokugawa rule. Many of the people whose heraldry was recorded in *O-umajirushi* were these new daimyō: rather than serving as a neutral account of battle participants, it focused on those close to the Tokugawa regime, and thus those who had power under the Tokugawa shōgunate. Focusing on the winners was practical: these were the samurai lords who were still around and considered worthy of respect. There nevertheless may have been a political motive: propagating a book focusing on the social order created by the Tokugawa directly supported the legitimacy of the new regime.

Recording Heraldry

O-umajirushi was far from the only work recording Japanese heraldry. The earliest known compendium of Japanese heraldry, *Kenmon Shokamon* (見聞諸家紋; "Various Observed Family Crests"), was published around 1467–1470. Rather than recording whole banners and devices, this work focused specifically on mon, Japanese heraldic crests that would often appear on curtains and banners. It recorded 300 mon used by 260 families.[2, p. 42] Notably, it recorded several names for many mon, reflecting the sharing of mon of the time, in part due to such practices of daimyō bestowing mon on loyal supporters and of samurai adopting mon based on a favored shrine or temple. Later in the Sengoku period (1467–1590), other books of mon were published. *Kantō Maku Chūmon* (関東幕注文; "Eastern Japan Curtain Orders"), compiled by Uesugi Kenshin in 1561, contained the mon of 251 families. 1570 brought a similar collection, *Awa Koku Kika Maku Mon Hikae* (阿波国旗下幕紋控; "Awa Province Commanded Troops' Curtain Crest Notes"), which recorded the mon of those who served the Miyoshi family.[12, p. ii] [2, p. 42]

The dawn of the Edo period, when *O-umajirushi* was published, saw great interest in recording and documenting heraldry, and other similar works were produced around the same time. *Shoshō Kisei Zu* (諸将旗旌図; "Various Commanders' Banner and Flag Illustrations") was a book published in 1637 that documented the heraldry used by individual samurai in a very similar way to *O-umajirushi*. The key difference is that *Shoshō Kisei Zu* was printed in black and white, with a single woodblock pass, as opposed to the multi-pass color of *O-umajirushi*. Instead of using color, the colors of banners are labeled with text. Because it covers many of the same individuals as *O-umajirushi*, *Shoshō Kisei Zu* provides an interesting comparison point. Different contemporaneous depictions of the same banner helps identify which details were seen as significant and which were not, and additional labels present in *Shoshō Kisei Zu* help identify materials used in some devices.

While books and scrolls were practical ways of spreading information, they were not the only way heraldry was documented. A 17th-century folding screen in the collection of the Ōsaka Castle Museum called "Shoshō Shōki Zu Byōbu" (諸将旌旗図屏風; "Various Commanders' Flag and Banner Illustrations Folding Screen") illustrates banners in color in

 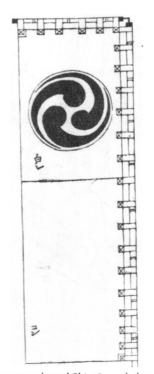 

Depictions from three different sources of tomoe, a comma-shaped Shintō symbol associated with Hachiman, god of archery and war. On the left is a banner with a three tomoe mon from O-umajirushi, *used by Matsudaira Nakazukasa (see p. 91). In the center is the same banner as shown in* Shoshō Kisei Zu, *published around the same time in 1637. It uses a separate circle around unconnected tomoe and has the bottom portion labeled navy blue, not black.[44, p. 1.32]. On the right is the same three tomoe mon as depicted in* Kenmon Shokamon, *published over 150 years earlier around 1470, with much the same shape as the* O-umajirushi *version.[20, p. 12]*

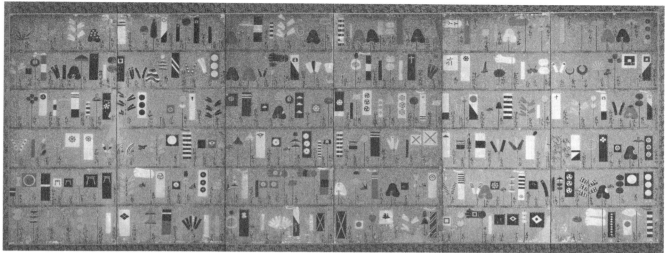

"Shoshō Shōki Zu Byōbu", a six-panel folding screen depicting the heraldry of 80 daimyō.
Ōsaka Castle Museum Collection

much the same way as *O-umajirushi*.[45][3, p. 298][31, p. 229] (There exist other similar screens with the same name.) Because a folding screen is generally kept at one residence and not easily carried when travelling, this was probably primarily a decorative item, rather than a reference. It has a style that shares elements with both *O-umajirushi* and *Shoshō Kisei Zu.* It contains almost the exact same set of daimyō as are contained in volumes 4, 5, and 6 of *O-umajirushi*, suggesting either that it was directly based on *O-umajirushi* or possibly that they were both based on some lost predecessor work. (This also suggests there was a lost companion screen that would correspond to volumes 1, 2, and 3.) There are enough differences in the heraldry shown, however, that it's clear that the screen is not a slavish copy of *O-umajirushi*. Either its creator was attempting to make corrections to *O-umajirushi*, or it's based on a predecessor work that *O-umajirushi*'s author was making corrections to. (For an example of a major graphical difference, refer to the section for Ota no Izumo-no-kami (see p. 142).)

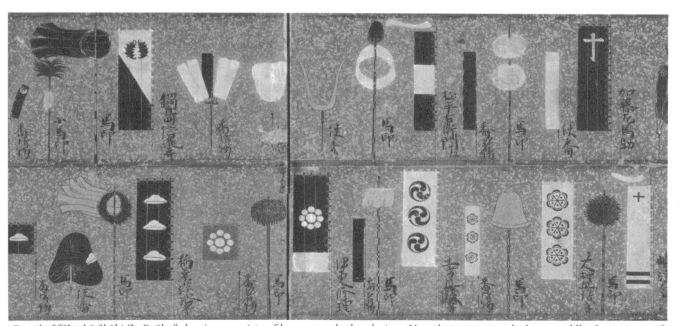

Detail of "Shoshō Shōki Zu Byōbu" showing a variety of banners and other devices. Note the tomoe near the lower middle, drawn in a style similar to those in O-umajirushi.
Ōsaka Castle Museum Collection

As mon spread from being used by just samurai to usage by other social classes and printing continued to expand throughout the Edo period, many more books of samurai heraldry, called *bukan* (武鑑), were published. At the same time, a similar quantity of books focused specifically on the heraldry of merchants, actors, or prostitutes, called *monchō* (紋帳), were also produced.[6, p. 17] These non-samurai individuals did not have any need for or tradition of battlefield identification compelling them to focus on colorful banners. Instead designing banners, they used mon on their own as a personal symbol. Mon allowed for detail-oriented artistry, could be made small for embellishments on personal objects or large for architectural use, and could be used in whatever color scheme was most convenient or elegant for the purpose at hand. This made mon alone the subject of non-samurai books of heraldry, and over time the focus became more on the mon specifically for samurai as well. Mon books generally provided either written descriptions or monochrome drawings of the mon (with specific colors sometimes noted), rather than the full-color banner presentation of *O-umajirushi*.[7]

About *O-umajirushi*

The Story of *O-umajirushi*

The contextual information in *O-umajirushi* is pretty sparse, focusing on names, titles, and descriptions of banners and other devices. This minimalist approach when it comes to text raises many questions. When, exactly, was it published? Who wrote and printed it? Why was this particular list of individuals included, and why were they put in this order? What was its intended purpose? Contextual information from other sources hints at answers to these questions and at the story underlying the text.

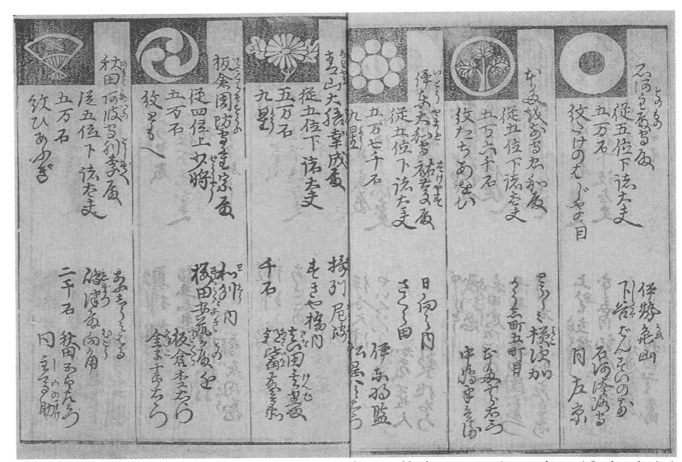

A bukan from 1658 showing just mon for samurai. The text notes information like domain income (measured in rice) for the individuals recorded.
Kokugakuin University

While presumably many copies of *O-umajirushi* were made and distributed at the time, it was a time of frequent fires, and like other books of the era most copies of *O-umajirushi* have been lost. In fact, until recently no complete copy of the original edition of *O-umajirushi* was known; individual volumes from different copies were known, but there was no known copy of Volume 6.[8, p. 23] The copy used in this translation, held at the National Diet Library of Japan, is the only known complete copy.

The scholarly consensus is that *O-umajirushi* was originally published in the Kan'ei (寛永) era, from 1624–1644.[8, p. 24] But *O-umajirushi* does not directly talk about its publication date within the text itself, and while theories have put its publication as early as 1629,[8, p. 24] no evidence from contemporary sources providing a specific date is known. So how can we date it more precisely? Well, we can identify the individuals included, and then look at other sources to determine when they acquired the titles *O-umajirushi* uses to refer to them. The clues that provide the clearest indication of date are the first two entries, which refer to Tokugawa shōguns by their posthumous names. From this, we know it was published after the death of Tokugawa Hidetada (entry 2 on p. 2) in 1632. Some scholars put its publication shortly after Hidetada's passing.[8, pp. 24–25] Identifying the more obscure individuals, there are quite a few samurai in *O-umajirushi* who received their titles during the Kan'ei era, but the latest such date according to my research is Kyōgoku Takakazu (entry 5 on p. 77), who received the title Lesser Assistant Director of the Ministry of Justice in 1639. Thus, the evidence I have been able to find suggests that *O-umajirushi* was published between 1639 and 1644. Given that it is possible that there is an alternate member of the Kyōgoku family who had the same title earlier, however, this is not completely certain. Since Takakazu's section is in the third volume, it's also possible that the first two volumes were published slightly earlier (though still after 1632).

Relatedly, we may wonder who wrote and published *O-umajirushi*. While woodblock printing generally involved teams of workers to do the actual carving, printing, coloring, and assembly, the consistency of the writing and art suggests that a single person created the designs the wood blocks were carved from, though it could have been a separate person from the person or team who actually gathered the necessary data. There is a second edition of *O-umajirushi*, published in 1656, that contains the same individuals and heraldry, but with a different foreword and afterword. The second edition's foreword clearly credits someone named Kyūan (久菴) with publishing it; however, the first edition contains no attribution. Kyūan is the pen name of Japanese mathematician Yoshida Mitsuyoshi (吉田光由), famous for publishing Jinkōki (塵劫記), the oldest extant Japanese book on mathematics, in 1627. Given that the two editions are almost identical, it initially seems

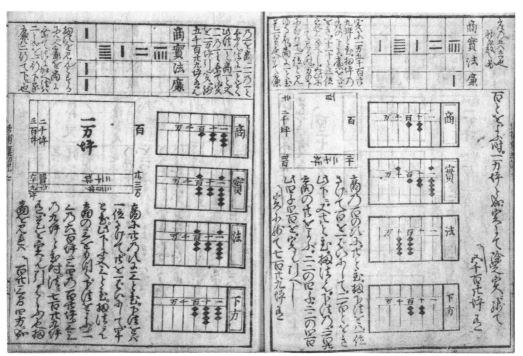

A page on abacus math from the 1689 revised edition of Yoshida Mitsuyoshi's Jinkōki.
National Diet Library

like they would have been published by the same person. However, the afterword to the second edition says "This *O-umajirushi* was previously published by a certain person, and a long time has passed. Elder Kyūan lamented that this book had not spread that much into the world, and visited the various families and recently completed an investigation..."[8, p. 25] This suggests that Kyūan is not the "certain person" who wrote the first edition, but rather Kyūan took it upon himself to publish a new edition to increase the reach of a book originally written by someone else. The style of the second edition is very close to the original, down to page numbering and the specific ways of writing characters in the captions, but that may just be because Kyūan was attempting a faithful copy. (In fact, he likely traced an original copy of *O-umajirushi* to prepare the blocks for the second edition.) The differences, particularly the color differences, may be a result of Kyūan's "investigation". This leaves the "certain person" behind the first edition unknown. Whoever it was must have had unusual dedication and resources to perform the necessary survey, create the various drawings, and print them in such quality using new and rare printing technology. Unfortunately, they did not see a need to sign their work, leaving this an unsolved mystery.

You may guess, from the previous discussion, that *O-umajirushi* was concerned primarily with the daimyō active in Japan when it was published, not the heroes of the preceding conflicts, many of whom had passed away. However, in actuality *O-umajirushi* contains a mix of both: in addition to present supporters of the Tokugawa, it portrays past allies and supporters as well, including individuals who died in battle or otherwise had passed away. The clearest example of this is the inclusion of Oda Nobunaga and his son Oda Nobutada, who had died dramatically in 1582 after being betrayed.[53, pp. 68–69] While this incident happened more than 50 years before *O-umajirushi* was published, they were still famous figures in Japan, and as allies of Tokugawa Ieyasu they may have been included to re-enforce the legitimacy of Tokugawa rule.

Given that individuals from different eras are included, you may wonder at the overall organization of *O-umajirushi*. The ordering is not completely random: Volume 1 starts with Tokugawa Ieyasu, the first Tokugawa shōgun, and his descendants, whereas Volume 4 starts with a focus on the unifiers of Japan who preceded Ieyasu and set the stage for Tokugawa rule. However, aside from these cases the organization is not made explicit. While individuals listed together often seem to have been active at similar times, there is no clear pattern based on chronology or societal position. The meaning behind the ordering of entries is one aspect of *O-umajirushi* that remains a mystery.

As for the purpose of *O-umajirushi*, that remains in the realm of conjecture. Given its use of ordinary quality materials such as mulberry paper, it was probably not intended as a gift to a lord nor to be distributed by a lord to his vassals, but was likely intended to be sold to well-off townspeople in the capital. Given its focus on Tokugawa supporters, it may have been

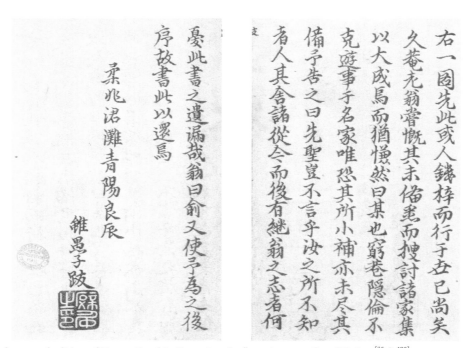

The afterword from the second edition of O-umajirushi, *discussing the "certain person" and Kyūan.*[35, p. 433]

specifically intended to spread awareness of the new political order to people other than the directly affected samurai. The second edition, interestingly enough, has a preface specifying its purpose as "to avoid forgetting war in a time of peace".[8, p. 25] However, despite the peaceful times, identifying banners had practical purposes. There were officials known as gezami (下座見), stationed at border crossings and castle gates, who were responsible for recognizing important individuals and commanding bystanders to pay appropriate respect. Samurai lords also had retainers with similar duties that accompanied them when travelling.[6, p. 16] Given that such officials needed to recognize mon, a compendium of heraldry such as this would have been a useful reference.

The Making of *O-umajirushi*

Rolled scrolls and bound books both have a long history in Japan, and both types of document were in use around the time of *O-umajirushi*. Scrolls were popular for many classic Japanese works because their continuous nature allowed for extended painted scenes not limited by the width of a page. Books, on the other hand, were a natural fit for printed works, since the size of the wood block corresponded naturally to the size of a page. *O-umajirushi*, however, is a woodblock-printed scroll. To achieve this efficiently, it was printed as a number of separate pages, as one would for a book, and the pages for each volume were then assembled into a continuous scroll.

The second edition was printed in 1656 in book form. It has the same contents and is almost identical, with some color changes but otherwise hardly any graphical differences. Unlike the original, it is hand-colored, and includes *Shoshō Kisei Zu*-style color labels to provide direction to the colorist.[8, p. 23])

Because of the way it's made up of book-like numbered pages, all of the same size, some have theorized that *O-umajirushi* was originally printed as a book and later reworked into a scroll, perhaps due to damage to the cover, as has been documented for other works. However, given the multiple separate scroll instances of *O-umajirushi* and the lack of evidence for any book version of the original edition, this seems unlikely.[8, pp. 23–24]

O-umajirushi uses a variety of different inks to capture the various colors used on the banners and other devices. The main ink used for text, outlines, and black areas is sumi, made from soot. The other main printed inks are indigo, red made from cinnabar, white from calcium carbonate, and yellow from Amur cork bark (also used as a traditional medicine). Normally, colors were not intended to overlap; however, for banners with white and red or white and black stripes, first the whole area was inked white, and then red or black stripes were placed on top of the white. Wood blocks were not used for all color; gold and silver paint were added by hand. Similarly, small details on helmets were also added manually.[8, p. 24]

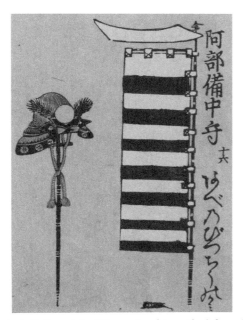 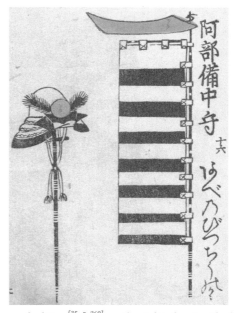

The same section in both the original O-umajirushi, on the left, and the second edition,[35, p. 260] on the right, showing the heraldry of Abe no Bitchū-no-kami (see p. 135). The second edition has notable color differences and reduced detail coloring on the helmet; however, the outlines and text are almost identical. Note the faint labels reading "aka", red, under the red paint.

Woodblock Printing

O-umajirushi is notable not only for its content, but for its medium. It was a pioneering work in Japanese color woodblock printing. Woodblock printing enabled a large number of banners and helmets to be captured in full color while making it practical to print and distribute many copies. This allowed *O-umajirushi* to be much more effective than hand-painted scrolls at spreading information. The color printing technique used in *O-umajirushi* would be further developed and refined, leading to the famous full-color woodblock prints that would come later in the Edo period.

Woodblock printing was originally introduced to Japan from China. Its first recorded use in Japan is in the 8th century, when Empress Shōtoku commissioned a million miniature pagodas, each containing a printed passage of Buddhist scripture.[47, pp. 1–2] Early religious prints were generally single sheets, though there are also examples of printed fans with religious designs in the late Heian period (794–1185).[27, p. 14] Use of woodblocks for Buddhist religious images dates back at least to the 11th century.[39, p. 82] Early prints were monochrome, using sumi (a black ink made from soot), and sometimes hand-colored after printing.[38, p. 9] The first known Japanese printed book, a copy of the constitution written by Prince Shōtoku in the 7th century, was printed in the 12th century.[39, p. 51] A printed version of the Chinese *Confucian Analects* dates to 1364,[39, p. 54] and an extant Japanese kanji dictionary dates to at least the 15th century.[39, p. 57] The earliest known Japanese illustrated printed book that was not a copy of a foreign book is a copy of *The Tales of Ise* which dates to 1610.[39, p. 82]

The early Edo period was a revolutionary time for Japanese publishing in many ways. Tokugawa Ieyasu was a big proponent of reproducing Japanese manuscripts, encouraging printed books to become more widespread.[39, p. 60] A growing merchant class and urbanization combined with cheaper, more efficient techniques for printing transformed books from something expensive reserved for wealthy nobles and notable samurai families to something widely available to ordinary

Two of the miniature pagodas of Empress Shōtoku, with two different block-printed passages of scripture. Each pagoda is 22 cm tall.
The Schøyen Collection, Oslo and London

An image of Fudō Myōō, a Buddhist guardian deity, from the 14th century, printed with woodblocks then hand-colored.
Metropolitan Museum of Art

A woodblock from the first half of the 18th century used to print an image of an actor. Note the mon of crossed oak leaves and three tomoe in the upper left.
Metropolitan Museum of Art

people. At the same time, the growing wealth of the lower classes and the idleness of the samurai in a time of peace led to a large demand for kabuki theater, which in turn created a large demand for individual images displaying popular actors, which also took advantage of wood block technology.

While Japan is famous for its woodblock prints, the technology for printing with movable type was also known in Japan. According to tradition, it was introduced in the 13th century,[39, p. 66] and the earliest known Japanese printed fiction book not a copy of an imported book, a version of *The Tales of Ise*, was published in 1597 using movable type.[39, p. 79] Nevertheless, *O-umajirushi* was printed with individually-carved blocks, not movable type, for both text and images. The thousands of characters used in Japanese made the creation of sets of type expensive and impractical. Having each page as a block that could be kept rather than needing to assemble a page each time it was printed also made it easier to print additional copies of a work, and reduced the chance of errors in later printings.[39, p. 79] In *O-umajirushi*'s case in particular, it would have been simpler to use the same technology for both text and images, and using individual woodblocks also allowed for the easy use of a cursive script involving connected and overlapping characters. These same reasons applied to other works, and thus movable type went out of fashion in Japan around the middle of the 17th century.

There were two methods of producing color prints in Japan. The earliest method was to print in black-and-white and then to color the resulting prints by hand. This was the common technique for printed books contemporary to *O-umajirushi*. Hand-colored manuscripts often used a reduced color palette to keep costs low.[56, p. 21] The second method, which developed later, used multiple blocks, one per color, using registration marks to align them precisely. This allowed for faster production of many copies, all colored in the same way. Using multiple blocks automated the process of making color prints, allowing for rapid production.[38, p. 10] *O-umajirushi* actually uses a hybrid approach: most color was applied with woodblocks, but gold and silver paint was applied by hand.[36] While *O-umajirushi* shows that this registration method was known in the first half of the 17th century, it was not until 1695 that color prints were mass-produced for general audiences.[39, p. 82] *O-umajirushi* was thus a work ahead of its time.

The Language

Japanese has three different alphabets, and all three are used in *O-umajirushi*.

Kanji (漢字) are logographic characters imported from China. Each kanji can be pronounced in a variety of ways, with both Chinese-origin "on" readings and Japanese-origin "kun" readings, and generally carry a particular meaning. Kanji readings can be one or more syllables, and many kanji share pronunciations. There are tens of thousands of Japanese kanji, but only a few thousand are used regularly.

Hiragana (ひらがな or 平仮名) is one alphabet of Japanese syllabic characters, used to write verb endings and some native Japanese words. They originated as simplifications of kanji, but are used purely phonetically. Each hiragana represents a mora, which is either just a vowel, a consonant followed by a vowel, a glottal stop, or a syllabic 'n'. (A mora is basically a Japanese syllable, but in cases of long vowels, doubled consonants, or syllabic 'n', what seems to an English speaker like one syllable will be multiple mora.)

The third alphabet, *katakana* (カタカナ), is similar to hiragana, using the same mora but with its own characters to represent them. In modern Japanese, it's mainly used for words of foreign origin and for emphasis, but in *O-umajirushi* it seems to sometimes replace hiragana to write particles (similar to English prepositions). Together, hiragana and katakana are referred to as kana. In modern Japanese, hiragana and katakana each have 46 characters, though there are a few additional historical kana characters used in *O-umajirushi*.

One side effect of different kanji sharing pronunciations is that Japanese writing can convey distinctions lost in the spoken language and in translation. In effect, Japanese is full of homophones that sound the same but are written differently and mean different things. They may have related meanings or be completely distinct. One example of this that features heavily in *O-umajirushi* is "kami". Three different titles, written with different kanji but all pronounced "kami", are used in *O-umajirushi*.

守 is the most common, attached to a province name and meaning "provincial governor", or more specifically, the "director" or top governor of a province. This title had come to be more of a honorary title, bestowed as a prestigious rank, rather than something based around practical responsibilities, in much the same way that modern British peers do not have any particular authority over the geographic area of their peerage.

頭 is the same kanji used (with a different pronunciation) for a person's literal head. It is used as "kami" in *O-umajirushi* to name the titles of the heads of the various *ryō* (寮), government bureaus.

正 usually means "correct". It's used to write "kami" for the head of a *shi* (司), or office, a government division beneath a *ryō*.

There are other words pronounced "kami" not used in *O-umajirushi*, including 上, meaning the upper part of something, 紙, meaning a sheet of paper, and 神, meaning a Shintō divinity.

Classical Japanese

The manuscript is written in Classical Japanese, and thus the language used has some noticeable differences from modern Japanese.

Sound Changes   This work predates the spelling reform of the early 20th century. Things that in modern Japanese would be long vowels are written differently. For example, "chū" is written ちう ("chiu") instead of ちゅう ("chuu").

Other long vowels are written in a manner similar to diphthongs. For example, the modern "bō" is written ばう ("bau") instead of ぼう ("bou"). This usage is inconsistent: the same word may be written with both "bou" and "bau" at different times in *O-umajirushi*, suggesting that at the time of publication these combinations were already pronounced the same, at least in mainstream accents.

Similarly, over time, h-sounds in the middle of words became w-sounds and w-sounds other than in 'wa' became dropped. This leads to, for example, the modern つかいばん ("tsukaiban") being written つかひばん ("tsukahiban") and the modern いしかわ ("Ishikawa") being written いしかは ("Ishikaha").

Another sound change that's less wide-ranging but frequently encountered here is to the mora 'mu'. It changed to 'u', in many cases, when at the start of a word before an m- or b-sound.[21, 補講202] Therefore, at the time of publication, *O-umajirushi* would have in fact been written *O-mumajirushi*, as the word for "battle standard" was "mumajirushi" instead of "umajirushi". As one might expect, this word is commonly used in the text. Nevertheless, I chose to keep the *O-umajirushi* spelling when referring to the work, as it is the common way to refer to the text in modern scholarship. (When transcribing the original text, I keep the "mumajirushi" pronunciation.)

Orthography   The way pronunciations are recorded is also less precise than is standard in modern Japanese. In the manuscript, の ('no'), meaning "of", is often left implied when writing with kanji. Similarly, dakuten (゛), marks indicating which syllables are voiced, were often left off of kana, presumably when the author thought the pronunciation was clear from context.

    The kurikaeshi, or kana repetition mark, is also used more frequently in *O-umajirushi* than in modern Japanese. For example, the sequence のの is written の ゝ, even when the two 'no' characters are parts of different words. There are cases, however, where the kurikaeshi is not used.

Character Changes   While some of the hiragana used in *O-umajirushi* look identical to those used in modern Japanese, some look completely different. These are hentaigana (変体仮名; "alternate characters"), which were used in Japan until script reform in 1900. These convey no semantic difference, but reflect that there were many different kanji that could be simplified for use in hiragana with the same pronunciation, and that formal simplification was not a focus of Japanese writing at the time. The same word may be found written using a variety of different hentaigana in *O-umajirushi*, sometimes even on the same page. (See Appendix A for a table of hentaigana used in *O-umajirushi*.)

    Similarly, while many of the kanji used in *O-umajirushi* are the same as modern kanji, there are also many variations. These can range from minor changes of a stroke or two to a substitution of a radical (a part of a kanji) with a similar radical or a rearrangement of radicals. (See Appendix B for a table of kanji variants.)

    While most kanji in *O-umajirushi* are written in a regular printed style similar to modern printing, the kanji used in captions and all the hiragana are written in *kuzushiji* (崩し字), or cursive (literally "broken") characters. This is a looser, flowing script closer to Japanese calligraphy. While hiragana, already being simplified forms, are not significantly different in their cursive forms, kanji are often simplified heavily in kuzushiji, which can make identifying cursive kanji challenging. Some of these characters are not just cursive but in fact ryakuji (略字, "abbreviated characters"), simplified forms that use fewer strokes.

    To transcribe these different variations accurately for this book, I turned to two main sources. While obsolete historical kanji variations are not of interest to most modern Japanese fonts, there is an online project, GlyphWiki, which aims to collect all kanji variations (and the equivalent in other Asian languages) in its database. It is the source of many of the historical glyphs used in my transcription. Furthermore, it provides a convenient tool for adding new variant glyphs, allowing me to get clean glyphs for historical characters that were not already in the database. You can visit it at `http://en.glyphwiki.org/`.

    While GlyphWiki does have some hentaigana characters, its focus is on printed kanji, not on cursive forms. To accurately represent the hentaigana used in *O-umajirushi*, I also took advantage of another font, Koin変体仮名外字明朝 (Koin Hentaigana Gaiji Minchō), which has solid coverage of hentaigana forms of hiragana.

From left to right, a hiragana 'no', a katakana 'no', a hentaigana for 'no', and a hiragana 'no' followed by the kurikaeshi (repetition mark) to produce the sequence "nono".

The kanji 松, meaning "pine tree" and pronounced "matsu". The version on the left corresponds to its modern form; the other two are variants.

The kanji 馬, meaning "horse" and pronounced "uma", and two different ways of writing it in kuzushiji.

Types of Heraldic Display

Part of the reason *O-umajirushi* became necessary was the proliferation of different kinds of banners and heraldic devices in the Sengoku period. Because mounted samurai could move across a battlefield quickly, distinctive banners were important to be able to quickly locate commanders and particular groups of soldiers.[8, p. 22] The heraldry created for war continued to be used in the peaceful times when *O-umajirushi* was published. Banners were for processions and other formal occasions, and heraldic designs were adapted for use off the battlefield.

The most common primary device for the daimyō in *O-umajirushi* was a nobori such as figure (a), below. A *nobori* (幟) is a tall identifying banner attached to a vertical pole and a top horizontal crosspiece. This level of support allowed the banner to remain visible regardless of wind. The banner's association with a particular commanding daimyō led to their frequent use to identify army subdivisions.[52, p. 22]

Even more prominent than the nobori on the battle field, however, were the battle standards. An *umajirushi* (馬印) was the battle standard used by a daimyō. Literally meaning "horse insignia", this could be an ordinary rectangular banner or a more elaborate object on a pole, and was generally carried alongside the daimyō. (While "umajirushi" is the modern pronunciation, at the time it was written "mumajirushi".) Examples are figures (b) and (c), below. Many daimyō had two: a great standard, or ō-umajirushi (大馬印) and a lesser standard, or ko-umajirushi (小馬印). These could use related designs, but were often completely different. They were large objects designed to be visible from a distance. Despite the name, they were generally too large to carry from horseback; they would often be carried by a foot soldier or held in a holder on a foot soldier's back and steadied by other foot soldiers with ropes.[52, pp. 27–29]

Since nobori and standards would generally be carried by foot soldiers, while they worked well for identifying large units or serving as rallying points, they couldn't easily keep up with individual mounted samurai, who could move quickly across the battlefield. This was particularly true when a samurai, to prove his courage or make a name for himself, was eager to be the first to engage. The Sengoku period introduced another type of heraldic device to address this. A *sashimono* (指物, "identifying thing" or 差物, "raised thing") was a banner or other identifying object on a pole that was attached to the back of armor, often used to indicate a samurai's daimyō or unit affiliation.[52, pp. 23–24] Sashimono in *O-umajirushi* are usually either for a particular unit type, like "guards" or "messengers", or as used for personal identification. Figure (d), opposite, is an example of a surviving sashimono.

Non-nobori banners are named by their proportions: square banners are called *shihō* (四方; "four sides") (see figure (e)) and banners half again as tall as they are wide are called *shihan* (四半; "four and a half", i.e., a square and a half) (see figure (f)).[31, p. 8]

Before nobori came into common use, a samurai would use a *nagare hata* (流れ旗; "flowing banner"), a loose banner attached only to a top crosspiece to identify himself on the battlefield (see figure (h)). (In contrast, banners attached to poles with loops, like the banners below, are are called *chitsuki bata* (乳付旗; "loop-attached banners").)[31, p. 8] Many banners are accompanied by a *maneki* (招き), a small nagare hata attached at the end of the pole of a larger banner (see figure (e)). Other banners are accompanied by a *dashi* (出し), a small non-banner object attached like a maneki (see figure (g)).[31, pp. 7–8] Dashi are most commonly fans or tassels made of feathers or yak hair. Both maneki and dashi served as additional details to help distinguish between banners.

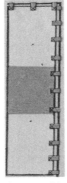  

(a) A nobori used by Sanada Kawachi-no-kami (see p. 30). *(b) A banner umajirushi used by Sakai Uta-no-kami (see p. 33).* *(c) A non-banner umajirushi used by Matsudaira Shimōsa-no-kami (see p. 35).*

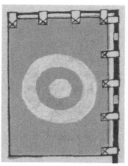

(d) A surviving dark blue sashimono from the 17th century. It bears a gold disc and the character 無 (mu, meaning "nothing") written in seal script.
Tokyo National Museum

(e) A shihō with a maneki, used by Makino Uma-no-jō (see p. 212).

(f) A shihan, used by Andō Ukyō (see p. 66).

(g) A nobori with a yak hair dashi, used by Kinoshita Emon-no-tayufu (see p. 159).

There were a few other non-banner devices common on the battlefield. A *fukinuki* (see figure (i), below) was a hollow streamer formed of strips of cloth attached to a ring, which would blow in the wind. They would often be used as standards but sometimes were used instead of a nobori as a primary device. A *horo*, on the other hand, was a type of canopy worn on the back and designed to inflate when riding a horse. It was thought to provide some protection against arrows. Horo were most often worn by messengers, but sometimes by other types of unit. An example of a horo is figure (j), below.

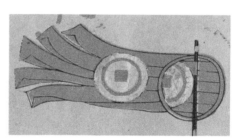

(i) A fukinuki used by Honda Ise-no-kami (see p. 192).

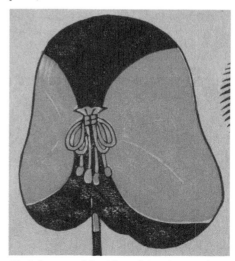

(h) A mounted samurai carrying a nagare hata. Detail from a 1517 scroll.
Tokyo National Museum

(j) A horo used by Matsudaira Awa-no-kami (see p. 174).

O-umajirushi has other types of heraldic devices beyond standards and banners. Most notable are helmets, which often had frontal crests or other elaborate embellishments making them identifiable from a distance. These could match the mon used on banners, but could just as easily be something specific to the helmet. Wearing a distinctive helmet would make it easy to identify a particular samurai on the battlefield, especially given that the helmet and face mask would otherwise obscure his features. There are even cases where a distinctive helmet itself was placed on a spear as a device in its own right.[52, p. 29] The helmets in *O-umajirushi* are drawn on poles, but it's unclear if this was actually a common way to display helmets or if this was just the style of the illustrator.

Mon were also used on weapons and scabbards. Since these decorations would not be visible across a battlefield, this sort of embellishment would have been more of a sign of wealth and position, though it could also help identify your possessions clearly in camp.

Mon could be used on armor, on fastenings or in larger designs formed by varying the colors of cord used to hold armor plates together. Though less visible and practical, these sorts of usages showed station and wealth. Ornamental uses of mon would become more of a focus later in the Edo period during the centuries of peace.

Detail of a 17th-century suit of armor showing the helmet. Note the moon-shaped helmet crest.
Metropolitan Museum of Art

A 17th-century sword guard with a paulownia mon.
Photograph ©2015 Museum of Fine Arts, Boston.

This 17th-century scabbard is decorated with three different mon: nine stars, paulownia, and wisteria.
Photograph ©2015 Museum of Fine Arts, Boston.

This 14th-century helmet features large fittings in the shape of a "horse's bit" mon, as used by Matsudaira Satsuma-no-kami (see p. 127). The helmet also has smaller instances of the same mon and a wisteria mon.
Metropolitan Museum of Art

A 17th-century helmet with an elaborate paper-mâché shell shape.
Ann and Gabriel Barbier-Mueller Museum

This 15th–16th-century helmet features a horned helmet crest similar to the one used by Aoyama Ōkura-no-shō -ifu (see p. 56). The neck guard turnbacks feature the geometric "sandbar" mon, as used by Hine no Oribe (see p. 84).
Metropolitan Museum of Art

The Structure of *O-umajirushi*

Above we see the first scroll of *O-umajirushi*, and below we see the start of it, unrolled. (The red stamp on the inside cover is a modern addition indicating ownership by the National Diet Library.) Each volume of *O-umajirushi* begins with a title and a table of contents. As is traditional in Japanese, the text is written vertically, in lines read right-to-left. Thus, the rightmost column, (a) below, is the volume title, followed by the first table of contents entry. The original document was a continuous scroll, with the first page rightmost and each following page following to the left.

Tables of Contents

Each table-of-contents entry has three parts. At the top of the page, labeled (b) below, is an individual's name, generally with a title, in kanji (logographic characters). Below that, labeled (c), is the entry number, also in kanji. At the bottom, labeled (d), is the same name's pronunciation given in hiragana (syllabic characters). Many of the hiragana are written with hentaigana (historical variant characters). In addition, these hiragana characters (but not the kanji) are written in kuzushiji (cursive characters), which can make them harder to identify. The entries will be transcribed, translated, and identified in the text.

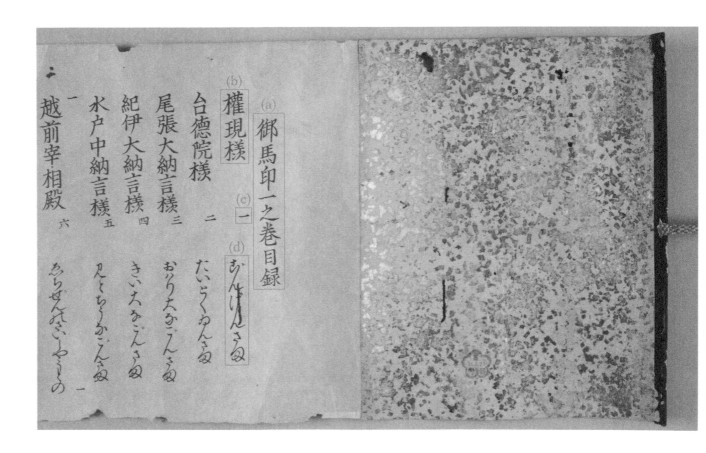

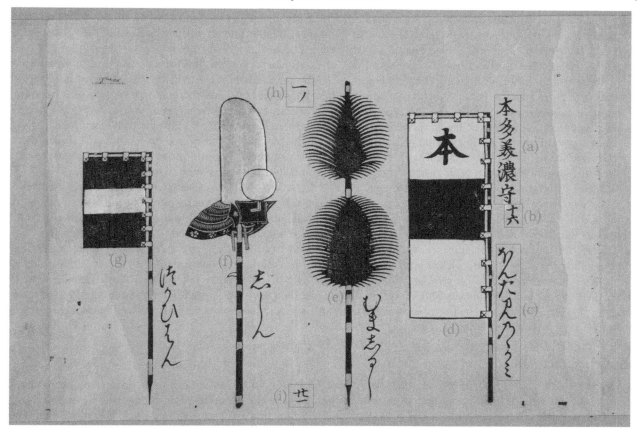

Heraldry Illustrations

Above is an example of an illustrated page from *O-umajirushi*. Here we have the heraldry illustrations for Honda Mino-no-kami. Each person's section starts with a label that matches the table of contents: his name in kanji, labeled (a) above; the entry number, labeled (b); and the name pronunciation, labeled (c). After that, we have a number of individual items of heraldry. In this particular case, we have from right to left: a nobori serving as his primary device, labeled (d); his standard, labeled (e); his personal helmet, labeled (f); and his messengers' device, labeled (g). Most devices after the primary device are labeled with a caption identifying what it is or its purpose; these captions will be transcribed, translated, and explained in the text.

Numbering in the Text

Note the volume number in the top middle, (h), and the page number in the bottom middle, (i). Here the volume number is 一, meaning 1, followed by a katakana 'no' (ノ), the possessive particle. The page number is 廿一, a historical way of writing 21. Together, the possessive particle makes the meaning "page 21 of the first volume". (The possessive particle is omitted in some cases.) Because *O-umajirushi* was printed as a continuous scroll, page boundaries were not very important to the reader, and the page numbers were probably just for collation.

    Note that while here Honda Mino-no-kami's section starts at the beginning of a page, that is not always the case; entries can continue for multiple pages and can both start and end in the middle of a page.

Names in *O-umajirushi*

While samurai had both family and personal names, only a few individuals in *O-umajirushi* are identified in that way. Other entries are identified in a number different ways.

    The most common pattern is family name + title, for example "Honda Mino-no-kami" ("Honda, Provincial Governor of Mino"). Provincial governor titles like this were the most common. These were honorary titles that provided a court rank but didn't relate to practical power over a province. (Actual control over regions of Japan was based on what daimyō

ruled a particular domain, an entirely separate system.) There are also many examples of titles referring to positions in government offices and bureaus. Sometimes a title just names an office or bureau without indicating the specific position within that division, for example "Sakai Kunai". In this case, I add the implied "official" to the translation, i.e., "Sakai, Imperial Household [official]". These divisions are part of the Ritsuryō system, the formal structure of Japanese court positions at the time. In this system, there are four administrative positions in each division. From highest to lowest, these are: director (長官, kami), assistant director (次官, suke), inspector (判官, jō), and secretary (主典, sakan). The exact title and the kanji used varies depending on the type of division, and some titles have greater and lesser variations. While positions like "Head of the Water, Ice, and Porridge Office" may seem strange for a samurai in a military feudal structure, the Ritsuryō system predates samurai rule of Japan and shows the feudal leadership's co-option of court ranks to reward supporters and formalize the practical military hierarchy. Like the provincial governor titles, these administrative positions were probably largely honorary, with practical responsibilities delegated to lower-ranked individuals.

Another pattern that looks similar to family name + title is used in names like "Mito Chūnagon" ("Mito Middle Councilor"); however, here "Mito" is not a family name but a reference to the Mito Domain, referring to the feudal domain the samurai was daimyō over. Domains (藩; han) were geographical subdivisions where daimyō had effective rulership and received income. They often shared names with provinces but had boundaries unrelated to province boundaries.

Finally, there are two different cases where individuals are referred to by a single name with an honorific suffix. The two former shōguns of the Tokugawa line are referred to by their formal posthumous names with the honorific suffix -sama (様). Similarly, some powerful daimyō who had effective rule over much of Japan before the Tokugawa came into power (but had died by the time of *O-umajirushi*) are referred to by just their given names with the less commonly used honorific suffix -kō (公). Like with the councilor names, these individuals would have been sufficiently well-known that indicating their family name was unnecessary.

For discussion of the order of names in *O-umajirushi*, see p. x.

About this Translation

In my translation, I maintain the traditional Japanese order for names, with family name first followed by personal name.

For name entries, I transcribe the entry as written, then provide the pronunciation in parentheses in both hiragana and roman characters. I insert middle dots (·) in the transcriptions to clarify word boundaries. When the kanji used in a name entry are different than the modern form of that kanji, I use the historical form in the transcription but also make note of the modern version.

For each caption, I've first given the transcription as written, with hentaigana and variant kanji, and then provided the modern version and the reading in parentheses.

My transcriptions of Japanese pronunciations are based on the Modified Hepburn romanization system. I always render the syllabic 'n' as 'n', never 'm', and only add an apostrophe after it when it is followed by a vowel or 'y'.

My transcriptions follow the post-sound-change pronunciation (see Sound Changes, p. xiv); however, when a sound change or ambiguous long vowel is present in a table-of-contents entry, I also provide a literal transcription. I apply the sound changes without regard to modern pronunciation; for example, I transcribe すぎはら as "Sugiwara (lit. Sugihara)" because of the w-sound change, even though the name is pronounced "Sugihara" in modern Japanese.

Dakuten (�゙), marks which indicate whether a syllable should be voiced, are applied inconsistently in *O-umajirushi*. My transcriptions only assume missing dakuten if there are other examples of the same word or name elsewhere in the text that include the dakuten; otherwise, I transcribe as written without regard to voicing in the modern pronunciation.

Annotations

Below each label in the original document giving an individual's name, I put a number. Below each other label, I put a letter. Matching the original document, these are read in right-to-left order. These correspond to the numbers and letters next to my translations of the label. Other annotations clarifying the label or the labeled image may follow.

At times, words are left implied in the Japanese text that are necessary to make the meaning clear in English. In these cases, I add the implied words in square brackets.

Since individuals are generally identified by title or otherwise in a way different from how they appear in modern sources, I annotate each entry with who the person referred to actually is according to my research in modern sources. When there are multiple possibilities, such as when multiple individuals in a family held the same title at different times, I list multiple options to give the reader the most information. In some cases, it's unclear whether they're intended to refer to the person with that title at the time *O-umajirushi* was published or whether they might refer to an earlier, more famous individual known under that title.

About Mon

To understand Japanese heraldry, one must understand mon. *Mon* (紋) are Japanese heraldic crests, similar to Western coats of arms, that identify particular families and institutions. *Kamon* (家紋), mon associated with a particular family, were the most common kind because Japan's feudal hierarchy was based on strong samurai family structures. In military situations, divisions would be identified by their commander, and thus the commander's mon was often used for identification on banners.

Family crests, however, were not the only type of mon. Mon were also used by Shintō shrines, with this type of usage dating back to the Kamakura period (1185–1333). These mon are called *shinmon* (神紋). The types of designs used for these mon were similar to those used by families. Shrines would sometimes adopt the mon of a patron family, and conversely a samurai might adopt the mon of a shrine he had a close connection to. Mon could also move between shrines, such as when an enshrined *kami* (Shintō deity) was transferred.[41] Buddhist temples also used mon in a similar way.[9, p. 127] Such mon are called *jimon* (寺紋).

The gentian-and-bamboo-leaf kamon of the Minamoto clan.
Drawing by 百楽兎; CC BY-SA 3.0

Design

Despite the widespread use of mon, they focused on a relatively fixed set of motifs, generally varying an existing motif rather than creating something totally different. Mon based on stylized depictions of plants were most common. Abstract geometric designs were also very popular, as were designs based on Japanese characters. Birds and butterflies were sometimes used, but other types of animals were uncommon, and human figures were very rare.

A crossed hawk's feather mon, used as a shrine mon by the Aso Shrine.[17, 鷹の羽]
Drawing by Mukai; CC BY-SA 3.0

A Buddhist treasure wheel mon,[20, p. 45] frequently used as a temple mon.[17, 輪宝]

In European heraldry it was common to combine many unrelated elements in a coat of arms or combine two entirely separate coats of arms into one ("marshalling" them). In Japanese heraldry, the common ways of varying mon were different, focused on simpler arrangements but treating smaller changes to individual elements as meaningful. Some variations would change the number of leaves, buds, or petals shown in an element. Others would make stylistic modifications to graphical details while leaving the overall design the same (compare figures (a) and (b)). Designs that featured multiple instances of a single element were more common than designs that combined unlike elements. Mon designs that did combine multiple elements usually followed set patterns, such as putting an element within an enclosure (see figure (c)), depicting a plant emerging from water (figure (d)), or decorating an item with another element (figure (e)). There are also examples of different mon being placed together in simple arrangements, often just in a vertical column (see figure (f)). A more elaborate type of variation was to arrange one element in the shape of another standard element (see figures (g) and (h)); while in the Edo period (1603–1868) these designs became very elaborate, before then this sort of mon generally only imitated simple geometrical designs.

In modern Japan, mon are thought of as being monochrome designs that have no particular color. At the time of *O-umajirushi*, however, color was often an important part of a samurai's heraldry. Banners were generally depicted with consistent colors, most commonly the five "lucky" colors: blue, yellow, red, white, and black.[52, p. 24] Different color combinations might be used to distinguish different members of a family or different families that used the same mon, so these distinctions were important. In some cases, the banner color seems to be more notable than the mon itself; for example, the troops of Doi no Ōi-no-kami (see p. 17) were known for their yellow banners, not for the water wheel mon on them. This makes sense, because on a hectic battlefield, banner color is easier to distinguish from a distance than mon design. Different units might be distinguished by different characters or colored bands on a consistently-colored flags. Conversely, in some cases a samurai commanding many units would give each unit a flag with a different background color but a consistent mon.[52, p. 24] In addition, a samurai might still use his mon with different colors in other situations, such as marking per-

(a) A sandbar design repeated three times.[20, p. 37] A similar mon was used by Hine no Oribe (see p. 84).

(b) A variant of the previous three-sandbar mon using a sharper depiction.[20, p. 43]

(c) A character 三 (san, meaning "three") in a square enclosure.[20, p. 14]

(d) A three-level pine tree emerging from water.[20, p. 45]

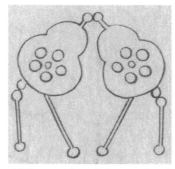

(e) Two gourds each decorated with a "plum bowl" design.[20, p. 21]

(f) Two unrelated elements: a character 大 (dai, meaning "great") and a China flower in a tortoise shell.[20, p. 50]

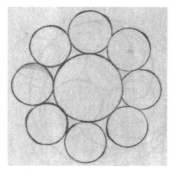

(g) As normally used, the nine stars mon is an arrangement of nine circles.[20, p. 10]

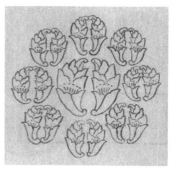

(h) In this mon, pairs of "apricot leaf" tassels replace the stars in the nine stars arrangement.[20, p. 41]

sonal possessions or on clothing, where another design aesthetic might take precedence and identification from a distance was not important. Thus, the color was not always an inseparable characteristic of the mon.[24, p. 15]

Regulation of Mon

Until 1642, after the Tokugawa peace had brought an end to the various samurai conflicts, there was no central authority registering mon;[16, p. 2] the motifs and types of designs used were limited only by custom and tradition. Because of this lack of formal restrictions, works such as *O-umajirushi* recorded the heraldry observed to be in use, rather than indicating what heraldry a given samurai lord was allowed to use. Mon could be created or abandoned easily, and while a son might use the mon of his father, he would not necessarily do so. In fact, since the fourteenth century, the practice was for the eldest son to inherit the family estate and holdings. This forced younger sons to create independent households, sometimes creating new surnames and/or mon as they did so.[6, p. 9] Some of these mon would be variations of the parent line's mon, while others would be completely different, perhaps reflecting animosity or a desire for independence.[6, p. 10] In addition, the same family would often adopt multiple "substitute mon" (kaemon; 替紋) in addition to its formal mon (jōmon; 定紋), leading to further complexity.[6, p. 10]

These variations and substitute mon were not just for variety: they had practical uses as well. At times, different members of the same family ended up on different sides in a battle, and they would need to use different heraldry to avoid confusion.[12, p. ii] In addition, a particular samurai lord might restrict the use of mon within the daimyō's domain. When a samurai traveled or was reassigned to a different province, their normal mon might violate such a restriction, forcing him to use a substitute mon instead.

In Europe, it was common for a College of Arms to be responsible for regulating who was eligible to use particular heraldry at a national level. In Japan, prior to 1642, there was no comparable mon authority assigning specific mon to specific individuals or families, and most restrictions were informal or local. Only two elements were restricted across Japan by law: the chrysanthemum mon, showing a chrysanthemum blossom most commonly with 16 petals or two layers of 16 petals each (see figure (h)), and the paulownia mon, showing the leaves and flowers of the fast-growing Asian tree (figure (i)). These two motifs were reserved for the Emperor and those he granted mon using the motif to (though, in practice, as the effective rulers of Japan, shōguns who were granted the paulownia mon sometimes granted it to their followers in turn).

Despite the relative lack of enforced formal restrictions, custom provided a sort of ownership of mon, and being granted the use of a prestigious mon by a noble or powerful family could be a significant social boost. Even mon without such prestige might be bestowed as a form of recognition and a way of solidifying the relationship between a daimyō and his vassals or between two allied clans.[6, pp. 12–14]

(h) An imperial chrysanthemum in a tortoise shell enclosure.[20, p. 49]

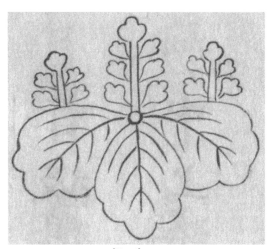

(i) A paulownia mon.[20, p. 4]

History of Mon

Mon were not originally used by warriors. The earliest mon were used by the imperial aristocracy, dating back to the Nara period (710–794).[52, pp. 6–7] Many early mon traced their designs back to fabric patterns and other decorative motifs imported from China. Mon were first specifically associated with particular noble families in the Heian period (794–1185).[12, p. v] The imperial chrysanthemum mon dates back to this time, but was not specifically reserved for the Emperor until the 13th century.[6, p. 53]

Mon were first used by samurai in the 12th-century Genpei Wars, where they were used on camp curtains and banners. They were also used on wooden mantlet shields, basically portable wooden walls used to provide cover against arrows, as shown below.[52, p. 8]

As the Edo period (1603–1868) progressed, mon usage began to spread from the warrior class down to lower classes

The "China flower" design started as a fabric pattern imported from China during the Nara period.[6, p. 138]
Drawing by Mukai; used under CC BY-SA 3.0

A detail of a late Heian illustrated scroll showing a kimono with a flower-in-hexagon pattern. This same pattern was used as a mon.
Tokugawa Art Museum

This "seven treasures" design came from a fabric pattern of overlapping circles in the late Heian period.[6, p. 134]

The butterfly mon.[20, p. 10] It was first used in the Nara period but was made famous by the Taira clan at the end of the Heian period.[6, p. 88]

Foot soldiers using mantlet shields, some bearing mon, at the 12th-century Battle of Yashima. Detail from a 17th-century screen.
Kobe City Museum

This detail of a scroll from 1347 depicting the Later Three-Year War shows a camp curtain with a dove[52, p. 7] or wild goose mon. Note also the vertical strips forming a tent in the background, on which a melon mon is faintly visible.
Tokyo National Museum

that were growing in influence during the time of peace. Mon became used by merchants by the Azuchi-Momoyama period (1573–1603), and from there became widely used by actors and courtesans.[6, p. 18]

Mon Origins

Mon Legends

Mon had many purposes, but one that became particularly important during the frequent upheavals of the Sengoku period was establishing legitimacy. Many samurai rose from humble roots to positions of power through skill, courage, luck, and well-chosen alliances. (Toyotomi Hideyoshi (entry 3 on p. 114), for example, was born a peasant but rose to become effective ruler of Japan.) And it was just as easy for a once-powerful lord to be stripped of his holdings or forced into suicide upon losing a war. Since mon had no formal regulation, the prestige and meaning of a mon was largely based on how convincingly a samurai could make a case for it. Daimyō found value in establishing illustrious ancestors and ties to prestigious and historically significant clans to justify their positions in society. Mon were one tool for doing so.

One particularly interesting facet of this is the pattern of mon origin legends. Many families had a dramatic story that gave a superficially simple motif added weight and meaning. It's hard to say to what extent these stories are actually the source of the mon in question, rather than an embellishment added by later generations. Regardless, these stories give insight into what various families considered important and legitimizing.

There are a few themes that emerge in these stories. Many involve supernatural elements, often establishing the blessing of a divine figure. Others involve more terrestrial bestowal, tying the device to a past Emperor or other notable family. Most commemorate heroic acts, daring, or victory in battle, an obviously attractive thing for a samurai to establish about his ancestors. In all these cases, the mon serves as a tool to symbolize worthiness of the holder.

One interesting example is the story of the dove mon of Kumagai Naozane. Naozane, although having previously sided with the Taira, secretly became loyal to Minamoto Yoritomo. When Yoritomo lost a battle and was on the run, he hid in a hollow tree while some Taira soldiers, including Naozane, searched for him. Naozane found the hiding place and disturbed some doves with his bow, who flew out with a commotion. He used this to convince his companions that no one could be hiding in the tree and thus saved his secret master.[52, p. 11] In thanks, Yoritomo supposedly gave Naozane a dove mon. One version specifically attributes the doves as a response to a prayer to Hachiman, god of war, who uses doves as messengers.[24, pp. 4–5]

To the right is a doves-with-mistletoe (寓生に鳩; hoya ni hato) mon used by the Kumagai family, from *Kenmon Shokamon*.[20, p. 31] Other versions include only two doves.[52, p. 11]

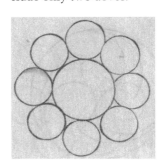

Another legend tells of the Chiba, on the brink of defeat in a 10th century battle. The Big Dipper constellation (北斗七星; hokuto shichisei) shone brightly in the night sky, so the Chiba prayed to Myōken Bosatsu, a Bodhisattva associated with the constellation. In response, they received a vision, and the next day proved victorious. The Chiba referred to this legend with various star-based mon, with either a larger circle or a crescent representing a moon.[52, p. 11]

To the left is a moon-and-stars mon recorded in *Kenmon Shokamon* as used by the Chiba family.[20, p. 10] Later this motif would be referred to as just "nine stars". The same arrangement was used by Matsudaira Yamashiro-no-kami (see p. 51).

For additional mon legends of divine aid, refer to the entries for Honda Inaba-no-kami (see p. 96), Hōjō Kyūtara (see p. 209), and Taketa no Shingen (see p. 207).

In other stories, supernatural elements are less explicit, and the legend focuses more on the victory itself. Mōri Motonari, in the 16th century, was approaching a battle when he is said to have, at a river bank, seen a dragonfly alight on a water plantain. Since a dragonfly was known as the victory insect, he took this as a positive sign and continued on to lead his men to victory. He then commemorated this event by adopting a water-plantain mon.[12, p. 14] The resulting mon is shown to the right.[14, 沢瀉紋]

An example of a mon story focused on human sources of prestige is that of Kusunoki Masashige. His brilliant defense of strongholds loyal to Emperor Go-Daigo was instrumental in restoring the emperor briefly to power in the Kenmu Restoration (1333-1336). Go-Daigo recognized Masashige by granting him a mon based on the normally-restricted imperial chrysanthemum, showing it supported by water. Go-Daigo explained that Masashige, in the same way, had kept him afloat by his support.[52, p. 13]

Unfortunately for them, one of Go-Daigo's key generals, Ashikaga Takauji, betrayed the emperor to seize rule over Japan for himself. Masashige knew that his forces in the capital were hopelessly outmatched and suggested that Go-Daigo retreat and regroup; however, Go-Daigo refused. Masashige then went into battle, knowing he was doomed, and willingly died for his emperor. Thus, he is remembered as a paragon of samurai loyalty.

Above is one chrysanthemum-and-water mon used by the Kusunoki family, from *Kenmon Shokamon*.[20, p. 14] Single-chrysanthemum variations were also used.[52, p. B1]

For another story of a mon commemorating imperial favor, refer to the section for Ogasawara Iki-no-kami (see p. 81).

An example of a story of victory with no supernatural elements is behind the hollyhock mon of the Tokugawa. Tokugawa Ieyasu claimed descent from the ancient Minamoto clan, a necessary qualification for officially becoming shōgun.[51, p. 144] However, he did not base his heraldry on the Minamoto mon of bamboo leaves and gentian flowers. Instead, the hollyhock mon used by the Tokugawa was of more recent origin. It is said that Ieyasu's father, Matsudaira Hirotada, returned victorious from battle in Mikawa in 1529 and was hosted for a celebratory feast by a vassal. Supposedly, he received a round tray with cakes placed on three hollyhock leaves as part of the victory celebrations, and was thus inspired to adopt the design as his mon in commemoration of the victory.[10, p. 160] The resulting mon, as recorded in *Shoshō Kisei Zu*, is on the right.[44, p. 1.8] (Another tradition holds that the Tokugawa hollyhock derives from the plant's association with the Kamo shrine.[12, p. 5])

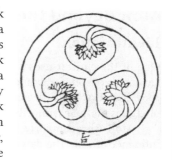

For another mon story about success in battle, refer to Nabeshima Ki-no-kami (see p. 220).

Shrine mon sometimes had interesting stories behind them as well. One Japanese deity with an interesting history is Tenjin, originally Sugawara no Michizane. Michizane was a courtier and poet of the 9th century and favored by Emperor Uda. When Uda abdicated, a rival engineered Michizane's exile to a remote province. After his death in exile, the imperial palace was repeatedly struck by lightning, and a series of disasters beset the capital. This was interpreted as being caused by Michizane's angry spirit. His rank was posthumously restored, a shrine was dedicated in his honor, and eventually he was deified as Tenjin, god of poetry, calligraphy, and scholarship. Sugawara no Michizane loved plum blossoms, so after he was deified, shrines dedicated to him adopted the plum blossom as a crest.[6, p. 75]

Drawing by Mukai; CC BY-SA 3.0

Mon origin stories provide a unique view into the various samurai families' desire to use ancestry and blessings, whether from gods or from notable mortal figures, to establish that their family rightfully deserved a high position in society and to gain the respect of other samurai. More than just an arbitrary design, mon helped remember and express important connections and facets of family history.

Heraldic Puns

Not all mon origins refer to particular stories. Another source for mon was making a reference to the family named involved, in a similar way to "canting", name-based puns in European heraldry. Some of these were very simple. Many samurai just used one of the kanji from their surname as a mon, for example Koide Tsushima-no-kami (see p. 155) used the "ko" (小) from "Koide".

Others were more elaborate. The Katō family put the character "ka" (加) from their name in a wisteria wreath, since the "tō" (藤) means "wisteria".[6, p. 82] "Aoyama" literally means "blue mountain", and their banners used the character 山 (yama, meaning "mountain") either in blue or with a blue background (see p. 55). The Torii family used a shrine gate because their name is the same as the word for shrine gate, "torii" (鳥居) (see p. 197). Kuroda means "black field", and so Kuroda Mankichi (see p. 83) used a black background on his banner.

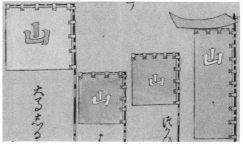

Koide Tsushima-no-kami's "ko" banner.

The Katō ka-in-wisteria mon, as drawn in Kenmon Shoka-mon.[20, p. 46]

Various Aoyama banners combining blue with the character "yama".

The shrine gate mon of the Torii.

Kuroda Mankichi's banner with a black field.

Mon Beyond the Battlefield

Identification

One of the earliest uses of mon was on Imperial oxcarts, long before mon were used on the battlefield.[52, p. 7] Since the carriage's passenger would be hidden, concealed by curtains, this could be a way of indicating who was travelling, though they also served as a decoration and wealth signifier. These early mon were simple designs, such as the "nine stars" cluster of circles on the carriage below.

Mon were similarly used on the curtains (幕; maku) surrounding military camps. As merchants gained practical influence around the dawn of the Edo period, merchants would display mon on their noren (暖簾), divided curtains used in doorways, that may have evolved from a type of divided banner by the same name used on the battlefield. Brothels in the pleasure districts also used noren in this way.

Similarly, mon might be displayed more permanently in architecture, a practice Toyotomi Hideyoshi pursued extravagantly during his rulership of Japan. In the Edo period, mon were used on castles and the houses of samurai everywhere from walls, roof tiles, and gates to stone lanterns in gardens. Given that domains were frequently reassigned, this led to considerable work renovating castles[6, p. 19]

Mon were also used on the sails of ships, a practice that became particularly common in the Edo period.[6, p. 19]

A 13th-century depiction of an Imperial oxcart decorated with a shadowed nine stars mon.
Tokyo National Museum

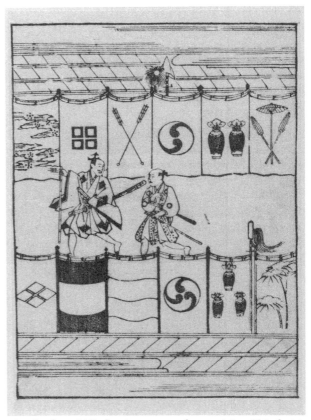

A print from 1663 showing mon used on curtains. This depicts preparations for a famous 1193 hunt by Shōgun Minamoto no Yoritomo, where curtains were used to block the path of fleeing animals.
Photograph ©2015 Museum of Fine Arts, Boston.

A late-1680s depiction of the Yoshiwara pleasure district of Edo, showing mon used on noren. From left to right, we have: an ivy mon with a hentaigana character 'ya', the same melon mon as on p. xxvi, and two characters reading "Yoshida". A screen in the background towards the left uses the seven treasures pattern, which was also used as a mon (see p. xxvi).
John C. Weber collection

Detail from a circa 1615 folding screen showing noren with mon in the doorways of shops or houses.
Tokyo National Museum

Detail from a Azuchi-Momoyama period (1573–1603) screen showing noren used by merchants in Kyōto.
Fukuoka City Museum

Detail of a roof tile from Nishi Honganji Temple, established in 1602, with a tomoe design.
Photo by Ciphers; used under CC BY-SA 3.0

Clothing

Mon were worn in various ways on clothing decoratively and to identify the wearer's family or affiliation. Most dramatic was the *daimon* (大紋; "great mon"), a large-sleeved kimono with enormous mon on the sleeves. Smaller mon were also worn on more every-day kimono. In the Edo period, mon size and placement became formalized and standardized, with mon about an inch and a half in diameter placed centered on the upper back, on the sleeves near the shoulders, and in some cases high on each side of the chest as well. The *jinbaori* (陣羽織), a long sleeveless coat worn over armor before battles, could also be decorated with mon.[6, pp. 11–12, 15]

While clothing decorated with mon was originally used only by the court nobility and samurai, in the early Edo period the practice of wearing mon spread to the lower classes and even to peasants.[6, p. 18]

A fragment of a Bugaku dance costume from the 12th or 13th century, featuring a five-petaled melon-with-flower mon.
Photograph ©2015 Museum of Fine Arts, Boston.

A samurai wearing a kataginu, a formal sleeveless jacket, decorated with mon. This hanging scroll dates to the late 16th century.
Metropolitan Museum of Art

A 17th-century jinbaori featuring a three oak leaves mon similar to those used by Matsudaira Tosa-no-kami (see p. 36) and Makino Uma-no-jō (see p. 212).
Metropolitan Museum of Art

A man wearing a kimono decorated with "three fish scales" mon, as used by Hōjō Kyūtara (see p. 209). Detail from a 1517 scroll.
Tokyo National Museum

An 1800 print showing a kabuki actor wearing a daimon while portraying 12th-century female samurai warrior Tomoe Gozen.
Toyokuni Utagawa I

A 16th-century portrait of a samurai commander, Naoe Kanetsugu, showing his kimono decorated with his mon of three tortoise shell enclosures each containing three oak leaves.
Yonezawa City Uesuki Museum

A woodblock print from the turn of the 18th century, showing a Kabuki actor with a kamon featured both on his kimono and hovering above him.
Metropolitan Museum of Art

Building Stones

Another interesting use for mon was marking blocks of stone. Building castles required large quantities of stone blocks, and various families were called upon to build castles under the Tokugawa. The samurai families contributing stones would carve symbols called kokuin (刻印; "carved mark") into the blocks at the quarry to identify the owner of the block.[34, 244] These carvings were most often mon or simplifications of mon. Since color was not used, mon were treated as tinctureless, contrasting with how they were used on banners. These carvings can still be seen in the walls of castles across Japan today.

A segment of a wall at Ōsaka Castle showing where construction responsibility transitioned from one family to another. The left portion has blocks with a circle-and-two-lines kokuin, which is a version of the circle with lines mon used by Honda Inaba-no-kami (see p. 96). The right portion uses a kokin of the common nine-stars mon, used by Matsudaira Yamashiro-no-kami (see p. 51) among others.
Photo by Eric Obershaw

Blocks from Edo Castle showing various kokuin. Note the line and circle on the light block, a simplification of the Mōri one-and-three-stars mon, as used by Nagai Shinano-no-kami (see p. 18).
Photo by Eric Obershaw

A block from Edo Castle showing a money changers' weight mon, as used by Horio Yamashiro-no-kami (see p. 203).
Photo by Eric Obershaw

Personal Objects

Personal items such as boxes and dishware would be decorated in a way somewhat similar to the decorative detailing on weapons. While this may have been used for practical identification purposes on ordinary chests and belongings in a camp, there are many examples on fancier items used more decoratively.

A 16th-century lacquer tray decorated with paulownia and chrysanthemum mon.
Photograph ©2015 Museum of Fine Arts, Boston.

An early-17th-century stationery box with paulownia mon.
Metropolitan Museum of Art

A 17th-century writing cabinet featuring Tokugawa hollyhock mon in both gold foil and in detail on the metal fittings.
Metropolitan Museum of Art

A 17th-century dish featuring the hollyhock mon, likely presented as a gift to the Shōgun.
Metropolitan Museum of Art

A 13th century abbot's seat with a circled gentian mon.
Tokyo National Museum

A 17th-century quiver with a dragonfly design.
Ann and Gabriel Barbier-Mueller Collection

This detail of an early-17th-century folding screen shows a fence decorated with an unusual variety of mon.
Metropolitan Museum of Art

A fan from circa 1600 showing shops with mon-bearing curtained doorways in front of a Christian church.
Wikimedia Commons

End of Contextual Information

To match the original source, the annotated translation is presented in right-to-left order. Thus, the next page is the end of the translation. For the start of the translation, turn to the far end of the red section.

O-umajirushi: **Annotated Translation**

Starting here, proceeding to the left, are all six scrolls of *O-umajirushi* with translation and annotations. To match the original work, this translation is presented in left-to-right order.

For more information about the structure of *O-umajirushi* and about reading this translation, see "Reading *O-umajirushi*" on page xx.

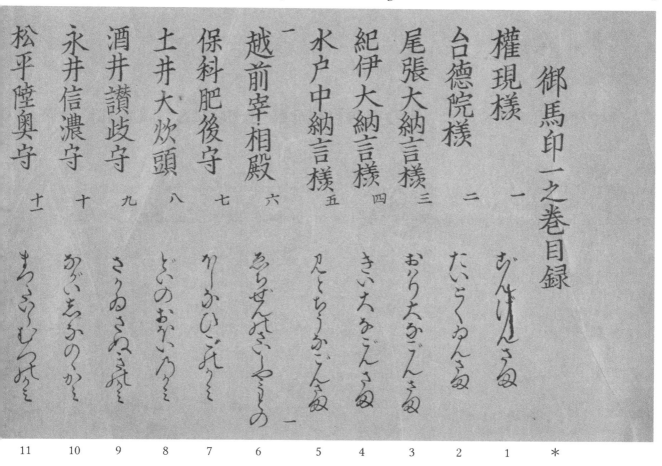

御馬印一之巻目録

*	一	二	三	四	五	六	七	八	九	十	十一
	權現様	台德院様	尾張大納言様	紀伊大納言様	水戸中納言様	越前宰相殿	保科肥後守	土井大炊頭	酒井讃岐守	永井信濃守	松平陸奥守
	ぎんげんさ	たいとくゐんさ	おり大なごんさ	きいたをごんさ	みとちうかごんさ	をちぜんさいやうの	かひこゑ	どいのおいい	さゐさぬき	あかいしなのく	まうたらむつの

| 11 | 10 | 9 | 8 | 7 | 6 | 5 | 4 | 3 | 2 | 1 | * |

These first three manuscript pages serve as a table of contents for Volume 1. While *O-umajirushi* numbers its pages, this table of contents doesn't label entries with page numbers, only with the order they appear in the document.

1. 權現様　一　ぎんげんさ (ごんげんさま; Gongen-sama):
Posthumous "god" name of Tokugawa Ieyasu (徳川家康) (1542–1616),[1, p. 540] referring to him as the manifestation of a Buddha in a Shintō Kami

    Sons include Yūki Hideyasu as well as Tokugawa Hidetada, Yoshinao, Yorinobu, and Yorifusa, all included later on this table-of-contents page. Half brother of Matsudaria Sadakatsu (entry 3 on p. 42). Stepbrother of Naitō Nobunari (entry 13 on p. 44).

    權現 is a historical variant of 権現.

Ieyasu became shōgun in 1603 after defeating various rival clans in battle, establishing Tokugawa rule that would last for 250 years.[53, p. 85]

2. 台德院様　二　たいとくゐんさ (たいとくゐんさま; Taitokuin-sama (lit. "Taitokuwin-sama")):
Posthumous name of Tokugawa Hidetada (徳川秀忠) (1579–1632)[1, p. 541]

    Third son and heir of Tokugawa Ieyasu[53, p. 85]. Father of Hoshina Masayuki (entry 7 on p. 3).[25, 連枝諸家（含む保科家）]

Hidetada's son and heir Tokugawa Iemitsu was shōgun at the time *O-umajirushi* was published, but does not have his own entry.

3. 尾張・大納言様　三　おハり大ゐごんさゐ (おはり大なごんさま;
        Owari Dainagon-sama (lit. "Ohari Dainagon-sama")):
  "Owari Major Councilor", i.e., Tokugawa Yoshinao (德川義直) (1600–1650)[25, 德川尾張家]
    Seventh son of Tokugawa Ieyasu[53, p. 86]
    大納言 is a historical variant of 大納言.

    "Owari" here refers to the domain Yoshinao ruled. (See p. xxii for discussion of provinces and feudal domains.)

4. 紀伊・大納言様　四　きい大ゐごんさゐ (きい大なごんさま; Kii Dainagon-sama):
  "Kii Major Councilor", i.e., Tokugawa Yorinobu (德川頼宣) (1602–1671)[25, 德川紀州家]
    Eighth son of Tokugawa Ieyasu[53, p. 86]

5. 水戸・中納言様　五　ゑとちうゐごんさゐ (みとちうなごんさま;
        Mito Chūnagon-sama (lit. "Mito Chiunagon-sama")):
  "Mito Middle Councilor", i.e., Tokugawa Yorifusa (德川頼房) (1603–1661)[1, p. 541]
    Ninth son of Tokugawa Ieyasu[53, p. 86]
    水戸 is a historical variant of 水戸, and 中納言 is a variant of 中納言.

6. 越前・宰相殿　六　ゑちぜん𛂧さいしやうとの (ゑちぜんのさいしやうとの;
        Echizen no Saishō-tono (lit. "Wechizen no Saishiyau-tono")):
  "State Councilor of Echizen", i.e., Yūki Hideyasu (結城秀康) (1574–1607)[1, p. 813]
    Second son of Tokugawa Ieyasu, brought up by Toyotomi Hideyoshi (entry 3 on p. 114).[53, p. 56] Father of
      Matsudaira Naomasa (entry 5 on p. 43).

7. 保科・肥後守　七　やくゐひご𛂧らゐ (ほしなひごのかみ; Hoshina Higo-no-kami):
  "Hoshina, Provincial Governor of Higo", i.e., Hoshina Masamitsu (保科正光) (1561–1631) or his adopted heir Hoshina
    Masayuki (保科正之) (1611–1672)[25, 連枝諸家（含む保科家）]
    Masayuki was the son of Tokugawa Hidetada (entry 2 on p. 2).

8. 土井・大炊頭　八　どいのおやい乃らゐ (どいのおほいのかみ;
        Doi no Ōi-no-kami (lit. "Doi no Ohoi-no-kami")):
  "Doi, Head of the Bureau of Palace Kitchens", i.e., Doi Toshikatsu (土井利勝) (1573–1644)[1, p. 532]
    Advisor to both Tokugawa Hidetada, above, and Hidetada's son Iemitsu.[40, DOI Toshikatsu]

    "Kami" (head) here uses 頭, unlike the 守 used for provincial governors. (See p. xiv.) Note also the 'no' between the
    family name and the title, which is sometimes used for bureaucratic titles but rarely for provincial governors.

9. 酒井・讃岐守　九　さゐゐさぬき𛂧らゐ (さかゐさぬきのかみ;
        Sakai Sanuki-no-kami (lit. "Sakawi Sanuki-no-kami")):
  "Sakai, Provincial Governor of Sanuki", i.e., Sakai Tadakatsu (酒井忠勝) (1587–1662)[25, 酒井若狭家]
    Cousin of Sakai Tadayo (entry 24 on p. 6)
    A Sakai Tadakatsu from a different Sakai family line appears on the next page.
    讃岐 is a historical variant of 讃岐.

10. 永井・信濃守　十　ゐぢいゐのゝかみ (ながいしなのゝかみ; Nagai Shinano-no-kami):
  "Nagai, Provincial Governor of Shinano", i.e., Nagai Naomasa (永井尚政) (1587–1668)[25, 永井家]
    Brother of Nagai Naokiyo (entry 21 on p. 79)
    信濃 is a historical variant of 信濃.
    This entry, unlike "Sakai" in the previous entry, uses 'i', not 'wi', as the pronunciation for 井, suggesting that 'wi'
      and 'i' already sound the same.

11. 松平・陸奥守　十一　まつさいゝむつ𛂧らゐ (まつたいらむつのかみ;
        Matsudaira Mutsu-no-kami (lit. "Matsutaira Mutsu-no-kami")):
  "Matsudaira, Provincial Governor of Mutsu", i.e., Matsudaira Masamune (松平政宗) (1567–1636)[25, 伊達家]
    Also known as Date Masamune (伊達政宗)
    Based on other examples, the pronunciation here is "Matsudaira" despite the omitted dakuten.

    Date Masamune was a powerful daimyō who ruled a large part of northern Japan and supported the Tokugawa
    campaign for power. He was also interested in Christianity and sent an embassy to Europe.[53, p. 33]

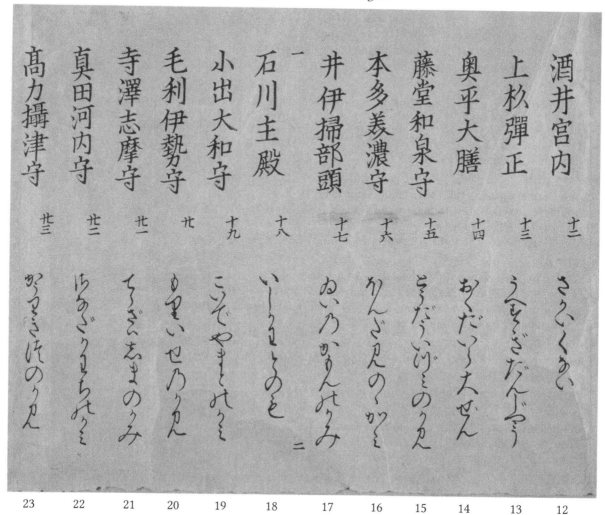

12. 酒井・宮内　十二　さくいくゐい (さかいくない; Sakai Kunai):
"Sakai, Imperial Household [official]", i.e., Sakai Ietsugu (酒井家次) (1564–1618), who became Greater Assistant
　　Director in 1589, or his son Sakai Tadakatsu (酒井忠勝) (1594–1647), who did so in 1609[25, 酒井左衛門家]
　This Sakai Tadakatsu is from a different branch than the one on the previous page.
　宮内 is a historical variant of 宮内.

13. 上杉・彈正　十三　うへもぎだん じやう (うへすぎだんじやう; Uesugi Danjō (lit. "Uesugi Danjiyau")):
"Uesugi, Imperial Prosecuting and Investigating [official]", i.e., Uesugi Kenshin (上杉謙信) (1530–1578), his adopted
　　son[1, p. 132] Uesugi Kagekatsu (上杉景勝) (1555–1623), or Kagekatsu's son Uesugi Sadakatsu (上杉定勝)
　　(1604–1645)[25, 上杉家]
　彈正 is a historical variant of 弾正.

　Uesugi Kenshin is known as one of the greatest commanders in Japanese history, involved in many of the conflicts
of Sengoku Japan. Kagekatsu won his inheritance by defeating Kenshin's biological son, Kagetora, militarily.[53, p. 89]

14. 奥平・大膳　十四　おくだい〻大ぜん (おくだいら大ぜん; Okudaira Daizen):
"Okudaira, Great Dining [official]", i.e., Okudaira Iemasa (奥平家昌) (1577–1614)[25, 奥平家]
　Brother of Matsudaira Tadaaki (entry 2 on p. 76)

15. 藤堂・和泉守　十五　とうだういげミのっろ (とうだいづみのかみ;
　　　　Tōdō Izumi-no-kami (lit. "Toudou Idzumi-no-kami")):
　　"Tōdō, Provincial Governor of Izumi", i.e., Tōdō Takatora (藤堂高虎) (1556–1630)[1, p. 534]
　　　藤堂 is a historical variant of 藤堂.

　　　Served Oda Nobunaga (entry 1 on p. 114) and later Toyotomi Hideyoshi (entry 3 on p. 114). Served as a commande
　　　during the invasion of Korea.

16. 本多・美濃守　十六　やんざゑのゝかミ (ほんだみのゝかみ; Honda Mino-no-kami):
　　"Honda, Provincial Governor of Mino", i.e., Honda Tadamasa (本多忠政) (1575–1631)[25, 本多平八家]
　　　From a different Honda line than Honda Toshimasa (entry 13 on p. 78) and from Honda Tadatoshi (entry 1 on p. 186
　　　美濃 is a historical variant of 美濃.

17. 井伊・掃部頭　十七　ゐい乃かゑんゑろみ (ゐいのかもんのかみ;
　　　　Ii no Kamon-no-kami (lit. "Wii no Kamon-no-kami")):
　　"Ii, Head of the Bureau of Palace Cleaning", i.e., Ii Naotaka (井伊直孝) (1590–1659)[1, p. 70]

　　The Kamon was responsible for the construction and cleaning of places for court ceremonies, dealing with such
　　things as tatami mats and bamboo blinds.[22, 掃部寮] While this may seem an strange position for a samurai lord,
　　keep in mind that these were formal court positions that conveyed court rank, and day-to-day operations were
　　presumably delegated.

18. 石川・主殿　十八　いしろゑとのゑ (いしかわとのも; Ishikawa Tonomo):
　　"Ishikawa, Palace Stores [official]", i.e., Ishikawa Tadafusa (石川忠総) (1582–1650)[25, 石川家]

19. 小出・大和守　十九　こいでやまとゑろみ (こいでやまとのかみ; Koide Yamato-no-kami):
　　"Koide, Provincial Governor of Yamato", i.e., Koide Yoshimasa (小出吉政) (1565–1613)[1, p. 319] or his son Koide
　　　　Yoshihide (小出吉英) (1587–1666)[25, 小出家]
　　　Yoshihide was Koide Yoshichika (entry 4 on p. 148)'s elder brother.

20. 毛利・伊勢守　廿　ゑゑいせ乃ろゑ (もりいせのかみ; Mori Ise-no-kami):
　　　廿 is a historical variation of 廿, another way of writing 二十 (20).
　　"Mori, Provincial Governor of Ise", i.e., Mōri Takamasa (毛利高政) (1559–1628)[25, 毛利佐伯家]
　　　In modern Japanese, the Mori clan is read as Mōri.

　　　Served Toyotomi Hideyoshi (entry 3 on p. 114) in Korea, and later fought against Tokugawa Ieyasu (entry 1 on p.
　　　2).[53, p. 63]

21. 寺澤・志摩守　廿一　てしざハゑまのゑみ (てらざはしまのかみ;
　　　　Terazawa Shima-no-kami (lit. "Terazaha Shima-no-kami")):
　　"Terazawa, Provincial Governor of Shima", i.e., Terazawa Hirotaka (寺沢広高) (1563–1633)[25, 二代で断絶した大名]
　　　寺澤 is a historical variant of 寺沢.

　　　Served Toyotomi Hideyoshi (entry 3 on p. 114) and later fought for Tokugawa Ieyasu (entry 1 on p. 2).[53, p. 84]

22. 真田・河内守　廿二　はゐざろゑちゑろミ (さなだかわちのかみ; Sanada Kawachi-no-kami):
　　"Sanada, Provincial Governor of Kawachi", i.e., Sanada Nobuyoshi (真田信吉) (1595–1635)[25, 真田家]
　　　Son of Sanada Nobuyuki (entry 34 on p. 191)
　　　真田 is a historical variant of 真田.

23. 髙力・攝津守　廿三　かうゑきほのゑゑ (かうりきつのかみ; Kōriki Tsu-no-kami (lit. "Kauriki Tsu-no-kami")):
　　"Kōriki, Provincial Governor of Tsu [i.e., Settsu]", i.e., Kōriki Tadafusa (高力忠房) (1584–1655)[25, 高力家]
　　　髙力 is a historical variant of 高力, and 攝津 is a variant of 摂津.
　　　"Tsu" is an alternate reading of "Settsu"; this is an unusual case of two kanji together read as a single mora (syllable

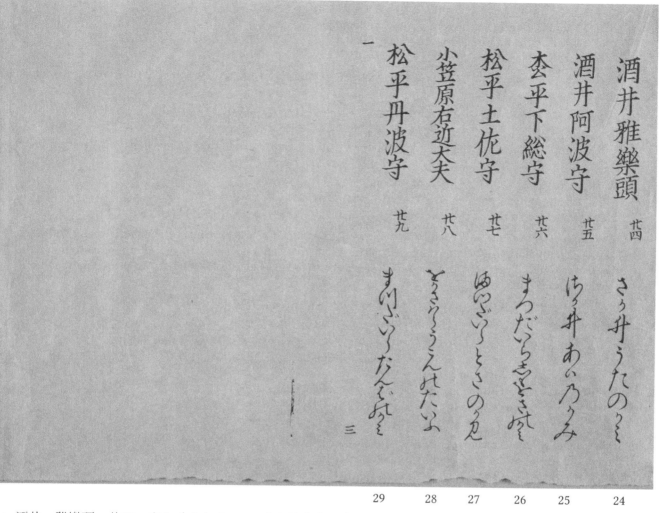

Vol. 1

4. 酒井・雅樂頭　廿四　さらⱦうたのⱦⱳⱦ (さかゐうたのかみ; Sakai Uta-no-kami (lit. "Sakawi Uta-no-kami")):
   "Sakai, Head of the Bureau of Court Music", i.e., Sakai Tadayo (酒井忠世) (1572–1636)[25, 酒井雅楽頭家]
   Father of Sakai Tadayuki, next entry. Cousin of Sakai Tadakatsu (entry 9 on p. 3).
   雅樂 is a historical variant of 雅楽.

5. 酒井・阿波守　廿五　ⱦらⱦあハ乃うみ (さかゐあはのかみ; Sakai Awa-no-kami (lit. "Sakawi Aha-no-kami")):
   "Sakai, Provincial Governor of Awa", i.e., Sakai Tadayuki (酒井忠行) (1599–1636)[25, 酒井雅楽頭家]
   Son of Sakai Tadayo

6. 杢平・下総守　廿六　まつだいら志ⱦをさ⺈ⱦⱦ (まつだいらしもをさのかみ;
   Matsudaira Shimōsa-no-kami (lit. "Matsudaira Shimowosa-no-kami")):
   "Matsudaira, Provincial Governor of Shimōsa", i.e., Matsudaira Tadaaki (松平忠明) (1583–1644)[25, 奥平家]
   Brother of Okudaira Iemasa (entry 14 on p. 4); adopted by Tokugawa Ieyasu (entry 1 on p. 2), his grandfather.[53, p. 57]
   杢平 is a historical variant of 松平.

7. 松平・土佐守　廿七　ⱳつざいⱦとさのⱦ⺈ (まつだいらとさのかみ; Matsudaira Tosa-no-kami):
   "Matsudaira, Provincial Governor of Tosa", i.e., Matsudaira Tadayoshi (松平忠義) (1592–1664)[25, 山内家]
   Also known as Yamauchi Tadayoshi (山内忠義)
   土佐 is a historical variant of 土佐.

28. 小笠原・右近大夫　廿八　をかさ ハ〵うこん ⟋たいふ (をかさはらうこんのたいふ;
    Ogasawara Ukon-no-taifu (lit. "Okasahara Ukon-no-taifu")):
    "Ogasawara, Greater Director of the Right Inner [Imperial Guard]", i.e., Ogasawara Tadazane (小笠原忠真)
    (1596–1667)[25, 小笠原小倉家]

    Brother of Ogasawara Tadanaga (entry 17 on p. 79) and Ogasawara Tadatomo (entry 1 on p. 76)

    While the clan name here is written "Okasawara", without the dakuten to make 'ka' into 'ga', other uses in
    O-umajirushi (e.g., Ogasawara Tadatomo (entry 1 on p. 76)) suggest that the "Ogasawara" pronunciation is correct.

29. 松平・丹波守　廿九　まつ ざい〵たんゞ ⟋ う ミ (まつだいらたんばのかみ; Matsudaira Tanba-no-kami):
    "Matsudaira, Provincial Governor of Tanba", i.e., Matsudaira Yasunaga (松平康長) (1562–1632), who received the title
    in 1592; his son, Matsudaira Yasunao (松平庸直) (1617–1634), who received it in 1633, or Yasunao's nephew,
    Matsudaira Mitsushige (松平光重) (1622–1668), who received it in 1635[25, 戸田家]
    Yasunaga is the father-in-law of Toda Ujikane (entry 17 on p. 117).
    丹波 is a historical variant of 丹波.

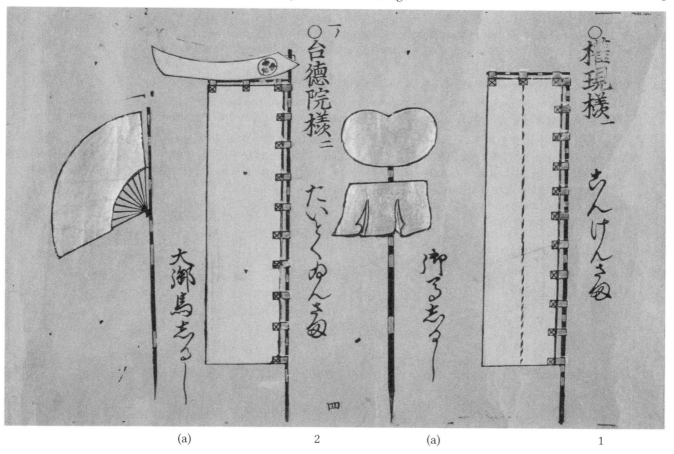

(a)   2   (a)   1

1. 權現様　一　さんけんさゑ (こんけんさま; Gongen-sama):
Posthumous "god" name of Tokugawa Ieyasu (徳川家康) (1542–1616),[1, p. 540] referring to him as the manifestation of a Buddha in a Shintō Kami

This simple white nobori (see p. xvi) features a line of visible stitching.

Note also the circular marks above the names. They may be registration marks to help line up multiple woodblocks.

(a) 御多志る� (御馬しるし; o-mumajirushi): honorable battle standard

This particular umajirushi (see p. xvi) is a gold-painted wooden shape above a hanging slashed banner. Banners slashed to divide them into streamers were common and are called kirisaki (切裂, "slashed thing"). This particular type is also called a noren (暖簾),[31, p. 166] a name also used for similar curtains used in doorways, and was frequently used in standards. While other sources give the top shape as a ball,[31, p. 161] here it seems to be a heart shape, possibly imitating the hollyhock leaf used in the Tokugawa mon (see p. 10).

2. 台徳院様　二　たいとくゐんさゑ (たいとくゐんさま; Taitokuin-sama):
Posthumous name of Tokugawa Hidetada (徳川秀忠) (1579–1632)[1, p. 541]

This maneki (see p. xvi) shows the Tokugawa hollyhock mon (see p. 10).

(a) 大御馬志る〳 (大御馬しるし; ō-o-mumajirushi): great honorable standard

Many daimyō would use two battle standards, an ō-*umajirushi* (大馬印), or great standard, and a ko-*umajirushi* (小馬印), or lesser standard. Standards were often large wooden objects, like this folding fan.[52, p. 27] Ieyasu, his father, famously used a seven-slat folding fan,[8, p. 22] but this fan has ten slats.

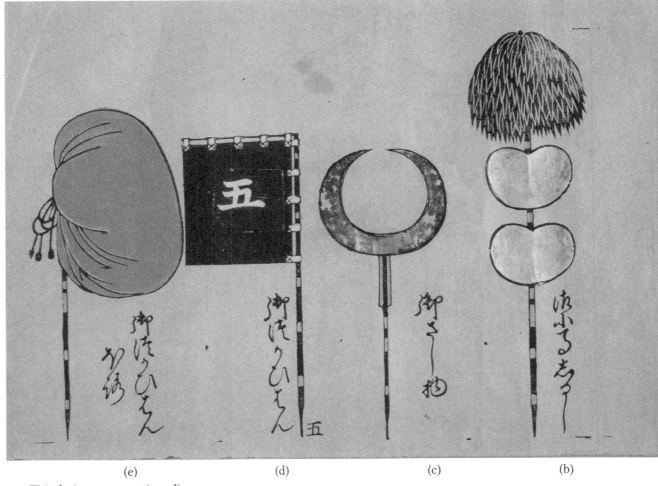

(e)   (d)   (c)   (b)

(Taitokuin-sama, continued)

(b) 御小多志るし (御小馬しるし; o-ko-mumajirushi): honorable lesser battle standard

The practice of having two different standards was common for more powerful daimyō. It was practical for coordinating large numbers of troops, and the added pageantry would also be more impressive both on the battlefield and when processing. In 1645, regulations officially reserved the practice of having two standards to daimyō of a certain station.[53, p. 23]

(c) 御さし物 (御さし物; o-sashimono): honorable identifying object

This sashimono (see p. xvi) is a wooden three-dimensional object, a silver crescent in the shape of a helmet crest (see p. 129).

(d) 御ほろひそん (御つかひはん; o-tsukaiban): honorable messengers

A *tsukaiban* (使番) was a battlefield messenger; this was a position given to distinguished samurai.[52, p. 30]

This banner is an example of a single character on a banner; here the character is 五 (go, meaning "five"). This ma‑ be a reference to the Buddhist deity Fudō.[52, p. 30]

(e) 御ほろひそん　不該 (御つかひはん　ほろ; o-tsukaiban horo): honorable messenger canopy.

A *horo* (母衣) was a sort of cloak or canopy worn on the back and designed to inflate when the wearer is riding a horse, used for identification and to protect against arrows. They were worn by messengers, bodyguards, and oth‑ elite samurai.[52, p. 30]

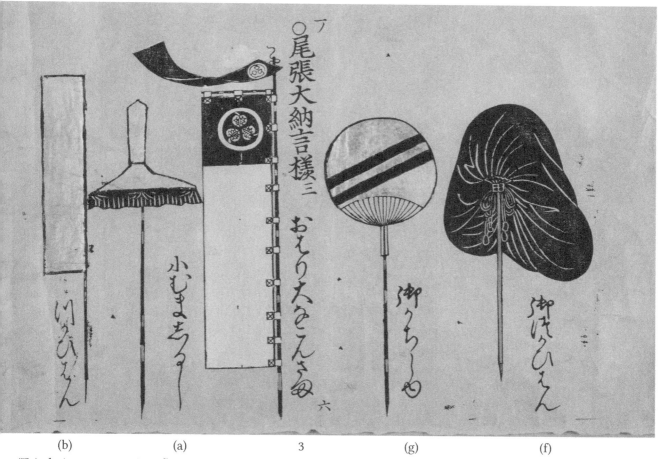

<table>
<tr><td>(b)</td><td>(a)</td><td>3</td><td>(g)</td><td>(f)</td></tr>
</table>

(Taitokuin-sama, continued)

f) 𛀁ほうひそん (御つかひはん; o-tsukaiban): honorable messengers

g) 𛀁うちしや (御かちしゆ; o-kachishu): honorable bodyguards

Kachishu (徒士衆, also read kachishū) were humble samurai who served as bodyguards on foot. The kanji literally mean "junior samurai multitude". This device is a rigid, non-folding fan (an "uchiwa") with two diagonal stripes.

---

3. 尾張・大納言様　三　おそり大ゐこんさゐ (おはり大なこんさま; Owari Dainagon-sama): "Owari Major Councilor", i.e., Tokugawa Yoshinao (徳川義直) (1600–1650)[25, 徳川尾張家]

The hollyhock is most strongly associated with the Tokugawa clan and the Tokugawa Shōgunate, which ruled Japan through the Edo period. The three-leaf design shown here was used both by the main Tokugawa line and by branch families under the name of Matsudaira, and occasionally granted to supporters as a sign of favor.[6, p. 58] Here it is used with a horizontal division from black to white. For the origin legend behind the hollyhock mon, see p. xxix.

a) 小むま志る〱 (小むましるし; ko-mumajirushi): lesser standard

むま (muma) is the historical reading of 馬 (modernly uma), meaning "horse"; see p. xiv.

This standard is a cloth umbrella with a sword blade shape on top.[53, p. 86]

b) つうひそん (つかひはん; tsukaiban): messengers

Instead of using strips like most banners in *O-umajirushi*, this banner's support poles are sewn into its edge; this style is called a *nuikurumi bata* (縫いくるみ旗; "sewn and covered banner").[31, p. 8]

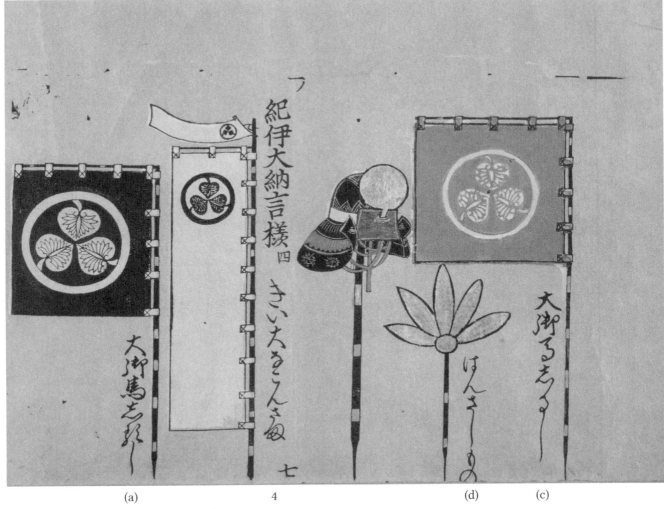

| (a) | 4 | | (d) | (c) |

(Owari Dainagon-sama, continued)

(c) 大御馬志るし (大御馬しるし; ō-o-mumajirushi): great honorable standard

This is an example of a large square banner as a standard, rather than a three-dimensional object.

(d) はんさしもの (はんさしもの; ban-sashimono): guard identifying object

A *ban-sashimono* (番指物) was a banner or other device worn on the back by samurai in a *ban* (guard) division.

This particular device is a gold sunburst of five flower-petal-like rays.[53, p. 86]

Unlabeled helmet

Note also the unlabeled helmet shown here. Samurai would often embellish their helmets with metal crests, wooden horns, three-dimensional paper-mâché shapes, and other designs to make them distinctive. A daimyō's helmet could also be carried on a spear as a form of heraldic display.[52, p. 29]

This particular helmet has a gold disc helmet crest emerging from a green peak.[53, p. 86]

4. 紀伊・大納言様　四　きい大ゐこんさゐ (きい大なこんさま; Kii Dainagon-sama):
   "Kii Major Councilor", i.e., Tokugawa Yorinobu (徳川頼宣) (1602–1671)[25, 徳川紀州家]

(a) 大御馬志るし (大御馬しるし; ō-o-mumajirushi): great honorable standard

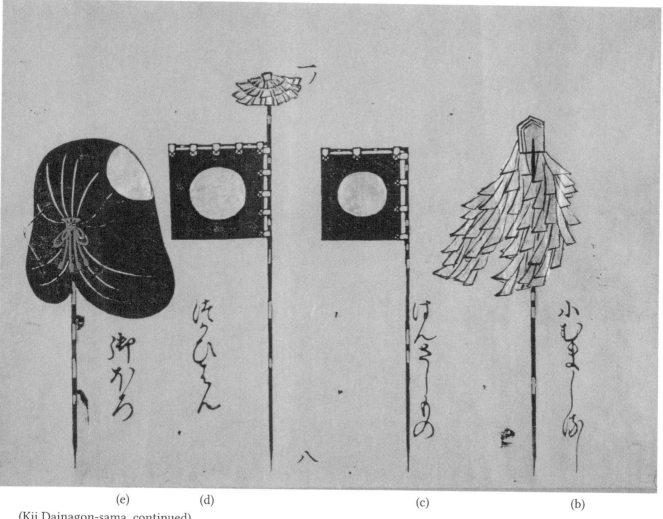

(e) (d) (c) (b)

(Kii Dainagon-sama, continued)

(b) 小むまくほく (小むましるし; ko-mumajirushi): lesser standard

This standard is a gold-painted version of a gohei. A *gohei* (御幣) is a Shintō ritual wand hung with paper strips.

(c) はんさくもの (はんさしもの; ban-sashimono): guard identifying object

These banners use a gold disc mon. This is the same design used on the modern Japanese flag, the *hi no maru* (日の丸; "sun disc"). The red sun disc on a white background wasn't a national flag until after the Meiji Restoration in 1868. Nevertheless, this plain circular disc was a popular motif, and similar designs were used by a wide variety of daimyō. It was not necessarily intended to represent only the sun; in addition to the sun,[31, p. 195] this motif is also identified as a mochi (餅), a type of sticky rice cake;[49, p. 280][31, p. 151] as an ensō (円相), a circle symbolizing enlightenment in Zen Buddhism;[49, p. 80] or simply as a circle.[31, p. 203]

(d) ほろひそん (つかひはん; tsukaiban): messengers

This banner adds a dashi of gold paper strips (see p. xvi), reminiscent of the large gohei used in the lesser standard.

(e) 御かろ (御ほろ; o-horo): honorable canopy

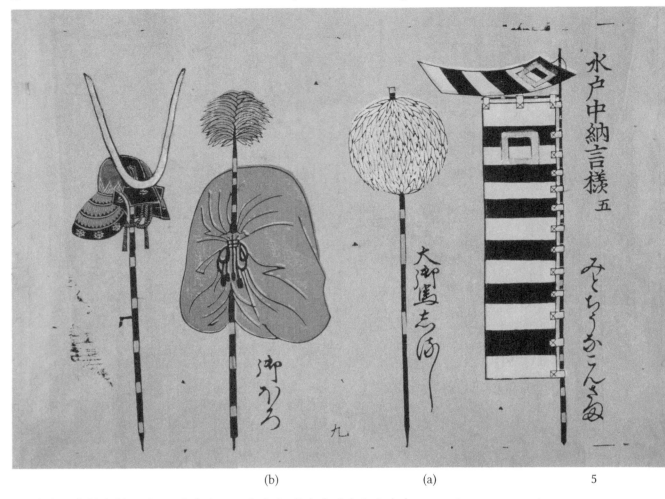

(b)　　　　　　　　　(a)　　　　　　　　5

5. 水戸・中納言様　五　みとちうゐこんさゐ (みとちうなこんさま; Mito Chūnagon-sama):
   "Mito Middle Councilor", i.e., Tokugawa Yorifusa (徳川頼房) (1603–1661)[1, p. 541]

   This banner uses a hollow square mon, called "one eye" (一つ目; hitotsu me).[19, p. 98] Mon like drawn with an outline rather than filled-in are described as "shadowed" (陰; kage). It's possibly related to the more well-known "nail puller" mon (see p. 220). It's also notable for its background of horizontal stripes, leading to a lower-contrast three-color design that's unusual for the display of a mon.

(a) 大㆐馬ゐほし (大御馬しるし; ō-o-mumajirushi): great honorable standard

   This standard is a white-painted feather ball.[53, p. 86]

(b) ㆐かろ (御ほろ; o-horo): honorable canopy

   Blue feathers above a red horo.[53, p. 86] According to the second edition, these are "asagi" (浅葱), a light blue.[35, p. 2●]

Unlabeled helmet

   This helmet has a helmet crest of large stylized horns. Tokugawa Ieyasu (entry 1 on p. 2) supposedly once had a dream in which he consulted with Oda Nobunaga (entry 1 on p. 114) and Toyotomi Hideyoshi (entry 3 on p. 114) about political matters. In the dream, all wore helmets with helmet horns. He interpreted the horns as a symbol o● unanimity and, according to tradition, gave them to his son Yorinobu (previous section).[12, p. 64] However, in *O-umajirushi* it is Yorifusa, here, who is shown using helmet horns, and Yūki Hideyasu (also a son of Ieyasu), in th● next section, who uses a mon based on helmet horns.

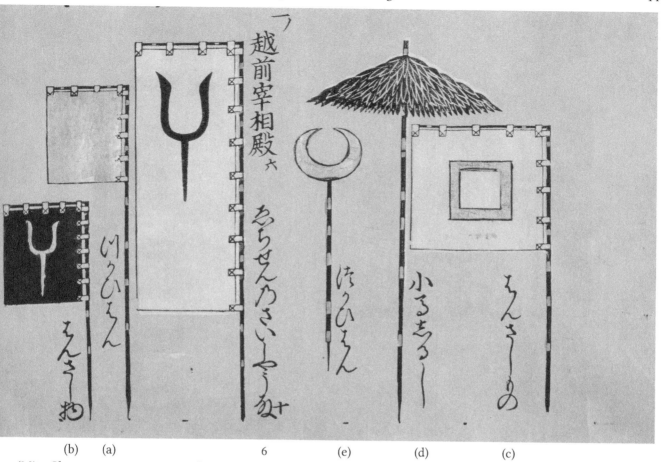

(b)　　(a)　　　　　6　　　(e)　　　　(d)　　　(c)

(Mito Chūnagon-sama, continued)

c) そんさくもの (はんさしもの; ban-sashimono): guard identifying object

d) 小马まるく (小馬しるし; ko-mumajirushi): lesser standard

This standard seems to be a thatched umbrella.

e) ほうひそん (つかひはん; tsukaiban): messengers

This device is a gold crescent in the style of a helmet crest.

---

6. 越前・宰相殿　六　ゑちせん乃さいくやう殿 (ゑちせんのさいしやう殿;
Echizen no Saishō-tono):

"State Councilor of Echizen", i.e., Yūki Hideyasu (結城秀康) (1574–1607)[1, p. 813]

The mon used here is a *tentsuki* (天衝),[31, p. 225] which is a particular shape of helmet crest patterned after a sasumata (刺股), a two-pronged weapon used to trap criminals non-lethally.[22, 天衝.1] It is also identified as an arrowhead (矢の根; ya-no-ne).[19, p. 230] (Forked arrowheads were used to hunt birds or disable horses.)

a) 川うひそん (つかひはん; tsukaiban): messengers

b) そんさく物 (はんさし物; ban-sashimono): guard identifying object

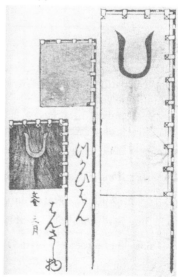

The same tentsuki banners from the second edition of O-umajirushi. *The lower points were painted over after printing for an unknown reason.*[35, p. 28]

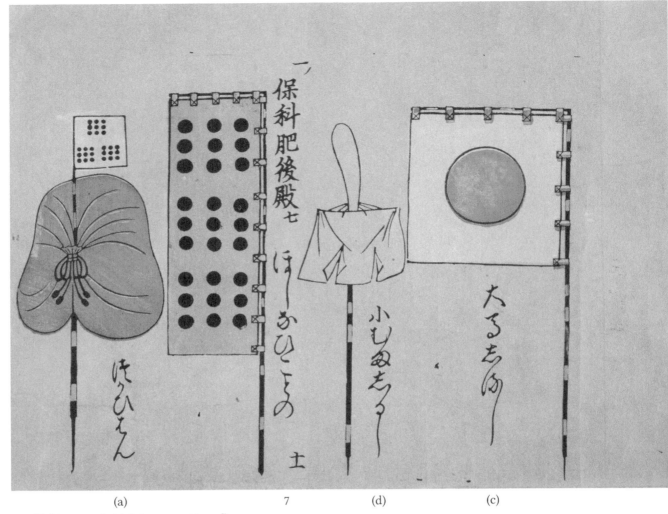

(a)   7   (d)   (c)

(Echizen no Saishō-tono, continued)

(c) 大馬志はし (大馬しるし; ō-mumajirushi): great standard

This disc standard looks identical to the modern Japanese flag. Again, this design wasn't used as a national flag until 1870, after the Meiji Restoration.

(d) 小むゐ志るし (小むましるし; ko-mumajirushi): lesser standard

A noren (see p. xxx) with a shape above it perhaps representing a formal cap.

7. 保科・肥後殿　七　ほしゐひことの (ほしなひことの; Hoshina Higo-tono):
"Hoshina, Provincial Governor of Higo", i.e., Hoshina Masamitsu (保科正光) (1561–1631) or his adopted heir Hoshina Masayuki (保科正之) (1611–1672)[25, 連枝諸家（含む保科家）]

This section label uses a slightly different title than the table of contents, which used "Higo-no-kami".

This banner consists of three mon, each consisting of nine stars forming a square. Stars function as the diminutive of the disc motif, suggesting a smaller circle and only used in groups of more than one.

While the banner appears blue here, in the second edition it's clearly green. Blue and green are traditionally considered the same color in Japanese.[35, p. 30]

(a) ほうひそん (つかひはん; tsukaiban): messengers

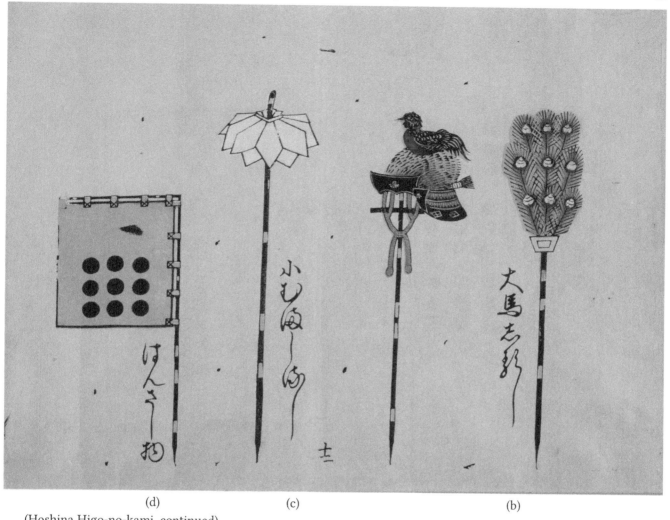

| (d) | (c) | (b) |

(Hoshina Higo-no-kami, continued)

(b) 大馬志れし (大馬しるし; ō-mumajirushi): great standard

This standard is made of peacock (孔雀; kujaku) feathers.[44, p. 3.30]

Unlabeled helmet

This helmet looks like it's intended to continue the peacock theme. *Shoshō Kisei Zu*, however, identifies it as a 黒鳥 (read "kokuchō" or "kurotori"),[44, p. 3.31] which could refer specifically to a black swan or more generally to any black bird.

(c) 小むほくほく (小むましるし; ko-mumajirushi): lesser standard

This standard has a bundle of paper shapes tied to it, possibly imitating paulownia leaves. A more elaborate standard using similar bundles was used by Ogasawara Ukon-no-taifu (see p. 38).

(d) はんさし物 (はんさし物; ban-sashimono): guard identifying object

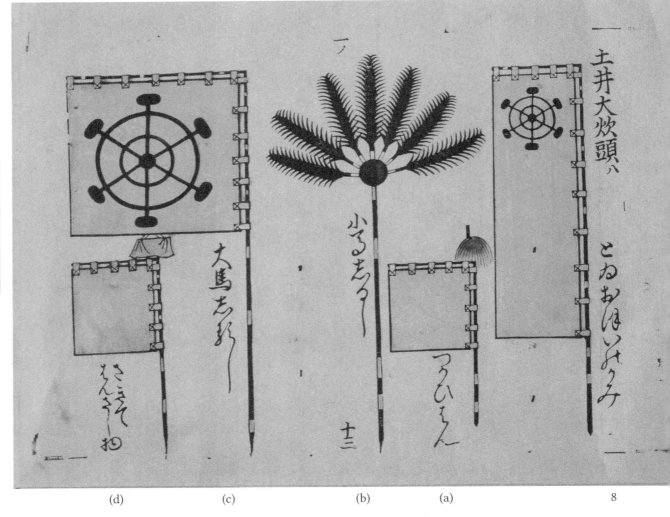

(d) (c) (b) (a) 8

8. 土井・大炊頭　八　とゐおほいゝらみ (とゐおほいのかみ; Doi no Ōi-no-kami):
"Doi, Head of the Bureau of Palace Kitchens", i.e., Doi Toshikatsu (土井利勝) (1573–1644)[1, p. 532]

This mon depicts a water wheel. Doi's troops were known as the "yellow regiment" due to their yellow banners.[53, p. 34] Note that the yellow color here is different than the gold used more frequently in *O-umajirushi*.

(a) つゝひそん (つかひはん; tsukaiban): messengers

A yellow banner with a tuft as the dashi.

(b) 小ゟまるゝ (小馬しるし; ko-mumajirushi): lesser standard

This standard consists of seven black chicken feather plumes.[53, p. 34]

(c) 大馬まれゝ (大馬しるし; ō-mumajirushi): great standard

(d) さきて　そんさゝ物 (さきて　はんさし物; sakite ban-sashimono): front-line guard identifying object

This yellow banner has a small unslashed hanging cloth rectangle as the dashi.

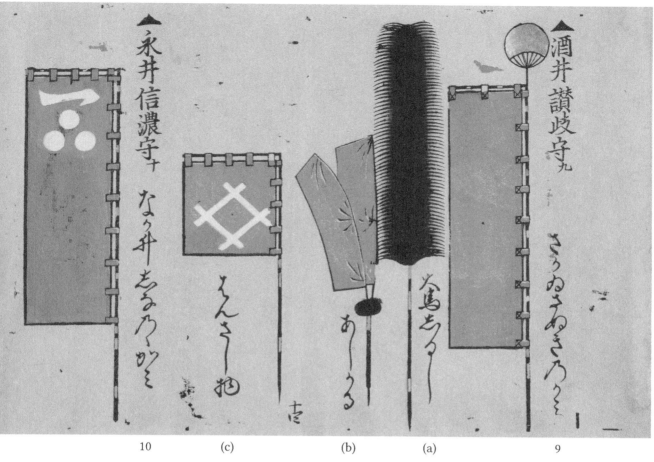

10　　　　(c)　　　　(b)　　　　(a)　　　　9

9. 酒井・讃岐守　九　さらゐさぬきのうミ (さかゐさぬきのかみ; Sakai Sanuki-no-kami): "Sakai, Provincial Governor of Sanuki", i.e., Sakai Tadakatsu (酒井忠勝) (1587–1662)[25, 酒井若狭家]

This nobori has a small gold non-folding fan added as a dashi (see p. xvi).

a) 大馬あるし (大馬しるし; ō-mumajirushi): great standard

This standard is a pole covered with black feathers.

b) あしらる (あしかる; ashigaru): foot soldiers

A red double banner.

c) そんさし物 (はんさし物; ban-sashimono): guard identifying object

The well frame mon is used here as a reference to the Sakai family name: the second kanji, 井 ('i'), means "well" and also visually resembles a well frame. (Traditional Japanese wells use a square design with extended posts; in this particular mon the frame is standing on its corner.)

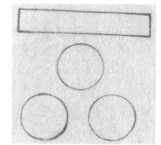

The version of the one-and-three-stars mon given in Ken-mon Shokamon.[20, p. 16]

---

10. 永井・信濃守　十　なうヰあるろゝかミ (なかゐしなのゝかみ; Nagai Shinano-no-kami): "Nagai, Provincial Governor of Shinano", i.e., Nagai Naomasa (永井尚政) (1587–1668)[25, 永井家]

This mon combines the kanji numeral 一 (ichi, meaning "one") with three stars. The stars reference the three stars of Orion's belt, traditionally called the "three warriors" or "general stars", and thus have martial connotations.[9, p. 41] This particular combination has a long history; it's also associated with the Mōri clan, and was used by the Nagai, Mōri, Takefuji, Hagi, and Kahata families at least as early as 1470.[20, pp. 16–17]

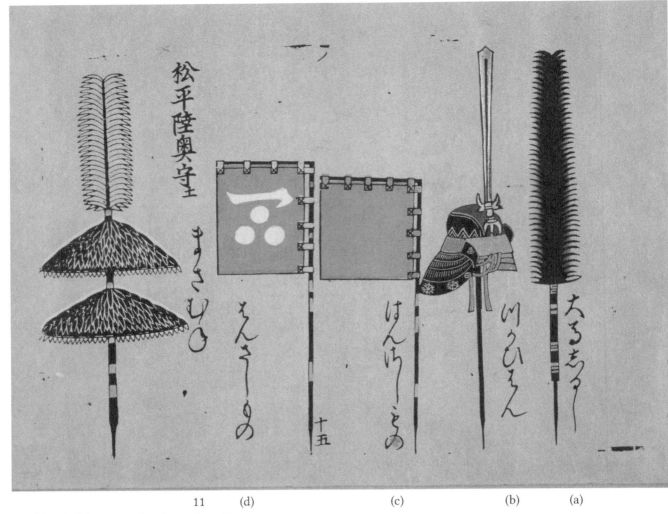

11   (d)   (c)   (b)   (a)

(Nagai Shinano-no-kami, continued)

(a) 大馬まるく (大馬しるし; ō-mumajirushi): great standard

This standard is a pole covered with black feathers.

(b) りっひそん (つかひはん; tsukaiban): messengers

Using a helmet as the device for messengers is unusual. This helmet features a large sword attachment.

(c) はんはくをの (はんさしもの; ban-sashimono): guard identifying object

(d) そんさくゆの (はんさしもの; ban-sashimono): guard identifying object

11. 松平・陸奥守　十一　まさむね (まさむね; Matsudaira Mutsu-no-kami: Masamune):
    "Matsudaira, Provincial Governor of Mutsu", i.e., Matsudaira Masamune (松平政宗) (1567–1636)[25, 伊達家]

    Unusually, the hiragana here identify the individual's *nanori*, or formal given name, rather than giving the reading of the kanji. (Note that this Masamune is not the legendary swordsmith Masamune from the 13th-14th centuries, but may have been named after him.)

    In addition, instead of a nobori as a primary device, Masamune here has a standard with a pillar of feathers above two black thatch umbrellas. Given that a lesser standard is indicated on the next page, this is implied to be his greater standard. Other sources show the feathers here to be gold.[31, p. 149] [53, p. 33]

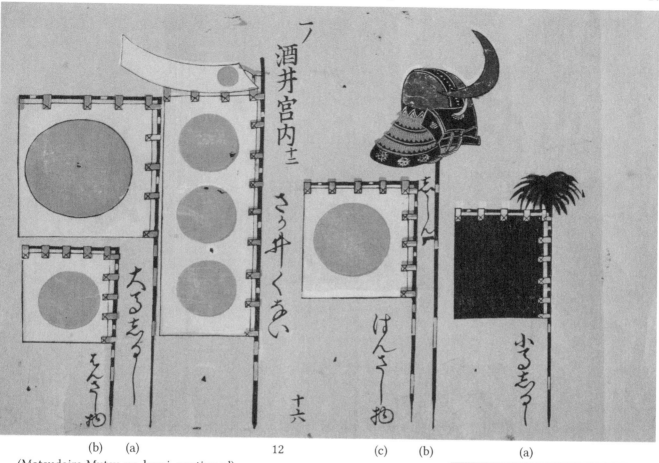

(b)   (a)   12   (c)   (b)   (a)

(Matsudaira Mutsu-no-kami, continued)

(a) 小馬まるし (小馬しるし; ko-mumajirushi): lesser standard

   This standard is a black banner with a dashi of a tuft of black feathers.

(b) まるん (ししん; jishin): personal [helmet]

   Since this caption is written without dakuten to indicate which syllables are voiced, this could be read in multiple ways: "shishin", "jishin", "shijin", and "jijin", all of which are Japanese words. Other captions (e.g., on p. 163) clarify that this is 自身 ("jishin"), meaning "personal".

   This helmet uses the shape of the moon as its helmet crest.

(c) はんさし抄 (はんさし物; ban-sashimono): guard identifying object

   Red disc on white.

---

12. 酒井・宮内　十二　さうゐくゐい (さかゐくない; Sakai Kunai): "Sakai, Imperial Household [official]", i.e., Sakai Ietsugu (酒井家次) (1564–1618), who became Greater Assistant Director in 1589, or his son Sakai Tadakatsu (酒井忠勝) (1594–1647), who did so in 1609[25, 酒井左衛門家]

(a) 大馬まるし (大馬しるし; ō-mumajirushi): great standard

(b) そんさし抄 (はんさし物; ban-sashimono): guard identifying object

A 17th-century helmet with a similar asymmetric moon shape.
Ann and Gabriel Barbier-Mueller Collection

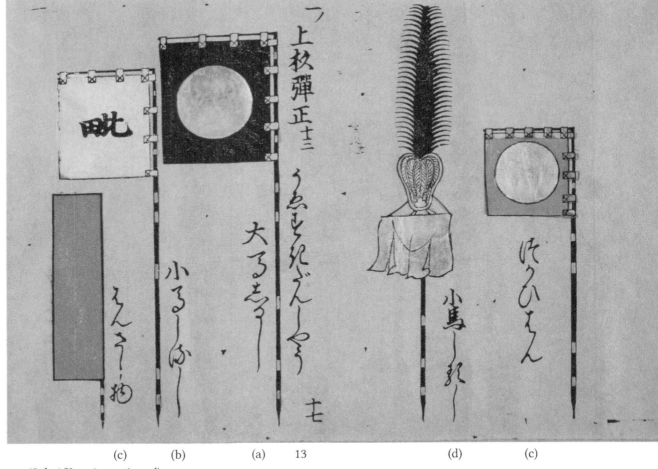

(c)   (b)   (a)   13   (d)   (c)

(Sakai Kunai, continued)

(c) ほかひそん (つかひはん; tsukaiban): messengers

> Contrasting with the preceding discs, this uses gold on blue. Another source gives this as red on green.[53, p. 75]

(d) 小馬しるし (小馬しるし; ko-mumajirushi): lesser standard

> This standard features a pillar of feathers, a wood war fan shape carved with a pattern that somewhat resembles wisteria leaves, and a hanging noren. (See p. 22 for more on war fans.)

---

13. 上杉・彈正　十三　うゑもねざん しやう (うゑすきだんしやう; Uesugi Danjō):

> "Uesugi, Imperial Prosecuting and Investigating [official]", i.e., Uesugi Kenshin (上杉謙信) (1530–1578), his adopted son[1, p. 132] Uesugi Kagekatsu (上杉景勝) (1555–1623), or Kagekatsu's son Uesugi Sadakatsu (上杉定勝) (1604–1645)[25, 上杉家]

> This samurai has no primary nobori listed. Other sources suggest that this is Kagekatsu's heraldry.[53, p. 89][31, p. 47]

(a) 大多ゐるし (大馬しるし; ō-mumajirushi): great standard (a gold disc on black)

(b) 小多くほく (小馬しるし; ko-mumajirushi): lesser standard

> This is an alternate way of writing the character 毘 (bi), the first kanji in the name of Bishamonten, Buddhist Guardian of the North.[53, p. 89] As a god of warfare and punisher of evildoers, he's fitting for samurai to invoke.

(c) そんさし物 (はんさし物; ban-sashimono): guard identifying object

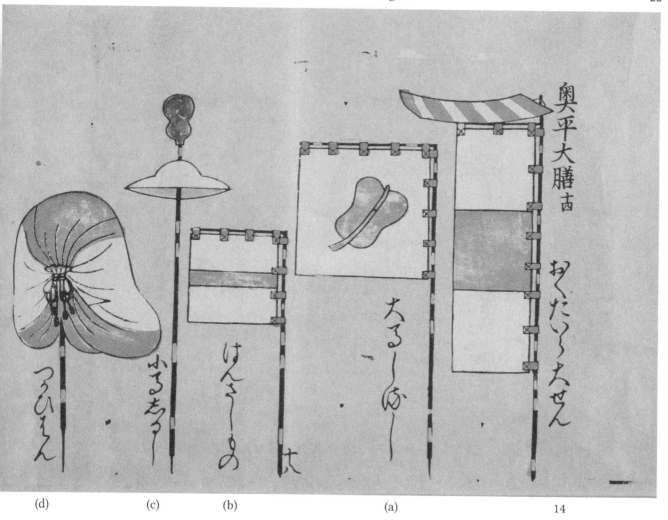

(d) (c) (b) (a) 14

4. 奥平・大膳　十四　おくたい〱大せん (おくたいら大せん; Okudaira Daizen):
"Okudaira, Great Dining [official]", i.e., Okudaira Iemasa (奥平家昌) (1577–1614)[25, 奥平家]

This nobori features a large red horizontal band on a white banner; the small accompanying maneki features several white horizontal stripes on red.

a) 大馬くはく (大馬しるし; ō-mumajirushi): great standard

This mon depicts a tō-uchiwa (唐団扇) or gunbai (軍配), a type of Japanese war fan used for signaling, to block arrows, and as a sun shade.[49, p. 71] Its use dates back to the 12th century.[12, p. 61]

b) はんさ〱ゐの (はんさしもの; ban-sashimono): guard identifying object

c) 小馬まるく (小馬しるし; ko-mumajirushi): lesser standard

This standard consists of a straw hat and a silver gourd.[53, p. 71]

d) つゥひそん (つかひはん; tsukaiban): messengers

A red and white horo.

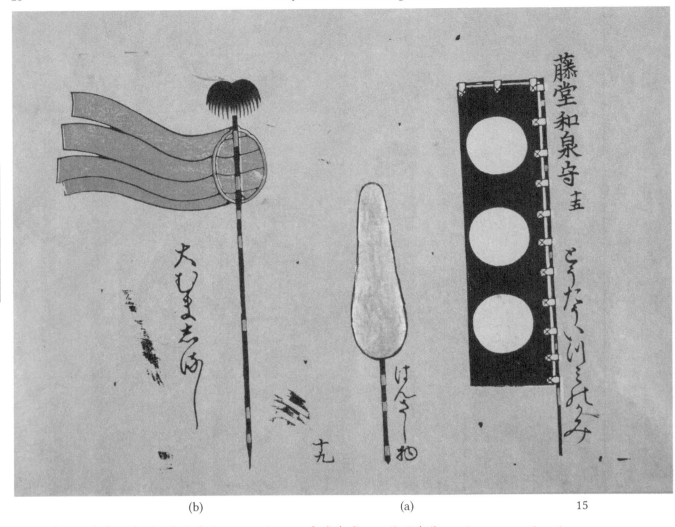

         (b)   (a)   15

15. 藤堂・和泉守　十五　とうたういりミ札ぅミ (とうたういつみのかみ; Tōdō Izumi-no-kami):
"Tōdō, Provincial Governor of Izumi", i.e., Tōdō Takatora (藤堂高虎) (1556–1630)[1, p. 534]

     White discs on black.

(a) はんさ〻物 (はんさし物; ban-sashimono): guard identifying object

     This device features a large, oblong gold-painted wood shape, possibly an elongated gourd.[53, p. 84]

(b) 大むま志はく (大むましるし; ō-mumajirushi): great standard

     This standard is a red *fukinuki* (吹貫), a large hollow streamer formed of strips of cloth attached to a ring, with a small plume of black feathers added.

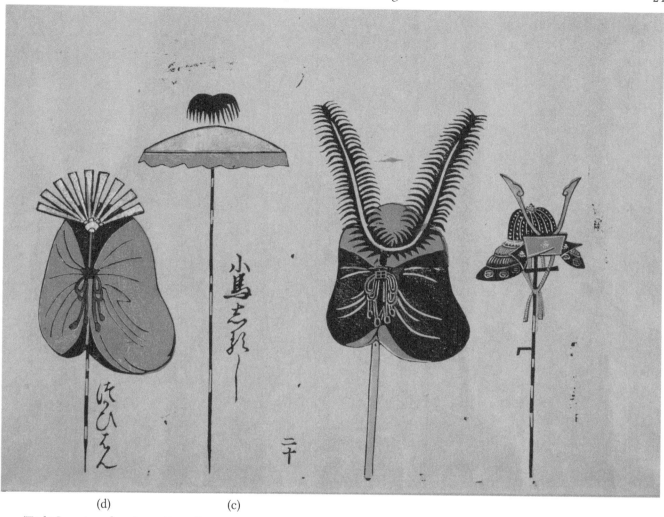

(d)　　　　　　　　(c)

(Tōdō Izumi-no-kami, continued)

Unlabeled helmet

Elaborate helmet horns and a red front piece.

Unlabeled horo (canopy)

Note the large, feather-covered helmet crest shape on this two-colored horo. Devices, like this horo and the preceding helmet, are sometimes left unlabeled in *O-umajirushi* since they can be identified by shape.

(c) 小馬志毬く (小馬しるし; ko-mumajirushi): lesser standard

This standard is a gold umbrella shape with a hanging red cloth border and a plume of black feathers on top. It seems to actually be a type of standard known as a *shidegasa* (四手笠; "four-hand conical hat"), a conical hat with Shintō paper strips hanging from its edge.[31, p. 157]

(d) ほうひそん (つかひはん; tsukaiban): messengers

This horo canopy has a shape made from wooden slats that resembles a widely spaced slatted fan. Unlike previous fans, a hiōgi (桧扇; "cypress fan") is a folding fan made of distinct wood slats not connected by silk or paper, associated with use by nobility.[12, p. 60] This design is also similar to a sunburst,[53, p. 84] such as the one used by Owari Dainagon-sama (see p. 11).

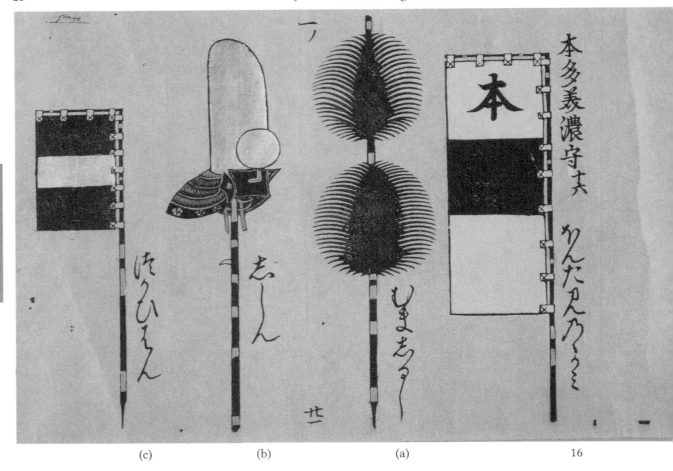

(c)　　　　　　　(b)　　　　　　　(a)　　　　　　　16

16. 本多・美濃守　十六　やんたみ乃ゝうミ (ほんたみのゝかみ; Honda Mino-no-kami):
    "Honda, Provincial Governor of Mino", i.e., Honda Tadamasa (本多忠政) (1575–1631)[25, 本多平八家]

    This banner uses the character 本 (hon, meaning "root"), the first kanji in the Honda name (and also the second character in Nihon/Nippon, the name of Japan). It also features a large black horizontal band.

(a) むま志るし (むましるし; mumajirushi): battle standard

    Two black feather balls.

(b) 志ゝん (ししん; jishin): personal [helmet]

    This helmet features a tall gold paper-mâché "catfish tail" (鯰尾; namazuo) shape[53, p. 39] and a disc mon.

(c) 本つひもん (つかひはん; tsukaiban): messengers

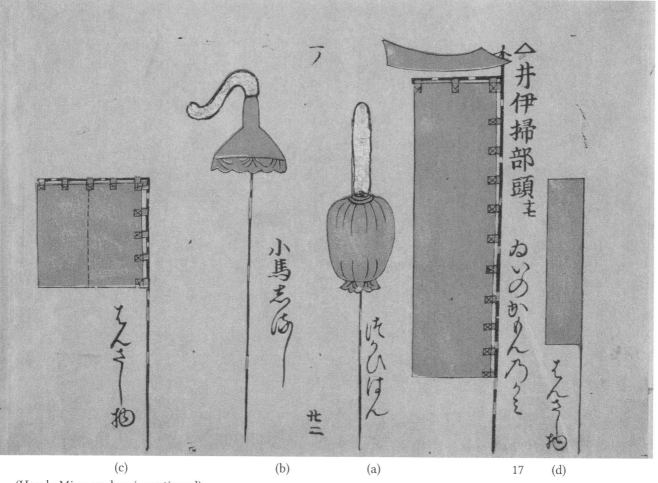

(c)   (b)   (a)   17   (d)

(Honda Mino-no-kami, continued)

d) そんさく物 (はんさし物; ban-sashimono): guard identifying object

7. 井伊・掃部頭　十七　ゐいのかゝんのうミ (ゐいのかもんのかみ; Ii no Kamon-no-kami): "Ii, Head of the Bureau of Palace Cleaning", i.e., Ii Naotaka (井伊直孝) (1590–1659)[1, p. 70]

Note the triangular mark above this name, different from the circular mark seen earlier. There's no indication that these marks had any particular purpose beyond helping to line up woodblocks properly.

Naotaka's army was known as the "red regiment" for its use of red banners.[53, p. 43]

a) ほうひはん (つかひはん; tsukaiban): messengers

A red cloth bundle with a gold top-pole.

b) 小馬志ほく (小馬しるし; ko-mumajirushi): lesser standard

While this looks like a similar umbrella shape to the shidegasa used by Tōdō Izumi-no-kami (see p. 24), it seems to actually be a fly trap (蠅取; haetori). A similar device with a gold main canopy and red tail was used by Naotaka's father, Naomasa (not included).[31, p. 31] The second edition has this device matching Naomasa's, so the color scheme here may be an error.[35, p. 52]

c) そんさく物 (はんさし物; ban-sashimono): guard identifying object

This red banner features a line of visible stitching.

Vol. 1

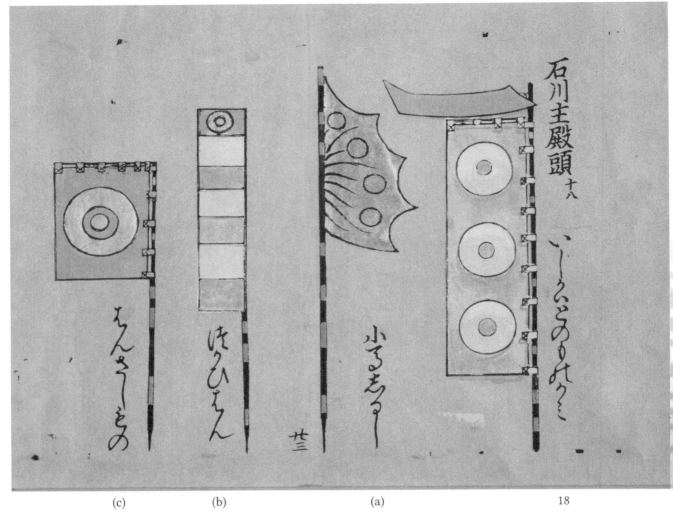

(c)   (b)   (a)   18

18. 石川・主殿頭　十八　いしかはとのものれうミ (いしかはとのものかみ; Ishikawa Tonomo-no-kami): "Ishikawa, Palace Stores [official]", i.e., Ishikawa Tadafusa (石川忠総) (1582–1650)[25, 石川家]

This section label adds an explicit "-no-kami" title; the table of contents named only the bureau, leaving the position within the bureau implied.

This geometric mon is known as a snake's eye ring (蛇の目輪; ja-no-me wa). It can also be called a *tsurumaki* ((弦巻) after a spool around which bowstrings would be wound to carry them;[6, p. 134] see p. 46.

(a) 小夛志る� (小馬しるし; ko-mumajirushi): lesser standard

This standard seems to be a large, gold-painted wooden butterfly wing.

(b) ほうひそん (つかひはん; tsukaiban): messengers

A gold snake's eye on a field of blue and white horizontal stripes.

(c) そんさしをの (はんさしもの; ban-sashimono): guard identifying object

This is a variant of the snake's eye motif with a disc or star added. This design is used by several samurai in *O-umajirushi*, but is not used as a mon in modern Japan.

A butterfly mon from Ken-mon Shokamon, *with similar detailing.*[20, p. 10]

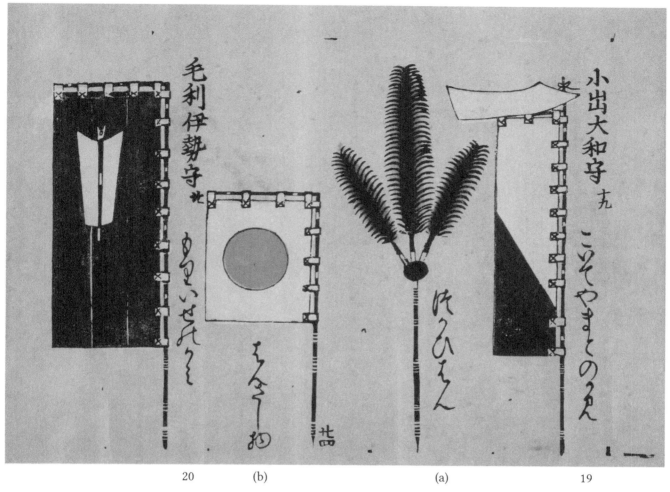

20 (b) (a) 19

19. 小出・大和守　十九　こいてやまとのうゑ (こいてやまとのかみ; Koide Yamato-no-kami):

"Koide, Provincial Governor of Yamato", i.e., Koide Yoshimasa (小出吉政) (1565–1613)[1, p. 319] or his son Koide Yoshihide (小出吉英) (1587–1666)[25, 小出家]

This nobori has a diagonal division, which is much rarer than horizontal divisions.

(a) ほうひそん (つかひはん; tsukaiban): messengers

This device consists of three feather-covered rods.

(b) そんさくね (はんさし物; ban-sashimono): guard identifying object

Another example of a disc mon.

20. 毛利・伊勢守　廿　もゑいせぬうミ (もりいせのかみ; Mori Ise-no-kami):

"Mori, Provincial Governor of Ise", i.e., Mōri Takamasa (毛利高政) (1559–1628)[25, 毛利佐伯家]

This mon shows the fletching and notch of an arrow. The way of the warrior was sometimes called "the way of the bow and arrow", and archery was an important skill for samurai.[6, p. 102]

A kokuin (see p. xxxiv) from Edo Castle featuring a simpler arrow fletching mon.
Photo by Eric Obershaw

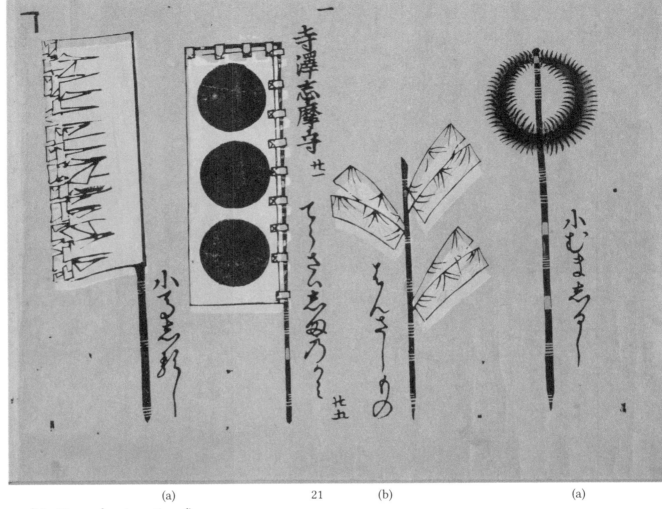

(a)   21   (b)   (a)

(Mori Ise-no-kami, continued)

(a) 小むま゙ゐる⌇ (小むましるし; ko-mumajirushi): lesser standard

This standard is a wreath covered in black feathers. The shape of the wreath, thicker at the bottom, is reminiscent of a helmet crest.

(b) そんさ⌇をの (はんさしもの; ban-sashimono): guard identifying object

Each color in *O-umajirushi* was printed separately. Here you can see that the black and white blocks were misaligned, so the white color doesn't match up correctly with the black outline.

The device itself consists of a "banner tree" of many small banners attached to a pole.

---

21. 寺澤・志摩守　廿一　て⌇さハ志ゐ乃ろミ (てらさはしまのかみ; Terazawa Shima-no-kami): "Terazawa, Provincial Governor of Shima", i.e., Terazawa Hirotaka (寺沢広高) (1563–1633)[25, 二代で断絶した大名]

Three discs.

(a) 小多゙ま゙欵⌇ (小馬しるし; ko-mumajirushi): lesser standard

This banner is in multiple layers and is slashed with many lines cut perpendicular to the far edge, creating a streamer effect that would move in the wind.

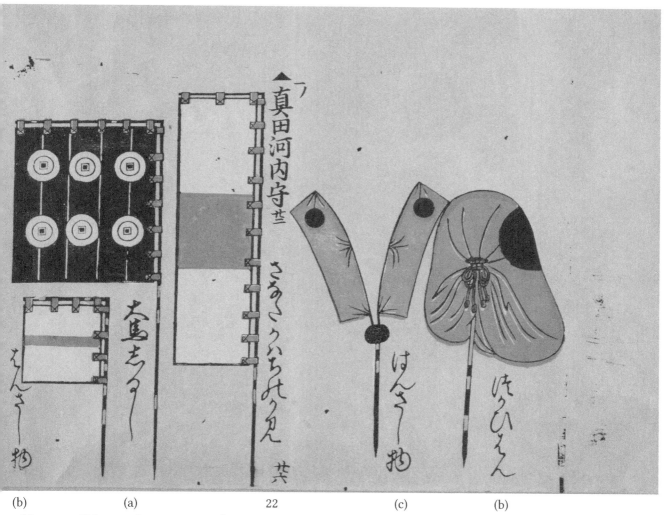

(b)   (a)   22   (c)   (b)

(Terazawa Shima-no-kami, continued)

b) ほうひそん (つかひはん; tsukaiban): messengers

Contrasting with the black disc on white of the nobori, these two devices use a black disc on red. Varying color scheme would help distinguish different banners on the battlefield, which could be important when different units were given different tasks.

c) はんさし物 (はんさし物; ban-sashimono): guard identifying object

---

22. 真田・河内守　廿二　さゐさゐハちねうゑ (さなたかはちのかみ; Sanada Kawachi-no-kami): "Sanada, Provincial Governor of Kawachi", i.e., Sanada Nobuyoshi (真田信吉) (1595–1635)[25, 真田家]

A white nobori with a thick red horizontal band.

a) 大馬まるし (大馬しるし; ō-mumajirushi): great standard

This banner shows six coins. This is the fee paid to cross the river of death, indicating that the samurai fighting under this standard are prepared to die.[52, p. 51]

b) そんさし物 (はんさし物; ban-sashimono): guard identifying object

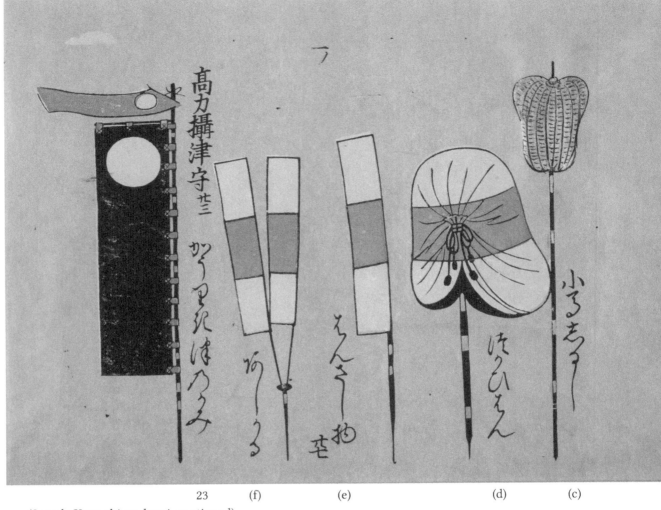

23   (f)   (e)   (d)   (c)

(Sanada Kawachi-no-kami, continued)

(c) 小马志るし (小馬しるし; ko-mumajirushi): lesser standard

This standard is a gold shape similar to a war fan, apparently woven out of something like reeds.

(d) ほうひそん (つかひはん; tsukaiban): messengers

This horo and the following banners follow the same horizontal band pattern as the nobori.

(e) そんさし物 (はんさし物; ban-sashimono): guard identifying object

(f) ほしうる (あしかる; ashigaru): foot soldiers

23. 髙力・攝津守　廿三　かう里記ほ乃ろみ (かうりきつのかみ; Kōriki Tsu-no-kami):
"Kōriki, Provincial Governor of Tsu [i.e., Settsu]", i.e., Kōriki Tadafusa (高力忠房) (1584–1655)[25, 高力家]

A white disc on two different backgrounds.

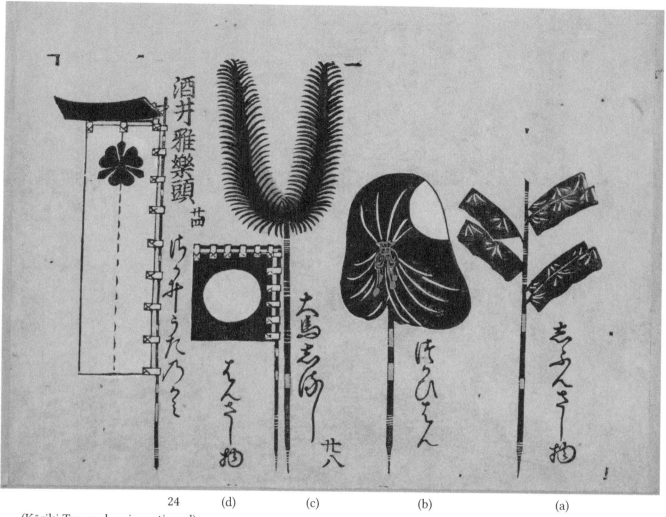

24   (d)   (c)   (b)   (a)

(Kōriki Tsu-no-kami, continued)

(a) 志ふん・さしおり (しふん・さし物; jibun sashimono): personal identifying object

    A "banner tree" of small black banners.

(b) ほうひそん (つかひはん; tsukaiban): messengers

(c) 大馬志はし (大馬しるし; ō-mumajirushi): great standard

    This standard is a very tall helmet crest shape, covered in feathers.

(d) そんさしおり (はんさし物; ban-sashimono): guard identifying object

---

24. 酒井・雅樂頭　廿四　ほう丹うた乃ろミ (さかゐうたのかみ; Sakai Uta-no-kami):
"Sakai, Head of the Bureau of Court Music", i.e., Sakai Tadayo (酒井忠世) (1572–1636)[25, 酒井雅楽頭家]

    This mon depicts wood sorrel leaves. Wood sorrel, also known as oxalis, is a small clover-like plant with edible leaves. This design dates back to the Heian period (794–1185). It's known for its fertile spreading, and in early Japan was used medicinally. It was later popular among warriors, largely for the stylized sword blades incorporated between the leaves.[6, p. 84] These sword designs, based on ancient Chinese swords rather than the Japanese katanas of the time, were incorporated into a variety of different mon designs.[12, p. 64] Another example is the "China flower" on p. 178.

    The banner also features visible stitching and a black maneki.

Vol. 1

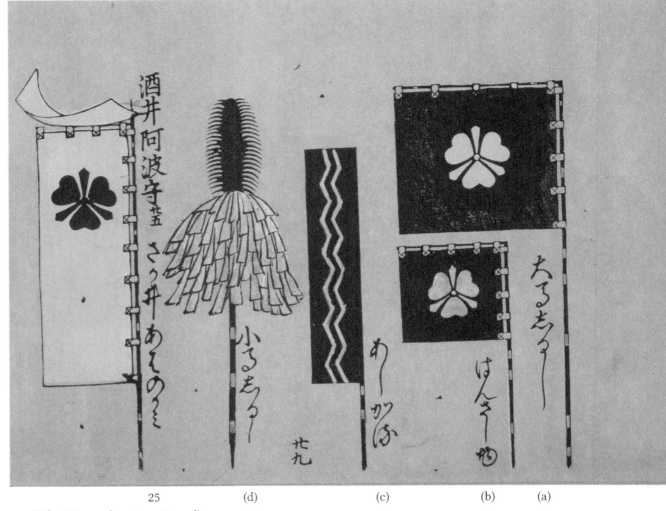

25   (d)   (c)   (b)   (a)

(Sakai Uta-no-kami, continued)

(a) 大多まるく (大馬しるし; ō-mumajirushi): great standard

(b) はんさくか (はんさし物; ban-sashimono): guard identifying object

(c) あくかっほ (あしかる; ashigaru): foot soldiers

    This banner has an unusual design of two vertical jagged lines.

(d) 小多まるく (小馬しるし; ko-mumajirushi): lesser standard

    This standard features a gohei-like collection of gold paper strips and a top-pole covered in feathers.

---

25. 酒井・阿波守　廿五　さろ斗あそのうミ (さかゐあはのかみ; Sakai Awa-no-kami):
    "Sakai, Provincial Governor of Awa", i.e., Sakai Tadayuki (酒井忠行) (1599–1636)[25, 酒井雅楽頭家]

    This Sakai nobori also uses the wood sorrel mon, but without the stitching and with a white maneki instead of a black one. The second edition gives the maneki as red, not white.[35, p. 66]

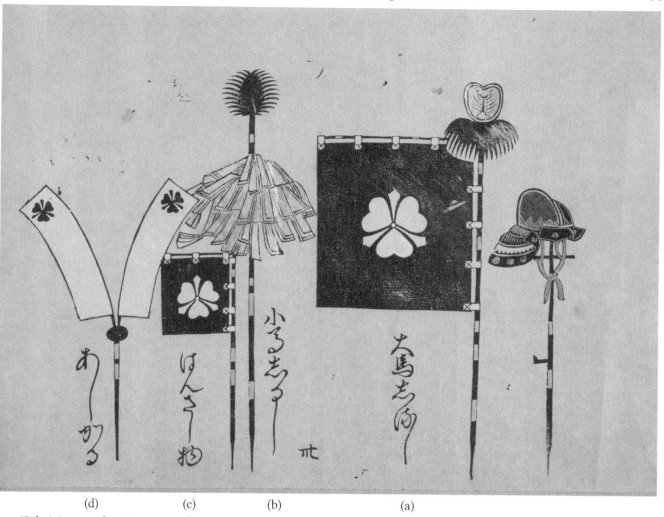

(d)   (c)   (b)   (a)

(Sakai Awa-no-kami, continued)

Unlabeled helmet

(a) 大馬志ほし (大馬しるし; ō-mumajirushi): great standard

This standard has a dashi of a tuft of black feathers and a gold-painted wooden war fan shape.

(b) 小夛志る〱 (小馬しるし; ko-mumajirushi): lesser standard

This standard is similar to the previous Sakai's lesser standard, with gohei-like paper strips; however, its feathered top-pole is shorter and it has a gap between the strips and the feathers.

(c) はんさ〱物 (はんさし物; ban-sashimono): guard identifying object

(d) あ〱かる (あしかる; ashigaru): foot soldiers

A double banner with the same wood sorrel mon, but in reverse colors. Reversing the color scheme was one common way for a samurai to distinguish their banners from each other.

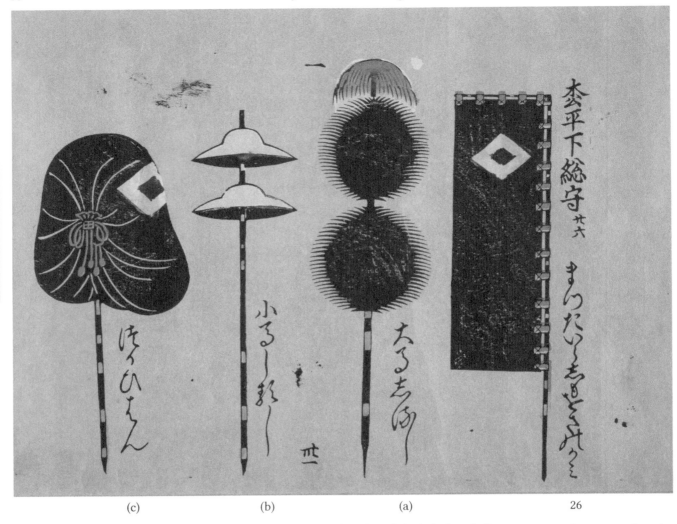

(c)　　　　(b)　　　　(a)　　　　26

26. 杢平・下総守　廿六　まつたい✓志をされうミ (まつたいらしもをさのかみ; Matsudaira Shimōsa-no-kami): "Matsudaira, Provincial Governor of Shimōsa", i.e., Matsudaira Tadaaki (松平忠明) (1583–1644)[25, 奥平家]

This shadowed (i.e., hollow) rhombus mon is very similar to the "nail puller" mon, an identically oriented hollow square (see p. 220). This rhombus design is described in Japanese as a hishi (菱), or water chestnut, whose leaves it resembles.[6, p. 136] It was used as a decorative pattern as early as the Nara period (710–794).[9, p. 110] An alternate translation is "caltrop", referring to small spiked objects which were scattered on the ground to injure and stop horses or infantry. This gives the mon a martial connotation. Effective caltrops could in fact be made from dried water chestnut seed pods, and the normal Japanese word for caltrop, makibishi (撒菱), literally means "scattered water chestnut".

(a) 大夢志はく (大馬しるし; ō-mumajirushi): great standard

Two balls covered in black feathers and a dashi of a tuft of red feathers.

(b) 小夢くれく (小馬しるし; ko-mumajirushi): lesser standard

This standard appears to consist of two straw hats painted white. Another source gives them as umbrellas.[53, p. 57]

(c) ほうひそん (つかひはん; tsukaiban): messengers

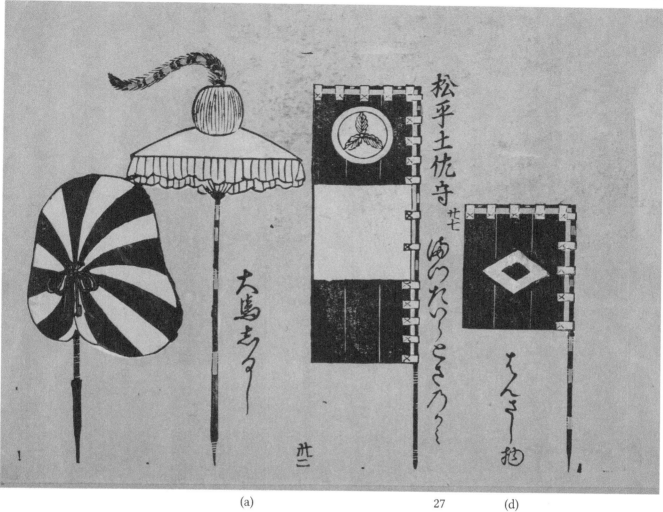

(a)　　　　　　27　　(d)

(Matsudaira Shimōsa-no-kami, continued)

(d) そんさ〻抱 (はんさし物; ban-sashimono): guard identifying object

27. 松平・土佐守　廿七　ゐつたい〻とさ乃ろﾐ (まつたいらとさのかみ; Matsudaira Tosa-no-kami):
"Matsudaira, Provincial Governor of Tosa", i.e., Matsudaira Tadayoshi (松平忠義) (1592–1664)[25, 山内家]

This mon shows three oak leaves in a ring enclosure. Oak leaves were used to present offerings to gods, and thus oak leaf mon were used for Shintō associations.[12, p. 38]

It's unusual that the space within the enclosure is the same color as the circle and the leaves, rather than contrasting with them, leaving the black outline alone to distinguish them.

(a) 大馬ゐる〻 (大馬しるし; ō-mumajirushi): great standard

This standard is a white cloth umbrella (a shidegasa; see p. 24) with what seems to a tiger's tail on top.

Unlabeled horo (canopy)

This type of multicolored design, with different colors radiating from a central point, was a common way of making a horo more distinctive.

A kokuin (see p. xxxiv) from a quarry in Izu featuring three oak leaves in a circle, along with a mon of two overlapping squares.
Photo by Eric Obershaw

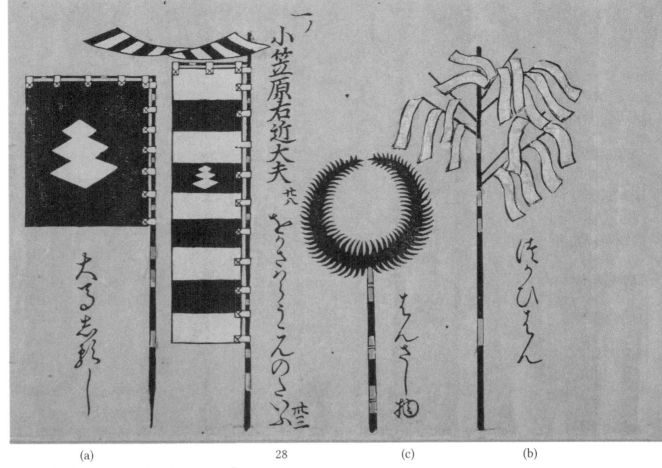

(a) 28 (c) (b)

(Matsudaira Tosa-no-kami, continued)

(b) ほうひそん (つかひはん; tsukaiban): messengers

This device imitates the branches of a tree tied with paper streamers. This type of device is called a *tanzaku etsuru* (短冊柄絃).[48, p. 73] A tanzaku is a narrow vertical strip on which poems are written, and etsuru means something like "shaft and strings". It resembles the later tradition of tying paper strips to bamboo to celebrate Tanabata, the star festival.[13, p. 20] It may have had religious significance, as similar strips can be used in Shintō contexts, or it may have reflected a love of poetry, which was common among samurai.

(c) そんさく物 (はんさし物; ban-sashimono): guard identifying object

This device consists of black feathers on a frame in the shape of the crescent helmet crest. This same wreath shape, without the feathers, was used by others in the Matsudaira clan and their Tokugawa relatives. (See, e.g., p. 9.)

---

28. 小笠原・右近大夫　廿八　をゝさはらうこんのさいふ (をかさはらうこんのたいふ; Ogasawara Ukon-no-taifu):

"Ogasawara, Greater Director of the Right Inner [Imperial Guard]", i.e., Ogasawara Tadazane (小笠原忠真) (1596–1667)[25, 小笠原小倉家]

This mon is a stack of three solid rhombuses, a common motif, on a background of horizontal stripes. For the story behind the Ogasawara mon, see p. 81.

(a) 大馬志るし (大馬しるし; ō-mumajirushi): great standard

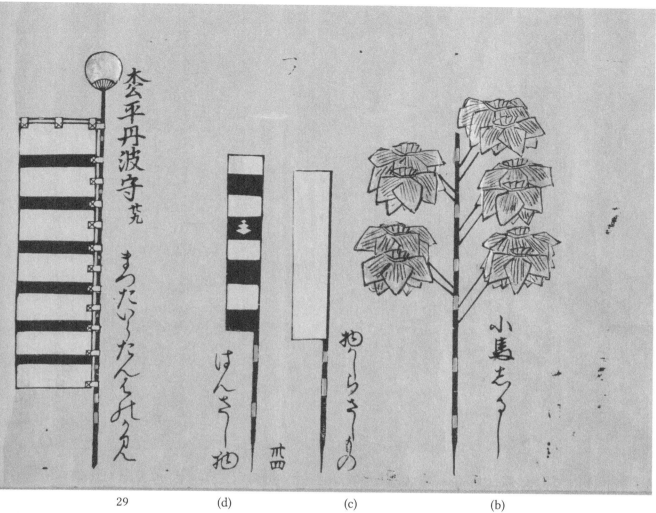

29   (d)   (c)   (b)

(Ogasawara Ukon-no-taifu, continued)

b) 小馬志るﾞ (小馬しるし; ko-mumajirushi): lesser standard

This tree-like standard is even more elaborate than the one on the previous page, with gold-painted leaves or paper shapes tied to the branches, possibly imitating paulownia leaves.[53, p. 70]

c) 物ぅくら・さしかの (物かしら・さしもの; monogashira sashimono): foot soldier commander identifying object

A *monogashira* (物頭) was a samurai who commanded a group of ashigaru (foot soldiers). A monogashira could also be called an ashigaru-taishō (足軽大将) or an ashigaru-gashira (足軽頭).

d) はんさくか (はんさし物; ban-sashimono): guard identifying object

9. 松平・丹波守　廿九　まつたいﾞたんそみぅえ (まつたいらたんはのかみ; Matsudaira Tanba-no-kami):
"Matsudaira, Provincial Governor of Tanba", i.e., Matsudaira Yasunaga (松平康長) (1562–1632), who received the title in 1592; his son, Matsudaira Yasunao (松平庸直) (1617–1634), who received it in 1633, or Yasunao's nephew, Matsudaira Mitsushige (松平光重) (1622–1668), who received it in 1635[25, 戸田家]

A small gold non-folding fan is added as a dashi, giving extra decoration to this nobori. Note also the uneven width of the horizontal stripes, unlike the more common even stripes of the preceding devices.

Vol. 1

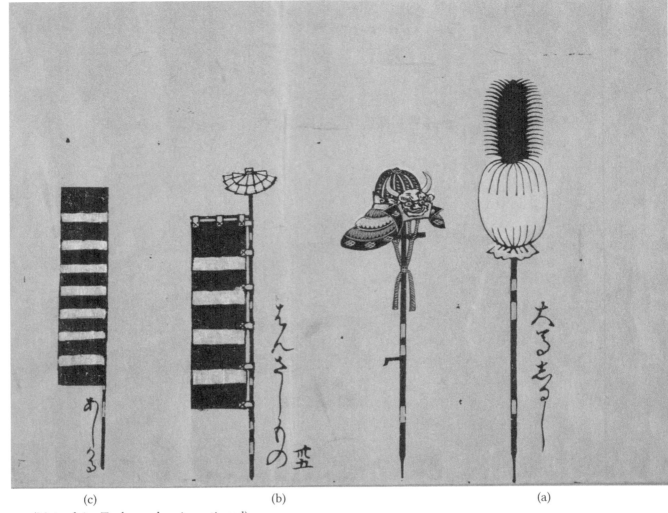

      (c)   (b)   (a)

(Matsudaira Tanba-no-kami, continued)

(a) 大馬志るし (大馬しるし; ō-mumajirushi): great standard

    This standard has a cloth bundle and a feathered top-pole.

Unlabeled helmet

    This helmet bears the face of an oni (demon).

(b) ゑんさしもの (はんさしもの; ban-sashimono): guard identifying object

    In addition to uneven horizontal stripes, this has a small paper dashi added.

(c) あしゐる (あしかる; ashigaru): foot soldiers

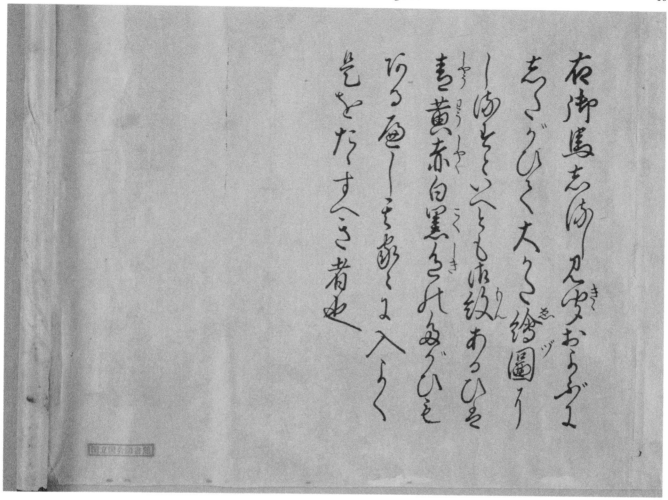

右・御馬志ほし・見聞・おらぶま
志さぐひく、大らさ・絵圖ら
しほもと・いへとも、御紋・あるひわ
青・黄・赤・白・黒・色此・ゑぐひを
ゐるゑし。其・あ々ま・入、よく
是を・たゝすへき・者・也。

右・御馬じるし・見聞・およぶに
したがひて、大かた・絵図に
しるすと・いへども、御紋・あるひは
青・黄・赤・白・黒・色の・たがひも
あるべし。其・家々に・入、よく
是を・たゞすべき・者・也。

Migi o-mumajirushi mikiki oyobu-ni
shitagai-te, ōkata wezu-ni
shirusu-to ie-domo, go-mon aruhi-wa
shō ō shaku haku koku shiki-no tagai-mo
aru-beshi. Sono ieie-ni iri, yoku
kore-wo tadasu-beki mono nari.

Even though I say I thoroughly observed the preceding battle standards and following right after recorded the greater part[1] with illustrations, there are surely even mistakes of[2] the noble crests or the blue, yellow, red, white, and black colors. The thing that should be done is to go into those various houses and correct this well.

---

[1] i.e., most of them
[2] i.e., errors in

This afterword is repeated at the end of each volume, and seems to basically be acknowledging that there may be mistakes. Note that it focuses on two areas where mistakes are particularly crucial: the mon, or crests, which often identify families, and the colors used. It specifically lists blue, yellow, red, white, and black (the five "lucky" colors[52, p. 24]) as the colors used. Black, white, yellow or gold, and red are frequently used in the manuscript, and blue to a lesser extent. Notably absent is green, used in the detailing of some of the helmets but in none of the banners, despite the popularity of plant motifs. Green was considered a shade of blue in Japan at this time, and some of the banners shown here as blue are elsewhere shown green. Purple is used in a few devices, but rarely.

The suggestion of visiting various families to verify the data seems to have prompted the investigation leading to the second edition. (See p. x.)

Other Japanese printed works from around the same time have similar postscripts acknowledging the possibility for mistakes.[39, p. 67] This probably reflects a cultural expectation of humbleness and self-deprecation, especially in the case of a work involving individuals of a higher social class.

The stamp in the lower left-hand corner identifies this as belonging to the National Diet Library of Japan; it is a modern addition.

Translation Notes:

1. This paragraph combines kuzushiji (cursive) hiragana and kanji, with furigana (small hiragana placed alongside a kanji) indicating the pronunciation of some of the kanji.
2. It uses dakuten inconsistently, including them at times but omitting them for more "obvious" voiced syllables, such as in "jirushi".
3. It also omits the suffixes from the kun readings of kanji when they'd normally be explicitly written with hiragana. Examples of this are 見聞 instead of 見聞き, 入 instead of 入り, and 其 instead of 其の.
4. As is common in Japanese, most pronouns are omitted, leaving the subjects of many verbs open to interpretation. The person writing the afterword could actually be different from the person doing the observing and recording, and it's unclear whether the author here is suggesting that he himself intends to go correct his own work or whether he thinks someone else should do so.
5. 見聞きおよぶ is made up of 見聞く (observe) and およぶ (reach). When およぶ is used as a helper verb, though, it can mean to do something thoroughly or completely.
6. あるひは is a common variation for あるいは, which can be pronounced the same way. In this usage, it just means "or", though in other uses it can refer to a certain thing, time, or situation.

End Volume 1

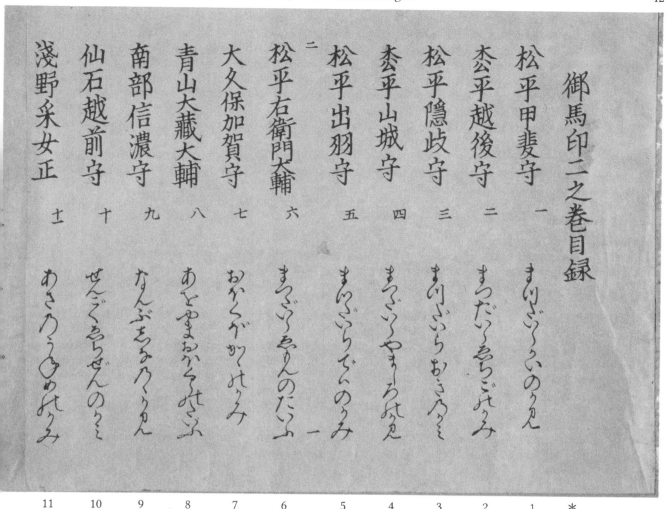

＊　御馬印・二之巻・目録 (O-umajirushi Ni-no-maki Mokuroku)
　　Honorable Battle Standards: Second Volume: Index

1. 松平・甲斐守　一　まりざい〜ろいのう忍 (まつだいらかいのかみ; Matsudaira Kai-no-kami):
　"Matsudaira, Provincial Governor of Kai", i.e., Matsudaira Tadayoshi (松平忠良) (1582–1624), who received the title in 1596,[25, 松平久松家] or (from a different line) Matsudaira Nagaoki (黒田長興) (1610–1665), who received it in 1626[25, 黒田家]

　　This is not the Matsudaira Tadayoshi that was a son of Tokugawa Ieyasu.
　　甲斐 is a historical variant of 甲斐.

2. 杢平・越後守　二　まつだい〜ゑちごれうみ (まつだいらゑちごのかみ;
　　Matsudaira Echigo-no-kami (lit. "Matsudaira Wechigo-no-kami")):
　"Matsudaira, Provincial Governor of Echigo", i.e., Matsudaira Mitsunaga (松平光長) (1615–1707)[25, 松平越前津山家]
　　杢平 is a historical variant of 松平.

3. 松平・隱歧守　三　まりざいらおき乃うミ (まつだいらおきのかみ; Matsudaira Oki-no-kami):
　"Matsudaira, Provincial Governor of Oki", i.e., Matsudaria Sadakatsu (松平定勝) (1560–1624), who received the title in 1601, or his son Matsudaira Sadayuki (松平定行) (1587–1668), who received it in 1626[25, 松平久松家]

　　Sadakatsu was the half brother of Tokugawa Ieyasu (entry 1 on p. 2).
　　隱歧 is a historical variant of 隠岐.

4. 杢平・山城守　四　まつざい◌やま◌ろ◌ら◌ゑ (まつだいらやましろのかみ; Matsudaira Yamashiro-no-kami):
   "Matsudaira, Provincial Governor of Yamashiro", i.e., Matsudaira Tadakuni (松平忠国) (1597–1659)[25, 松平藤井家]
       杢平 is a historical variant of 松平.

5. 松平・出羽守　五　まりざいらでハのらみ (まつだいらではのかみ;
       Matsudaira Dewa-no-kami (lit. "Matsudaira Deha-no-kami")):
   "Matsudaira, Provincial Governor of Dewa", i.e., Matsudaira Naomasa (松平直政) (1601–1666)[25, 松平越前松江家]
       Son of Yūki Hideyasu (entry 6 on p. 3)
       出羽 is a historical variant of 出羽.

6. 松平・右衛門大輔　六　まつざい◌ゑ◌んのたいふ (まつだいらゑもんのたいふ;
       Matsudaira Emon-no-taifu (lit. "Matsudaira Wemon-no-taifu")):
   "Matsudaira, Greater Assistant [Director] of the Right Gate Guards", i.e., Matsudaira Masatsuna (松平正綱)
       (1576–1648)[1, p. 729]

7. 大久保・加賀守　七　おゝくぞかゝ◌ろ◌み (おほくぼかゝのかみ;
       Ōkubo Kaga-no-kami (lit. "Ohokubo Kaga-no-kami")):
   "Ōkubo, Provincial Governor of Kaga", i.e., Ōkubo Tadatsune (大久保忠常) (1580–1611), who received the title in
       1600, or his son Ōkubo Tadamoto (大久保忠職) (1604–1670), who received it in 1626[25, 大久保家]
       Tadatsune served Tokugawa Hidetada (entry 2 on p. 2).[53, p. 70]

8. 青山・大藏大輔　八　あやゆまおゝく◌◌さいふ (あほやまおほくらのたいふ;
       Aoyama Ōkura-no-taifu (lit. "Ahoyama Ohokura-no-taifu")):
   "Aoyama, Greater Assistant [Director] of Finance", i.e., Aoyama Yoshinari (青山幸成) (1586–1643)[25, 青山家]
       大藏 is a historical variant of 大蔵.

9. 南部・信濃守　九　なんぶ◌ゑ◌ろゝらゑ (なんぶしなのゝかみ; Nanbu Shinano-no-kami):
   "Nanbu, Provincial Governor of Shinano", i.e., Nanbu Toshinao (南部利直) (1576–1632)[25, 南部家]
       南部 is a historical variant of 南部, and 信濃 is a variant of 信濃.

10. 仙石・越前守　十　せんごくゑちぜんのらミ (せんごくゑちぜんのかみ;
        Sengoku Echizen-no-kami (lit. "Sengoku Wechizen-no-kami")):
    "Sengoku, Provincial Governor of Echizen", i.e., Sengoku Hidehisa (仙石秀久) (1551–1614), who received the title in
        1583, or his grandson Sengoku Masatoshi (仙石政俊) (1617–1674), who received it in 1634[25, 仙石家]
        Hidehisa served Toyotomi Hideyoshi (entry 3 on p. 114).[53, p. 77]

    The Sengoku family, written 仙石, uses different characters than the Sengoku historical period (which is written
    戦国), and is unrelated.

11. 淺野・采女正　十一　あさ乃うゝめ◌ろ◌み (あさのうねめのかみ; Asano Uneme-no-kami):
    "Asano, Head of the Imperial Ladies-in-waiting", i.e., Asano Nagashige (浅野長重) (1588–1632)[1, p. 32]
        Uncle of Matsudaira Mitsuakira (entry 10 on p. 115)
        淺野 is a historical variant of 浅野.

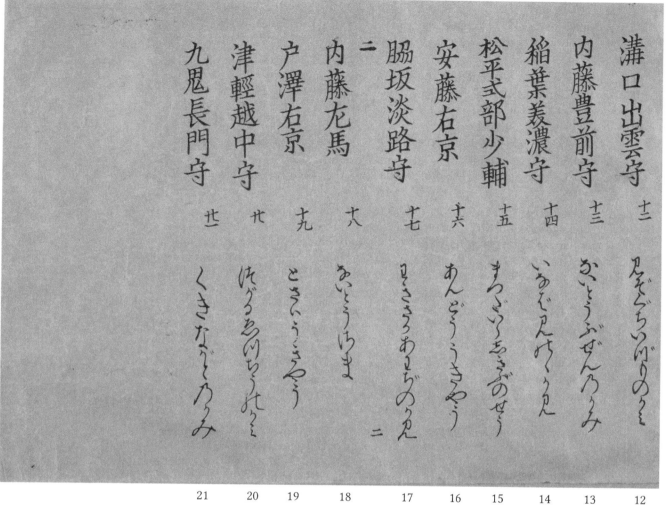

| 21 | 20 | 19 | 18 | 17 | 16 | 15 | 14 | 13 | 12 |

12. 溝口・出雲守　十二　ゑぞぐちいげゑのうミ (みぞぐちいづものかみ;
　　　Mizoguchi Izumo-no-kami (lit. "Mizoguchi Idzumo-no-kami")):
　　"Mizoguchi, Provincial Governor of Izumo", i.e., Mizoguchi Nobunao (溝口宣直) (1605–1676)[25, 溝口家]
　　　Son of Mizoguchi Nobukatsu (entry 18 on p. 79)
　　　溝口 is a historical variant of 溝口, and 出雲 is a variant of 出雲.

13. 内藤・豊前守　十三　ゐいとうぶぜんのうみ (ないとうぶぜんのかみ;
　　　Naitō Buzen-no-kami (lit. "Naitou Buzen-no-kami")):
　　"Naitō, Provincial Governor of Buzen", i.e., Naitō Nobunari (内藤信成) (1545–1612), who received the title in 1603, or
　　　his grandson Naitō Nobuteru (内藤信照) (1592–1665), who received it in 1621[25, 内藤延岡家]
　　　Nobunari was the stepbrother of Tokugawa Ieyasu (entry 1 on p. 2), adopted into the Naitō family, and served his
　　　stepbrother.[53, p. 66]
　　　内藤 is a historical variant of 内藤.

14. 稲葉・美濃守　十四　いゐぞゑぬゝうゑ (いなばみのゝかみ; Inaba Mino-no-kami):
　　"Inaba, Provincial Governor of Mino", i.e., Inaba Masanori (稲葉正則) (1623–1696)[25, 稲葉家]
　　　From a different Inaba line than Inaba Ittetsu (entry 33 on p. 153)
　　　美濃 is a historical variant of 美濃.

15. 松平・式部少輔　十五　まつざい＼志きぶのせう (まつだいらしきぶのせう;

        Matsudaira Shikibu-no-shō (lit. "Matsudaira Shikibu-no-seu")):

"Matsudaira, Lesser Assistant [Director] of the Ministry of Ceremonies", i.e., Matsudaira Tadatsugu (松平忠次)

    (1605–1665)[11][25, 榊原家]

    Also known as Sakakibara Tadatsugu (榊原忠次); distinct from Matsudaira Geki, also named Matsudaira

        Tadatsugu (entry 28 on p. 80).

    式部 is a historical variant of 式部.

    Tadatsugu became Greater Assistant Director in 1616, well before *O-umajirushi* was published,[25, 榊原家] but is referred to in some sources by the "Lesser Assistant Director" title.[11]

    少輔 are together read as "shō", the result of a sound change. Separately, the kanji are read "seu" ("shō" after the ō sound change) and "fu". "Seu-fu" became "shō-u" and then was shortened to just "shō". This results in a two-kanji title that is pronounced with a reading that's a reading the first kanji has by itself.

16. 安藤・右京　十六　あんどううきやう (あんどううきやう; Andō Ukyō (lit. "Andou Ukiyau")):

    "Andō, Right Capital Administration [official]", i.e., Andō Shigenaga (安藤重長) (1600–1657)[25, 安藤家]

        Served Tokugawa Hidetada (entry 2 on p. 2) and his son Iemitsu (who was shōgun at time of publication but does

            not have his own entry).

      安藤 here uses the same variant 藤.

17. 脇坂・淡路守　十七　ゑきさ｀ぁゑぢのゝゑ (わきさかあわぢのかみ;

        Wakisaka Awaji-no-kami (lit. "Wakisaka Awadji-no-kami")):

    "Wakisaka, Provincial Governor of Awaji", i.e., Wakisaka Yasumoto (脇坂安元) (1584–1653)[25, 脇坂家]

      脇坂 is a historical variant of 脇坂.

18. 内藤・左馬　十八　ふいとうほま (ないとうさま; Naitō Sama (lit. "Naitou Sama")):

    "Naitō, Left Horses [official]", i.e., Naitō Masanaga (内藤政長) (1568–1634)[1, p. 559]

      内藤 here uses the same variant 藤.

      左馬 is a historical variant of 左馬.

      "Sama" here, referring to the Left Horses Bureau, is unrelated to the honorific suffix "-sama" (様). The Horses Bureau was responsible for the raising and training of the Imperial Court's horses; it was made up of left and right divisions.

19. 戸澤・右京　十九　とさハうきやう (とさはうきやう; Tosawa Ukyō (lit. "Tosaha Ukiyau")):

    "Tosawa, Right Capital Administration [official]", i.e., Tozawa Masamori (戸沢政盛) (1585–1648)[1, p. 544]

      Fought on the side of the Tokugawa.[53, p. 88]

      戸澤 is a historical variant of 戸沢.

    In modern Japanese, this family name is pronounced "Tozawa".

20. 津軽・越中守　廿　ほぐるゑりちうゝろゝ (つがるゑつちうのかみ;

        Tsugaru Etchū-no-kami (lit. "Tsugaru Wetsuchiu-no-kami")):

    "Tsugaru, Provincial Governor of Etchū", i.e., Tsugaru Nobuhira (津軽信牧) (1586–1631)[1, p. 516]

      津軽 is a historical variant of 津軽.

    The tsu (ツ) here at some point underwent a sound change to a glottal stop, as is represented by a "small tsu" (っ) in modern Japanese. It's unclear whether this was the pronunciation at the time of *O-umajirushi* or not.

21. 九鬼・長門守　廿一　くきなぢとゝろゝみ (くきながとのかみ; Kuki Nagato-no-kami):

    "Kuki, Provincial Governor of Nagato", i.e., Kuki Moritaka (九鬼守隆) (1573–1632)[1, p. 298]

      Sided with Tokugawa Ieyasu (entry 1 on p. 2), opposing his own father, Kuki Yoshitaka (not listed).[53, p. 53]

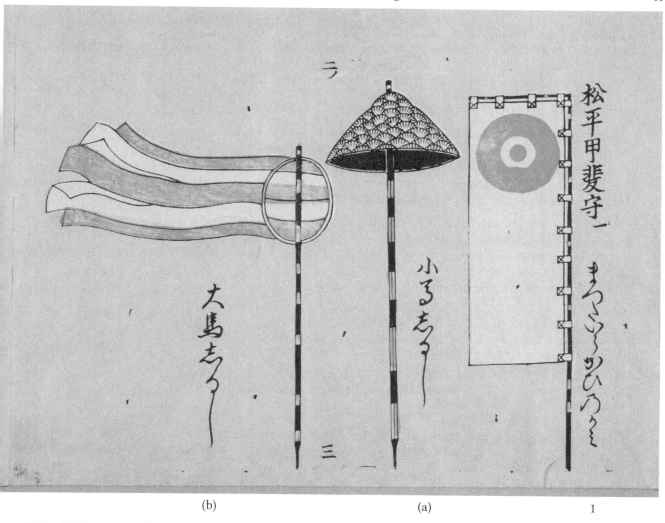

(b)   (a)   1

1. 松平・甲斐守　一　まつさい�し かひ乃うミ (まつたいらかひのかみ; Matsudaira Kai-no-kami):
   "Matsudaira, Provincial Governor of Kai", i.e., Matsudaira Tadayoshi (松平忠良) (1582–1624), who received the title in 1596,[25, 松平久松家] or (from a different line) Matsudaira Nagaoki (黒田長興) (1610–1665), who received it in 1626[25, 黒田家]

   A snake's eye with a disc or star inside. A snake's eye can also be called a *tsurumaki* (弦巻) after a spool around which bowstrings would be wound to carry them.[6, p. 134]

a) 小馬しるし (小馬しるし; ko-mumajirushi): lesser standard

   This standard consists of a cone shape with a white feather covering. *Shoshō Kisei Zu* describes these as 白鳥の羽 (read "hakuchō no hane" or "shiratori no hane"),[44, p. 2.25] which can mean specifically a swan's feathers or might just refer to the feathers of any white bird. This type of of flat feather design contrasts with the more common use of protruding feathers.

b) 大馬しるし (大馬しるし; ō-mumajirushi): great standard

   This standard is a red and white fukinuki.

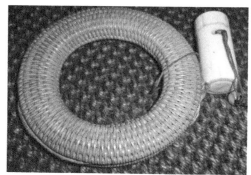

A tsurumaki.
Photo by Samuraiantiqueworld; CC BY 3.0

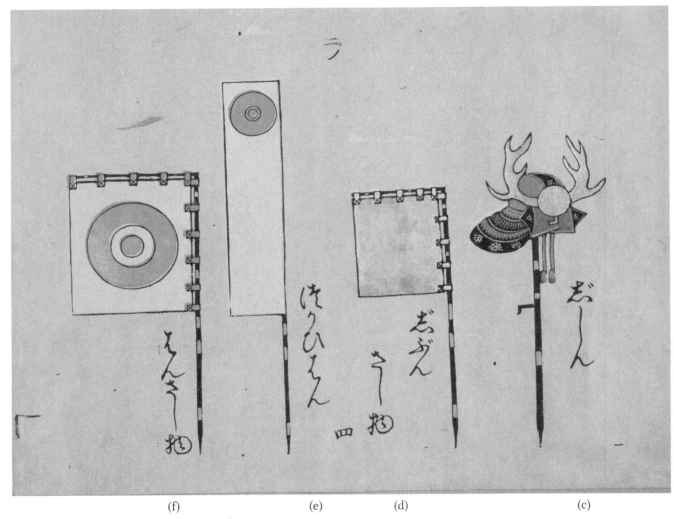

(f)　　　　　　　　(e)　　　(d)　　　　　　　　(c)

(Matsudaira Kai-no-kami, continued)

(c) ぢしん (じしん; jishin): personal [helmet]

　This helmet features both gold-painted antlers and a gold disc mon.

(d) ぢぶん　さし物 (じぶん　さし物; jibun sashimono): personal identifying object

(e) つかひはん (つかひはん; tsukaiban): messengers

(f) ゑんさし物 (はんさし物; ban-sashimono): guard identifying object

　Note the red smudge above this device, product of a printing error possibly because that portion of the block was not carved deeply enough.

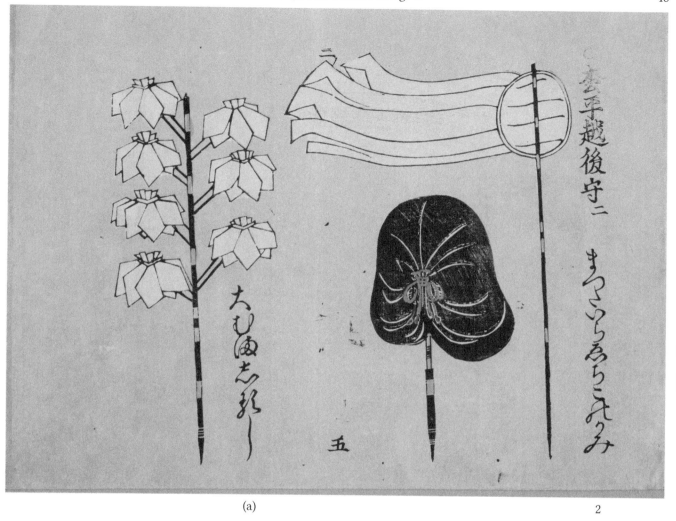

(a)

2

2. 杢平・越後守　二　まつさいらゑちこのうみ (まつたいらゑちこのかみ; Matsudaira Echigo-no-kami):
"Matsudaira, Provincial Governor of Echigo", i.e., Matsudaira Mitsunaga (松平光長) (1615–1707)[25, 松平越前津山家]

The primary device here is a white fukinuki. While less common, there are numerous examples in *O-umajirushi* where the primary device is a fukinuki or a standard-like device instead of a nobori.

Unlabeled horo (canopy)

(a) 大むゑ志釈く (大むましるし; ō-mumajirushi): great standard

This tree standard consists of seven white paper paulownia leaf shapes similar to those used by Ogasawara Ukon-no-taifu (see p. 38).

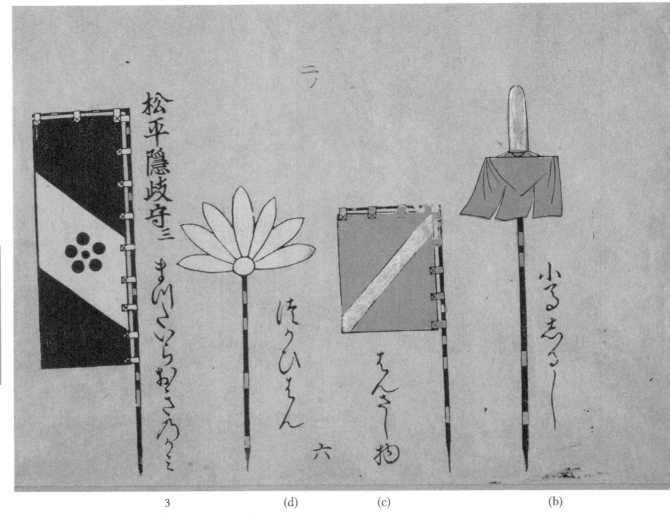

3   (d)   (c)   (b)

(Matsudaira Echigo-no-kami, continued)

(b) 小まゐるし (小馬しるし; ko-mumajirushi): lesser standard

     A red cloth noren and a gold-painted wooden top-shape.

(c) そんさゝ抅 (はんさし物; ban-sashimono): guard identifying object

     A gold diagonal stripe on a red field.

(d) ほうひそん (つかひはん; tsukaiban): messengers

     A white sunburst[52, p. 57] or flower shape.

---

3. 松平・隠歧守　三　まりさいらおき乃ゝミ (まつたいらおきのかみ; Matsudaira Oki-no-kami):
     "Matsudaira, Provincial Governor of Oki", i.e., Matsudaria Sadakatsu (松平定勝) (1560–1624), who received the title
         in 1601, or his son Matsudaira Sadayuki (松平定行) (1587–1668), who received it in 1626[25, 松平久松家]

     A diagonal band with a pattern of circles. While similar to the stars motif (also made of circles around a central
     circle), this particular pattern, with the smaller middle circle, is a simple version of the "plum bowl" (梅鉢;
     umebachi) motif. It comes from a simplified five-petaled plum blossom. The plum blossom is a common subject of
     Japanese poetry. It is associated with Tenjin (the deified Sugawara no Michizane), god of poetry, calligraphy, and
     scholarship.[12, p. 25] (For more on Tenjin, see p. xxix.)

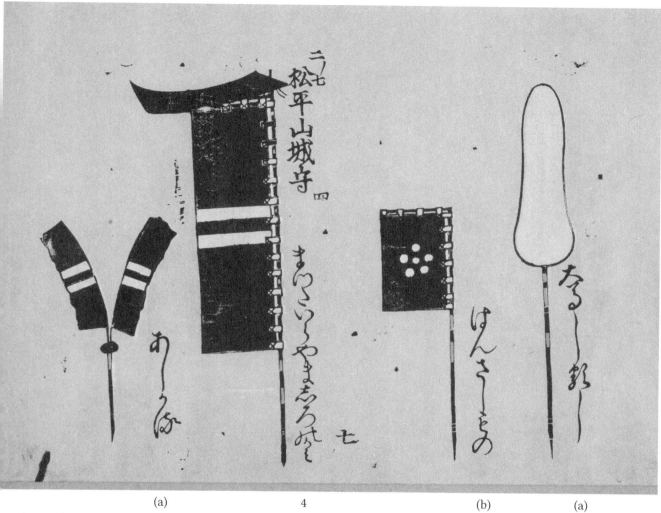

(a)   4   (b)   (a)

(Matsudaira Oki-no-kami, continued)

a) 大夛く𛁈るく (大馬しるし; ō-mumajirushi): great standard

   A tall, oblong wooden shape, possibly a long gourd.[53, p. 56]

b) はんさくをの (はんさしもの; ban-sashimono): guard identifying object

---

4. 杢平・山城守　四　まつさいくやま志ろれろミ (まつたいらやましろのかみ; Matsudaira Yamashiro-no-kami): "Matsudaira, Provincial Governor of Yamashiro", i.e., Matsudaira Tadakuni (松平忠国) (1597–1659)[25, 松平藤井家]

   A black nobori with two white horizontal stripes.

a) あくろ𛂢 (あしかる; ashigaru): foot soldiers

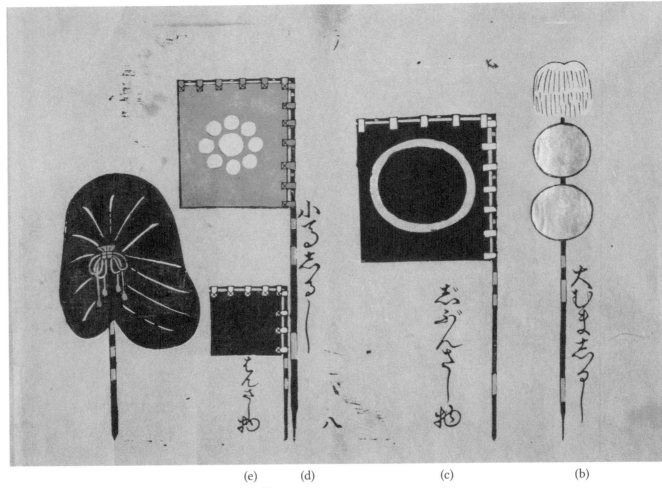

       (e)   (d)   (c)   (b)

(Matsudaira Yamashiro-no-kami, continued)

(b) 大むま志る�\ (大むましるし; ō-mumajirushi): great standard

    This standard has two golden balls, reminiscent of the disc mon, and a dashi of a tuft of white feathers.

(c) ぎぶん・さ�\抱 (じぶん・さし物; jibun sashimono): personal identifying object

    This device features a large ring, proportionally larger and thinner than the snake's eye ring.

(d) 小馬志る�\ (小馬しるし; ko-mumajirushi): lesser standard

    This arrangement of nine stars, with one larger one in the middle, is more common than the nine stars grid seen earlier (see p. 15). In fact, it is one of the earliest motifs found in mon, dating back at least to 1160.[52, p. 4] In addition to number, the stars motif is distinguished from the visually similar "plum bowl" motif by having the central circle larger than the ones around it.

    For a story about this mon from the Chiba family, see p. xxviii.

(e) そんさ�\抱 (はんさし物; ban-sashimono): guard identifying object

    Unlabeled horo (canopy)

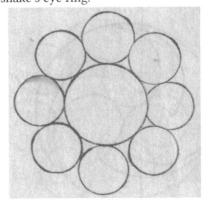

The same mon as recorded in Kenmon Shokamon.[20, p. 10]

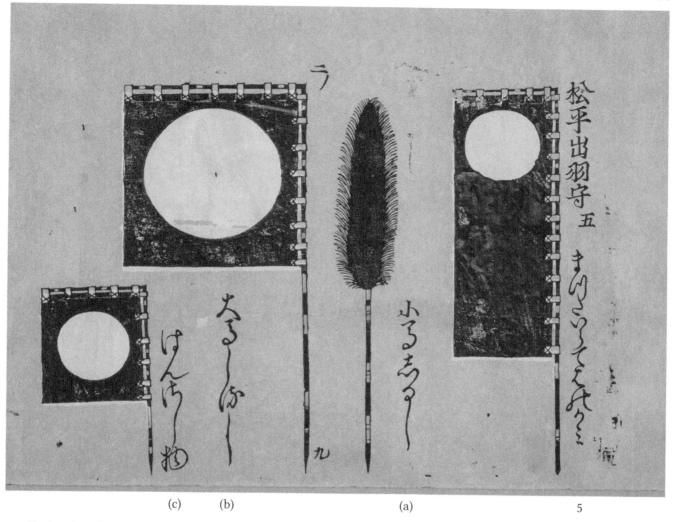

(c)　　　(b)　　　　　　　　(a)　　　　　　　　5

5. 松平・出羽守　五　まりさいくてそ九ろミ (まつたいらてはのかみ; Matsudaira Dewa-no-kami):
"Matsudaira, Provincial Governor of Dewa", i.e., Matsudaira Naomasa (松平直政) (1601–1666)[25, 松平越前松江家]

A white disc on black.

(a) 小多まるく (小馬しるし; ko-mumajirushi): lesser standard

A tapered pillar of black feathers.

(b) 大多くほく (大馬しるし; ō-mumajirushi): great standard

This standard resembles the nobori. This pattern of having a banner for the greater standard and a different sort of device for the lesser standard was common, though far from universal.

(c) はんほくわ (はんさし物; ban-sashimono): guard identifying object

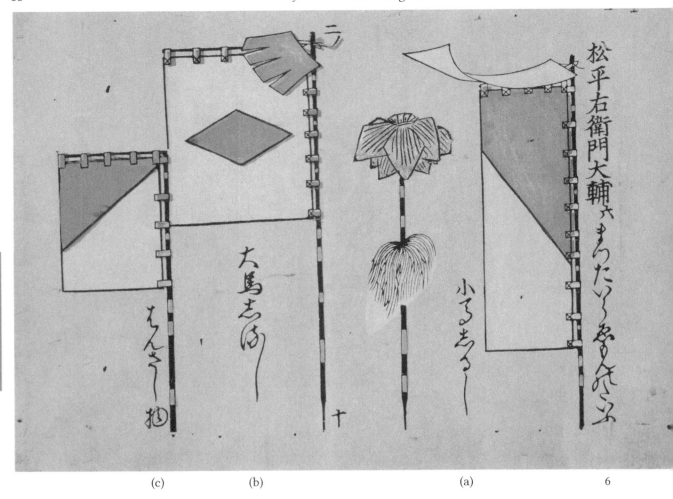

(c)　　　　　　　(b)　　　　　　　　　　　　　(a)　　　　　　　6

6. 松平・右衛門大輔　六　まつたい〱ゑゐんのたいふ (まつたいらゑもんのたいふ; Matsudaira Emon-no-taifu): "Matsudaira, Greater Assistant [Director] of the Right Gate Guards", i.e., Matsudaira Masatsuna (松平正綱) (1576–1648)[1, p. 729]

This nobori has a diagonal division into red and white. The black outline is not always included in these drawings; it's unclear if that's just artistic inconsistency or if it represents something like black stitching.

(a) 小�548るし (小馬しるし; ko-mumajirushi): lesser standard

This standard combines a paulownia leaf shape and a hanging white yak hair (白熊; haguma) plume.

"Haguma", white yak hair, is used by *Shoshō Kisei Zu* to refer to undyed yak hair,[44, p. 3.23] whereas "shaguma" (赤熊), literally "red yak hair", is used to refer to yak hair dyed either black or red.[44, p. 2.48] The kanji literally mean "white bear" and "red bear", respectively, but unintuitively actually refer to yak hair.

In addition to the sort of plume shown here, yak hair could be used as a helmet decoration, often imitating hairstyles or moustaches. This usage is not seen in *O-umajirushi*, however.

(b) 大馬志はし (大馬しるし; ō-mumajirushi): great standard

A solid rhombus or water chestnut mon, contrasting with the shadowed rhombus on p. 35. This standard also has a noren attached on top.

(c) ゑんさ〱抄 (はんさし物; ban-sashimono): guard identifying object

The diagonal division here goes in the opposite direction from the nobori.

(b)   (a)   7   (d)

(Matsudaira Emon-no-taifu, continued)

d) あしかる (あしかる; ashigaru): foot soldiers

     Like the nobori, the diagonal division on this double banner goes down towards the support poles.

---

7. 大久保・加賀守　七　大くぞかゝのうミ (大くほかゝのかみ; Ōkubo Kaga-no-kami):

     "Ōkubo, Provincial Governor of Kaga", i.e., Ōkubo Tadatsune (大久保忠常) (1580–1611), who received the title in 1600, or his son Ōkubo Tadamoto (大久保忠職) (1604–1670), who received it in 1626[25, 大久保家]

     This nobori features a ring motif with similar proportions to the one used by Matsudaira Yamashiro-no-kami (see p. 51). While shared motifs could indicate a family connection, that a daimyō had granted a mon to a vassal, or that two samurai were tied to the same shrine or temple, in other cases samurai adopted similar designs by coincidence.

a) 小馬まるく (小馬しるし; ko-mumajirushi): lesser standard

     This standard seems to be a closed umbrella, contrasting with the more common open umbrella standards.

b) 大馬まるく (大馬しるし; ō-mumajirushi): great standard

     This standard consists of a plume of feathers, some paper strips, and two black noren. Lines on the noren indicate folds in the fabric.

Vol. 2

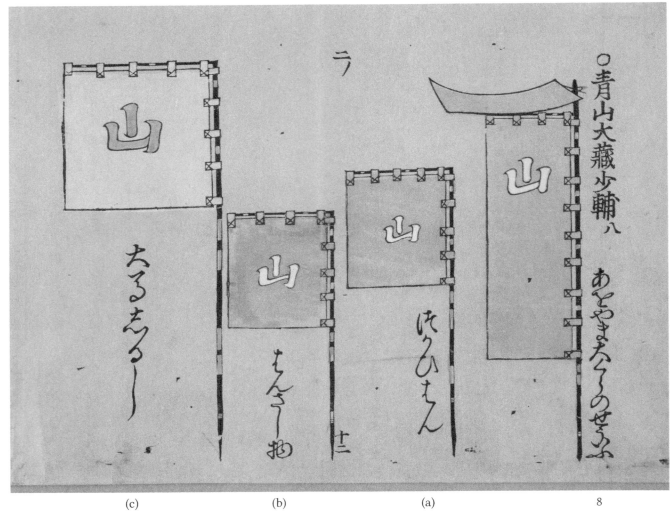

(c)   (b)   (a)   8

8. 青山・大藏少輔　八　あをやま大く〵のせういふ (あをやま大くらのせういふ; Aoyama Ōkura-no-shō -ifu): "Aoyama, Greater Assistant [Director] of Finance", i.e., Aoyama Yoshinari (青山幸成) (1586–1643)[25, 青山家]

This section label differs from the table of contents, which has 大輔 (taifu, greater assistant) rather than 少輔 (shō, lesser assistant). The reading here also has an extraneous いふ (ifu), the final morae of "taifu", which are not in the kanji. Genealogical information from *Kansei Chōshū Shoka Fu* indicates that "lesser assistant" is the correct title. The confusion here suggests that the inaccuracy in the table of contents was noticed by the time this page was prepared but extra hiragana were accidentally retained when correcting it.[25, 青山家]

Aoyama literally means "blue mountain", and these devices reflect that by combining the character 山 (yama, meaning "mountain") with the color blue. This is a particularly good example of a Japanese heraldic pun.

(a) ほうひそん (つかひはん; tsukaiban): messengers

(b) ゑんさ〵物 (はんさし物; ban-sashimono): guard identifying object

(c) 大多まるし (大馬しるし; ō-mumajirushi): great standard

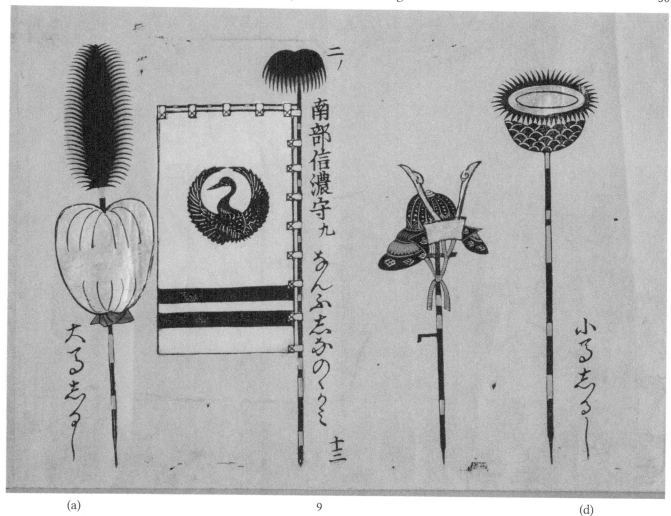

(a)　　　　　　　　　9　　　　　　　　　(d)

(Aoyama Ōkura-no-taifu, continued)

(d) 小乃まるし (小馬しるし; ko-mumajirushi): lesser standard

This standard resembles a basket or cut-open fruit. It's covered in flat black feathers, with protruding feathers along the rim.

Unlabeled helmet

This helmet has a helmet crest with a rectangular base and a more intricate shape for the horns.

9. 南部・信濃守　九　ゐんふまゐのゝらミ (なんふしなのゝかみ; Nanbu Shinano-no-kami):
"Nanbu, Provincial Governor of Shinano", i.e., Nanbu Toshinao (南部利直) (1576–1632)[25, 南部家]

This nobori features a crane and two horizontal stripes. It also has a top plume. Birds are one of the main types of animals found in Japanese heraldry. The crane in particular represents longevity, and this crane circle has been used since the Kamakura period (1185–1333).[12, p. 48]

(a) 大乃まるし (大馬しるし; ō-mumajirushi): great standard

A feather-covered top-pole and a cloth bundle.

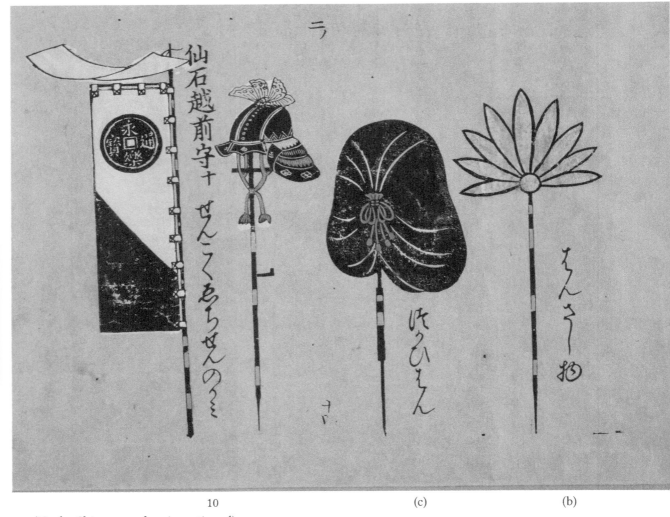

10   (c)   (b)

(Nanbu Shinano-no-kami, continued)

(b) そんさり抪 (はんさし物; ban-sashimono): guard identifying object

     A nine-rayed gold sunburst.

(c) ほうひそん (つかひはん; tsukaiban): messengers

     A black horo.

Unlabeled helmet

     This helmet has a butterfly on top, likely made out of paper-mâché.

---

10. 仙石・越前守　十　せんこくゑちせんのうミ (せんこくゑちせんのかみ; Sengoku Echizen-no-kami):
     "Sengoku, Provincial Governor of Echizen", i.e., Sengoku Hidehisa (仙石秀久) (1551–1614), who received the title in
         1583, or his grandson Sengoku Masatoshi (仙石政俊) (1617–1674), who received it in 1634[25, 仙石家]

     This nobori has a single coin. The kanji on the coin, 永楽通寶, identify it as a Ming dynasty coin imported from
     China but widely used in Japan.[37, p. 19] The field has a diagonal division.

     The second edition colors the center hole of this coin red, leading to a three-color design.[35, p. 112]

     Other sources give Hidehisa a banner with the character 無 (mu, meaning "nothing").[31, p. 123]

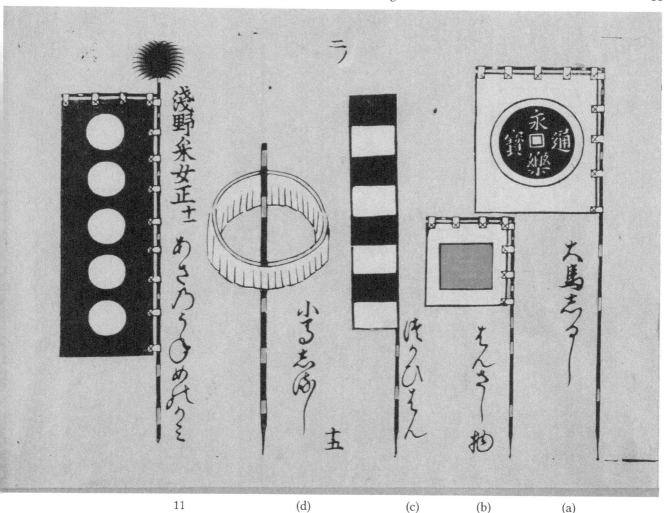

11   (d)   (c)   (b)   (a)

(Sengoku Echizen-no-kami, continued)

(a) 大馬志る く (大馬しるし; ō-mumajirushi): great standard

This standard interestingly has the outer rim of the coin in white, with the rest white kanji on black as before. The second edition colors the center and the top kanji on this coin red.[35, p. 112]

(b) そんさく抄 (はんさし物; ban-sashimono): guard identifying object

A red square on a white background.

(c) ほうひそん (つかひはん; tsukaiban): messengers

Black and white horizontal stripes.

(d) 小多志はく (小馬しるし; ko-mumajirushi): lesser standard

This standard is a ring with a hanging slashed cloth.

The same banner in the second edition.

1. 淺野・采女正 十一 あさ乃うゝめ丸うミ (あさのうねめのかみ; Asano Uneme-no-kami): "Asano, Head of the Imperial Ladies-in-waiting", i.e., Asano Nagashige (浅野長重) (1588–1632)[1, p. 32]

Five discs, with a plume of feathers on top.

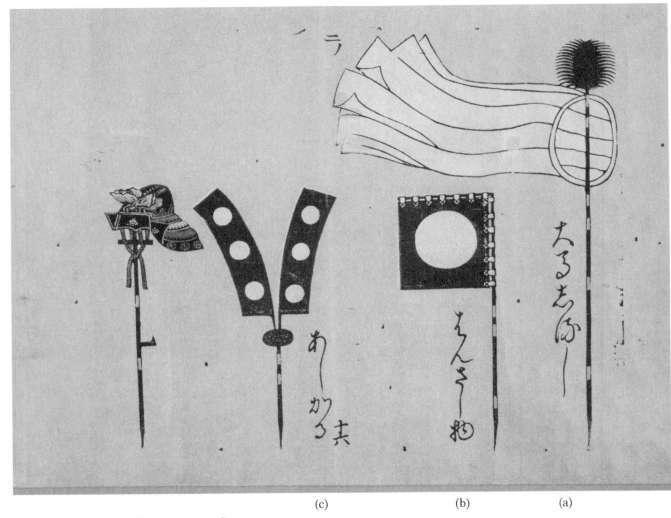

                        (c)   (b)   (a)

(Asano Uneme-no-kami, continued)

(a) 大多志はく (大馬しるし; ō-mumajirushi): great standard

    A white fukinuki and a plume of black feathers.

(b) ゑんさくわ (はんさし物; ban-sashimono): guard identifying object

(c) あくかる (あしかる; ashigaru): foot soldiers

    A single white disc on a black shihō.

Unlabeled helmet

    This helmet also features a butterfly, positioned lower down on the helmet than the one used by Nanbu Shinano-no-kami (see p. 57).

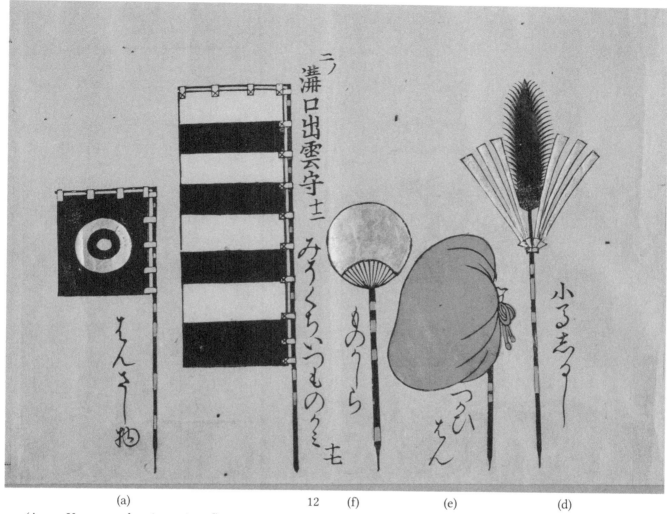

(a)   12 (f)   (e)   (d)

(Asano Uneme-no-kami, continued)

(d) 小多ぁる︿ (小馬しるし; ko-mumajirushi): lesser standard

A feathered top-pole and an array of gold wooden slats.

(e) つゎひ そん (つかひ はん; tsukaiban): messengers

(f) ゐのゥ︿ら (ものかしら; monogashira): foot soldier commanders

A gold non-folding fan ("uchiwa").

---

12. 溝口・出雲守　十二　みろくちいつものゥミ (みそくちいつものかみ; Mizoguchi Izumo-no-kami):
"Mizoguchi, Provincial Governor of Izumo", i.e., Mizoguchi Nobunao (溝口宣直) (1605–1676)[25, 溝口家]

White and black horizontal stripes.

(a) そんさ︿抄 (はんさし物; ban-sashimono): guard identifying object

A snake's eye with disc. The second edition shows an interesting thin black circle dividing
the snake's eye.[35, p. 117]

*The same banner in
the second edition.*

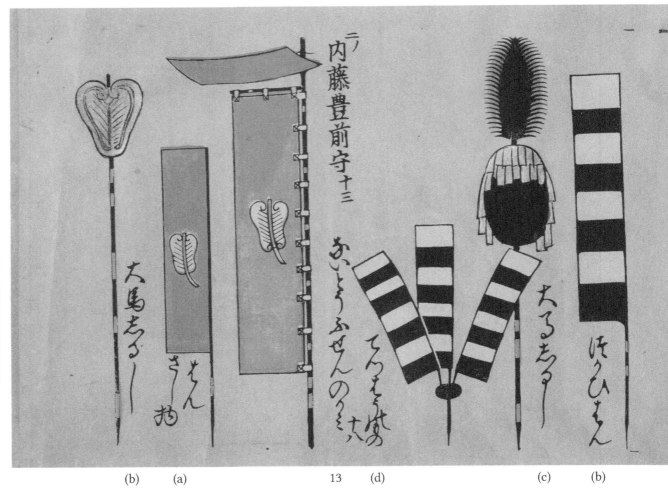

(b)   (a)   13   (d)   (c)   (b)

(Mizoguchi Izumo-no-kami, continued)

(b) ほうひそん (つかひはん; tsukaiban): messengers

(c) 大ゑまるし (大馬しるし; ō-mumajirushi): great standard

> This unusual standard has a feather-covered top-pole and gold paper strips draped over a black shape, creating the impression of a head with hair.

(d) てつそうねもの (てつはうのもの; tetsubō-no-mono): spiked club men

> A tetsubō (鉄棒) is a long thin wood or iron club with metal studs or spikes that came in a wide variety of lengths. This triple banner is an obvious but unusual extension of the double banner; triple banners seem to have been frequently used with tetsubō units.

---

13. 内藤・豊前守　十三　ゐいとうふせんのうミ (ないとうふせんのかみ; Naitō Buzen-no-kami): "Naitō, Provincial Governor of Buzen", i.e., Naitō Nobunari (内藤信成) (1545–1612), who received the title in 1603, or his grandson Naitō Nobuteru (内藤信照) (1592–1665), who received it in 1621[25, 内藤延岡家]

> This nobori depicts a gunbai war fan. (See p. 22.)

(a) そん　さしㇻ物 (はん　さし物; ban-sashimono): guard identifying object

(b) 大馬ゑるし (大馬しるし; ō-mumajirushi): great standard

> This standard is a gold-painted wooden representation of the same war fan motif.

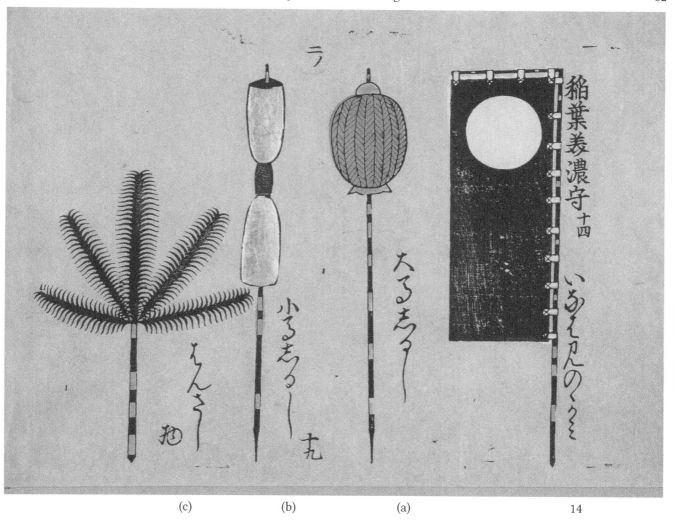

(c)   (b)   (a)   14

14. 稲葉・美濃守　十四　いゐそゑのゝうミ (いなはみのゝかみ; Inaba Mino-no-kami):
"Inaba, Provincial Governor of Mino", i.e., Inaba Masanori (稲葉正則) (1623–1696)[25, 稲葉家]

    A white disc on black.

(a) 大多志る� (大馬しるし; ō-mumajirushi): great standard

    A red bundle-shape, apparently woven from reeds.

(b) 小多志る〱 (小馬しるし; ko-mumajirushi): lesser standard

    An interesting wood shape representing a wooden pestle (杵; kine).[49, p. 128] It may be a reference to a vajra, the "diamond thunderbolt" Buddhist divine weapon, which can be referred to with the same word.[22, 杵]

(c) そんさし　物 (はんさし　物; ban-sashimono): guard identifying object

    Five feather-covered prongs.

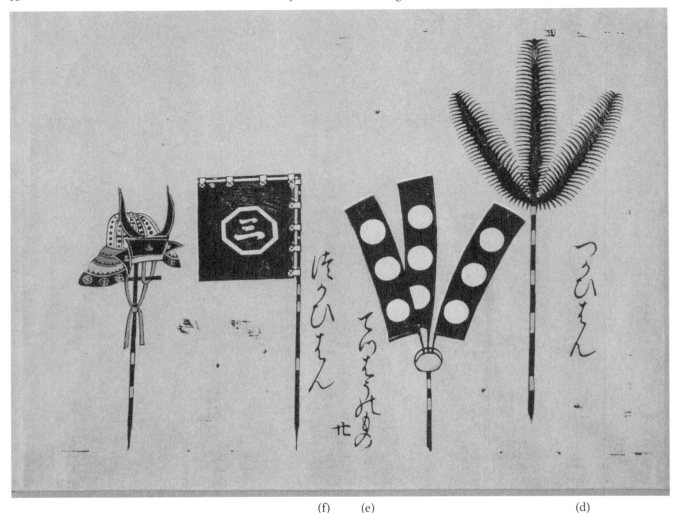

(f)   (e)   (d)

(Inaba Mino-no-kami, continued)

(d) つゝひそん (つかひはん; tsukaiban): messengers

Three feather-covered prongs, perhaps imitating a helmet crest.

(e) てつそうぇもの (てつはうのもの; tetsubō-no-mono): spiked club men

See p. 61 for an explanation of tetsubō. This triple banner has three discs on each banner.

(f) ほうひそん (つかひはん; tsukaiban): messengers

This device features a kanji 三 (san, meaning "three") in an octagon enclosure. The octagon actually represents an *oshiki* (折敷), a wooden tray used to make offerings to Shintō gods. The three character is a reference to the name of the Ōmishima Shrine (大三島神社), which literally means "Great Three Islands Shrine". This mon was used by the Kōno (河野氏) family by the 14th century.[4, 河野氏]

A kokuin (see p. xxxiv) from Edo Castle featuring the same three-in-octagon mon.
Photo by Eric Obershaw

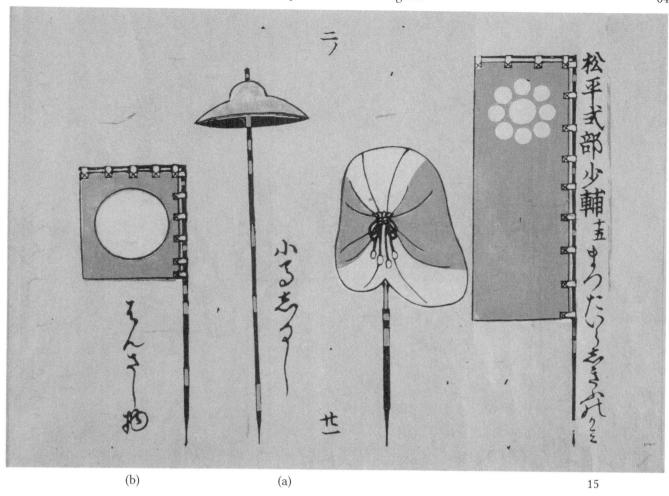

(b)　　　　　　　(a)　　　　　　　　　　　　15

15. 松平・式部少輔　十五　まつたい�işきふ札ゥξ (まつたいらしきふのかみ; Matsudaira Shikibu-no-kami):
    "Matsudaira, Lesser Assistant [Director] of the Ministry of Ceremonies", i.e., Matsudaira Tadatsugu (松平忠次)
    (1605–1665)[11][25, 榊原家]

    This section label gives the erroneous pronunciation "Shikibu-no-kami" instead of the correct "Shikibu-no-shō"; the pronunciation was given correctly in the table of contents.

    The nobori uses the common "nine stars" motif; see p. 51.

    Unlabeled horo (canopy)

(a) 小夢志る〻 (小馬しるし; ko-mumajirushi): lesser standard
    A straw hat.

(b) そんさ〻物 (はんさし物; ban-sashimono): guard identifying object
    A white disc on red.

Vol. 2

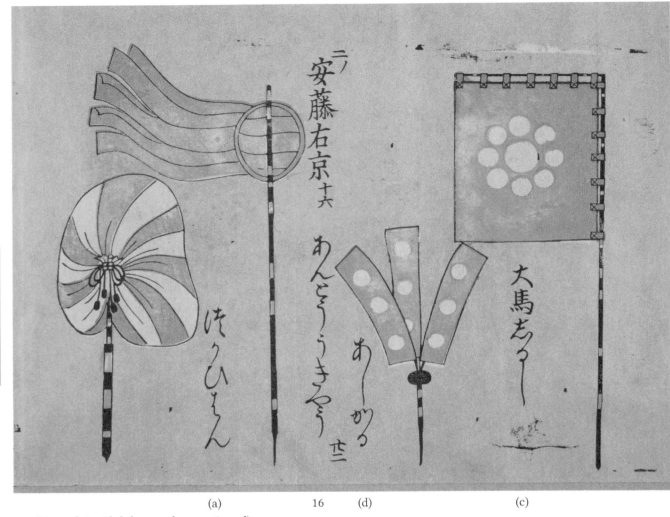

(a)　　　16　(d)　　　　　(c)

(Matsudaira Shikibu-no-shō, continued)

(c) 大馬ゝるく (大馬しるし; ō-mumajirushi): great standard

(d) あくかる (あしかる; ashigaru): foot soldiers

---

16. 安藤・右京　十六　あんとううきやう (あんとううきやう; Andō Ukyō):
    "Andō, Right Capital Administration [official]", i.e., Andō Shigenaga (安藤重長) (1600–1657)[25, 安藤家]

    A red fukinuki.

(a) ほうひそん (つかひはん; tsukaiban): messengers

Unlabeled horo (canopy)

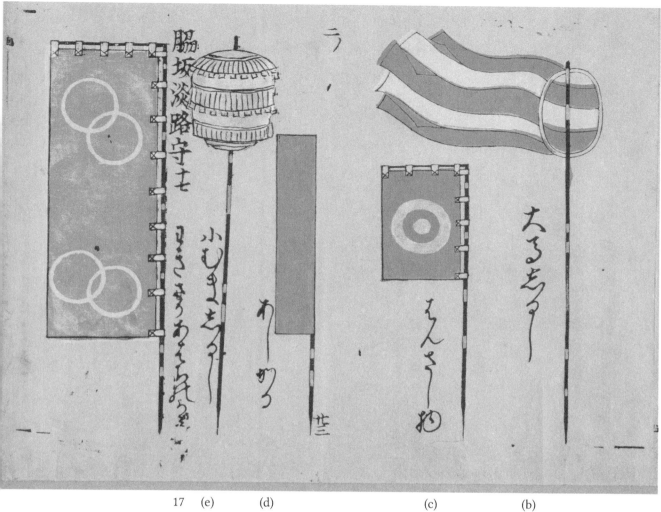

17　(e)　　　(d)　　　　　　　　(c)　　　　　　(b)

(Andō Ukyō, continued)

(b) 大多志る� (大馬しるし; ō-mumajirushi): great standard

　Contrasting with the solid red fukinuki used for the primary device, this standard is a red and white fukinuki.

(c) そんさく抄 (はんさし物; ban-sashimono): guard identifying object

　A snake's eye with disc.

(d) あくかる (あしかる; ashigaru): foot soldiers

(e) 小むま志る public (小むましるし; ko-mumajirushi): lesser standard

　A large gold object shaped roughly like a paper lantern.

.7. 脇坂・淡路守　十七　そきさゥあそちゎらミ (わきさかあはちのかみ; Wakisaka Awaji-no-kami):
　"Wakisaka, Provincial Governor of Awaji", i.e., Wakisaka Yasumoto (脇坂安元) (1584–1653)[25, 脇坂家]

　The 'wa' in Awaji is written with a 'ha' here, but was written with a 'wa' in the table of contents. (See p. xiv for more on w-sounds.)

　This nobori features two instances of a mon of two interlocked rings.

Vol. 2

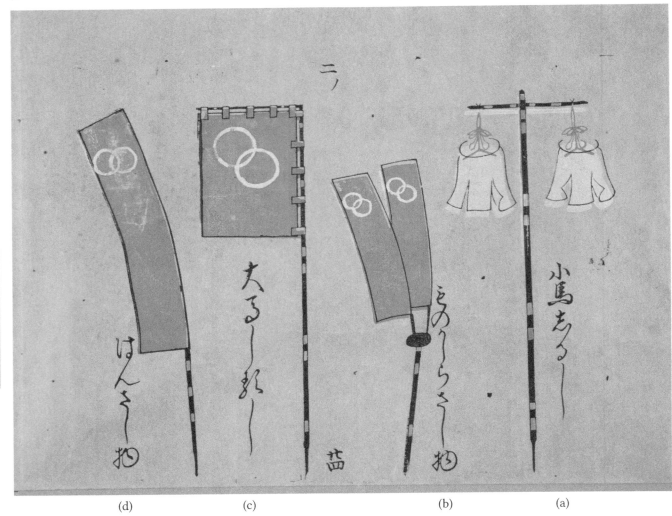

(d)   (c)   (b)   (a)

(Wakisaka Awaji-no-kami, continued)

(a) 小馬志るく (小馬しるし; ko-mumajirushi): lesser standard

    Two circular noren hanging from a cross pole.

(b) をのうくら・さく物 (ものかしら・さし物; monogashira sashimono): foot soldier commander identifying object

(c) 大 多く秋く (大 馬しるし; ō-mumajirushi): great standard

(d) はんさく物 (はんさし物; ban-sashimono): guard identifying object

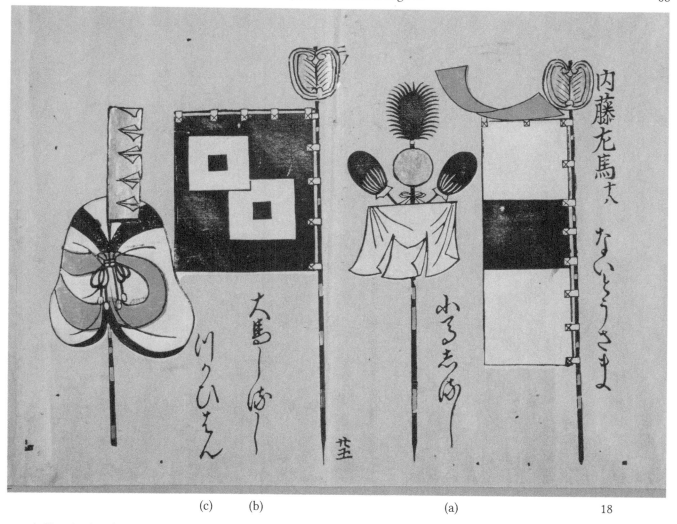

(c)   (b)   (a)   18

18. 内藤・左馬　十八　ないとうさま (ないとうさま; Naitō Sama):
   "Naitō, Left Horses [official]", i.e., Naitō Masanaga (内藤政長) (1568–1634)[1, p. 559]

   This nobori features a black horizontal band on white, a red maneki, and a war fan dashi.

(a) 小多志はく (小馬しるし; ko-mumajirushi): lesser standard

   This complex standard features a feathered top pole, a gold ball, two black bundles, and a white noren.

(b) 大馬志はく (大馬しるし; ō-mumajirushi): great standard

   This standard features two overlapping shadowed squares.

(c) ツうひそん (つかひはん; tsukaiban): messengers

   A slashed gold banner and a horo with a three-color design. The red portion forms an unusual curved shape.

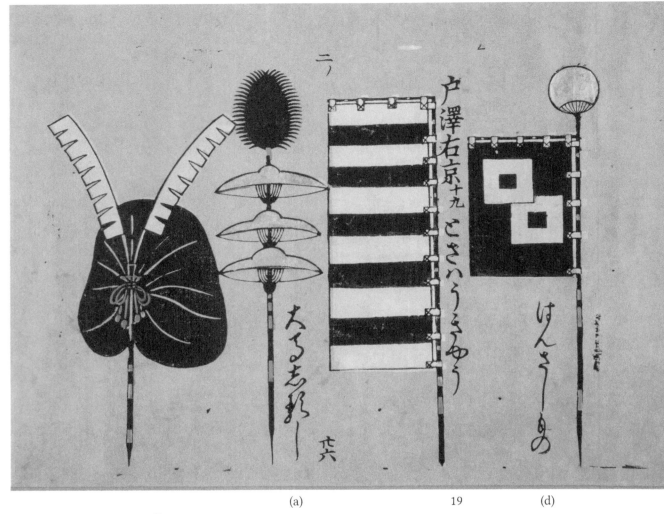

(a) 19 (d)

(Naitō Sama, continued)

(d) はんさ〱〱の (はんさしもの; ban-sashimono): guard identifying object

Unlike the preceding standard, which used a war fan, this uses an "uchiwa" non-folding fan.

---

19. 戸澤・右京　十九　とさハうき〿う (とさはうきやう; Tosawa Ukyō):
"Tosawa, Right Capital Administration [official]", i.e., Tozawa Masamori (戸沢政盛) (1585–1648)[1, p. 544]

White and black horizontal stripes.

(a) 大亐志〽〱 (大馬しるし; ō-mumajirushi): great standard

A black feathered top pole and three umbrellas. While these look similar to hats (e.g., p. 22), the supports against the pole make it clear that this represents an umbrella.

Unlabeled horo (canopy)

A black horo with two small slashed banners.

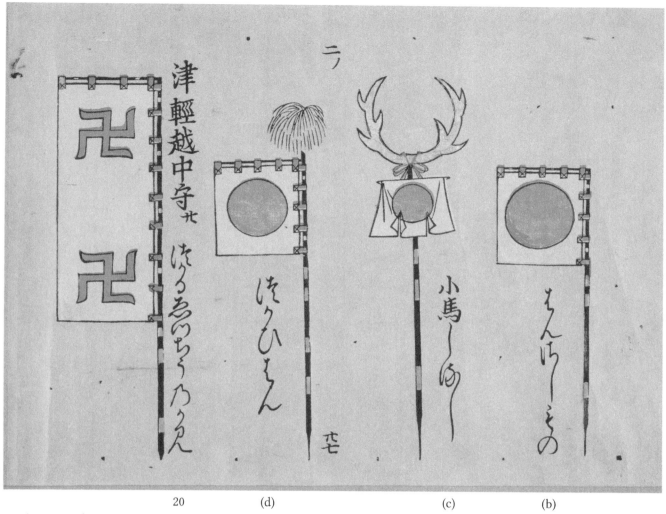

津軽越中守 卅

| 20 | (d) | (c) | (b) |

(Tosawa Ukyō, continued)

(b) そんはらしをの (はんさしもの; ban-sashimono): guard identifying object

A red disc on white.

(c) 小馬らしほら (小馬しるし; ko-mumajirushi): lesser standard

A gold-painted pair of antlers and a white noren with a red disc.

(d) ほうひそん (つかひはん; tsukaiban): messengers

A red disc on white and a yak hair dashi.

---

20. 津軽・越中守　卅　ほうるゑつちう乃うゑ (つかるゑつちうのかみ; Tsugaru Etchū-no-kami):
"Tsugaru, Provincial Governor of Etchū", i.e., Tsugaru Nobuhira (津軽信牧) (1586–1631)[1, p. 516]

This nobori uses two red swastikas. The swastika is a traditional Buddhist symbol dating back to ancient times, used in Japan and elsewhere in Asia and India.[6, p. 148] In Japan, it represents Fudō, the Immovable Wisdom King,[24, p. 12] and is called a *manji* (卍). It is still used widely in Japan today to represent Buddhism. Its use in Japan is unrelated to its use as a Nazi symbol. It also may have been used by "hidden Christians" in Japan after Christianity was banned by the Tokugawa because of the cross shape it contains.[6, p. 32]

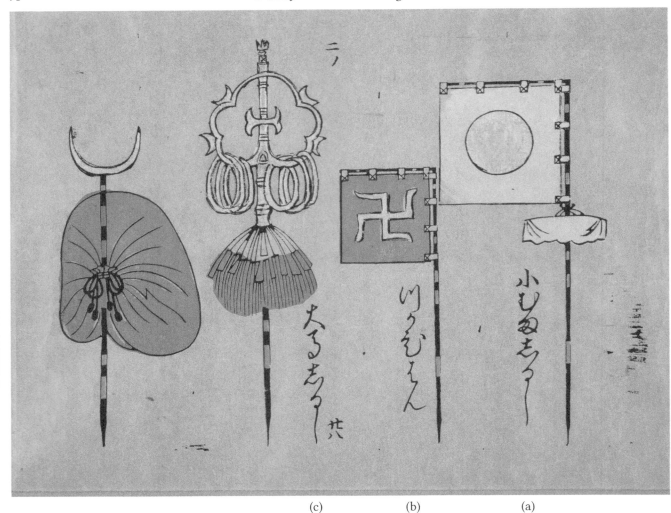

(c)   (b)   (a)

(Tsugaru Etchū-no-kami, continued)

(a) 小む𛀙志るく (小むましるし; ko-mumajirushi): lesser standard

   A gold disc on white and a hanging cloth shape.

(b) 川ろむそん (つかひはん; tsukaiban): messengers

(c) 大多志るく (大馬しるし; ō-mumajirushi): great standard

   This ornate standard represents a shakujō,[53, p. 88] a metal staff
   used by Buddhist monks that made a rattling noise and could
   also be used as a weapon.

Unlabeled horo (canopy)

   This horo is accompanied by a helmet crest or moon shape.

*A kokuin (see p. xxxiv) from Edo Castle featuring
a swastika (manji) mon.*
Photo by Eric Obershaw

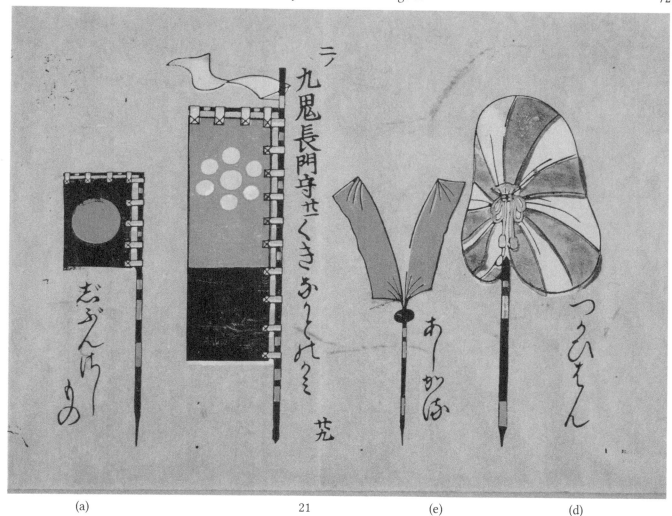

(a)　　　　　　　　21　　　　　(e)　　　　　(d)

(Tsugaru Etchū-no-kami, continued)

(d) つゝひそん (つかひはん; tsukaiban): messengers

The shade of red on this multicolored horo is different, suggesting more of a brown color. The second edition identifies this specifically as purple.[35, p. 140] It likely used ink that was originally purple but has since faded to brown.

(e) あしかつは (あしかる; ashigaru): foot soldiers

---

21. 九鬼・長門守　廿一　くきゐらとれらミ (くきなかとのかみ; Kuki Nagato-no-kami): "Kuki, Provincial Governor of Nagato", i.e., Kuki Moritaka (九鬼守隆) (1573–1632)[1, p. 298]

This banner feathers a horizontal division between red and black and a seven stars motif in white. It is accompanied by a white maneki.

(a) ぎぶん・はし　のの (じぶん・さし　もの; jibun sashimono): personal identifying object

A red disc on black.

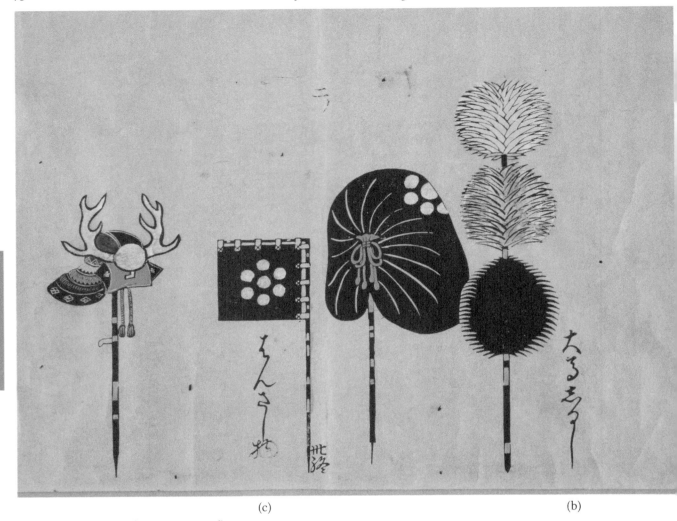

(c)   (b)

(Kuki Nagato-no-kami, continued)

(b) 大多ゝまるし (大馬しるし; ō-mumajirushi): great standard

Three balls of feathers, in white, gold, and black.

Unlabeled horo (canopy)

(c) そんさくも (はんさし物; ban-sashimono): guard identifying object

Unlabeled helmet

An antlers and disc combination, very similar to that on p. 47.

Note also the page number here. In addition to 卅 (thirty), it also includes a cursive form of 終 (owari), meaning "the end", indicating the last page of this volume. (The following closing paragraph page is not numbered.) This convention is also used in volumes 3–5, but not in volumes 1 or 6.

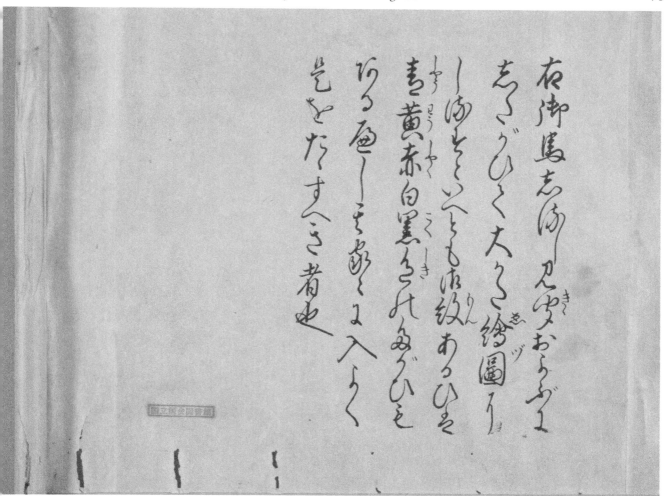

The closing paragraph here is printed with the same block as in the other volumes. This page being added to each volume is the only clear example of intentionally reused blocks in *O-umajirushi*. For translation and discussion, see p. 40.

End Volume 2

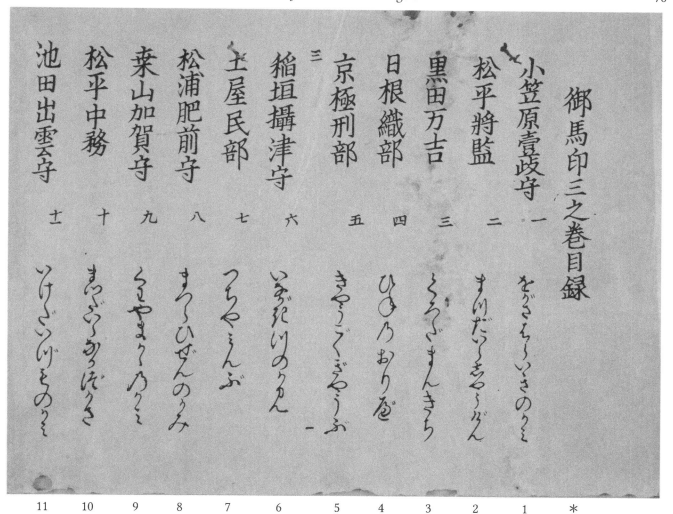

| | 11 | 10 | 9 | 8 | 7 | 6 | 5 | 4 | 3 | 2 | 1 | * |

* 御馬印・三之巻・目録 (O-umajirushi San-no-maki Mokuroku)
  Honorable Battle Standards: Third Volume: Index

1. 小笠原・壹歧守　一　をぐさそ〱いきのかミ (をがさはらいきのかみ;
       Ogasawara Iki-no-kami (lit. "Wogasahara Iki-no-kami")):
   "Ogasawara, Provincial Governor of Iki", i.e., Ogasawara Tadatomo (小笠原忠知) (1599–1663)[25, 小笠原小倉家]
       Brother of Ogasawara Tadanaga (entry 17 on p. 79) and Ogasawara Tadazane (entry 28 on p. 7)
       壹歧 is a historical variant of 壱岐.

   Unlike some other instances of this clan in *O-umajirushi*, the pronunciation given here is "Ogasawara", with a
   voiced 'ga', not "Okasawara". This suggests that the clan was pronounced "Ogasawara" in all cases, but dakuten
   were omitted in the other entries.

2. 松平・將監　二　まりだい〱志やうげん (まつだいらしやうげん;
       Matsudaira Shōgen (lit. "Matsudaira Shiyaugen")):
   "Matsudaira, Commander [of the Imperial Guards]", i.e., Matsudaira Narishige (松平成重) (1594–1633), who
       commanded the Right Inner Guard starting in 1608, or his son Matsudaira Tadaaki (松平忠昭) (1617–1693), who
       commanded the Left Inner Guard starting in 1640[25, 松平大給家]
       將監 is a historical variant of 将監.

3. 黒田・万吉　三　くろざまんきち (くろだまんきち; Kuroda Mankichi):
   Referring to Kuroda Yoshitaka (黒田孝高) (1546–1604)[1, p. 311]
       Grandfather of Matsudaira Tadayuki (entry 5 on p. 186)

4. 日根・織部　四　ひ♭乃おりゑ (ひねのおりべ; Hine no Oribe):
   "Hine, Weaving Bureau [official]", i.e., Hineno Takahiro (日根野高弘) (1539–1600) or his son Hineno Yoshiaki
       (日根野吉明) (1587–1656)[1, pp. 653–654]
       織部 is a historical variant of 織部.

   The Hine clan is also called the Hineno (日根野) clan, but here the absence of a kanji for 'no' make it clear that it represents the possessive particle here.

5. 京極・刑部　五　きやうごくぎやうぶ (きやうごくぎやうぶ; Kyōgoku Gyōbu (lit. "Kiyaugoku Giyaubu")):
   "Kyōgoku, Ministry of Justice [official]", i.e., Kyōgoku Takakazu (京極高和) (1619–1662)[25, 京極家]
       Grandnephew to Kyōgoku Takatomo (entry 19 on p. 151)
       京極 is a historical variant of 京極.

   Kyōgoku Takakazu received the title Lesser Assistant Director of the Ministry of Justice (刑部少輔; kyōgoku-no-shō) in 1639. This is the latest such date among individuals in *O-umajirushi*, suggesting the book was published shortly thereafter. (See p. ix.)

6. 稲垣・攝津守　六　いながきつのかゑ (いながきつのかみ; Inagaki Tsu-no-kami):
   "Inagaki, Provincial Governor of Tsu [i.e., Settsu]", i.e., Inagaki Shigetsuna (稲垣重綱) (1583–1654)[25, 稲垣家]
       攝津 is a historical variant of 摂津.

       Shigetsuna received this title in 1623. Three years later, Kōriki Tadafusa (entry 23 on p. 5) took it over, but
         Shigetsuna still seems to have been known by it. Again, the "Tsu" reading here is an example of two kanji
         together being read as a single mora.

7. 土屋・民部　七　つちやゑんぶ (つちやみんぶ; Tsuchiya Minbu):
   "Tsuchiya, Ministry of Popular Affairs [official]", i.e., Tsuchiya Tadanao (土屋忠直) (1578–1612), who became Lesser
       Assistant in 1599, or his son Tsuchiya Toshinao (土屋利直) (1607–1675), who did so in 1621[25, 土屋家]

8. 松浦・肥前守　八　まつ〱ひぜんのうみ (まつらひぜんのかみ; Matsura Hizen-no-kami):
   "Matsura, Provincial Governor of Hizen", i.e., Matsura Takanobu (松浦隆信) (1591–1637), who received the title in
       1612, or his son Matsura Shigenobu (松浦鎮信) (1622–1703), who received it in 1635[25, 松浦家]

9. 桒山・加賀守　九　くそやまらゝ乃うゑ (くわやまかゝのかみ; Kuwayama Kaga-no-kami):
   "Kuwayama, Provincial Governor of Kaga", i.e., Kuwayama Sadaharu (桑山貞晴) (1604–1629)[25, 桑山家]
       Sadaharu received this title in 1623, three years before Ōkubo Tadamoto (entry 7 on p. 43) took it over.

10. 松平・中務　十　まつざい〱ゐろぼうさ (まつだいらなかづかさ;
        Matsudaira Nakazukasa (lit. "Matsudaira Nakadzukasa")):
    "Matsudaira, Ministry of the Center [official]", i.e., Matsudaira Tadatomo (松平忠知) (1605–1634)[25, 江戸初期国持ち大名家]
        Son of Matsudaira Hideyuki (entry 17 on p. 189). Granted the Matsudaira name in 1612.
        中務 is a historical variant of 中務.
        In modern Japanese, 中務 is pronounced "Nakatsukasa".

11. 池田・出雲守　十一　いけざいげゑのうゑ (いけだいづものかみ;
        Ikeda Izumo-no-kami (lit. "Ikeda Idzumo-no-kami")):
    "Ikeda, Provincial Governor of Izumo", i.e., Ikeda Nagatsune (池田長常) (1609–1641)[25, 池田岡山家]
        出雲 is a historical variant of 出雲.

Vol. 3

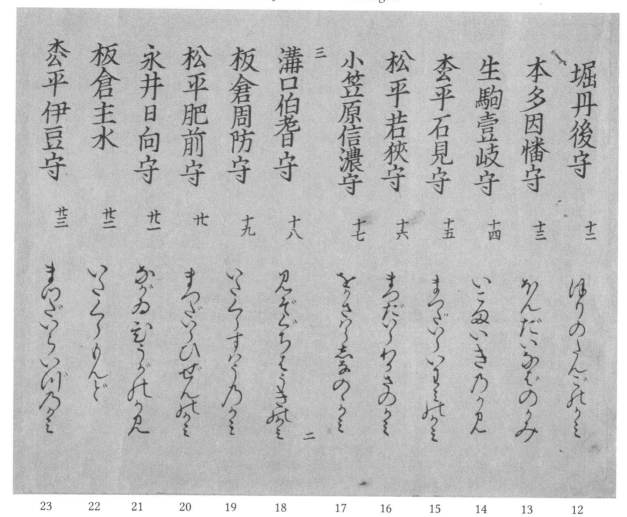

| 23 | 22 | 21 | 20 | 19 | 18 | 17 | 16 | 15 | 14 | 13 | 12 |

12. 堀・丹後守　十二　ほりのさんごのうミ (ほりのたんごのかみ; Hori no Tango-no-kami):
    "Hori, Provincial Governor of Tango", i.e., Hori Naoyori (堀直寄) (1577–1639)[1, p. 700]
    丹後 is a historical variant of 丹後.

    His father, Hori Naomasa (not listed), served Hori Chikayoshi (entry 4 on p. 186)'s father, Hori Hidemasa (also not listed), and adopted their family name.

    Unusually for a provincial governor title, the title here includes a 'no' ("of") between the family name and the title.

13. 本多・因幡守　十三　やんだいゐぐのうみ (ほんだいなばのかみ; Honda Inaba-no-kami):
    "Honda, Provincial Governor of Inaba", i.e., Honda Toshimasa (本多俊政) –1608) or his son Honda Masatake
    (本多政武) (1598–1637)[25, 本多高取家]
    From a different Honda line than Honda Tadamasa (entry 16 on p. 5) and from Honda Tadatoshi (entry 1 on p. 186)
    因幡 is a historical variant of 因幡.

14. 生駒・壹岐守　十四　いこゐいきのうゑ (いこまいきのかみ; Ikoma Iki-no-kami):
    "Ikoma, Provincial Governor of Iki", i.e., Ikoma Takatoshi (生駒高俊) (1611–1659)[25, 江戸初期国持ち大名家]
    壹岐 is a historical variant of 壱岐.
    Note this uses the modern 岐, not the variant form 歧 used previously for Iki on p. 76.

15. 杢平・石見守　十五　まつざい〱いそミ𛀁ろミ (まつだいらいわみのかみ; Matsudaira Iwami-no-kami):
    "Matsudaira, Provincial Governor of Iwami", i.e., Matsudaira Yasuyasu (松平康安) (1555–1623)[1, p. 730] or (from a different branch) Matsudaira Teruzumi (松平輝澄) (1604–1662)[25, 池田因幡家]
    杢平 is a historical variant of 松平.

16. 松平・若狭守　十六　まつだい〱わ𛀁さのろミ (まつだいらわかさのかみ; Matsudaira Wakasa-no-kami):
    "Matsudaira, Provincial Governor of Wakasa", i.e., Matsudaira Yasunobu (松平康信) (1600–1682)[25, 松平形原家および松平竹谷家]
    若狭 is a historical variant of 若狭.

17. 小笠原・信濃守　十七　をゥさハ〱志るのゝろミ (をかさはらしなのゝかみ; Ogasawara Shinano-no-kami (lit. "Wokasahara Shinano-no-kami")):
    "Ogasawara, Provincial Governor of Shinano", i.e., Ogasawara Tadanaga (小笠原忠脩) (1594–1615), who received the title in 1606, or his son Ogasawara Nagatsugu (小笠原長次) (1615–1666), who received it in 1629[25, 小笠原小倉家]
    Tadanaga was the brother of Ogasawara Tadazane (entry 28 on p. 7) and Ogasawara Tadatomo (entry 1 on p. 76)
    信濃 is a historical variant of 信濃.

    While the clan name here is written "Okasawara", without the dakuten to make 'ka' into 'ga', the pronunciation given in the actual section includes the dakuten, suggesting that the "Ogasawara" pronunciation is correct.

18. 溝口・伯耆守　十八　ゑぞぐちそうき𛀁ろミ (みぞぐちはうきのかみ; Mizoguchi Hōki-no-kami (lit. "Mizoguchi Hauki-no-kami")):
    "Mizoguchi, Provincial Governor of Hōki", i.e., Mizoguchi Hidekatsu (溝口秀勝) (1548–1610) or his son Mizoguchi Nobukatsu (溝口宣勝) (1582–1628)[25, 溝口家]
    Nobukatsu was the father of Mizoguchi Nobunao (entry 12 on p. 44)
    溝口 is a historical variant of 溝口.

19. 板倉・周防守　十九　いさく〱すハう乃ろミ (いたくらすはうのかみ; Itakura Suō-no-kami (lit. "Itakura Suhau-no-kami")):
    "Itakura, Provincial Governor of Suō", i.e., Itakura Shigemune (板倉重宗) (1586–1656)[25, 板倉家]
    Elder brother of Itakura Shigemasa (entry 22 on p. 79)
    板㲯 is a historical variant of 板倉.

20. 松平・肥前守　廿　まつざい〱ひぜん𛀁ろミ (まつだいらひぜんのかみ; Matsudaira Hizen-no-kami):
    "Matsudaira Provincial Governor of Hizen", i.e., Matsudaira Tadanao (松平忠直) (1613–1635), who received the title in 1622,[25, 鍋島家] or Matsudaira Toshitsune (松平利常) (1593–1658), who received it in 1629.[25, 前田家] (The two individuals were from different Matsudaira branches.)

21. 永井・日向守　廿一　ゐぐゐゑうづ𛀁ろゑ (ながゐひうがのかみ; Nagai Hyūga-no-kami (lit. "Nagawi Hiuga-no-kami")):
    "Nagai, Provincial Governor of Hyūga", i.e., Nagai Naokiyo (永井直清) (1591–1671)[25, 永井家]
    Brother of Nagai Naomasa (entry 10 on p. 3)

22. 板倉・主水　廿二　いさく〱ゐんど (いたくらもんど; Itakura Mondo):
    "Itakura, Water, Ice, and Porridge Office [official]", i.e., Itakura Shigemasa (板倉重昌) (1588–1638)[1, p. 96]
    Younger brother of Inoue Masashige (entry 31 on p. 191)
    Unlike the previous Itakura entry (item 19), this does not use the variant form 㲯 for 倉.

    Personally led an attack against the Shimabara rebels in 1638 and was killed by an arrow.[53, p. 46]

23. 杢平・伊豆守　廿三　まつざいらいげろろミ (まつだいらいづのかみ; Matsudaira Izu-no-kami (lit. "Matsudaira Idzu-no-kami")):
    "Matsudaira, Provincial Governor of Izu", i.e., Matsudaira Nobukazu (松平信一) (1539–1624), his son Matsudaira Nobuyoshi (松平信吉) (1575–1620),[25, 松平藤井家] or (from a different branch) Matsudaira Terutsuna (松平輝綱) (1620–1671)[25, 松平大河内家]

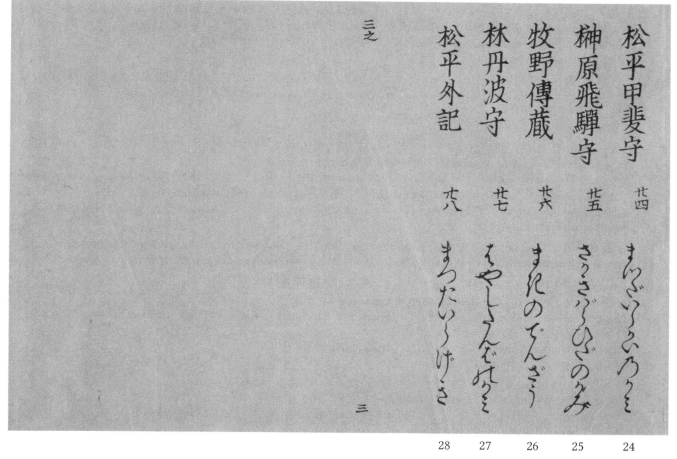

24. 松平・甲斐守　廿四　まつざい〵ろいゐ〵ミ (まつだいらかいのかみ; Matsudaira Kai-no-kami):
    甲斐 is a historical variant of 甲斐.
    Matsudaira Kai-no-kami also had an entry in volume 2 (see p. 46); this may be an addendum.

25. 榊原・飛驒守　廿五　さゝきバ〵ひざのゝみ (さかきばらひだのかみ; Sakakibara Hida-no-kami):
    "Sakakibara, Provincial Governor of Hida", i.e., Sakakibara Motonao (榊原職直) (1586–1648)[28, 27]
    榊原 is a historical variant of 榊原, and 飛驒 is a variant of 飛驒.

26. 牧野・傳蔵　廿六　ま㐂のでんざう (まきのでんざう; Makino Denzō (lit. "Makino Denzau")):
    Referring to Makino Shigesato (牧野成里) (1556–1614)[1, p. 714]
    牧野 is a historical variant of 牧野, and 傳蔵 is a variant of 傳蔵.
    傳蔵 can also be written 伝蔵, with a different initial kanji.

27. 林・丹波守　廿七　そやしさんぞゝ〵ミ (はやしたんばのかみ; Hayashi Tanba-no-kami):
    "Hayashi, Provincial Governor of Tanba", i.e., Hayashi Katsumasa (林勝正)[11][15, #1119]
    丹波 is a historical variant of 丹波.

28. 松平・外記　廿八　まつたい〵げき (まつたいらげき; Matsudaira Geki (lit. "Matsutaira Geki")):
    Referring to Matsudaira Tadatsugu (松平忠次) (1521–1547)[22, 松平忠次]
    Distinct from Matsudaira Shikibu-no-shō, also named Matsudaira Tadatsugu (entry 15 on p. 45).
    外記 is a historical variant of 外記.

    Geki was Tadatsugu's tsūshō, or informal given name.

    This entry gives the clan name pronunciation as "Matsutaira", with an unvoiced 'ta' instead of the usual 'da'. Given the many "Matsudaira" examples, this is probably just an omitted dakuten.

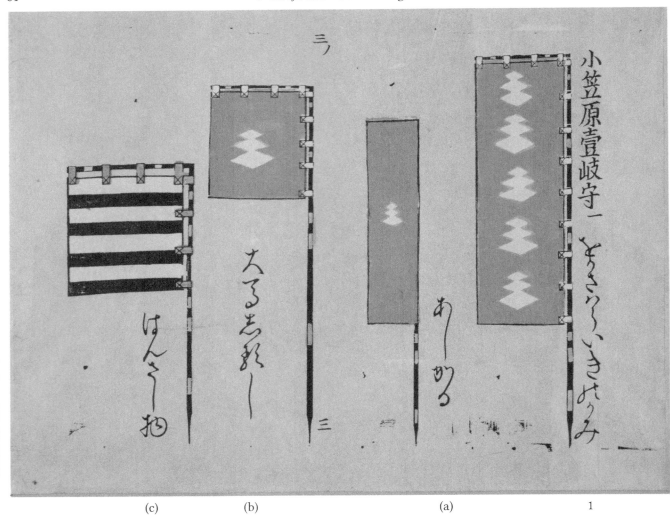

(c)   (b)   (a)   1

1. 小笠原・壹岐守　一　をゝさハ〱いきゟろみ (をかさはらいきのかみ; Ogasawara Iki-no-kami):
   "Ogasawara, Provincial Governor of Iki", i.e., Ogasawara Tadatomo (小笠原忠知) (1599–1663)[25, 小笠原小倉家]

   This section label does not use the variant 歧 for 岐 found in the table of contents, highlighting how interchangeable this variation is.

   This combination of three stacked rhombuses resembles 王 (ō), the Japanese character for king, adding an auspicious connotation. According to tradition, this mon was given to the Ogasawara by Emperor Go-Daigo, who originally wanted to give them the 王 character as a mon but thought that level of favoritism would cause strife. Instead, he gave them a mon that resembled the character, hiding a secret meaning in an unobjectionable geometric shape.[32, p. 1201] (For more on rhombuses in general, see p. 35.)

(a) あしかる (あしかる; ashigaru): foot soldiers

(b) 大馬志るし (大馬しるし; ō-mumajirushi): great standard

(c) はんさし抱 (はんさし物; ban-sashimono): guard identifying object

   White and black horizontal stripes.

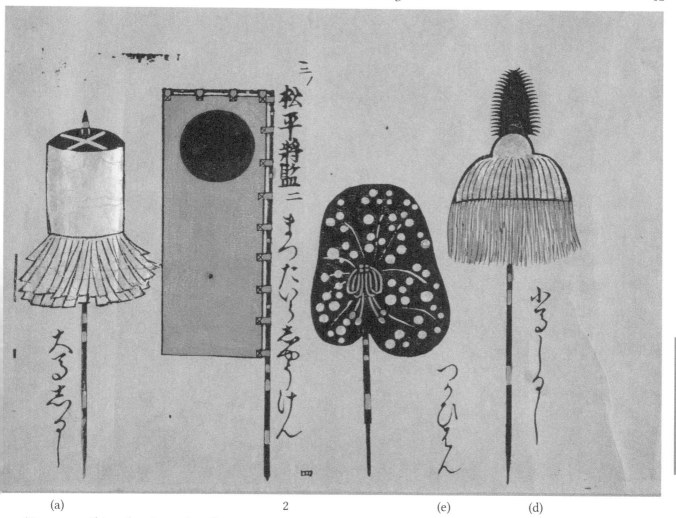

(a) 2 (e) (d)

(Ogasawara Iki-no-kami, continued)

(d) 小多くるし (小馬しるし; ko-mumajirushi): lesser standard

A black feathered top pole, a gold wooden shape that may represent a chrysanthemum or other flower, and red cord.

(e) つゝひそん (つかひはん; tsukaiban): messengers

A black horo splattered with variously-sized gold stars.

---

2. 松平・将監　二　まつたいらしゆうけん (まつたいらしやうけん; Matsudaira Shōgen):

"Matsudaira, Commander [of the Imperial Guards]", i.e., Matsudaira Narishige (松平成重) (1594–1633), who commanded the Right Inner Guard starting in 1608, or his son Matsudaira Tadaaki (松平忠昭) (1617–1693), who commanded the Left Inner Guard starting in 1640[25, 松平大給家]

将監 is a slightly different variant of 将監 than 将監, used in the table of contents.

A black disc on red.

(a) 大多志るし (大馬しるし; ō-mumajirushi): great standard

A gold cylinder with hanging paper strips. Compare the cylinder used by Matsushita Iwami-no-kami (see p. 205).

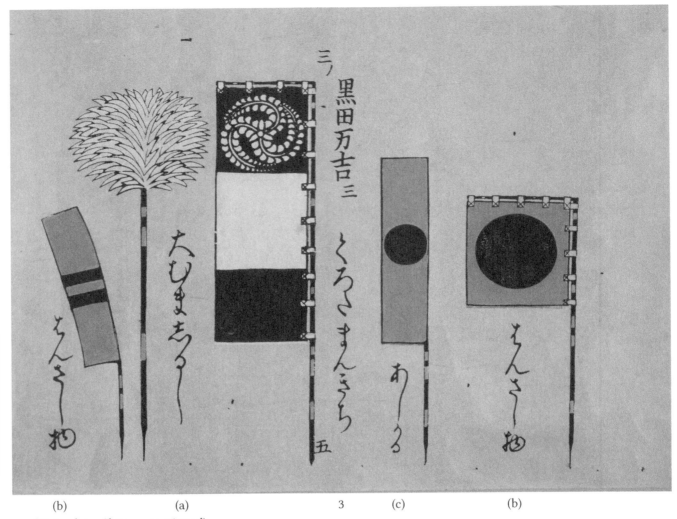

(b)   (a)   3   (c)   (b)

(Matsudaira Shōgen, continued)

(b) そんさし物 (はんさし物; ban-sashimono): guard identifying object

(c) あしかる (あしかる; ashigaru): foot soldiers

---

3. 黒田・万吉　三　くろさまんきち (くろたまんきち; Kuroda Mankichi):
   Referring to Kuroda Yoshitaka (黒田孝高) (1546–1604)[1, p. 311]

   This nobori has a mon of wisteria branches in the shape of tomoe above a white horizontal band. (See p. 91 for more on tomoe.) This type of "element in the shape of another element" design was rare at the time of *O-umajirushi*, but became popular later in the Edo period.

   The black background is a reference to the Kuroda name, which means "black field".

(a) 大むましるし (大むましるし; ō-mumajirushi): great standard

   A large plume of white feathers.

(b) そんさし物 (はんさし物; ban-sashimono): guard identifying object

   Two horizontal stripes.

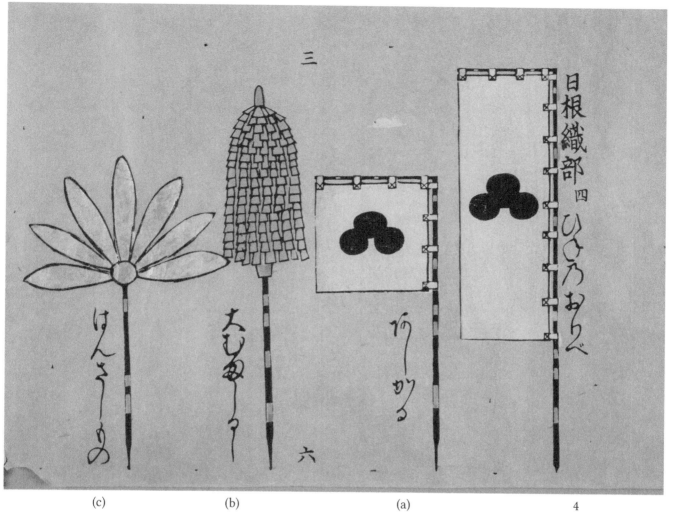

(c)　　　　　　(b)　　　　　　(a)　　　　　　4

4. 日根・織部　四　ひゐ乃おりべ (ひねのおりべ; Hine no Oribe):
"Hine, Weaving Bureau [official]", i.e., Hineno Takahiro (日根野高弘) (1539–1600) or his son Hineno Yoshiaki
(日根野吉明) (1587–1656)[1, pp. 653–654]

This design, called suhama (洲浜 or 州浜), supposedly represents a wavy sandbar that projects out into the ocean, but is functionally geometrical.

(a) ゐ�dくかる (あしかる; ashigaru): foot soldiers

(b) 大むゐしるし (大むましるし; ō-mumajirushi): great standard

This standard has blue paper strips hanging in a form reminiscent of a bell.

(c) はんさしゐの (はんさしもの; ban-sashimono): guard identifying object

A gold sunburst with seven rays.

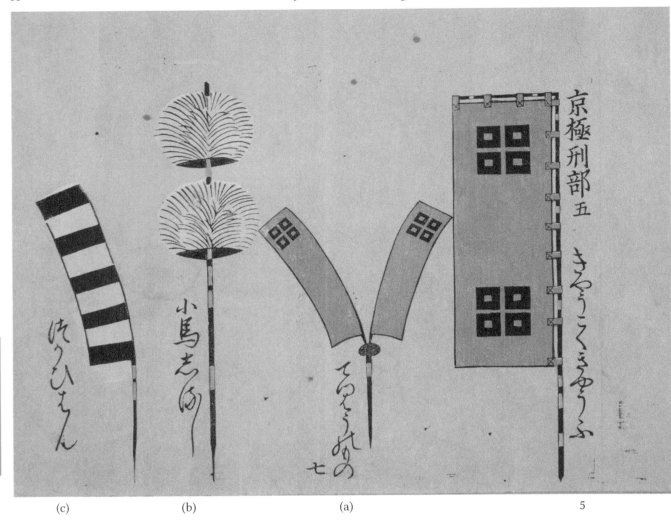

(c)   (b)   (a)   5

5. 京極・刑部　五　きやうこくきゆうふ (きやうこくきやうふ; Kyōgoku Gyōbu):
"Kyōgoku, Ministry of Justice [official]", i.e., Kyōgoku Takakazu (京極高和) (1619–1662)[25, 京極家]

This mon is described as a flat "four eyes joined" (四つ目結; yotsu me yui) mon.[44, p. 2.25] An "eye" is a small shadowed square, effectively the diminutive of the nail puller (see p. 220). It's "flat" because the default orientation would be rotated 45 degrees, with a corner pointed down.

(a) てつそう比もの (てつはうのもの; tetsubō-no-mono): spiked club men

(b) 小馬志はく (小馬しるし; ko-mumajirushi): lesser standard

Two hollow balls of white feathers.

(c) ほうひそん (つかひはん; tsukaiban): messengers

Black and white horizontal stripes.

A kokuin (see p. xxxiv) from Yodo Castle featuring a four eyes mon.
Photo by Eric Obershaw

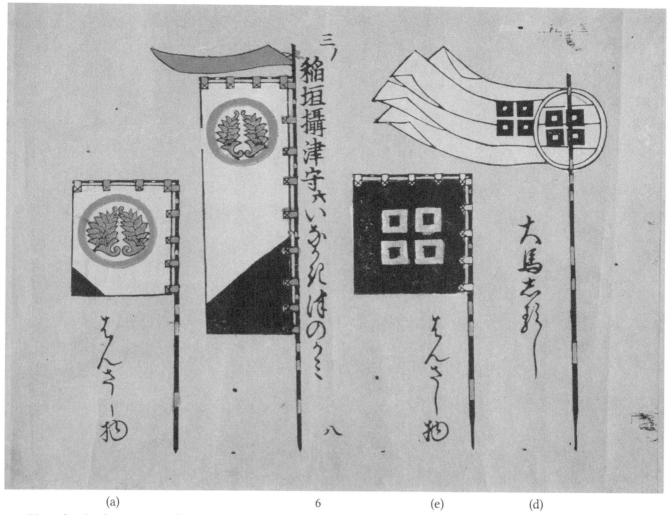

(a)   6   (e)   (d)

(Kyōgoku Gyōbu, continued)

(d) 大馬志犁く (大馬しるし; ō-mumajirushi): great standard

   The same mon, black on white, on a fukinuki.

(e) そんさく抝 (はんさし物; ban-sashimono): guard identifying object

---

6. 稲垣・攝津守　六　いゐう記ほのうミ (いなかきつのかみ; Inagaki Tsu-no-kami):
   "Inagaki, Provincial Governor of Tsu [i.e., Settsu]", i.e., Inagaki Shigetsuna (稲垣重綱) (1583–1654)[25, 稲垣家]

   This mon features two red apricot leaf (杏葉; gyōyō) shapes in a ring enclosure on a field with a diagonal division into white and black. The "apricot leaf" referred to a decorative tassel used on carriages, horse barding, and armor,[6, p. 126] which gave it a martial connotation. A red maneki accompanies.

(a) そんさく抝 (はんさし物; ban-sashimono): guard identifying object

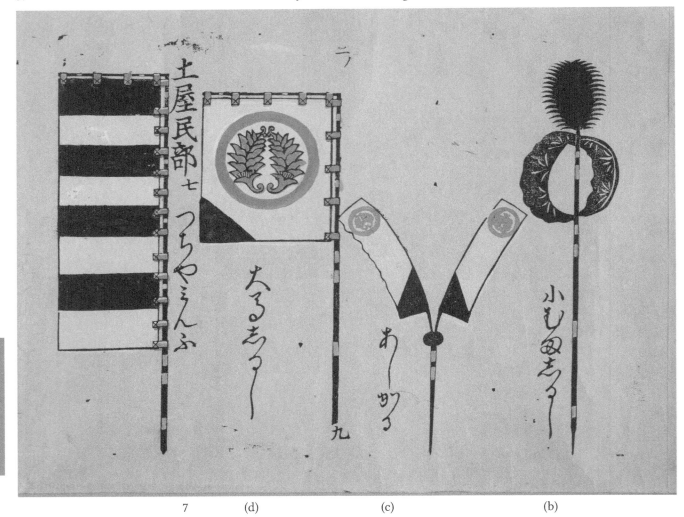

7 (d) (c) (b)

(Inagaki Tsu-no-kami, continued)

(b) 小むゐ志る〱 (小むましるし; ko-mumajirushi): lesser standard

A feathered top-pole and a cloth-covered hoop.

(c) あ〱かる (あしかる; ashigaru): foot soldiers

This double banner uses the same mon; it's just drawn with less detail here due to the smaller size.

(d) 大馬志る〱 (大馬しるし; ō-mumajirushi): great standard

---

7. 土屋・民部　七　つちやゝんふ (つちやみんふ; Tsuchiya Minbu):
"Tsuchiya, Ministry of Popular Affairs [official]", i.e., Tsuchiya Tadanao (土屋忠直) (1578–1612), who became Lesser Assistant in 1599, or his son Tsuchiya Toshinao (土屋利直) (1607–1675), who did so in 1621[25, 土屋家]

This nobori consists of black and white horizontal stripes.

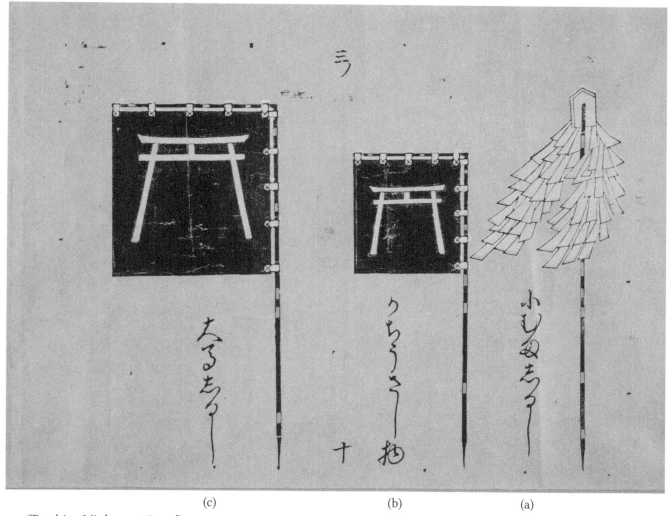

(c) (b) (a)

(Tsuchiya Minbu, continued)

(a) 小むぬまるし (小むましるし; ko-mumajirushi): lesser standard

This standard is a white gohei.

(b) ろちうさし物 (かちうさし物; kachū sashimono): whole family identifying object

This banner would have been worn by other members of the Tsuchiya family. It depicts a white shrine gate (鳥居; torii), which, like the preceding gohei, is a Shintō religious symbol. This suggests the Tsuchiya family had strong Shintō ties or ties to a particular shrine.

(c) 大多まるし (大馬しるし; ō-mumajirushi): great standard

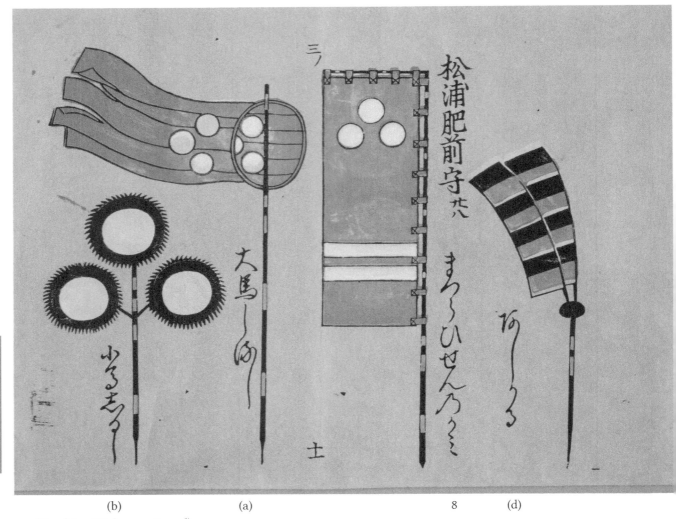

(b)   (a)   8   (d)

(Tsuchiya Minbu, continued)

(d) ��る (あしかる; ashigaru): foot soldiers

A three-color design combining black and red horizontal stripes with much thinner white stripes.

8. 松浦・肥前守　廿八　まつらひせんのうミ (まつらひせんのかみ; Matsura Hizen-no-kami):
"Matsura, Provincial Governor of Hizen", i.e., Matsura Takanobu (松浦隆信) (1591–1637), who received the title in 1612, or his son Matsura Shigenobu (松浦鎮信) (1622–1703), who received it in 1635[25, 松浦家]

An error here gives the entry number as 廿八, 28, instead of just 八, 8.

This nobori features a three stars mon and two horizontal stripes. Compare the more famous Nagai mon, p. 18.

(a) 大馬しるし (大馬しるし; ō-mumajirushi): great standard

The same mon, on a fukinuki.

(b) 小馬しるし (小馬しるし; ko-mumajirushi): lesser standard

This standard reflects the shape of the same mon with three white balls each with a border of black feathers.

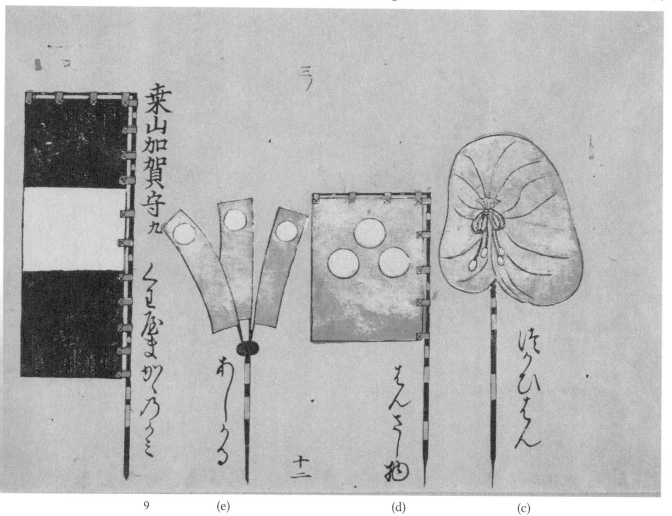

9　　　(e)　　　　　　　　(d)　　　　　　(c)

(Matsura Hizen-no-kami, continued)

(c) ほうひそん (つかひはん; tsukaiban): messengers

(d) そんさし物 (はんさし物; ban-sashimono): guard identifying object

(e) あしうる (あしかる; ashigaru): foot soldiers

　　This triple banner takes the unique tactic of splitting the three stars mon, putting one star on each banner.

---

9. 桒山・加賀守　九　くゑまかゝろうミ (くわやまかゝのかみ; Kuwayama Kaga-no-kami):
　　"Kuwayama, Provincial Governor of Kaga", i.e., Kuwayama Sadaharu (桑山貞晴) (1604–1629)[25, 桑山家]

　　A black nobori with a white horizontal band.

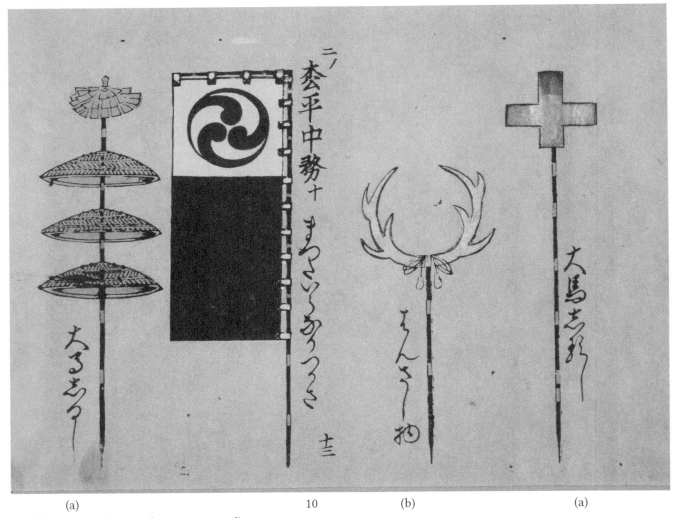

(a)   10   (b)   (a)

(Kuwayama Kaga-no-kami, continued)

(a) 大馬志�りし (大馬しるし; ō-mumajirushi): great standard

    This standard is a silver wooden cross, possibly suggesting that this samurai was Christian.

(b) そんさくり物 (はんさし物; ban-sashimono): guard identifying object

    This device consists of a pair of gold-painted antlers.

---

10. 松平・中務 　十　まつさいりゐうつうさ (まつたいらなかつかさ; Matsudaira Nakazukasa):
    "Matsudaira, Ministry of the Center [official]", i.e., Matsudaira Tadatomo (松平忠知) (1605–1634)[25, 江戸初期国持ち大名家]

    This nobori features a black mon of three tomoe on a field with a horizontal division between white and black. Tomoe are a Shintō symbol, associated with Hachiman, god of archery and war. Tomoe are variously associated with whirlpools, with the comma-shaped "magatama" jewels of ancient Japan (one of which serves as part of the imperial regalia), or with a type of leather wrist guard used by archers.[6, pp. 145-146] Their whirlpool interpretation led to them being credited as protecting from fire, and they were thus used on roof tiles.[12, p. 76] They have also been said to represent a whirling snowfall.[24, p. 12] This motif has been used since at least the 11th century.[12, p. v]

    Shoshō Kisei Zu describes the bottom portion as navy blue, not black.[44, p. 1.32]

(a) 大夛志るし (大馬しるし; ō-mumajirushi): great standard

    This standard consists of a dashi of paper strips and three woven straw hats.

(d)　　　　　　　　　　(c)　　　　　　　　　　(b)

(Matsudaira Nakazukasa, continued)

(b) そんさゝ抱 (はんさし物; ban-sashimono): guard identifying object

A large banner tree with black and white horizontal stripes.

(c) 志ふん (しふん; jibun): personal [device]

(d) しふん (しふん; jibun): personal [helmet]

This helmet has a very tall bowl, presumably enhanced with paper-mâché, and a crest featuring a similar tomoe design.

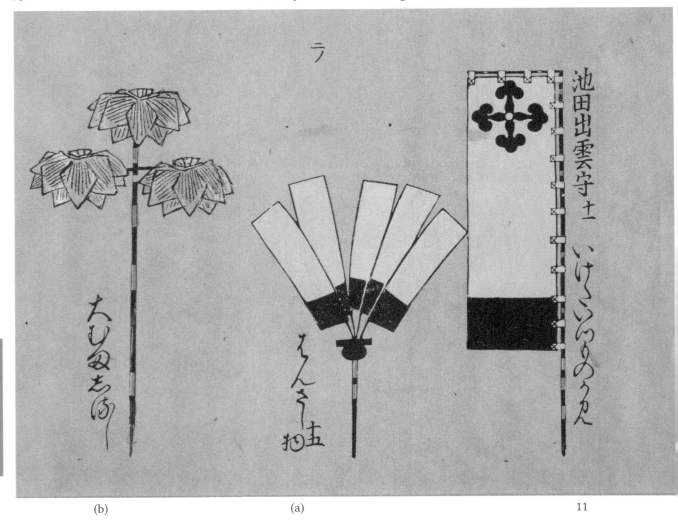

(b)　　　　　　　　　　　　　　　　　(a)　　　　　　　　　　　　　　　　11

11. 池田・出雲守　十一　いけさいつ�のらえ (いけたいつものかみ; Ikeda Izumo-no-kami):
　　　"Ikeda, Provincial Governor of Izumo", i.e., Ikeda Nagatsune (池田長常) (1609–1641)[25, 池田岡山家]

　　　Contrasting with the Shintō theme of the previous section, this nobori features a black cross mon, presumably a Christian design, and a low horizontal division from white to black.

(a) そんさくわ (はんさし物; ban-sashimono): guard identifying object

(b) 大むゑ志はく (大むましるし; ō-mumajirushi): great standard

　　　This standard uses three paulownia leaf shapes. Compare the standard used by Ogasawara Ukon-no-taifu (see p. 38).

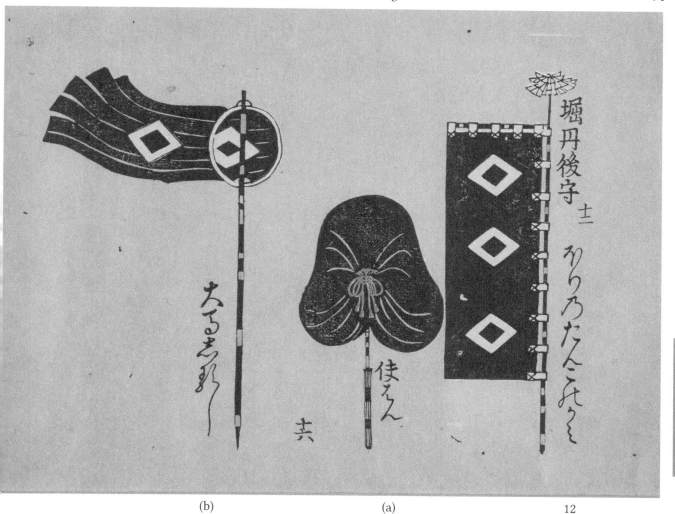

(b)   (a)   12

12. 堀・丹後守　十二　ぞり乃たんこのかみ (ほりのたんこのかみ; Hori no Tango-no-kami): "Hori, Provincial Governor of Tango", i.e., Hori Naoyori (堀直寄) (1577–1639)[1, p. 700]

This black nobori features three white shadowed rhombus mon identical except for color to the Matsudaira mon on p. 35. Attached at the top is a dashi of white paper strips.

(a) 使ざん (使はん; tsukaiban): messengers

(b) 大多志れく (大馬しるし; ō-mumajirushi): great standard

This standard is a fukinuki with the same mon.

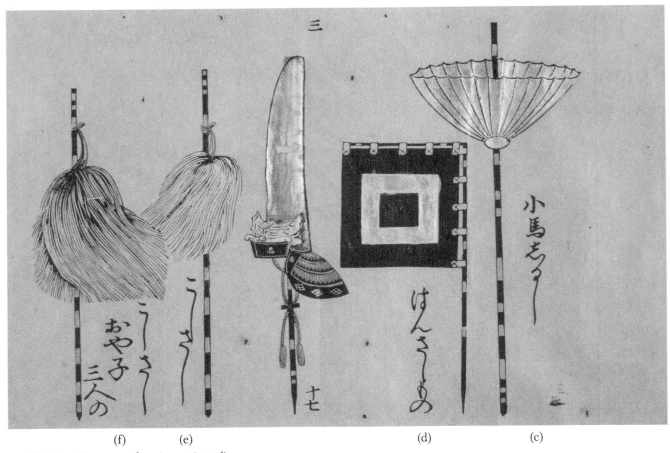

(f)   (e)   (d)   (c)

(Hori no Tango-no-kami, continued)

(c) 小馬志るし (小馬しるし; ko-mumajirushi): lesser standard

This standard is an unusual gold inverted umbrella.[53, p. 41]

(d) はんさしもの (はんさしもの; ban-sashimono): guard identifying object

This sashimono uses a similar but distinct mon, a hollow square, instead of the rhombus.

Unlabeled helmet

This very tall "catfish tail" helmet features a butterfly crest.

(e) こしさし (こしさし; koshisashi): lower-back identification

A *koshisashi* (腰指し) was an identifying object attached by a cord to a pole, which was worn stuck in the back of the obi of a mounted samurai. The kanji literally mean "lower-back identifying [thing]". Later koshisashi were square badges,[46, p. 375] but these ones seems to be made of yak hair, making them similar to saihai, commanders' batons with tassels made of leather or paper strips or yak hair.[46, p. 535]

(f) こしさし　おや子　三人の (こしさし　おや子　三人の; koshisashi oyako sannin-no): lower-back identifying object, parents-and-child, three people's

Oyako (親子) is a Japanese word that can mean "mother and child" or "parents and child" and is often used metaphorically, for example as the name of a popular rice bowl made with chicken and egg.[29, p. 5.746] Here "three people's" is specified almost as an afterthought, unusually ending with the connective particle 'no'; it may have been added after the rest of the caption to clarify that there are three hanging plumes and not two, which would otherwise be unclear both from the caption and from the image.

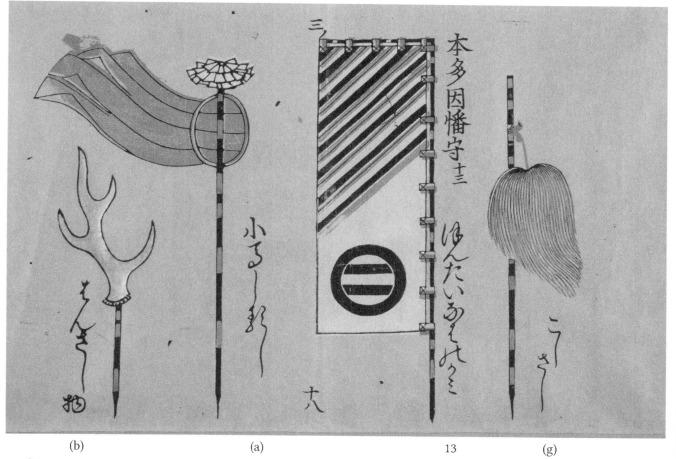

(b) (a) 13 (g)

(Hori no Tango-no-kami, continued)

(g) こしさし (こしさし; koshisashi): lower-back identification

A red yak hair koshisashi.

---

13. 本多・因幡守　十三　ほんたいゐそねうミ (ほんたいなはのかみ; Honda Inaba-no-kami):
"Honda, Provincial Governor of Inaba", i.e., Honda Toshimasa (本多俊政) –1608) or his son Honda Masatake
(本多政武) (1598–1637)[25, 本多高取家]

This nobori has elaborate, three-color diagonal stripes and a "rice bowl" circle with lines (引|両; hikiryō) mon.
Literally, "hiki" (引) means "pulled", referring to the horizontal lines, and "ryō" (両) can mean "both" or refer to an
old coin. The unclear meaning of "ryō" has contributed to various interpretations, including a deceased spirit
(written 霊, "ryō" can mean "spirit") or a submerged dragon (written 龍, "ryō" can mean "dragon").[49, p. 231]

According to legend, a variation on this mon was first used by the founder of the Narita family. Out of provisions
on a long campaign, he was famished on the way to battle when he came across a small shrine where a bowl of rice
had been left as an offering. Driven by hunger, he stole the offering and devoured it. Thus fortified, he accounted
himself well in the battle and emerged victorious. Crediting the deity whose rice he'd stolen with his victory, he
adopted this mon, a circular rice bowl with two horizontal stripes to represent chopsticks.[24, p. 6]

(a) 小馬しるし (小馬しるし; ko-mumajirushi): lesser standard

A red fukinuki and a dashi of white paper strips.

(b) そんさし物 (はんさし物; ban-sashimono): guard identifying object

This sashimono is a single antler.

14   (c)

(Honda Inaba-no-kami, continued)

(c) 大馬ゑはし (大馬しるし; ō-mumajirushi): great standard

14. 生駒・壹岐守　十四　いこゐいきのうミ (いこまいきのかみ; Ikoma
      Iki-no-kami):
    "Ikoma, Provincial Governor of Iki", i.e., Ikoma Takatoshi (生駒高俊) (1611–1659)[25,
      江戸初期国持ち大名家]

    This nobori has three one-third cart wheel mon. These cart wheels are known as
    "Genji wheels" after the classic Heian-period Japanese novel *The Tale of Genji*,[6,
    p. 130] where ox-carts are used by the nobility for transportation. This motif is also
    sometimes identified with the Buddhist "wheel of the law".[52, pp. 59–60] The
    one-third portion may be based on the shape of an open folding fan.

    Unlabeled horo (canopy)

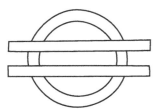

*The Narita variation of the rice
bowl mon.*[24, p. 22a]

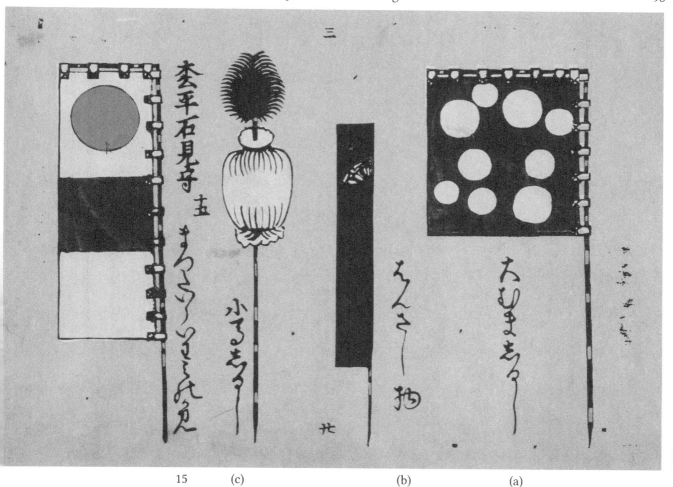

15   (c)   (b)   (a)

(Ikoma Iki-no-kami, continued)

(a) 大むま志る⎰ (大むましるし; ō-mumajirushi): great standard

An array of variously-sized stars.

(b) そんさ⎰抄 (はんさし物; ban-sashimono): guard identifying object

The design here is unclear due to the small size; it's actually just a smaller portion of the same cart wheel.

(c) 小多志る⎰ (小馬しるし; ko-mumajirushi): lesser standard

A feathered top-pole and a white cloth bundle.

---

15. 杢平・石見守　十五　まつさい⎰いそミ北っ见 (まつたいらいわみのかみ; Matsudaira Iwami-no-kami):

"Matsudaira, Provincial Governor of Iwami", i.e., Matsudaira Yasuyasu (松平康安) (1555–1623)[1, p. 730] or (from a different branch) Matsudaira Teruzumi (松平輝澄) (1604–1662)[25, 池田因幡家]

This nobori has a red disc on white and a black horizontal band.

A clearer version of the same wheel sashimono, from Shoshō Kisei Zu.[44, p. 1.25]

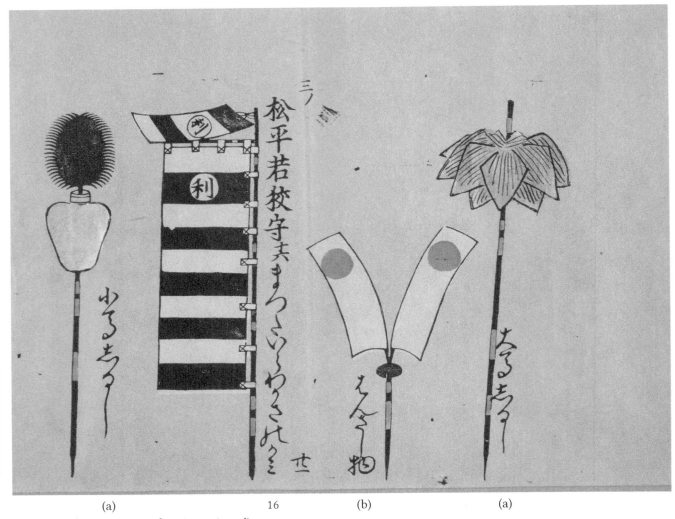

(a)   16   (b)   (a)

(Matsudaira Iwami-no-kami, continued)

(a) 大夢志るく (大馬しるし; ō-mumajirushi): great standard

    A single large paulownia leaf shape, similar to that used by Hoshina Higo-tono (see p. 16).

(b) そんさくや (はんさし物; ban-sashimono): guard identifying object

---

16. 松平・若狭守　十六　まつさいくわうさねうミ (まつたいらわかさのかみ; Matsudaira Wakasa-no-kami): "Matsudaira, Provincial Governor of Wakasa", i.e., Matsudaira Yasunobu (松平康信) (1600–1682)[25, 松平形原家および松平竹谷家]

    This section label uses a different variant 狭 for 狭, not the 狭 variant found in the table of contents.

    This banner features a mon of a white disc pierced with a black character 利 (ri, meaning "advantage") on a field of white and black horizontal stripes. Note the accompanying maneki, which suggests that whether a black or white stripe comes first is not important but that the colors of the mon are.

(a) 小夢志るく (小馬しるし; ko-mumajirushi): lesser standard

    A feathered top-pole and a smooth gold shape similar to a war fan.

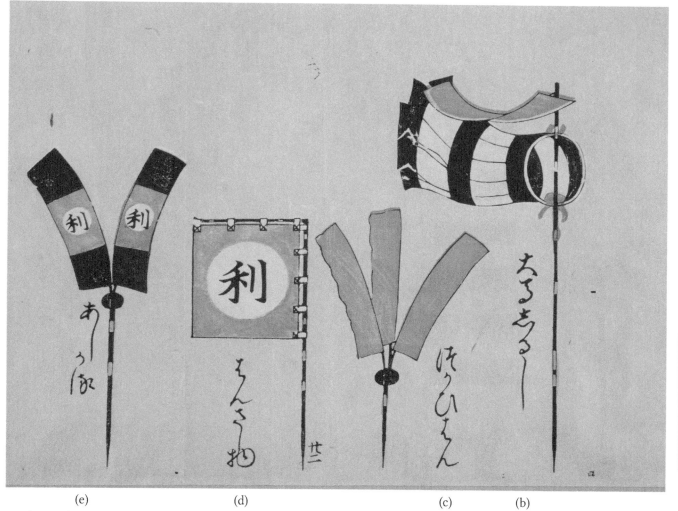

(e) (d) (c) (b)

(Matsudaira Wakasa-no-kami, continued)

(b) 大多志るく (大馬しるし; ō-mumajirushi): great standard

A white and black striped fukinuki accompanied by a red maneki. Unlike previous multicolored fukinuki, where different streamers were different colors, this one has stripes that go around the fukinuki.

(c) ほうひそん (つかひはん; tsukaiban): messengers

(d) そんさく扨 (はんさし物; ban-sashimono): guard identifying object

The same black character on white disc mon, this time on a red field.

(e) あくうは (あしかる; ashigaru): foot soldiers

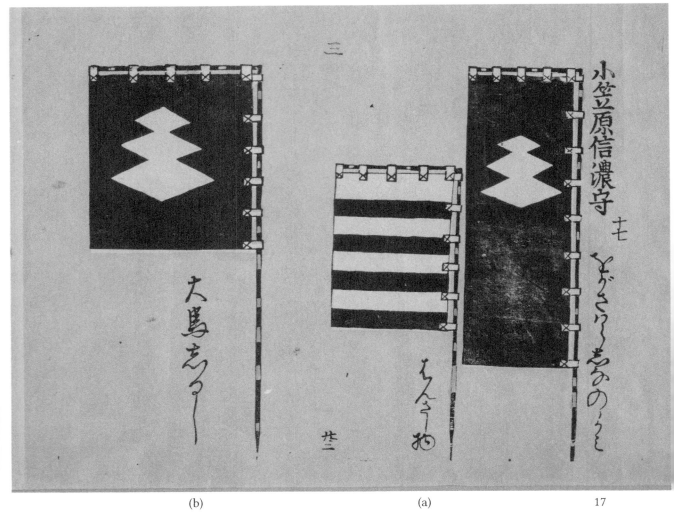

(b)   (a)   17

17. 小笠原・信濃守　十七　をゞさハ〱゙をゐのゝゥミ (をがさはらしなのゝかみ; Ogasawara Shinano-no-kami): "Ogasawara, Provincial Governor of Shinano", i.e., Ogasawara Tadanaga (小笠原忠脩) (1594–1615), who received the title in 1606, or his son Ogasawara Nagatsugu (小笠原長次) (1615–1666), who received it in 1629[25, 小笠原小倉家]

Another example of the Ogasawara three stacked rhombuses mon. (See p. 81.)

(a) そんさ〱抣 (はんさし物; ban-sashimono): guard identifying object
    White and black horizontal stripes.

(b) 大馬まる〱 (大馬しるし; ō-mumajirushi): great standard

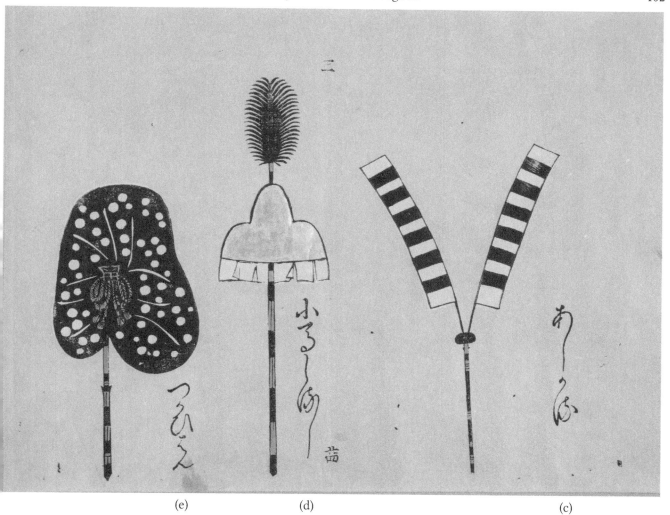

(e)　　　　　　　　(d)　　　　　　　　　　　　　　(c)

(Ogasawara Shinano-no-kami, continued)

(c) あしろは (あしかる; ashigaru): foot soldiers

(d) 小多しはし (小馬しるし; ko-mumajirushi): lesser standard

    A feathered top-pole and a gold mountain shape with a a border of slashed white cloth.

(e) つゥひそん (つかひはん; tsukaiban): messengers

    A black horo covered with white stars, similar to that used by Ogasawara Iki-no-kami (see p. 82).

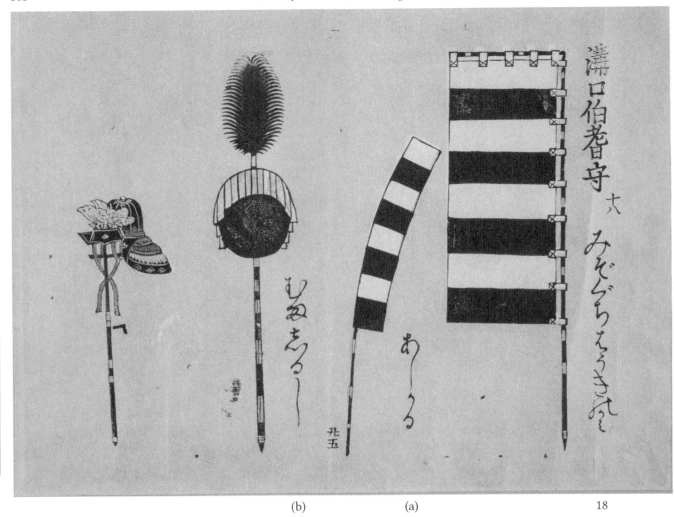

(b)   (a)   18

18. 溝口・伯耆守　十八　みぞぐちそうきねうミ (みぞぐちはうきのかみ; Mizoguchi Hōki-no-kami): "Mizoguchi, Provincial Governor of Hōki", i.e., Mizoguchi Hidekatsu (溝口秀勝) (1548–1610) or his son Mizoguchi Nobukatsu (溝口宣勝) (1582–1628)[25, 溝口家]

White and black horizontal stripes.

(a) あしうる (あしかる; ashigaru): foot soldiers

(b) むゐ志るし (むましるし; mumajirushi): battle standard

This standard is basically identical to the Mizoguchi standard used by Nobukatsu's son, Mizoguchi Izumo-no-kami (see p. 61).

Unlabeled helmet

A butterfly helmet crest.

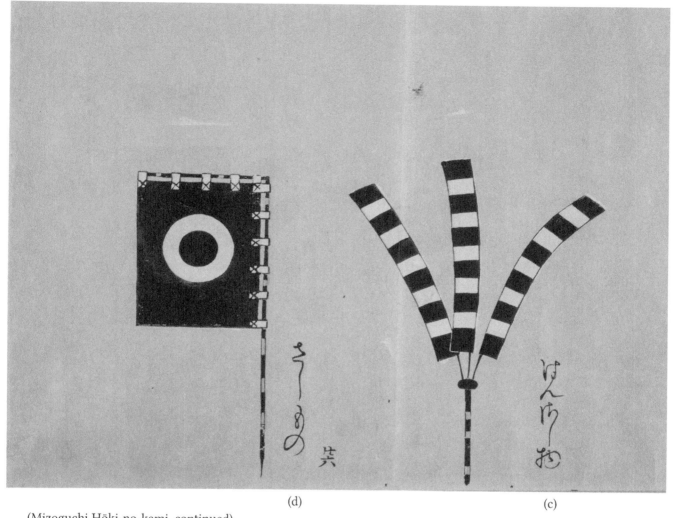

(d)

(c)

(Mizoguchi Hōki-no-kami, continued)

(c) はんほくあ (はんさし物; ban-sashimono): guard identifying object

(d) さくあの (さしもの; sashimono): identifying object

    This is an unusual case of a sashimono label that does not identify the specific purpose of the sashimono.

    The sashimono has a white snake's eye on a black field.

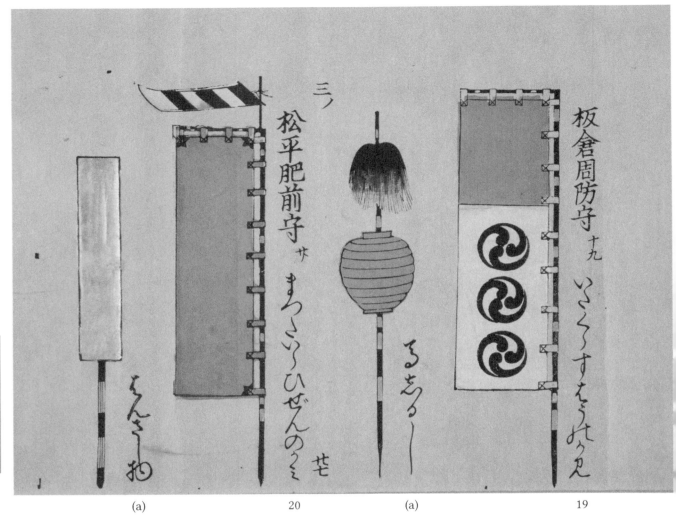

(a)   20   (a)   19

19. 板倉・周防守　十九　いさくゝすそうぬらゑ (いたくらすはうのかみ; Itakura Suō-no-kami):
"Itakura, Provincial Governor of Suō", i.e., Itakura Shigemune (板倉重宗) (1586–1656)[25, 板倉家]

This nobori has a field with a horizontal division from red to white, with three triple tomoe mon in black on the lower portion.

(a) 夢志るく (馬しるし; mumajirushi): battle standard

A black yak hair plume and a red paper lantern.

20. 松平・肥前守　廿　まつさいゝひぜんのうミ (まつたいらひぜんのかみ; Matsudaira Hizen-no-kami):
"Matsudaira Provincial Governor of Hizen", i.e., Matsudaira Tadanao (松平忠直) (1613–1635), who received the title in 1622,[25, 鍋島家] or Matsudaira Toshitsune (松平利常) (1593–1658), who received it in 1629.[25, 前田家] (The two individuals were from different Matsudaira branches.)

A solid red nobori with a maneki with black and white horizontal stripes.

(a) そんさくおゑ (はんさし物; ban-sashimono): guard identifying object

This sashimono seems to be a gold nagare hata.

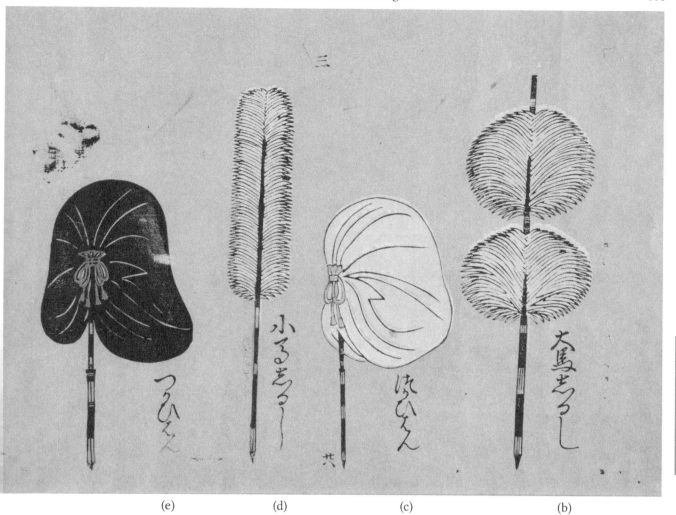

(e)   (d)   (c)   (b)

(Matsudaira Hizen-no-kami, continued)

(b) 大馬まるし (大馬しるし; ō-mumajirushi): great standard

    This standard is two large white balls of feathers.

(c) ほうひそん (つかひはん; tsukaiban): messengers

(d) 小马まるし (小馬しるし; ko-mumajirushi): lesser standard

    The lesser standard is a column of white feathers.

(e) つらひそん (つかひはん; tsukaiban): messengers

Vol. 3

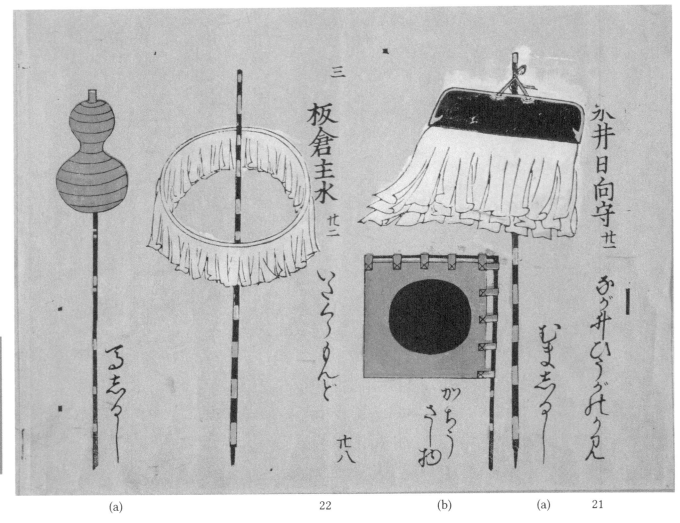

(a)   22   (b)   (a)   21

21. 永井・日向守　廿一　ゐぐ斗ひうゞれぅゑ (ながゐひうがのかみ; Nagai Hyūga-no-kami):
"Nagai, Provincial Governor of Hyūga", i.e., Nagai Naokiyo (永井直清) (1591–1671)[25, 永井家]

(a) むまゑるく (むましるし; mumajirushi): battle standard

     This standard is a similar to a very large noren hanging from a rigid black base.

(b) かっちう　さくｼ物 (かちう　さし物; kachū sashimono): whole family identifying object

     A black disc on red.

22. 板倉・主水　廿二　いさくゝゐんと (いたくらもんと; Itakura Mondo):
"Itakura, Water, Ice, and Porridge Office [official]", i.e., Itakura Shigemasa (板倉重昌) (1588–1638)[1, p. 96]

     Instead of a nobori, the primary device here is a hoop with slashed cloth hanging from it, similar to the shidewa used by Akitsuki Nagato-no-kami (see p. 157).

(a) 馬ゑるく (馬しるし; mumajirushi): battle standard

     A red gourd-shaped paper lantern.

(b)　　　　　　　　　　　　(a)　　　　　　　　23

23. 杢平・伊豆守　廿三　まつだい〳〵いづ北ろ三 (まつだいらいづのかみ; Matsudaira Izu-no-kami):
"Matsudaira, Provincial Governor of Izu", i.e., Matsudaira Nobukazu (松平信一) (1539–1624), his son Matsudaira
Nobuyoshi (松平信吉) (1575–1620),[25, 松平藤井家] or (from a different branch) Matsudaira Terutsuna (松平輝綱)
(1620–1671)[25, 松平大河内家]

A ladder.

(a) そんさ〳〵物 (はんさし物; ban-sashimono): guard identifying object

This double banner features a mon of three folding fans. One tradition is that a folding fan, in the way it opens,
represents a broadening of perspective.[12, p. 58]

(b) 小馬志�er〳〵 (小馬しるし; ko-mumajirushi): lesser standard

A tree with hanging cloth bundles possibly imitating blossoms.

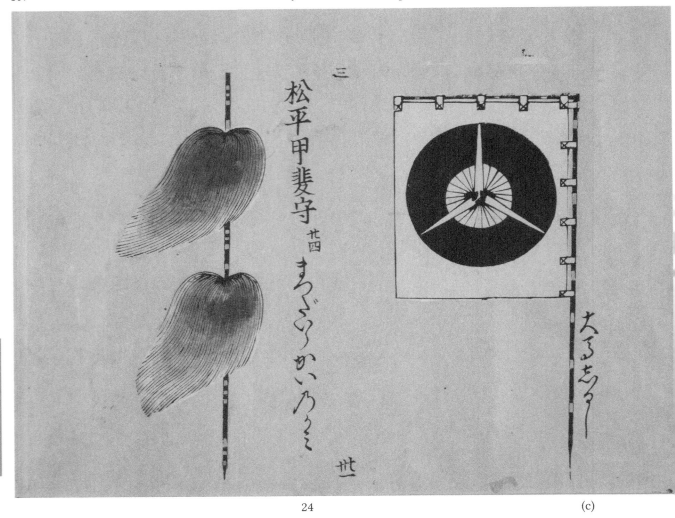

24   (c)

(Matsudaira Izu-no-kami, continued)

(c) 大夛志る⌇ (大馬しるし; ō-mumajirushi): great standard

    A larger version of the three folding fan mon.

---

24. 松平・甲斐守　廿四　まつざい⌇かい乃ろミ (まつだいらかいのかみ; Matsudaira Kai-no-kami):

    This may be an addendum to the previous section for Matsudaira Kai-no-kami (see p. 46), adding a device of two yak hair plumes. Given that there were two possible Matsudaira Kai-no-kami, Matsudaira Tadayoshi and Matsudaira Nagaoki, it could also be a section for the one not given in the previous section.

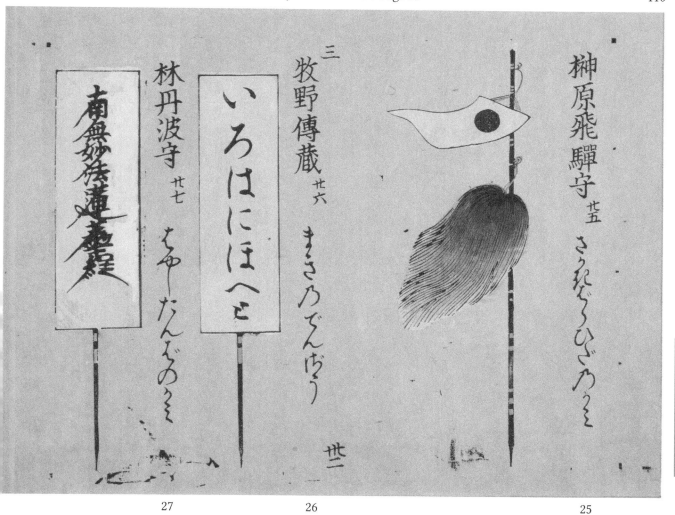

27   26   25

25. 榊原・飛驒守　廿五　さうねぐらひざろうミ (さかきばらひだのかみ; Sakakibara Hida-no-kami):
"Sakakibara, Provincial Governor of Hida", i.e., Sakakibara Motonao (榊原職直) (1586–1648)[28, 27]

The primary device here is a maneki with a black disc and a yak hair plume.

26. 牧野・傳蔵　廿六　まきろでんばう (まきのでんざう; Makino Denzō):
Referring to Makino Shigesato (牧野成里) (1556–1614)[1, p. 714]

This nagare hata reads いろはにほへと, "Iro ha nihoheto". This is the first line of the poem commonly called "Iroha", an ancient Japanese poem that uses every Japanese mora exactly once. Because of this, it was traditionally used for Japanese alphabetical order and also to count various things, like the notes in the scale.

27. 林・丹波守　廿七　そゆりたんぞのうミ (はやしたんばのかみ; Hayashi Tanba-no-kami):
"Hayashi, Provincial Governor of Tanba", i.e., Hayashi Katsumasa (林勝正)[11][15, #1119]

This nagare hata reads 南無妙法蓮華経, "Namu Myōhō Renge Kyō", meaning "Glory to the Lotus Sutra", a Nichiren mantra.[53, p. 37] Note the attention to detail reproducing the characters here, which are in a different style than other characters in *O-umajirushi*.

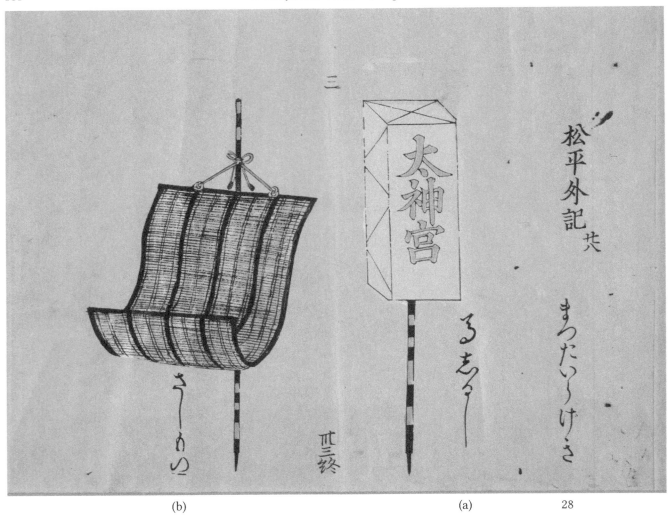

(b)   (a) 28

28. 松平・外記　廿八　まつたい〱げき (まつたいらげき; Matsudaira Geki):
Referring to Matsudaira Tadatsugu (松平忠次) (1521–1547)[22, 松平忠次]

(a) 馬しるし (馬しるし; mumajirushi): battle standard

This standard is a white cloth- or paper-covered box with gold characters reading 太神宮, "dai jingū", meaning "great shrine", a Shintō reference. Specifically, it refers to Ise Shrine, particularly its inner shrine, Kōtai Shrine, where Amaterasu Ōmikami, the sun goddess, is enshrined.[22, 太神宮]

In modern Japanese, 大 would usually be used for "great" and 太 for "thick" or "plump", but they seem to have been more interchangeable at the time of *O-umajirushi*.

(b) さ〱もの (さしもの; sashimono): identifying object

This sashimono is a bamboo blind. In Japanese, these are called either *misu* (御簾) or *sudare* (簾). This motif would later be used as a mon.[49, p. 268]

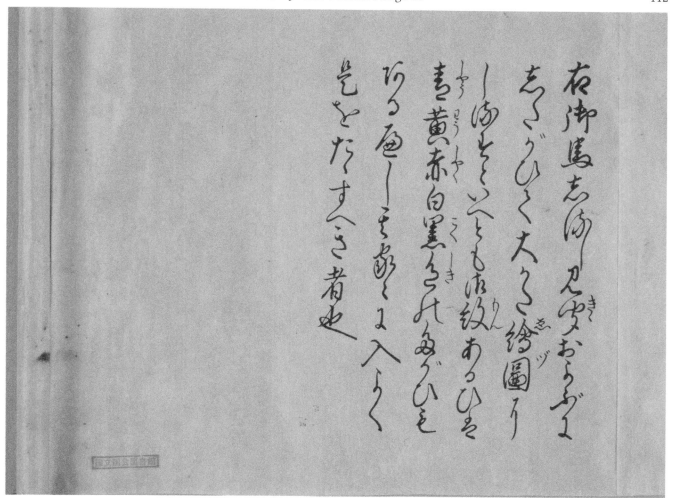

The closing paragraph here is printed with the same block as in the other volumes. This page being added to each volume is the only clear example of intentionally reused blocks in *O-umajirushi*. For translation and discussion, see p. 40.

End Volume 3

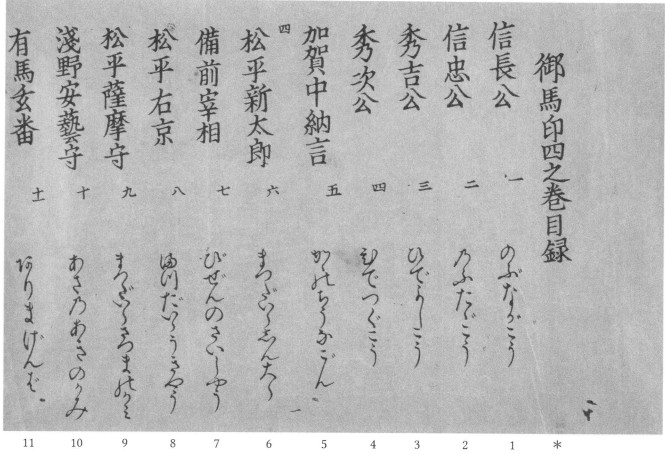

* 御馬印・四之巻・目録 (O-umajirushi Shi-no-maki Mokuroku)
　Honorable Battle Standards: Fourth Volume: Index

1. 信長公　一　のぶながこう (のぶながこう; Nobunaga-kō (lit. "Nobunaga-kou")):
　Referring to Oda Nobunaga (織田信長) (1534–1582)[1, p. 217]
　　　Father of Oda Nobutada, below, and Oda Nobutaka (entry 21 on p. 189). Grandson, via another son not included, of
　　　　Oda Takanaga (entry 21 on p. 117). Uncle of Oda Nobunori (entry 27 on p. 190).

　　-kō (〜公) is a honorific suffix. Here it is applied the formal given names (nanori) of lords who once held great
　　power in Japan but had passed away by the time of *O-umajirushi*. Nobunaga is known as the Japan's first great
　　unifier, conquering much of it and setting the stage for Toyotomi Hideyoshi, below, to finish unifying Japan.

2. 信忠公　二　乃ふたゞこう (のふたゞこう; Nobutada-kō (lit. "Nobutada-kou")):
　Referring to Oda Nobutada (織田信忠) (1557–1582)[1, p. 216]
　　First son of Oda Nobunaga

　　Although lack of dakuten make the pronunciation literally "Nofutada", the preceding name makes the modern
　　"Nobutada" pronunciation more likely, and this the "Nobutada" pronunciation is what's given in the actual section
　　label.

3. 秀吉公　三　ひでゝしこう (ひでよしこう; Hideyoshi-kō (lit. "Hideyoshi-kou")):
　Referring to Toyotomi Hideyoshi (豊臣秀吉) (1536–1598)[1, p. 553]
　　Uncle of Toyotomi Hidetsugu

　　Toyotomi Hideyoshi succeeded Oda Nobunaga, above, avenging his assassination, and finished the conquest and
　　unification of Japan started by his predecessor. He also led the failed invasion of Korea.

4. 秀次公　四　ひでつぐこう (ひでつぐこう; Hidetsugu-kō (lit. "Hidetsugu-kou")):
   Referring to Toyotomi Hidetsugu (豊臣秀次) (1568–1595)[1, pp. 552–553]
   Nephew of Toyotomi Hideyoshi
   秀次 is a historical variant of 秀次.

5. 加賀・中納言　五　かゝのちうゐごん (かゝのちうなごん; Kaga no Chūnagon (lit. "Kaga no Chiunagon")):
   "Kaga Middle Councilor", i.e., Maeda Toshitsune (前田利常) (1593–1658)[1, p. 711]
   中納言 is a historical variant of 中納言.

6. 松平・新太郎　六　まつだいらしん太ら (まつだいらしん太ら;
      Matsudaira Shintara (lit. "Matsudaira Shintara")):
   Referring to Matsudaira Mitsumasa (松平光政) (1609–1682)[25, 池田岡山家]
      Also known as Ikeda Mitsumasa (池田光政)
      新太郎 is a historical variant of 新太郎.

   新太郎 would today be pronounced "Shintarō"; however that's not the pronunciation given here. The
   pronunciation given includes a kuzushiji character that looks like 大; however, it's slightly different from kuzushiji
   大 characters elsewhere in *O-umajirushi* and is either just a kuzushiji 太[23, p. 255] or a hentaigana "ta" derived from
   that kanji (i.e., an ancestor of the modern hiragana ta, た, which is derived from the same kanji). Either way, the
   reading indicated is most likely "Shintara". While there are extant place names suggesting that "Oira" and "Dairo"
   are also historical readings of 太郎, "Tara" is a rare alternate reading of the name today, and consistent with how
   太 is normally pronounced in this combination.

   This name is also notable for using not just a given name but a *yobina*, the informal or child name, rather than a
   title or the more formal nanori. While Mitsumasa became Major General (少将; shōshō) in 1626, he may have lost
   that position by the time of *O-umajirushi* or otherwise have been better known by his informal name.

7. 備前・宰相　七　びぜんのさい〱ゆう (びぜんのさいしやう; Bizen no Saishō (lit. "Bizen no Saishiyau")):
   "State Councilor of Bizen", i.e., Ukita Hideie (宇喜多秀家) (1572–1655)[26, p. 273][1, p. 140]

8. 松平・右京　八　ゐりだい〱うきやう (まつだいらうきやう; Matsudaira Ukyō (lit. "Matsudaira Ukiyau")):
   "Matsudaira, Right Capital Administration [official]", i.e., Matsudaira Masatsuna (松平政綱) (1606–1631), also known
      as Ikeda Masatsuna (池田政綱), who became Greater Director in 1623,[25, 池田岡山家] or (from another line)
      Matsudaira Yorishige (松平頼重) (1622–1695), who did so in 1638[25, 徳川水戸家]

   Yorishige became chamberlain (侍従; jijū) instead of Greater Director of the Right Capital Administration
   (右京大夫; ukyō-no-taifu) in 1640; however, since this entry may refer to Masatsuna, and *O-umajirushi* sometimes
   uses past titles to refer to individuals, it does not definitively establish *O-umajirushi* as published before 1640.

9. 松平・薩摩守　九　まつだい〱さつまゐろミ (まつだいらさつまのかみ; Matsudaira Satsuma-no-kami):
   "Matsudaira, Provincial Governor of Satsuma", i.e., Matsudaira Iehisa (松平家久) (1576–1638), who received the title
      in 1617, or his son Matsudaira Mitsuhisa (松平光久) (1616–1694), who received it in 1631[25, 島津家]
      Both also used the surname Shimazu (島津)
      薩摩 is a historical variant of 薩摩.

10. 淺野・安藝守　十　あさゐあきのゝみ (あさのあきのかみ; Asano Aki-no-kami):
    "Asano, Provincial Governor of Aki", i.e., Matsudaira Mitsuakira (松平光晟) (1617–1693)[25, 浅野家]
       Nephew of Asano Nagashige (entry 11 on p. 43)
       淺野 is a historical variant of 浅野, and 安藝 is a variant of 安芸.

    Mitsuakira was granted the Matsudaira surname in 1627, but is still referred to as "Asano" here, suggesting that
    being granted a new surname did not necessarily completely replace your original surname.

11. 有馬・玄番　十一　ゐりまげんぞ (ありまげんば; Arima Genba):
    "Arima, Priests and Foreigners Bureau [official]", i.e., Arima Toyōji (有馬豊氏) (1569–1642)[25, 有馬久留米家]
       Toyōji was the son of Arima Noriyori (entry 12 on p. 116) and father of Arima Tadayori (entry 12 on p. 116).
       玄番 is a historical variant of 玄番.

    This bureau name is today written 玄蕃, suggesting inconsistency in the kanji used.

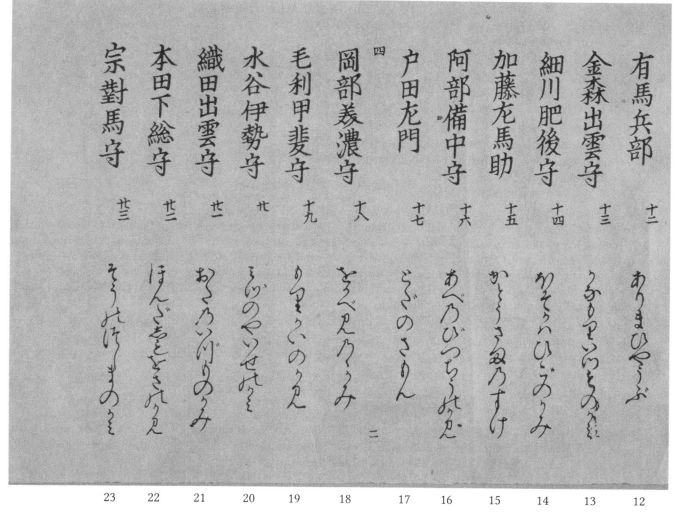

23	22	21	20	19	18	17	16	15	14	13	12

12. 有馬・兵部　十二　ありまひやうぶ (ありまひやうぶ; Arima Hyōbu (lit. "Arima Hiyaubu")):
"Arima, Ministry of War [official]", i.e., Arima Noriyori (有馬則頼) (1533–1602) or his grandson Arima Tadayori
(有馬忠頼) (1603–1655)[25, 有馬久留米家]
Noriyori was the father of Arima Toyōji (entry 11 on p. 115), and Tadayori was Toyōji's son.

13. 金森・出雲守　十三　かなもりいつをのかみ (かなもりいつものかみ;
Kanamori Izumo-no-kami (lit. "Kanamori Itsumo-no-kami")):
"Kanamori, Provincial Governor of Izumo", i.e., Kanamori Yoshishige (金森可重) (1558–1615) or his son Kanamori
Shigeyori (金森重頼) (1594–1650)[1, pp. 251–252]
出雲 is a historical variant of 出雲.

Although the pronunciation given here lacks the dakuten that would make "Itsumo" into "Izumo", the
pronunciation given in the actual section label and uses elsewhere in *O-umajirushi* suggest that "Izumo" is the
intended pronunciation.

14. 細川・肥後守　十四　ゃそらハひごのらみ (ほそかはひごのかみ;
Hosokawa Higo-no-kami (lit. "Hosokaha Higo-no-kami")):
"Hosokawa, Provincial Governor of Higo", i.e., Hosokawa Mitsunao (細川光尚) (1619–1649)[25, 細川家]
細川 is a historical variant of 細川.

15. 加藤・㔫馬助　十五　かとうさゐ乃すけ (かとうさまのすけ; Katō Sama-no-suke (lit. "Katou Sama-no-suke")):
"Katō, Assistant [Director] of the Left Horses", i.e., Katō Yoshiaki (加藤嘉明) (1563–1631)[1, p. 249]
　　From a different Katō line than Katō Yasuoki (entry 11 on p. 149) and from Katō Kiyomasa (entry 14 on p. 188)
　　加藤 is a historical variant of 加藤, and 㔫馬 is a variant of 左馬.

16. 阿部・備中守　十六　あべ乃びつちう㔫らゑ (あべのびつちうのかみ;
　　　　Abe no Bitchū-no-kami (lit. "Abe no Bitsuchiu-no-kami")):
"Abe, Provincial Governor of Bitchū", i.e., Abe Masatsugu (阿部正次) (1569–1647)[1, p. 51]
　　備中 is a historical variant of 備中.

17. 戸田・㔫門　十七　とざのさゐん (とだのさもん; Toda no Samon):
Referring to Toda Kazuaki (戸田一西) (1541–1602) or his son Toda Ujikane (戸田氏鉄) (1576–1655)[25, 戸田大垣家]
　　Ujikane is the son-in-law of Matsudaira Yasunaga (entry 29 on p. 7).
　　戸田 is a historical variant of 戸田, and 㔫門 is a variant of 左門.

Samon (左門) means "Left Gate" and would seem to imply an association with the Left Gate Guards, but seems to have been a nickname or informal given name rather than a title. During his time as ruler of the Zeze Domain, Kazuaki encouraged red clam fishing; he became so known for this that the clams started being called "Samon clams" after his informal name.[55, p. 167]

18. 岡部・美濃守　十八　をゝべ乬乃ゝらみ (をかべみのゝかみ;
　　　　Okabe Mino-no-kami (lit. "Wokabe Mino-no-kami")):
"Okabe, Provincial Governor of Mino", i.e., Okabe Nobukatsu (岡部宣勝) (1597–1668)[25, 岡部家]
　　美濃 is a historical variant of 美濃.

19. 毛利・甲斐守　十九　ゐ乬らいの乃ゑ (もりかいのかみ; Mori Kai-no-kami):
"Mori, Provincial Governor of Kai", i.e., Mōri Hidemoto (毛利秀元) (1579–1650)[1, p. 774]
　　甲斐 is a historical variant of 甲斐.
　　In modern Japanese, the Mori clan is read as Mōri.

20. 水谷・伊勢守　廿　ミげのやいせ㔫らミ (みづのやいせのかみ;
　　　　Mizunoya Ise-no-kami (lit. "Midzunoya Ise-no-kami")):
"Mizunoya, Provincial Governor of Ise", i.e., Mizunoya Katsutoshi (水谷勝俊) (1542–1606)[1, p. 744] or his son Mizunoya
　　Katsutaka (水谷勝隆) (1597–1664)[25, 水谷家]

21. 織田・出雲守　廿一　おさ乃いげゐの乃ゐ (おたのいづものかみ;
　　　　Ota no Izumo-no-kami (lit. "Ota no Idzumo-no-kami")):
"Ota, Provincial Governor of Izumo", i.e., Oda Takanaga (織田高長) (1590–1674)[25, 織田家]
　　Grandson of Oda Nobunaga (entry 1 on p. 114)
　　織田 is a historical variant of 織田, and 出雲 is a variant of 出雲.

22. 本田・下総守　廿二　ほんざゑををさ㔫らゑ (ほんだしもをさのかみ;
　　　　Honda Shimōsa-no-kami (lit. "Honda Shimowosa-no-kami")):
"Honda, Provincial Governor of Shimōsa", i.e., Honda Toshitsugu (本多俊次) (1595–1668)[25, 本多膳所家]
　　Written with different kanji than the other Honda families in *O-umajirushi*; however, given that *Kansei Chōshū Shoka Fu* uses 本多, this may not be a significant difference.

23. 宗・對馬守　廿三　そう㔫ほゝまのらゑ (そうのつしまのかみ;
　　　　Sō no Tsushima-no-kami (lit. "Sou no Tsushima-no-kami")):
"Sō, Provincial Governor of Tsushima", i.e., Sō Yoshitoshi (宗義智) (1568–1615) or his son Sō Yoshinari (宗義成)
　　(1604–1657)[25, 宗家]
　　對馬 is a historical variant of 対馬.

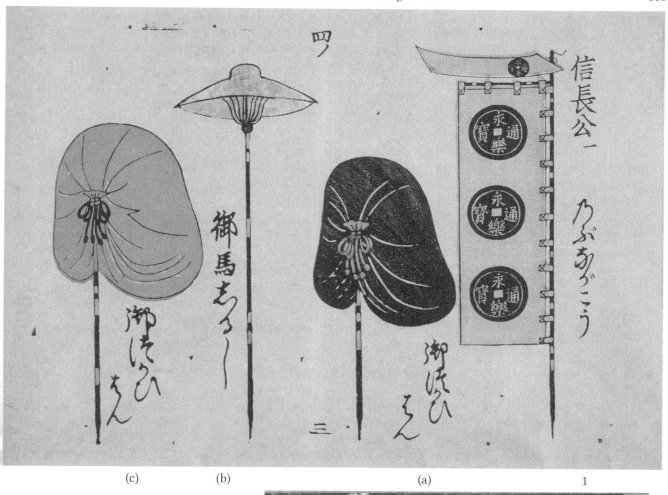

(c)   (b)   (a)   1

1. 信長公　一　のぶゐグこう
　　(のぶながこう; Nobunaga-kō):
　　Referring to Oda Nobunaga (織田信長)
　　(1534–1582)[1, p. 217]

　　This nobori has three coin mon, using
　　the same Ming dynasty coin as p. 57.
　　The maneki uses the same mon.

(a) 御ほうひ　そん (御つかひ　はん;
　　o-tsukaiban): honorable
　　messengers

(b) 御馬志るし (御馬しるし;
　　o-mumajirushi): honorable battle
　　standard

　　A gold-painted umbrella.

(c) 御ほうひ　そん (御つかひ　はん;
　　o-tsukaiban): honorable
　　messengers

Nobunaga's heraldry from "Shoshō Shōki Zu Byōbu".[45, 1] *The nobori here is white, and instead of a mon on the maneki, it reads* 南無妙法蓮華経, *"Glory to the Lotus Sutra", the same Nichiren mantra used by Hayashi Tanba-no-kami (see p. 110).*
Ōsaka Castle Museum Collection

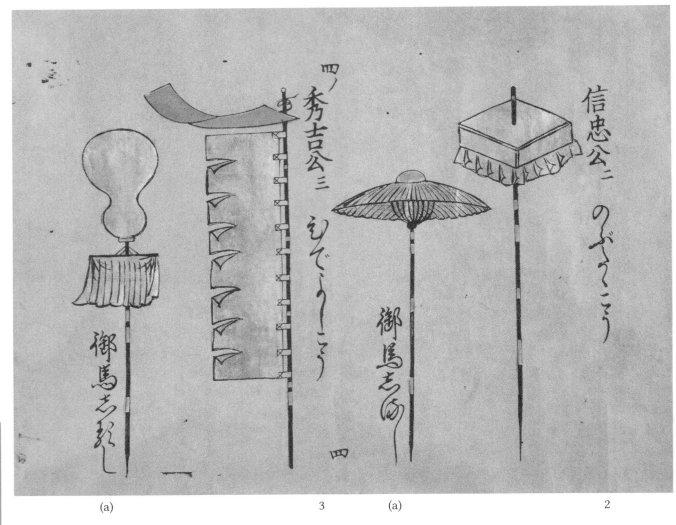

(a)   3   (a)   2

2. 信忠公　二　のぶさゝこう (のぶたゝこう; Nobutada-kō):
Referring to Oda Nobutada (織田信忠) (1557–1582)[1, p. 216]

The primary device here is cloth-covered square frame with slashed cloth at the edges.

(a) 御馬志はく (御馬しるし; o-mumajirushi): honorable battle standard

A slightly more complex umbrella than the one used by Nobunaga, his father (previous section).

3. 秀吉公　三　むでゝりこう (ひでよしこう; Hideyoshi-kō):
Referring to Toyotomi Hideyoshi (豊臣秀吉) (1536–1598)[1, p. 553]

A gold slashed nobori and a red maneki.

(a) 御馬志れし (御馬しるし; o-mumajirushi): honorable battle standard

A large gold gourd and a noren with many slashes. Some traditions indicate that Hideyoshi would add one gourd to his standard for each victory; however, *O-umajirushi* and other sources show only one gourd.[53, p. 87]

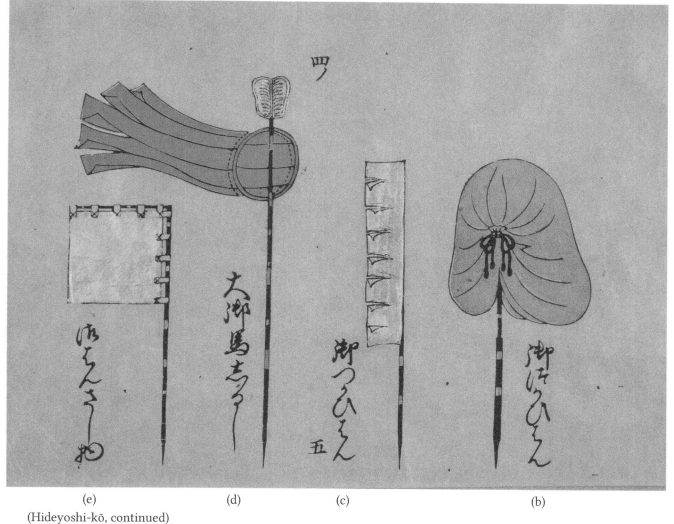

(e)　　　　　　(d)　　　　　(c)　　　　　　　　(b)

(Hideyoshi-kō, continued)

(b) 御ほろひそん (御つかひはん; o-tsukaiban): honorable messengers

　　This horo seems to be an unusual yellow or tan color, instead of the more common gold.

(c) 御つろひそん (御つかひはん; o-tsukaiban): honorable messengers

(d) 大御馬志るし (大御馬しるし; ō-o-mumajirushi): great honorable standard

　　This standard is a red fukinuki and a gold wooden war fan.

(e) ほそんさし物 (御はんさし物; o-ban-sashimono): honorable guard identifying object

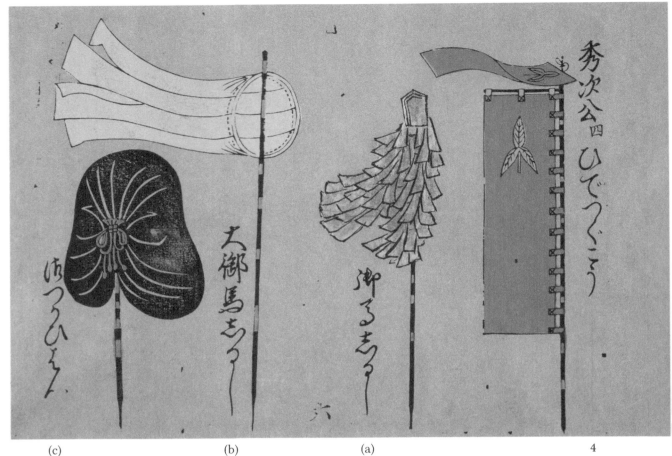

(c)　　　　　　　　(b)　　　　　　　　(a)　　　　　　　　4

4. 秀次公　四　ひでつぐこう (ひでつぐこう;
    Hidetsugu-kō):
    Referring to Toyotomi Hidetsugu (豊臣秀次)
    (1568–1595)[1, pp. 552–553]

    This mon depicts the three-leaf arrowhead plant (沢瀉),
    a marsh plant with edible tubers. This mon is
    considered one of Japan's 10 great crests due to its
    frequent use, though this version has more internal
    detailing than modern depictions.[49, p. 88]

(a) 御多まるし (御馬しるし; o-mumajirushi): honorable
    battle standard

    This standard consists of a gold gohei.

(b) 大御馬まるし (大御馬しるし; ō-o-mumajirushi): great
    honorable standard

    A white fukinuki.

(c) 御つかひはん (御つかひはん; o-tsukaiban): honorable
    messengers

*Some of Hidetsugu's heraldry from "Shoshō Shōki Zu
Byōbu".*[45, 4] *This version shows mon on the fukinuki as well.*
Ōsaka Castle Museum Collection

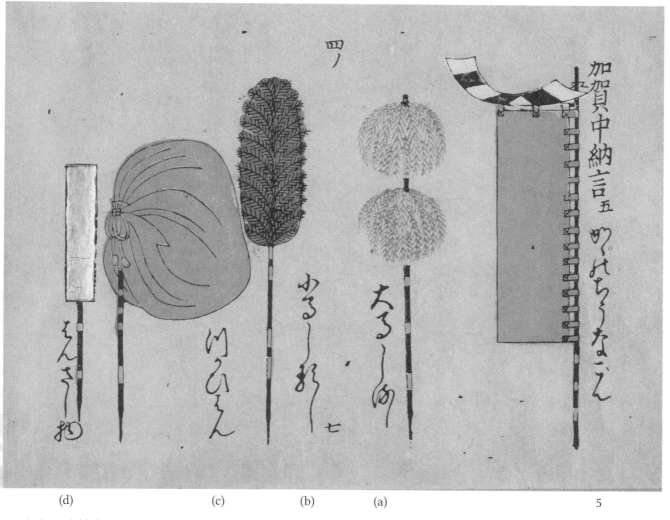

(d)　　　　　　　(c)　　　(b)　　　(a)　　　　　　　　　5

5. 加賀・中納言　五　かゞれちうなごん (かゞのちうなごん; Kaga no Chūnagon):
   "Kaga Middle Councilor", i.e., Maeda Toshitsune (前田利常) (1593–1658)[1, p. 711]

   A red nobori and a maneki with white and black horizontal stripes.

(a) 大うくほく (大馬しるし; ō-mumajirushi): great standard

   Two balls with blue feathers.

(b) 小うく払く (小馬しるし; ko-mumajirushi): lesser standard

   An oblong pillar covered in blue feathers.

(c) りうひそん (つかひはん; tsukaiban): messengers

(d) そんさく抄 (はんさし物; ban-sashimono): guard identifying object

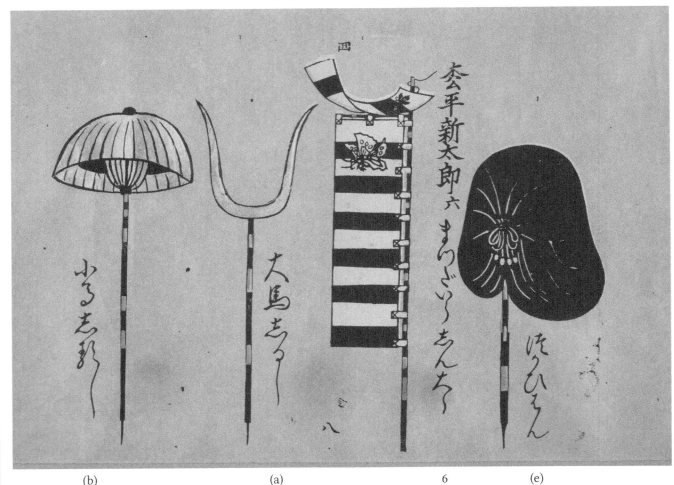

(b)   (a)   6   (e)

(Kaga no Chūnagon, continued)

(e) ほうひそん (つかひはん; tsukaiban): messengers

6. 杢平・新太郎　六　まつざい〱あん太〱 (まつだいらしん太ら;
Matsudaira Shintara):
Referring to Matsudaira Mitsumasa (松平光政) (1609–1682)[25, 池田岡山家]

A nobori with a butterfly mon on a background of white and black
horizontal stripes. The butterfly mon is strongly associated with the
Taira family, one side in the 12th century Genpei War (although the mon
may have come into use later).[52, p. 9] While his family was granted the
name Matsudaira, Mitsumasa comes from the Ikeda family; they were
granted the use of the butterfly mon by Oda Nobunaga (entry 1 on p.
114), a Taira descendant.[12, p. 55]

(a) 大馬志るし (大馬しるし; ō-mumajirushi): great standard

A wood standard in the shape of a helmet crest.

(b) 小馬志敕し (小馬しるし; ko-mumajirushi): lesser standard

A bowl-shaped umbrella.

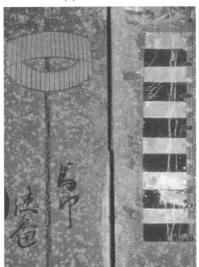

*In "Shoshō Shōki Zu Byōbu", Mit-
sumasa's nobori lacks the mon, the
maneki lacks stripes, and the umbrella is
replaced with a hoop shape.*[45, 6]
Ōsaka Castle Museum Collection

Vol. 4

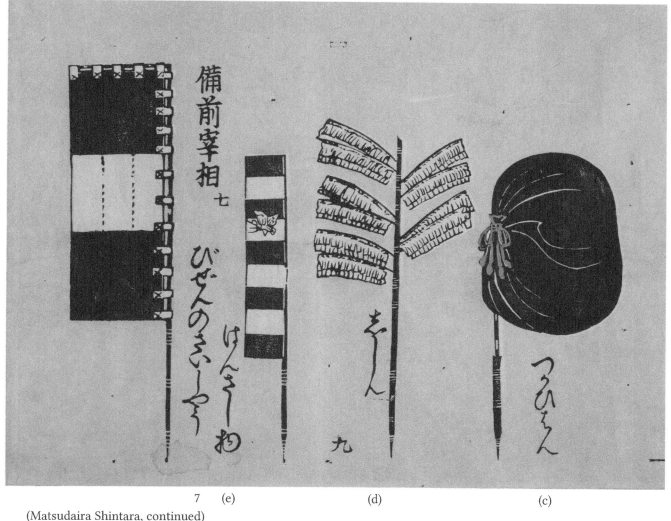

7   (e)   (d)   (c)

(Matsudaira Shintara, continued)

(c) つゝひそん (つかひはん; tsukaiban): messengers

(d) ましん (ししん; jishin): personal [helmet]

   A banner tree of white slashed banners.

(e) はんさゝ物 (はんさし物; ban-sashimono): guard identifying object

   A banner similar to the nobori, with the same butterfly mon.

---

7. 備前・宰相　七　びぜんのさいゝやう (びぜんのさいしやう; Bizen no Saishō):
   "State Councilor of Bizen", i.e., Ukita Hideie (宇喜多秀家) (1572–1655)[26, p. 273][1, p. 140]

   A black nobori with a white horizontal band with stitching.

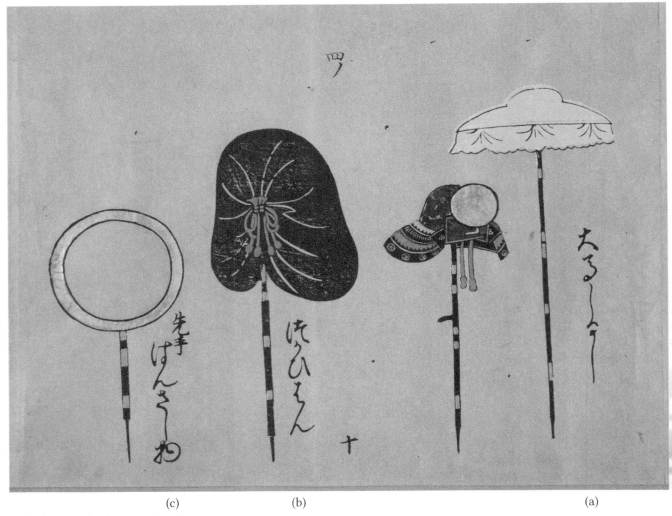

(c)   (b)   (a)

(Bizen no Saishō, continued)

(a) 大多くるし (大馬しるし; ō-mumajirushi): great standard

    A white cloth umbrella.

Unlabeled helmet

    A helmet with a disc crest.

(b) ほうひそん (つかひはん; tsukaiban): messengers

(c) 先手　はんさし物 (先手　はんさし物; sakite ban-sashimono): front-line guard identifying object

    A gold ring-shaped standard.

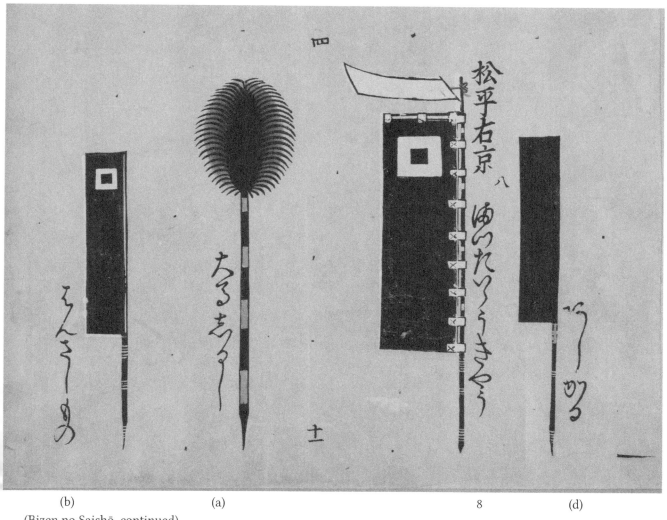

(b)   (a)   8   (d)

(Bizen no Saishō, continued)

(d) ほしかる (あしかる; ashigaru): foot soldiers

8. 松平・右京　八　ゐつたいしうきやう (まつたいらうきやう; Matsudaira Ukyō):
"Matsudaira, Right Capital Administration [official]", i.e., Matsudaira Masatsuna (松平政綱) (1606–1631), also known
as Ikeda Masatsuna (池田政綱), who became Greater Director in 1623,[25, 池田岡山家] or (from another line)
Matsudaira Yorishige (松平頼重) (1622–1695), who did so in 1638[25, 徳川水戸家]

A shadowed square mon on a black nobori, accompanied by a white maneki.

(a) 大あ志るし (大馬しるし; ō-mumajirushi): great standard

A feathered oblong top shape.

(b) そんさしもの (はんさしもの; ban-sashimono): guard identifying object

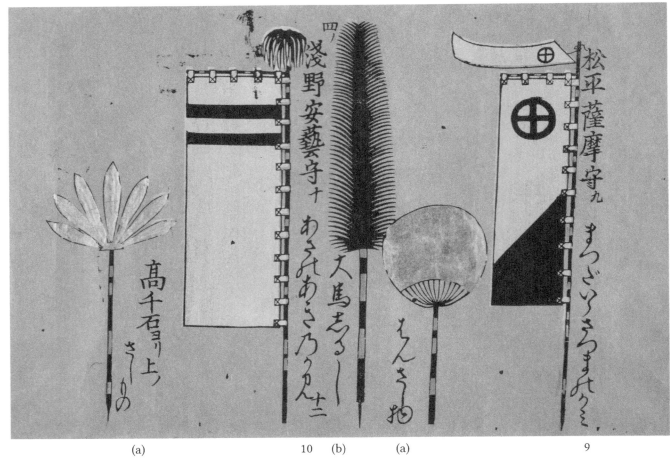

(a)   10 (b)   (a)   9

9. 松平・薩摩守　九　まつざい〳さつま𛂛ろゑ (まつだいらさつまのかみ; Matsudaira Satsuma-no-kami):
   "Matsudaira, Provincial Governor of Satsuma", i.e., Matsudaira Iehisa (松平家久) (1576–1638), who received the title
   in 1617, or his son Matsudaira Mitsuhisa (松平光久) (1616–1694), who received it in 1631[25, 島津家]

   This uses a horse's bit (轡; kutsuwa) mon. While predating Christianity, it was later used as a Christian symbol;
   such "hidden crosses" were used by hidden Christians to safely affirm their faith.[6, p. 32]

(a) そんさ〳抇 (はんさし物; ban-sashimono): guard identifying object (a gold non-folding fan)

(b) 大馬志る〳 (大馬しるし; ō-mumajirushi): great standard (a feathered pole)

10. 淺野・安藝守　十　あさ𛂛あき乃ろゑ (あさのあきのかみ; Asano Aki-no-kami):
    "Asano, Provincial Governor of Aki", i.e., Matsudaira Mitsuakira (松平光晟) (1617–1693)[25, 浅野家]

    Two horizontal stripes and a dashi of a tuft of feathers.

(a) 髙千石ヨリ上ノ　さ〳ぬの (髙千石ヨリ上ノ　さしもの; taka sen-koku yori ue no): identifying object of [those]
    amounting from one thousand koku up (a seven-ray sunburst)

    A koku (石) was a measure of rice, supposedly the amount of rice that would feed one person for a year. It
    measured about 280 liters. Income and wealth in feudal Japan was measured in of rice.

    Note that ヨ リ (yori) and ノ (no) are here written in small katakana, not hiragana, which is unusual for
    O-umajirushi (with the exception of the katakana 'no' for the volume number on each page). While katakana in
    modern Japanese is used for phonetic writing, the names of plant and animal species, and for foreign loan words,
    here small katakana characters seem to be used for particles. Similar is the use of a small katakana ke (ケ) in
    modern Japanese as a counter for durations in months. (E.g., 一ヶ月, ikkagetsu, meaning "one month".)

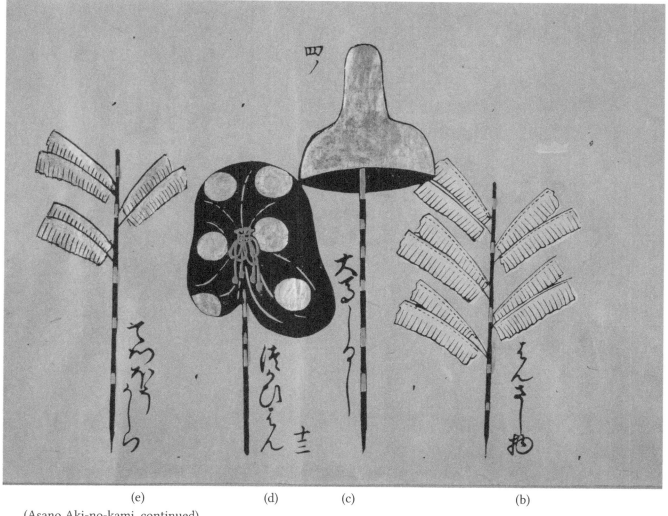

(e)   (d)   (c)   (b)

(Asano Aki-no-kami, continued)

(b) そんさ〻抄 (はんさし物; ban-sashimono): guard identifying object

A banner tree of white slashed banners.

(c) 大多しるし (大馬しるし; ō-mumajirushi): great standard

A gold "Chinese person hat" (唐人笠; dōjingasa) shape;[31, p. 105] compare the one used by Satake Ukyō-no-tayufu (see p. 165).

(d) ほうひそん (つかひはん; tsukaiban): messengers

A black horo with gold discs.

(e) てつゐう　ろくら (てつほう　かしら; tetsubō kashira): spiked club head

Unlike previous instances of "tetsubō-no-mono", spiked club men, this device is specifically for the commander of a spiked club unit. (See p. 61 for an explanation of this weapon.)

This instance of tetsubō spells the final two mora "hou", not "hau", suggesting that at the time of *O-umajirushi* these were already interchangeable. (See p. xiv for more on this sound change.)

A banner tree of gold slashed banners.

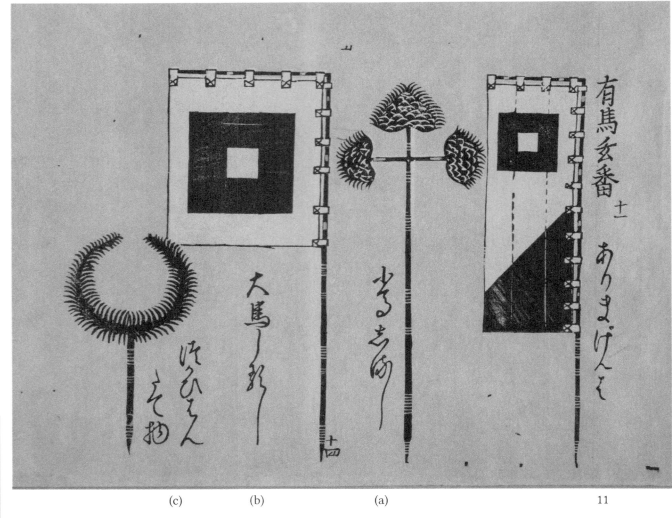

(c)   (b)   (a)   11

11. 有馬・玄番　十一　ありまげんそ (ありまげんは; Arima Genba):
"Arima, Priests and Foreigners Bureau [official]", i.e., Arima Toyōji (有馬豊氏) (1569–1642)[25, 有馬久留米家]

A shadowed black square mon on a white nobori with stitching and a diagonal division to black.

(a) 小多志はく (小馬しるし; ko-mumajirushi): lesser standard

A black standard with three wooden shapes, possibly representing hollyhock leaves, with black feathers both laid flat and protruding from the edge. Compare the standard used by Koide Tsushima-no-kami (see p. 156) and the heart shape used by Gongen-sama (see p. 8).

(b) 大馬志釣く (大馬しるし; ō-mumajirushi): great standard

(c) ほうひそん　さて物 (つかひはん　たて物; tsukaiban tatemono): messenger helmet crest [-shaped device]

A tatemono or datemono (立物) was a type of crest made of metal and attached to a samurai's helmet; the term literally means "standing thing". These crests could be mon but were often simple designs resembling horns. This label clarifies that devices of this shape are intended to resemble helmet crests, rather than a crescent moon. While the actual tatemono shown on helmets in *O-umajirushi* vary widely in shape, this crescent shape seems to be one of only a few styles used for devices imitating helmet crests. (See, e.g., p. 9.) This one in particular is covered in black feathers.

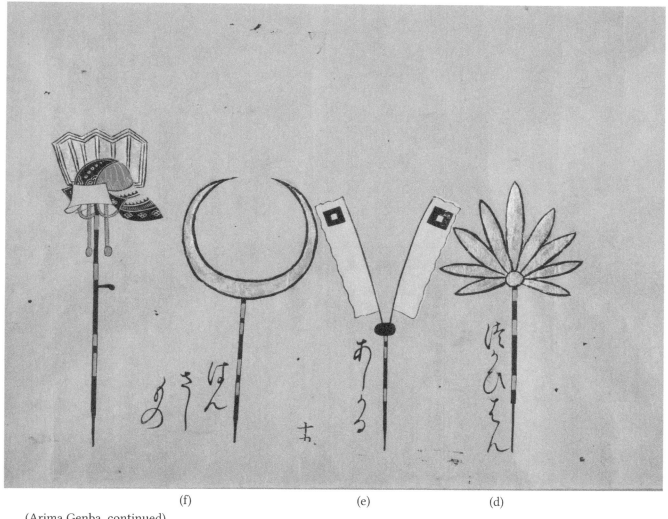

(f) (e) (d)

(Arima Genba, continued)

(d) ほうひそん (つかひはん; tsukaiban): messengers

A nine-rayed sunburst.

(e) あしかる (あしかる; ashigaru): foot soldiers

(f) はん さし かの (はん さし もの; ban-sashimono): guard identifying object

The same helmet crest shape, in gold wood, without the feathers.

Unlabeled helmet

Note that Toyōji's helmet doesn't actually feature the helmet crest shape used in some of his devices. Instead, it features a white trapezoid and three gold arrow fletching shapes.

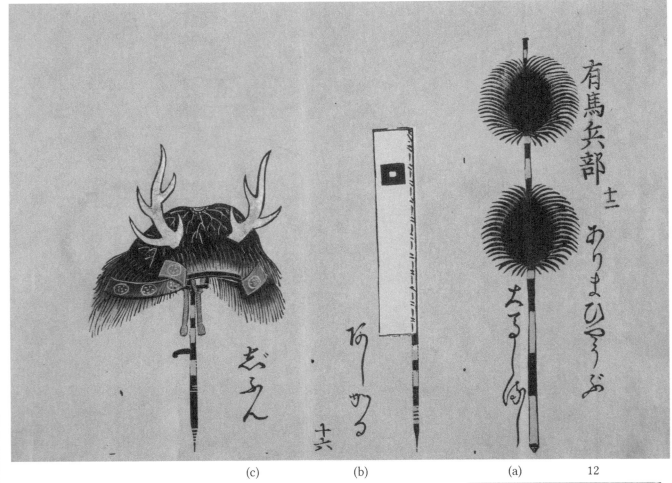

(c)   (b)   (a)   12

12. 有馬・兵部　十二　ありまひやうぶ (ありまひやうぶ; Arima Hyōbu):
    "Arima, Ministry of War [official]", i.e., Arima Noriyori (有馬則頼)
    (1533–1602) or his grandson Arima Tadayori (有馬忠頼)
    (1603–1655)[25, 有馬久留米家]

(a) 大多くほく (大馬しるし; ō-mumajirushi): great standard

    Two feather balls.

(b) ほくかる (あしかる; ashigaru): foot soldiers

    This samurai uses the same square mon as Arima Genba (see p. 129).

(c) ぎふん (じふん; jibun): personal [helmet]

    This helmet is covered with fur and features two antlers.

In "Shoshō Shōki Zu Byōbu", this standard is shown with white balls and the helmet is drawn differently, with black antlers.[45, 12]

Ōsaka Castle Museum Collection

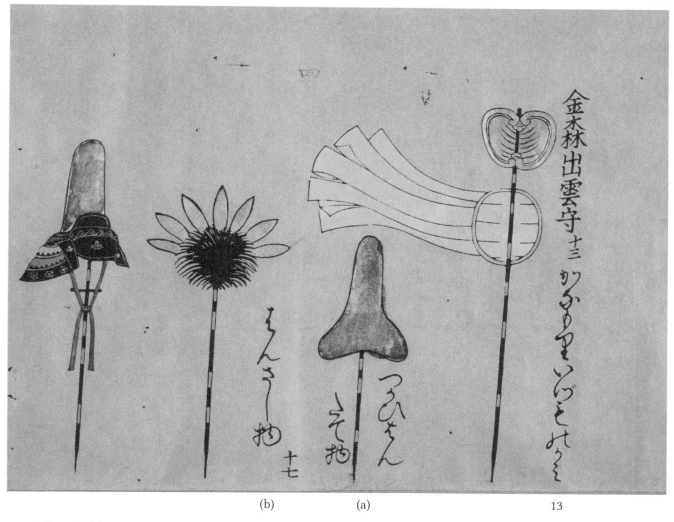

(b)　　　　　(a)　　　　　13

13. 金森・出雲守　十三　かゐゕ을いづを丸ゥﾐ (かなもりいづものかみ; Kanamori Izumo-no-kami):
"Kanamori, Provincial Governor of Izumo", i.e., Kanamori Yoshishige (金森可重) (1558–1615) or his son Kanamori Shigeyori (金森重頼) (1594–1650)[1, pp. 251–252]

This primary device is a fukinuki and a gold war fan.

(a) つゥひそん　さて抄 (つかひはん　たて物; tsukaiban tatemono): messenger helmet crest [-shaped device]

This device uses a more unique helmet crest shape.

(b) そんさ‍く抄 (はんさし物; ban-sashimono): guard identifying object

This sashimono resembles a seven-ray sunburst emerging from a ball of feathers.

Unlabeled helmet

Note how in this case, the rear crest on the helmet is similar to the helmet crest-shaped device shown previously.

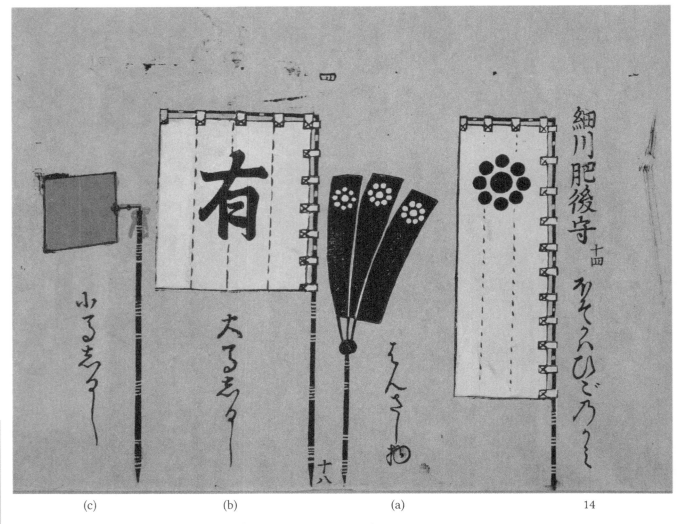

(c)   (b)   (a)   14

14. 細川・肥後守　十四　やそゝハひごゐゥミ (ほそかはひごのかみ; Hosokawa Higo-no-kami): "Hosokawa, Provincial Governor of Higo", i.e., Hosokawa Mitsunao (細川光尚) (1619–1649)[25, 細川家]

This nobori features a black nine stars mon (see p. 51) on a white background with stitching.

(a) そんさゝ物 (はんさし物; ban-sashimono): guard identifying object

(b) 大馬志るゝ (大馬しるし; ō-mumajirushi): great standard

This standard uses a similar background but instead uses the character 有 (ari, meaning "existence").

(c) 小馬志るゝ (小馬しるし; ko-mumajirushi): lesser standard

This unusual standard is a rigid red square extended a short distance from the support pole.

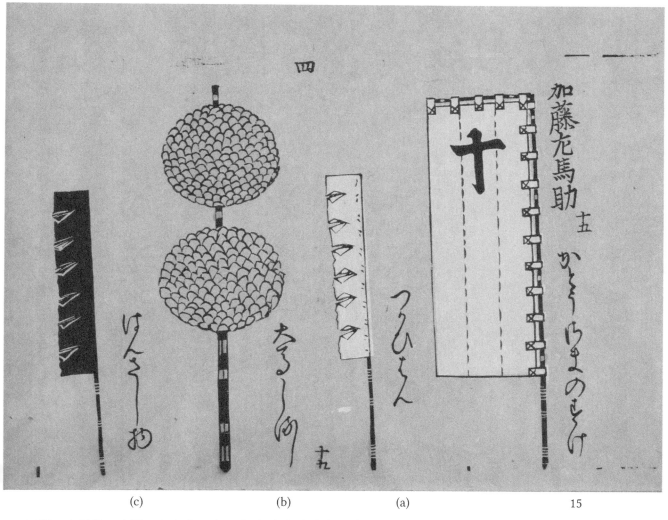

(c) (b) (a) 15

15. 加藤・左馬助　十五　かとうはものそけ (かとうさものすけ; Katō Sama-no-suke):
"Katō, Assistant [Director] of the Left Horses", i.e., Katō Yoshiaki (加藤嘉明) (1563–1631)[1, p. 249]

A brushwork-style cross suggests a Christian affiliation. The nobori background is white with stitching.

(a) つゝひそん (つかひはん; tsukaiban): messengers

A white slashed banner.

(b) 大夛くほく (大馬しるし; ō-mumajirushi): great standard

Two balls covered in flat feathers.

(c) はんさくお (はんさし物; ban-sashimono): guard identifying object

A black slashed banner.

(a)   16

16. 阿部・備中守 十六 ㄌべ乃びつちうㄣㄅㄥ (あべのびつちうのかみ; Abe no Bitchū-no-kami):

"Abe, Provincial Governor of Bitchū", i.e., Abe Masatsugu (阿部正次) (1569–1647)[1, p. 51]

White and black horizontal stripes and a white maneki. The maneki is red in the second edition.[35, p. 260]

Unlabeled helmet

The helmet features a white disc front crest and two feathered "eyebrows". The disc is red in the second edition.[35, p. 260]

(a) 大多くㄹし (大馬しるし; ō-mumajirushi): great standard

The し here interestingly is placed partially alongside the previous character, rather than below it, which the following pages show was a deliberate part of the kuzushiji used in this section of *O-umajirushi*.

A white disc on black.

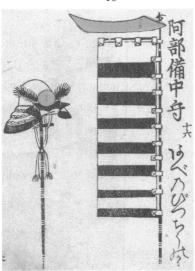

The same section in the second edition, replacing some white areas with red and with reduced color on the helmet.

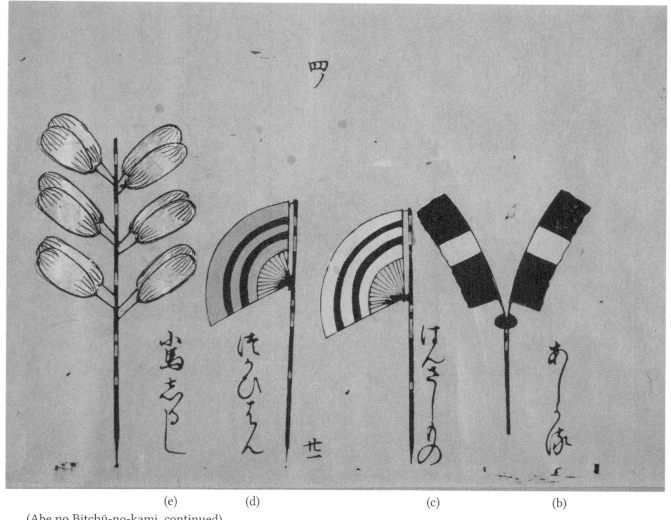

(e)   (d)   (c)   (b)

(Abe no Bitchū-no-kami, continued)

(b) あしうほ (あしかる; ashigaru): foot soldiers

A double banner, each black with a white horizontal band.

(c) はんさしゆの (はんさしもの; ban-sashimono): guard identifying object

A white folding fan with two black curved stripes.

(d) ほうひそん (つかひはん; tsukaiban): messengers

The same device, but with a blue background.

(e) 小馬志るし (小馬しるし; ko-mumajirushi): lesser standard

A tree of bundles.

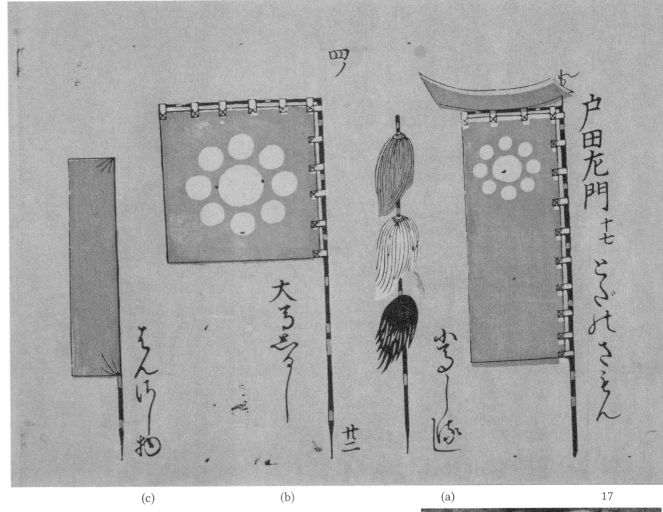

(c)   (b)   (a)   17

17. 戸田・左門　十七　とざれさをん (とだのさもん; Toda no Samon):

Referring to Toda Kazuaki (戸田一西) (1541–1602) or his son Toda Ujikane (戸田氏鉄) (1576–1655)[25, 戸田大垣家]

A white nine stars motif on red, with a red maneki. "Shoshō Shōki Zu Byōbu" shows the inverse color scheme.[45, 51]

(a) 小馬しるし (小馬しるし; ko-mumajirushi): lesser standard

Three yak hair plumes in three colors: red, white, and black.

(b) 大馬志るく (大馬しるし; ō-mumajirushi): great standard

(c) そんはくわ (はんさし物; ban-sashimono): guard identifying object

A kokuin (see p. xxxiv) from Edo Castle featuring a nine stars mon.
Photo by Eric Obershaw

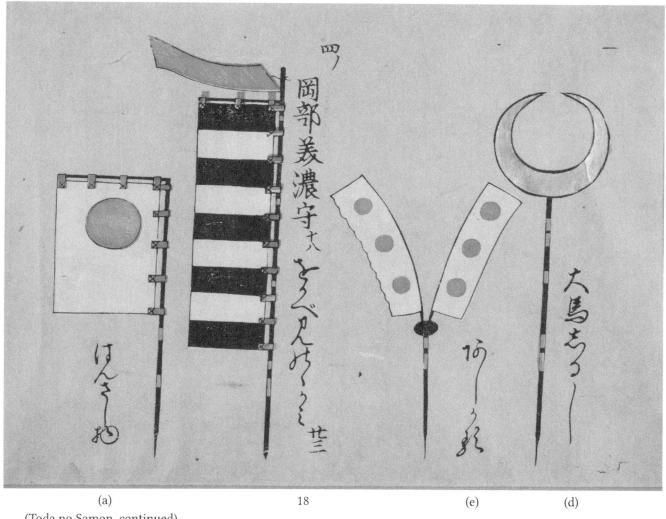

(a)　　　　　　　　　18　　　　　　　　　(e)　　　(d)

(Toda no Samon, continued)

(d) 大馬ゑるく (大馬しるし; ō-mumajirushi): great standard

   A gold helmet crest-shaped device.

(e) あしうゑ (あしかる; ashigaru): foot soldiers

   A double banner, each with three red disc mon on white.

---

18. 岡部・美濃守　十八　をうべゑ北ゝうミ (をかべみのゝかみ; Okabe Mino-no-kami):
   "Okabe, Provincial Governor of Mino", i.e., Okabe Nobukatsu (岡部宣勝) (1597–1668)[25, 岡部家]

   Black and white horizontal stripes, with a red maneki.

(a) はんさくゑ (はんさし物; ban-sashimono): guard identifying object

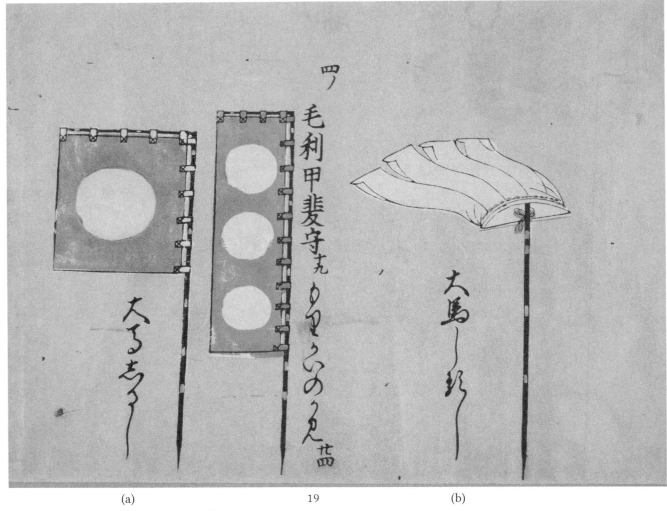

(a)   19   (b)

(Okabe Mino-no-kami, continued)

(b) 大馬〱〱 (大馬しるし; ō-mumajirushi): great standard

　　A white fukinuki shown with an unusual orientation or possibly a differently-shaped hoop.

---

19. 毛利・甲斐守　十九　〱〱いのろ〱 (もりかいのかみ; Mori Kai-no-kami):
　　"Mori, Provincial Governor of Kai", i.e., Mōri Hidemoto (毛利秀元) (1579–1650)[1, p. 774]

　　White discs on red.

(a) 大夛志る〱 (大馬しるし; ō-mumajirushi): great standard

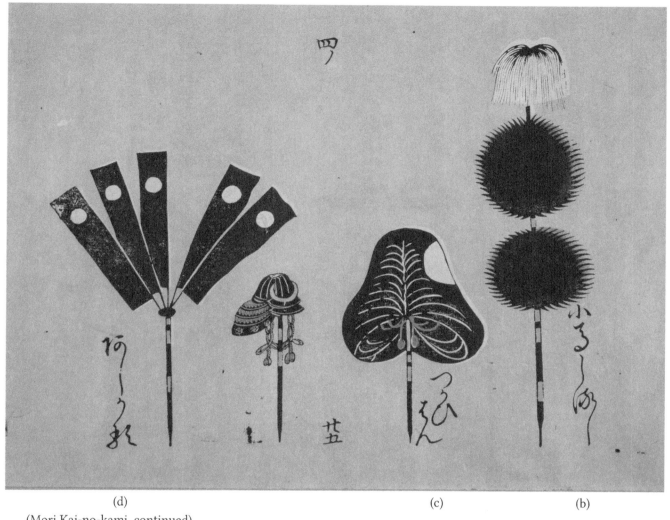

(d) (c) (b)

(Mori Kai-no-kami, continued)

(b) 小馬しるし (小馬しるし; ko-mumajirushi): lesser standard

   Two black feather balls and a white top plume.

(c) つかひ　はん (つかひ　はん; tsukaiban): messengers

   A horo with a white disc on black.

   Unlabeled helmet

   This helmet's crest has the same crescent shape seen in many helmet crest-shaped devices, such as on p. 129 or p. 138.

(d) あしかる (あしかる; ashigaru): foot soldiers

   A rare quintuple banner.

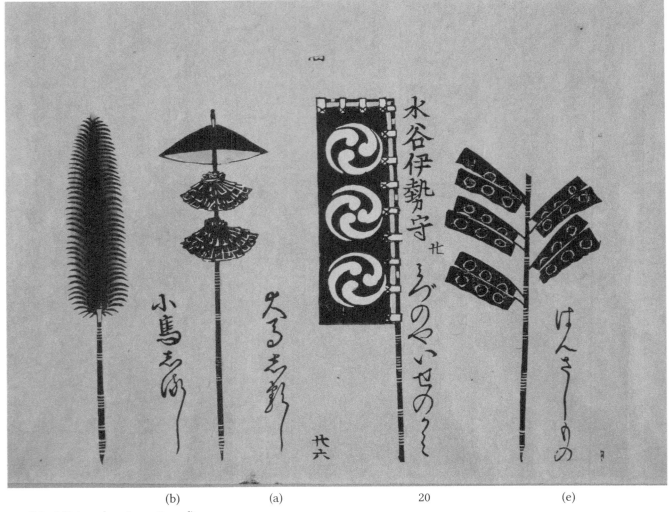

(b)   (a)   20   (e)

(Mori Kai-no-kami, continued)

(e) はんさ〱ㇷ゚の (はんさしもの; ban-sashimono): guard identifying object

The banners in this banner tree seem to each have three white ring mon on black.

20. 水谷・伊勢守　廿　ミづのやいせのㇰミ (みづのやいせのかみ; Mizunoya Ise-no-kami):
"Mizunoya, Provincial Governor of Ise", i.e., Mizunoya Katsutoshi (水谷勝俊) (1542–1606)[1, p. 744] or his son Mizunoya Katsutaka (水谷勝隆) (1597–1664)[25, 水谷家]

Three white tomoe mon on black.

(a) 大夢志れ〱 (大馬しるし; ō-mumajirushi): great standard

A black hat and two saihai-like tassels of paper strips.

(b) 小馬志はく (小馬しるし; ko-mumajirushi): lesser standard

A feathered pole.

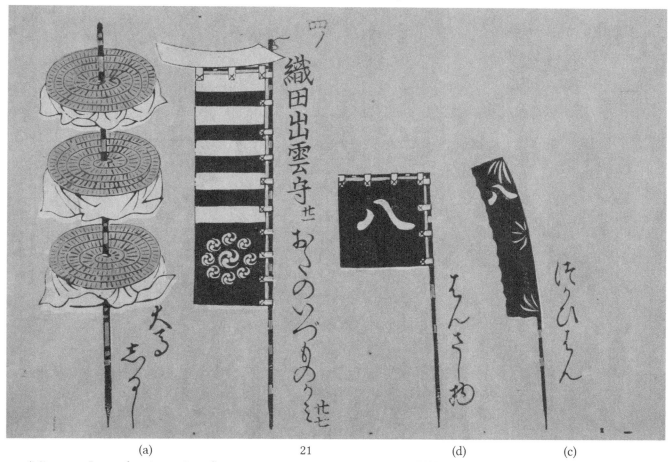

(a)   21   (d)   (c)

(Mizunoya Ise-no-kami, continued)

(c) ほうひそん (つかひはん; tsukaiban): messengers

A banner with the character 八 (hachi, meaning "eight"). Detail lines show folds in the cloth.

(d) そんさ〳物 (はんさし物; ban-sashimono): guard identifying object

---

21. 織田・出雲守　廿一　おさのいづかのうミ
(おたのいづものかみ; Ota no Izumo-no-kami):
"Ota, Provincial Governor of Izumo", i.e., Oda Takanaga
(織田高長) (1590–1674)[25, 織田家]

This nobori features horizontal stripes and a horizontal division to a black field with a white mon on it. The mon is a nine stars design with each star replaced by a swirl of three tomoe. This type of motif mimicry, also used on p. 83, was rare at this time, but became popular later.

(a) 大㐧　あるく (大馬　しるし; ō-mumajirushi): great standard

Three coiled mats with hanging cloth.

In "Shoshō Shōki Zu Byōbu", Takanaga's nobori has the mon in black-on-white instead of white on black.[45, 54]
Ōsaka Castle Museum Collection

Vol. 4

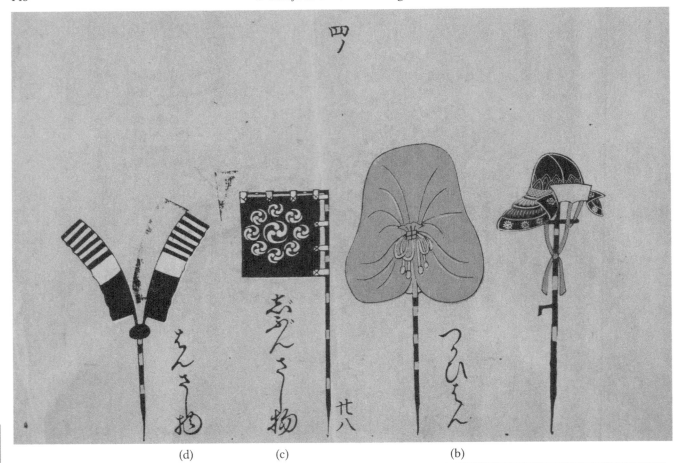

(d)　　　　(c)　　　　　　　　(b)

(Ota no Izumo-no-kami, continued)

Unlabeled helmet

A white crest similar to the one on p. 130.

(b) つゝひそん (つかひはん; tsukaiban): messengers

(c) ぢぶんさゝ物 (じぶんさし物; jibun sashimono): personal identifying object

(d) そんさゝ物 (はんさし物; ban-sashimono): guard identifying object

A double banner each divided into horizontal stripes and black by a white horizontal band.

Similarly, his ban-sashimono lacks the black bottom part in "Shoshō Shōki Zu Byōbu". However, his jibun sashimono remains white-on-black. [45, 54]

Ōsaka Castle Museum Collection

Vol. 4

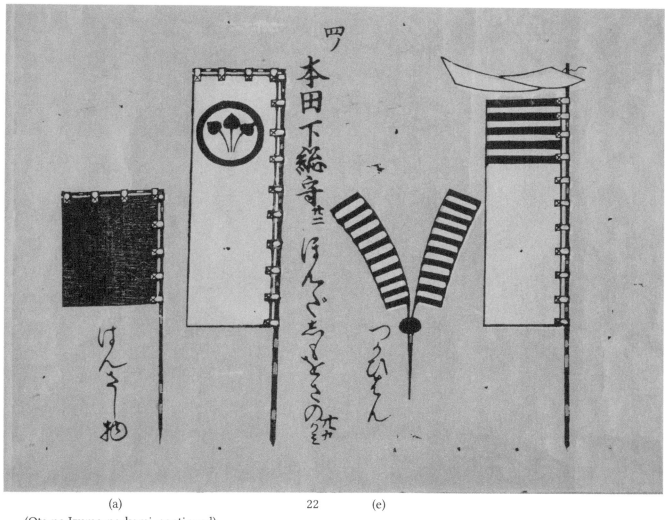

(a)   22   (e)

(Ota no Izumo-no-kami, continued)

Unlabeled banner

This nobori perhaps was an alternate nobori for Takanaga. Like the preceding double banner, it features horizontal stripes and a horizontal division.

(e) つゝひそん (つかひはん; tsukaiban): messengers

---

22. 本田・下総守　廿二　ほんざゑゕをさのゝ三 (ほんだしもをさのかみ; Honda Shimōsa-no-kami): "Honda, Provincial Governor of Shimōsa", i.e., Honda Toshitsugu (本多俊次) (1595–1668)[25, 本多膳所家]

Three hollyhock leaves in a ring enclosure. This leaf arrangement is known as "tachi aoi" (立ち葵; "standing hollyhock"); compare the Tokugawa hollyhock arrangement, p. 10. The hollyhock mon is associated with the Kamo Shrine.[18, 葵紋]

(a) はんさくゝ抣 (はんさし物; ban-sashimono): guard identifying object

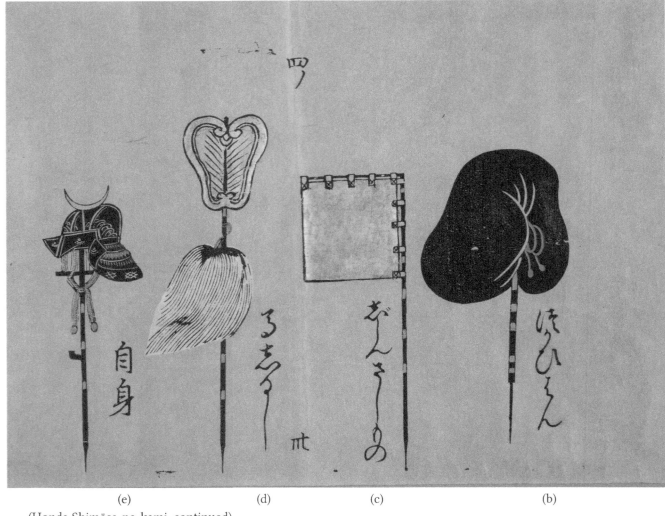

(e)   (d)   (c)   (b)

(Honda Shimōsa-no-kami, continued)

(b) ほうひそん (つかひはん; tsukaiban): messengers

(c) をりんさしもの (じしんさしもの; jishin sashimono): personal identifying object

(d) うまるし (馬しるし; mumajirushi): battle standard

    A gold wooden war fan shape and a white yak hair (白熊; haguma) plume.[44, p. 3.23]

(e) 自身 (jishin): personal [helmet]

    A moon-shaped helmet crest.

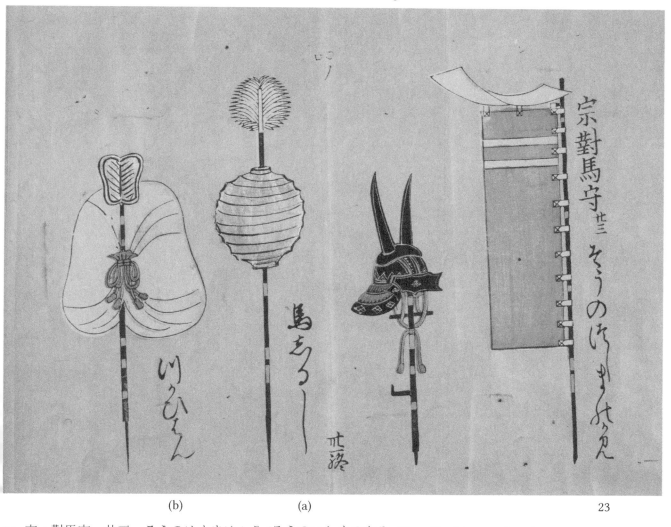

(b)　　　　　　　　(a)　　　　　　　　23

23. 宗・對馬守　廿三　そうのほくしまねうえ (そうのつしまのかみ; Sō no Tsushima-no-kami):
    "Sō, Provincial Governor of Tsushima", i.e., Sō Yoshitoshi (宗義智) (1568–1615) or his son Sō Yoshinari (宗義成) (1604–1657)[25, 宗家]

    A red nobori with two horizontal stripes and a white maneki.

    Unlabeled helmet

    This helmet features two tall pointy "ears".

(a) 馬まるく (馬しるし; mumajirushi): battle standard

    A dashi of a tuft of white feathers and a gold paper lantern.

(b) りうひそん (つかひはん; tsukaiban): messengers

    A gold war fan shape accompanying a white horo.

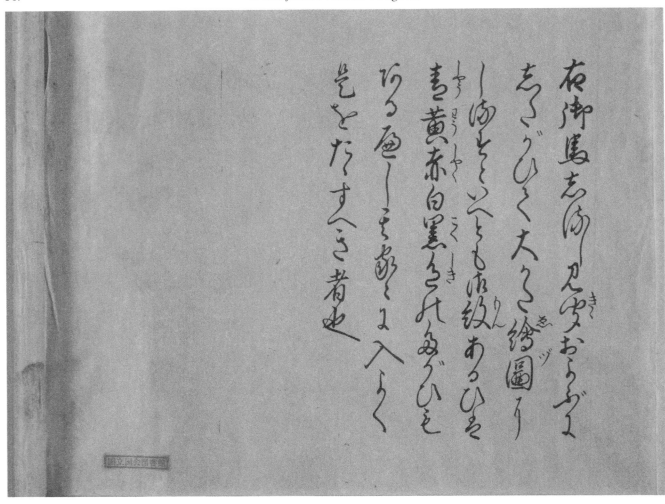

The closing paragraph here is printed with the same block as in the other volumes. This page being added to each volume is the only clear example of intentionally reused blocks in *O-umajirushi*. For translation and discussion, see p. 40.

End Volume 4

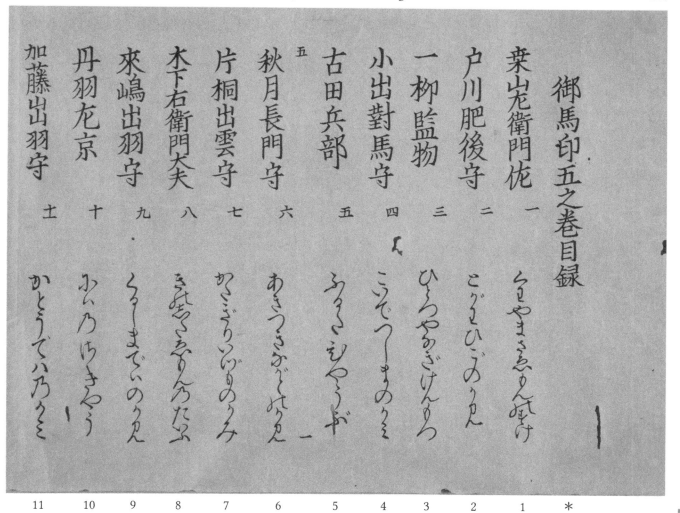

| 11 | 10 | 9 | 8 | 7 | 6 | 5 | 4 | 3 | 2 | 1 | * |

* 御馬印・五之巻・目録 (O-umajirushi Go-no-maki Mokuroku)
　　Honorable Battle Standards: Fifth Volume: Index

1. 菜山・厷衛門佐　一　くてゆまさゑゐ从もけ (くわやまさゑもんのすけ;
　　　Kuwayama Saemon-no-suke (lit. "Kuwayama Sawemon-no-suke")):
　"Kuwayama, Assistant [Director] of the Left Gate Guards", i.e., Kuwayama Kazunao (桑山一直) (1578–1636)[25, 桑山家]
　　Kuwayama Kazunao is a first cousin of Kuwayama Sadaharu (entry 9 on p. 77).
　　菜山 is a historical variant of 桑山, 厷衛門 is a variant of 左衛門, and 佗 is a variant of 佐.

　　The character used for "suke" (Assistant Director) varies based on the type of office being referred to.

2. 戸川・肥後守　二　とぐてひごのろ尺 (とがわひごのかみ; Togawa Higo-no-kami):
　"Togawa, Provincial Governor of Higo", i.e., Togawa Michiyasu (戸川達安) (1567–1627)[25, 戸川家]
　　戸川 is a historical variant of 戸川.

3. 一柳・監物　三　ひとつやゐぎけんゝつ (ひとつやなぎけんもつ; Hitotsuyanagi Kenmotsu):
　"Hitotsuyanagi, Goods Oversight [official]", i.e., Hitotsuyanagi Naomori (一柳直盛) (1564–1636)[1, p. 652]
　　監物 is a historical variant of 監物.

4. 小出・對馬守　四　こいでつしまのうミ (こいでつしまのかみ; Koide Tsushima-no-kami):
   "Koide, Provincial Governor of Tsushima", i.e., Koide Yoshichika (小出吉親) (1590–1668)[25, 小出家]
   　　Younger brother to Koide Yoshihide (entry 19 on p. 5)
   　　對馬 is a historical variant of 対馬.

5. 古田・兵部　五　ふるさむやうぶ (ふるたひやうぶ; Furuta Hyōbu (lit. "Furuta Hiyaubu")):
   "Furuta, Ministry of War [official]", i.e., Furuta Shigekatsu (古田重勝) (1560–1606) or his son Furuta Shigetsune
   　　(古田重恒) (1603–1648)[25, 古田家]

6. 秋月・長門守　六　あきつきながとのうゑ (あきつきながとのかみ; Akitsuki Nagato-no-kami):
   "Akitsuki, Provincial Governor of Nagato", i.e., Akizuki Tanenaga (秋月種長) (1587–1614) or his adopted grandson
   　　Akizuki Taneharu (秋月種春) (1610–1659)[25, 秋月家]

7. 片桐・出雲守　七　かさぎりいづものうみ (かたぎりいづものかみ;
   　　Katagiri Izumo-no-kami (lit. "Katagiri Idzumo-no-kami")):
   "Katagiri, Provincial Governor of Izumo", i.e., Katagiri Takatoshi (片桐孝利) (1601–1638)[25, 片桐家]
   　　出雲 is a historical variant of 出雲.

8. 木下・右衛門大夫　八　きのしさゑんのたいふ (きのしたゑもんのたいふ;
   　　Kinoshita Emon-no-taifu (lit. "Kinoshita Wemon-no-taifu")):
   "Kinoshita, Greater Director of the Right Gate Guards", i.e., Kinoshita Nobutoshi (木下延俊) (1577–1642)[1, p. 284]
   　　Younger brother of Kinoshita Toshifusa (entry 24 on p. 190)

   Unusually for a kanji, the 右 in 右衛門 is silent: it does not add anything to the pronunciation of "emon". This
   seems to have resulted from the "uwemon" pronunciation getting shortened to just "wemon", in a similar way to
   the i sound change (see p. xiv). In modern pronunciation, "wemon" is just "emon".

9. 來嶋・出羽守　九　くるしまでハのうゑ (くるしまではのかみ;
   　　Kurushima Dewa-no-kami (lit. "Kurushima Deha-no-kami")):
   "Kurushima, Provincial Governor of Dewa", i.e., Kurushima Michifusa (来島通総) (1561–1597)[22, 来島氏.3, 来島通総.1]
   　　來嶋 is a historical variant of 来島, and 出羽 is a variant of 出羽.

10. 丹羽・左京　十　ふハろはきやう (にはのさきやう; Niwa no Sakyō (lit. "Niha no Sakiyau")):
    "Niwa, Left Capital Administration [official]", i.e., Niwa Mitsushige (丹羽光重) (1621–1701)[25, 二本松丹羽家]
    　　丹羽 is a historical variant of 丹羽, and 左京 is a variant of 左京.

11. 加藤・出羽守　十一　かとうでハろうミ (かとうではのかみ; Katō Dewa-no-kami (lit. "Katou Deha-no-kami")):
    "Katō, Provincial Governor of Dewa", i.e., Katō Yasuoki (加藤泰興) (1611–1677)[25, 加藤大洲家]
    　　From a different Katō line than Katō Yoshiaki (entry 15 on p. 116) and from Katō Kiyomasa (entry 14 on p. 188)
    　　加藤 is a historical variant of 加藤, and 出羽 is a variant of 出羽.

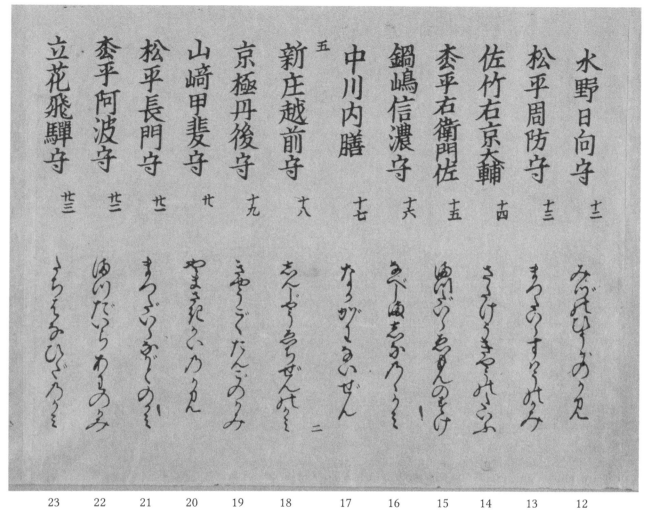

| 23 | 22 | 21 | 20 | 19 | 18 | 17 | 16 | 15 | 14 | 13 | 12 |

12. 水野・日向守　十二　みづ𛂕ひうぐのらゑ (みづのひうがのかみ;
   Mizuno Hyūga-no-kami (lit. "Midzuno Hiuga-no-kami")):
   "Mizuno, Provincial Governor of Hyūga", i.e., Mizuno Katsunari (水野勝成) (1564–1651)[25, 水野日向家]
   水野 is a historical variant of 水野.

13. 松平・周防守　十三　まつさいぃすハう𛂕らみ (まつたいらすはうのかみ;
   Matsudaira Suō-no-kami (lit. "Matsutaira Suhau-no-kami")):
   "Matsudaira, Provincial Governor of Suō", i.e., Matsudaira Yasushige (松平康重) (1568–1640), who received the title in
   1595, or his son Matsudaira Yasuteru (松平康映) (1615–1674), who received it in 1640[25, 松平松井家]

14. 佐竹・右京大輔　十四　さゝけうきやう𛂕さいふ (さたけうきやうのたいふ;
   Satake Ukyō-no-taifu (lit. "Satake Ukiyau-no-taifu")):
   "Satake, Greater Assistant [Director] of Right Capital Administration", i.e., Satake Yoshiaki (佐竹義昭) (1531–1565) or
   his grandson Satake Yoshinobu (佐竹義宣) (1570–1633)[1, pp. 369–371]

15. 杢平・右衛門佐　十五　ゐりさいぃゑゐんのそけ (まつだいらゑもんのすけ;
   Matsudaira Emon-no-suke (lit. "Matsudaira Wemon-no-suke")):
   "Matsudaira, Assistant [Director] of the Right Gate Guards", i.e., Matsudaira Tadayuki (松平忠之) (1602–1654)[25,
   黒田家]
   杢平 is a historical variant of 松平.

16. 鍋嶋・信濃守　十六　ゐべくゐ志ゐ乃丶ゟミ (なべしましなのゝかみ; Nabeshima Shinano-no-kami):
    "Nabeshima, Provincial Governor of Shinano", i.e., Nabeshima Katsushige (鍋島勝茂) (1580–1657)[25, 鍋島家]
      Father of Nabeshima Motoshige (entry 33 on p. 191)
      鍋嶋 is a historical variant of 鍋島, and 信濃 is a variant of 信濃.

17. 中川・内膳　十七　なゝかうそゐいぜん (なかがわないぜん; Nakagawa Naizen):
    "Nakagawa, Inner Dining [official]", i.e., Nakagawa Hisamori (中川久盛) (1594–1653)[25, 中川家]

    The Inner Dining Office (内膳司; Naizen Shi) was specifically responsible for cooking for the Emperor. It was a separate division from the Great Dining Agency (大膳職; Daizen Shiki), which was responsible for court banquets (see Okudaira Daizen, p. 4).

18. 新庄・越前守　十八　ゑん゛じやうゑちぜん比らミ (しんじやうゑちぜんのかみ; Shinjō Echizen-no-kami (lit. "Shinjiyau Wechizen-no-kami")):
    "Shinjō, Provincial Governor of Echizen", i.e., Shinjō Naosada (新庄直定) (1562–1618) or his son Shinjō Naoyoshi (新庄直好) (1599–1662)[25, 新庄家]

19. 京極・丹後守　十九　きゆうごくたんごのゟみ (きやうごくたんごのかみ; Kyōgoku Tango-no-kami (lit. "Kiyaugoku Tango-no-kami")):
    "Kyōgoku, Provincial Governor of Tango", i.e., Kyōgoku Takatomo (京極高知) (1572–1622) or his son Kyōgoku Takahiro (京極高広) (1599–1677)[25, 京極家]
      Takatomo was the granduncle of Kyōgoku Takakazu (entry 5 on p. 77)
      京極 is a historical variant of 京極, and 丹後 is a variant of 丹後.

20. 山﨑・甲斐守　廿　やまさ祀らい乃らゑ (やまさきかいのかみ; Yamasaki Kai-no-kami):
    "Yamasaki, Provincial Governor of Kai", i.e., Yamazaki Ieharu (山崎家治) (1594–1648)[25, 山崎家]
      山﨑 is a historical variant of 山崎, and 甲斐 is a variant of 甲斐.

21. 松平・長門守　廿一　まつざい〱うぐとのゟミ (まつだいらながとのかみ; Matsudaira Nagato-no-kami):
    "Matsudaira, Provincial Governor of Nagato", i.e., Matsudaira Hidenari (松平秀就) (1595–1651)[25, 毛利家]
      Also known as Mōri Hidenari (毛利秀就)[1, p. 773]

22. 杢平・阿波守　廿二　ゐりだいらあそのらミ (まつだいらあわのかみ; Matsudaira Awa-no-kami):
    "Matsudaira, Provincial Governor of Awa", i.e., Matsudaira Yoshishige (松平至鎮) (1586–1620) or his son Matsudaira Tadatsune (松平忠英) (1611–1652)[25, 蜂須賀家]
      杢平 is a historical variant of 松平.

23. 立花・飛驒守　廿三　さちそゐひざ乃らミ (たちはなひだのかみ; Tachihana Hida-no-kami):
    "Tachihana, Provincial Governor of Hida", i.e., Tachibana Muneshige (立花宗茂) (1569–1642)[25, 立花家]
      飛驒 is a historical variant of 飛騨.
      In modern Japanese, "Tachihana" is pronounced "Tachibana".

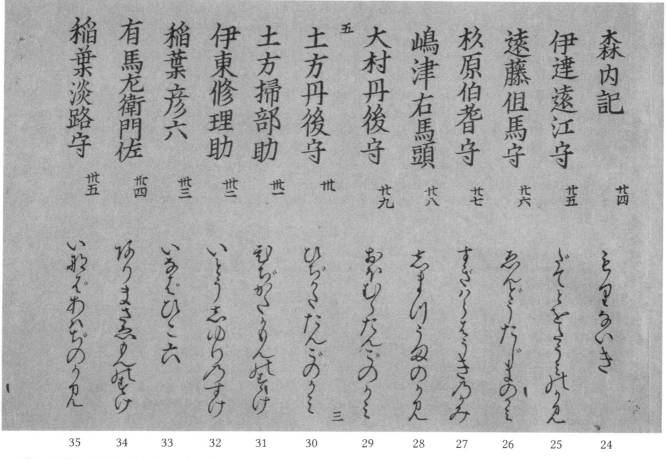

24. 森・内記　廿四　をりないき (もりないき; Mori Naiki):
    "Mori, Imperial Documents Agency [officer]", i.e., Mori Nagatsugu (森長継) (1610–1698)[25, 森家]
    内記 is a historical variant of 内記.

25. 伊達・遠江守　廿五　さてとをさうミ北らん (だてとをたうみのかみ;
    Date Tōtōmi-no-kami (lit. "Date Towotaumi-no-kami")):
    "Date, Provincial Governor of Tōtōmi", i.e., Date Hidemune (伊達秀宗) (1591–1658) or his son Date Munetoshi
    (伊達宗利) (1634–1708)[25, 伊達家]
    伊達 is a historical variant of 伊達, and 遠江 is a variant of 遠江.

26. 遠藤・但馬守　廿六　ゑんどうたじまのうミ (ゑんどうたじまのかみ;
    Endō Tajima-no-kami (lit. "Wendou Tajima-no-kami")):
    "Endō, Provincial Governor of Tajima", i.e., Endō Yoshitaka (遠藤慶隆) (1550–1632) or his heir Endō Yoshitoshi
    (遠藤慶利) (1609–1646)[25, 遠藤家]
    遠藤 is a historical variant of 遠藤, and 但馬 is a variant of 但馬.

27. 杦原・伯耆守　廿七　すぎハ〻そうきのうみ (すぎはらはうきのかみ;
    Sugiwara Hōki-no-kami (lit. "Sugihara Hauki-no-kami")):
    "Sugiwara, Provincial Governor of Hōki", i.e., Sugihara Nagafusa (杉原長房) (1574–1629), who received the title in
    1589, or his son Sugihara Shigenaga (杉原重長) (1616–1644), who received it in 1640[25, 杉原家]
    杦原 is a historical variant of 杉原.

    Unlike other instances where 'ha' in the middle of a name became 'wa' in modern Japanese due to the w-sound
    change (see p. xiv), this name is pronounced "Sugihara" today.

28. 嶋津・右馬頭　廿八　ゑまゐうゐのかゑ (しまつうまのかみ;
     Shimazu Uma-no-kami (lit. "Shimatsu Uma-no-kami")):
"Shimazu, Head of the Right Horse Bureau", i.e., Shimazu Tadanaga (島津忠長) (1551–1610),[1, p. 398] his cousin
     Shimazu Yukihisa (島津以久) (1550–1610), or Yukihisa's son Shimazu Tadaoki (島津忠興) (1599–1637)[25, 島津家]
     嶋津 is a historical variant of 島津.
     Dakuten in the actual section label give the modern pronunciation, "Shimazu".

29. 大村・丹後守　廿九　おやむらたんごのかゑ (おほむらたんごのかみ;
     Ōmura Tango-no-kami (lit. "Ohomura Tango-no-kami")):
"Ōmura, Provincial Governor of Tango", i.e., Ōmura Sumitada (大村純忠) (1533–1587),[1, p. 192] his son Ōmura Yoshiaki
     (大村嘉前) (1569–1616), or Yoshiaki's grandson Ōmura Suminobu (大村純信) (1618–1650)
     丹後 is a historical variant of 丹後.

     Sumitada was the first Christian daimyō, baptized Bartolomeo. Yoshiaki and Suminobu were also baptized.
     Yoshiaki fought against the Tokugawa. Suminobu later in life turned against the Christians and helped defeat them
     in the Shimabara Rebellion.[53, p. 71] Because of his alliance with the Tokugawa, he is likely the one represented here.

30. 土方・丹後守　卅　ひぢらさたんごのかゑ (ひぢかたたんごのかみ;
     Hijikata Tango-no-kami (lit. "Hidjikata Tango-no-kami")):
"Hijikata, Provincial Governor of Tango", i.e., Hijikata Katsūji (土方雄氏) (1583–1638)[1, p. 650]
     Brother to Hijikata Katsushige, next entry[25, 土方家]
     丹後 is a historical variant of 丹後.

31. 土方・掃部助　卅一　むぢかさらゐんゐそけ (ひぢかたかもんのすけ;
     Hijikata Kamon-no-suke (lit. "Hidjikata Kamon-no-suke")):
"Hijikata, Assistant [Dir.] of the Bureau of Palace Cleaning", i.e., Hijikata Katsushige (土方雄重) (1592–1628)[25, 土方家]
     Brother to Hijikata Katsūji, previous entry

     Edo Jidai Daimyō Sōran lists Katsushige as kami, head, rather than suke, assistant director. However, he is the only
     Hijikata associated with the bureau at the proper time, and may have been suke before getting promoted.

32. 伊東・修理助　卅二　いとうゑゆりのすけ (いとうしゆりのすけ;
     Itō Shūri-no-suke (lit. "Itou Shiyuri-no-suke")):
"Itō, Assistant [Director] of the Repairing Agency", i.e., Itō Yoshisuke (伊東義祐) (1512–1585)[1, p. 110] or his grandson
     Itō Sukenori (伊東祐慶) (1589–1636)[1, p. 107]

33. 稲葉・彦六　卅三　いゐぞひこ六 (いなばひこ六; Inaba Hikoroku):
Referring to Inaba Ittetsu (稲葉一鉄) (1515–1588) or his son Inaba Sadamichi (稲葉貞通) (1546–1603)[1, pp. 113–114]
     Sadamichi was the father of Inaba Norimichi (entry 35 on p. 153). Inaba Masanori (entry 14 on p. 44) is from a
     different line.

     "Hikoroku" was the informal given name of three members of the Inaba family; it was also used by Inaba Norimichi
     (entry 35 on p. 153). It means "boy six" or "young scholar six".[50, p. 200] Ittetsu was actually a sixth son, but neither
     of his descendants who used it were.

     Unusually, the pronunciation here repeats the kanji 六, six, rather than giving its reading in hiragana.

34. 有馬・左衛門佐　卅四　ありまさゑゐんゐそけ (ありまさゑもんのすけ;
     Arima Saemon-no-suke (lit. "Arima Sawemon-no-suke")):
"Arima, Assistant [Director] of the Left Gate Guards", i.e., Arima Naozumi (有馬直純) (1586–1641)[25, 有馬丸岡家]
     左衛門 is a historical variant of 左衛門.

     Naozumi was from a separate line than the previous Arima family headed by Arima Noriyori (entry 12 on p. 116).
     His father, Arima Harunobu (not listed) was baptized, but Naozumi opposed Christianity.[53, p. 30]

35. 稲葉・淡路守　卅五　いゐぞあハぢのかゑ (いなばあはぢのかみ;
     Inaba Awaji-no-kami (lit. "Inaba Ahadji-no-kami")):
"Inaba, Provincial Governor of Awaji", i.e., Inaba Norimichi (稲葉紀通) (1603–1648)[25, 稲葉家]
     稲葉 is a historical variant of 稲葉.

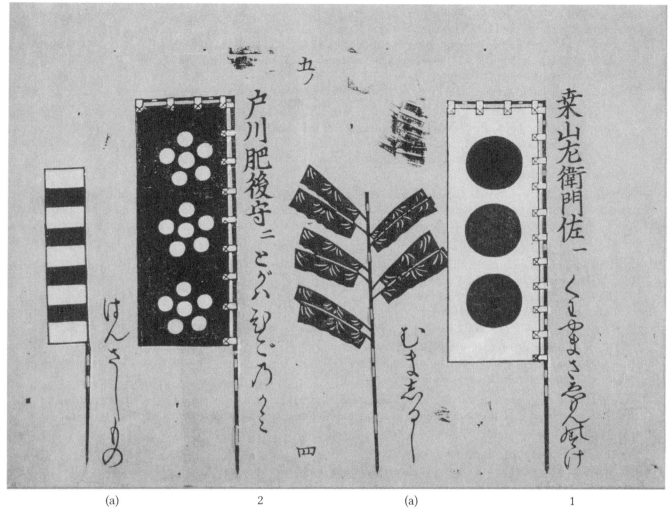

(a)   2   (a)   1

1. 桑山・左衛門佐　一　くゑやまさゑゐん北もけ (くわやまさゑもんのすけ; Kuwayama Saemon-no-suke): "Kuwayama, Assistant [Director] of the Left Gate Guards", i.e., Kuwayama Kazunao (桑山一直) (1578–1636)[25, 桑山家]

(a) むまゑるく (むましるし; mumajirushi): battle standard

     A banner tree of black banners.

2. 戸川・肥後守　二　とぐハむごろうミ (とがはひごのかみ; Togawa Higo-no-kami): "Togawa, Provincial Governor of Higo", i.e., Togawa Michiyasu (戸川逹安) (1567–1627)[25, 戸川家]

     A five stars mon that shows similarity to the plum bowl mon used by Matsudaira Oki-no-kami (see p. 49).

(a) はんさくゐの (はんさしもの; ban-sashimono): guard identifying object

     White and black horizontal stripes.

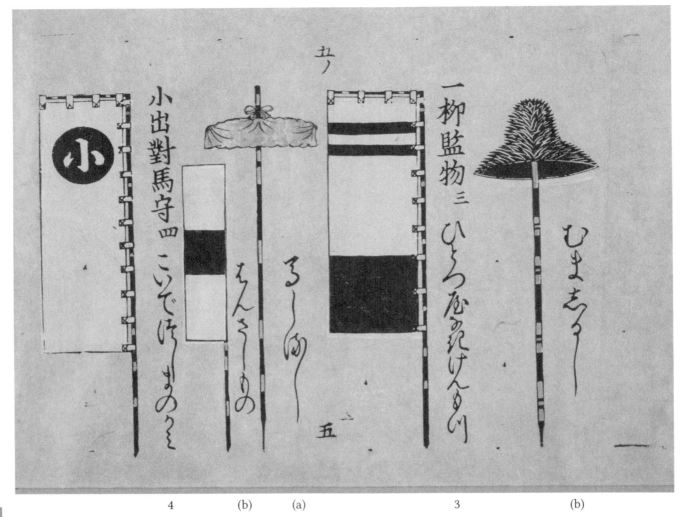

| 4 | (b) | (a) | 3 | (b) |

(Togawa Higo-no-kami, continued)

(b) むま志る〳 (むましるし; mumajirushi): battle standard

    A black feathered hat.

---

3. 一柳・監物　三　ひとつ圅み记けん𛀁り (ひとつやなきけんもつ; Hitotsuyanagi Kenmotsu):
    "Hitotsuyanagi, Goods Oversight [official]", i.e., Hitotsuyanagi Naomori (一柳直盛) (1564–1636)[1, p. 652]

    Two black horizontal stripes on white and a horizontal division to black.

(a) 㐂〱ほ〱 (馬しるし; mumajirushi): battle standard

    A short gold cloth hanging of a slightly-curved pole.

(b) そんさ〱かの (はんさしもの; ban-sashimono): guard identifying object

    A black horizontal band on white.

---

4. 小出・對馬守　四　こいでほ〱まのうミ (こいでつしまのかみ; Koide Tsushima-no-kami):
    "Koide, Provincial Governor of Tsushima", i.e., Koide Yoshichika (小出吉親) (1590–1668)[25, 小出家]

    The mon here is a disc pierced with the character 小 (ko, meaning "small"), the first character of the Koide family name. It's interesting that a character that might be seen as at odds with the fierce, strong samurai was highlighted in this banner.

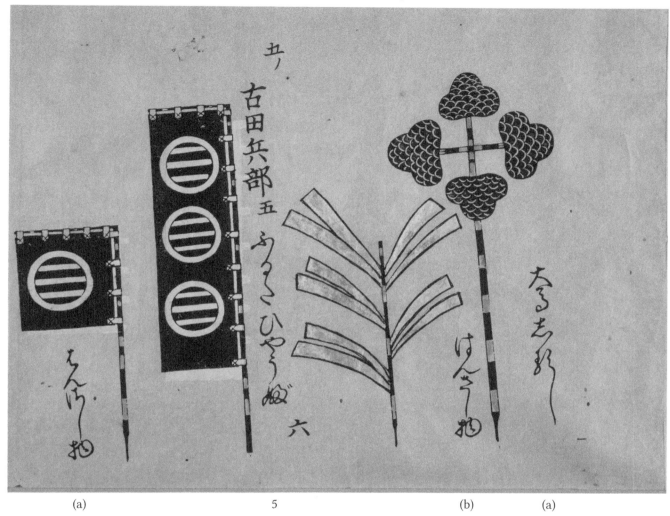

(a)　　　　　　　　　　　5　　　　　　　　　　(b)　　　(a)

(Koide Tsushima-no-kami, continued)

(a) 大馬志るし (大馬しるし; ō-mumajirushi): great standard

This standard is four wood shapes covered in flat black feathers. They somewhat resemble the sandbar mon used by, e.g., Hine no Oribe (see p. 84). Compare the standard used by Arima Genba (see p. 129).

(b) はんさし物 (はんさし物; ban-sashimono): guard identifying object

Rigid gold rays of some sort come out from the pole in this sashimono in a tree-like pattern.

---

5. 古田・兵部　五　ふるさひやうぶ (ふるたひやうぶ; Furuta Hyōbu):
"Furuta, Ministry of War [official]", i.e., Furuta Shigekatsu (古田重勝) (1560–1606) or his son Furuta Shigetsune (古田重恒) (1603–1648)[25, 古田家]

A variation of the rice bowl mon, with three lines. (See p. 96.)

(a) そんはし物 (はんさし物; ban-sashimono): guard identifying object

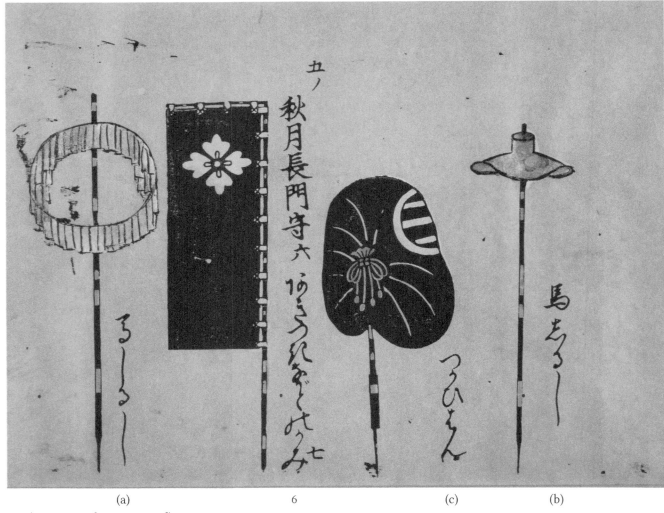

(a)　　　　　6　　　　　(c)　　　　　(b)

(Furuta Hyōbu, continued)

(b) 馬あるし (馬しるし; mumajirushi): battle standard

　　A different kind of hat device, possibly made from leather.

(c) つゝひそん (つかひはん; tsukaiban): messengers

---

6. 秋月・長門守　六　あきつ記ゐ⿹とれうみ (あきつきながとのかみ; Akitsuki Nagato-no-kami): "Akitsuki, Provincial Governor of Nagato", i.e., Akizuki Tanenaga (秋月種長) (1587–1614) or his adopted grandson Akizuki Taneharu (秋月種春) (1610–1659)[25, 秋月家]

　　A flower square (花角, "hanakaku") mon, a four-petaled version of the "China flower" mon. This depiction is closer to the modern China flower than the flower used by Ōmura Tango-no-kami (see p. 178).

(a) あしるし (馬しるし; mumajirushi): battle standard

　　This standard is a hoop hung with paper strips. This type of standard is called a "shidewa" (四手輪),[48, p. 14] using the same type of Shintō paper strips as a shidegasa (see p. 24).

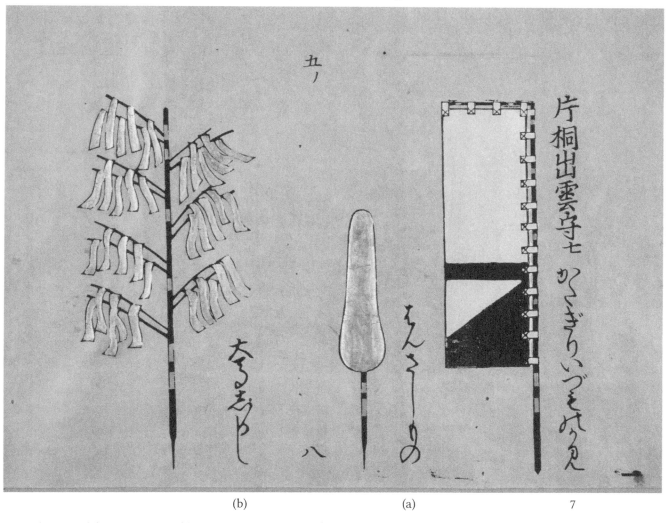

(b)   (a)   7

7. 片桐・出雲守　七　かさぎりいづをれうえ (かたぎりいづものかみ; Katagiri Izumo-no-kami):
   "Katagiri, Provincial Governor of Izumo", i.e., Katagiri Takatoshi (片桐孝利) (1601–1638)[25, 片桐家]

   A white nobori with an interesting black shape that combines a horizontal stripe and a diagonal division.

(a) そんさくもの (はんさしもの; ban-sashimono): guard identifying object

   An oblong wooden device.

(b) 大多まるし (大馬しるし; ō-mumajirushi): great standard

   A tree-shaped device hung with paper streamers; a similar device was used by Matsudaira Tosa-no-kami (see p. 37).

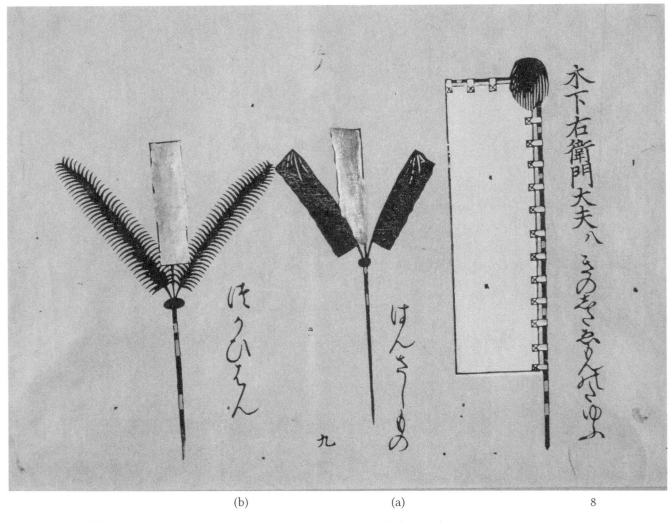

(b)   (a)   8

8. 木下・右衛門大夫　八　きのゑさゑ⼀んゑさゆふ (きのしたゑもんのたゆふ; Kinoshita Emon-no-tayufu): "Kinoshita, Greater Director of the Right Gate Guards", i.e., Kinoshita Nobutoshi (木下延俊) (1577–1642)[1, p. 284]

大夫, normally pronounced "taifu", is here instead read "tayufu", a historical alternate reading. (In the table of contents, the "taifu" reading is used.) This sound change is similar to the change from "yuku" to "iku" for the common Japanese verb meaning "to go".

The nobori is white with a black dyed yak hair (赤熊; shaguma) dashi.[44, p. 2.48]

(a) はんさ⼁の (はんさしもの; ban-sashimono): guard identifying object

Nobutoshi unusually used non-uniform triple devices. This one is a silver banner between two black ones.

(b) ⼾っひそん (つかひはん; tsukaiban): messengers

This device is a gold nagare hata between two feather-covered poles.

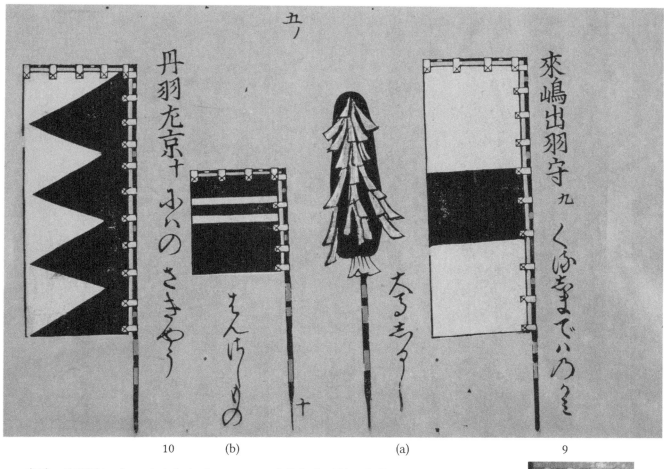

10   (b)   (a)   9

9. 來嶋・出羽守　九　くほゑまでハ乃うミ (くるしまではのかみ; Kurushima
　　Dewa-no-kami):
　　"Kurushima, Provincial Governor of Dewa", i.e., Kurushima Michifusa (来島通総)
　　(1561–1597)[22, 来島氏.3, 来島通総.1]

　　A black horizontal band on a white nobori.

(a) 大多ゑるく (大馬しるし; ō-mumajirushi): great standard

　　This standard combines gold gohei-like strips with a black cloth bundle.

(b) そんほくゆの (はんさしもの; ban-sashimono): guard identifying object

　　Two white horizontal stripes on black.

10. 丹羽・左京　十　ふハのさきやう (にはのさきやう; Niwa no Sakyō):
　　"Niwa, Left Capital Administration [official]", i.e., Niwa Mitsushige (丹羽光重)
　　(1621–1701)[25, 二本松丹羽家]

　　This nobori has an unusual jagged division between white and black.

*In "Shoshō Shōki Zu Byōbu",
Mitsushige's nobori has a completely different design featuring a triangle mon.*[45, 45]
Ōsaka Castle Museum Collection

Vol. 5

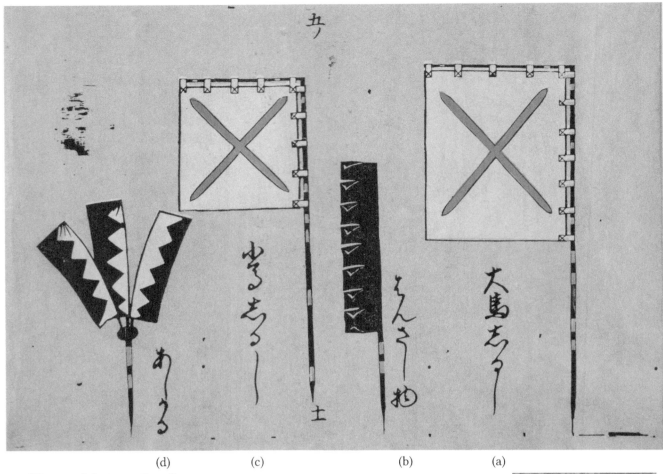

(d)　(c)　(b)　(a)

(Niwa no Sakyō, continued)

(a) 大馬志る�ix(大馬しるし; ō-mumajirushi): great standard

This standard uses a bold red X shape on white.

Supposedly, this Niwa mon came about because of an ancestor who killed so many foes in battle that wiping his sword off on his hakama (pleated trousers) left a broad X shape of blood.[24, pp. 5–6] This shape is also said to represent the ornamental gables, called *chigi* (千木), on the roof a Shintō shrine.[49, p. 181]

(b) そんさ志物 (はんさし物; ban-sashimono): guard identifying object

A black slashed banner.

(c) 小馬志るix (小馬しるし; ko-mumajirushi): lesser standard

(d) あ志かる (あしかる; ashigaru): foot soldiers

This triple banner follows the nobori; however, note here the white is against the support pole of each banner, whereas in the nobori the black was against the support pole.

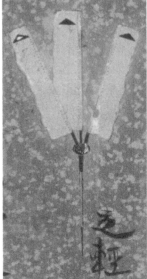

Similarly, his ashigaru device bears the same mon instead of the jagged division.[45, 45]
Ōsaka Castle Museum Collection

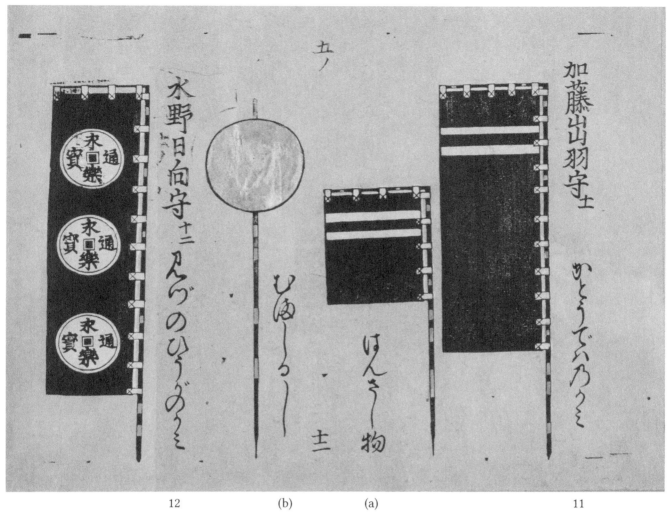

11. 加藤・出羽守　十一　かとうでハ乃ろ三 (かとうではのかみ; Katō Dewa-no-kami):
"Katō, Provincial Governor of Dewa", i.e., Katō Yasuoki (加藤泰興) (1611–1677)[25, 加藤大洲家]

Two white horizontal stripes on black, closely imitating the ban-sashimoto of Kurushima Michifusa, who held the same title earlier. (See p. 160.)

(a) はんさくわ (はんさし物; ban-sashimono): guard identifying object

(b) むゐくるく (むましるし; mumajirushi): battle standard

A gold wooden ball standard.

12. 水野・日向守　十二　ゑづのひうゞのろ三 (みづのひうがのかみ; Mizuno Hyūga-no-kami):
"Mizuno, Provincial Governor of Hyūga", i.e., Mizuno Katsunari (水野勝成) (1564–1651)[25, 水野日向家]

Three Ming coin mon; see p. 57.

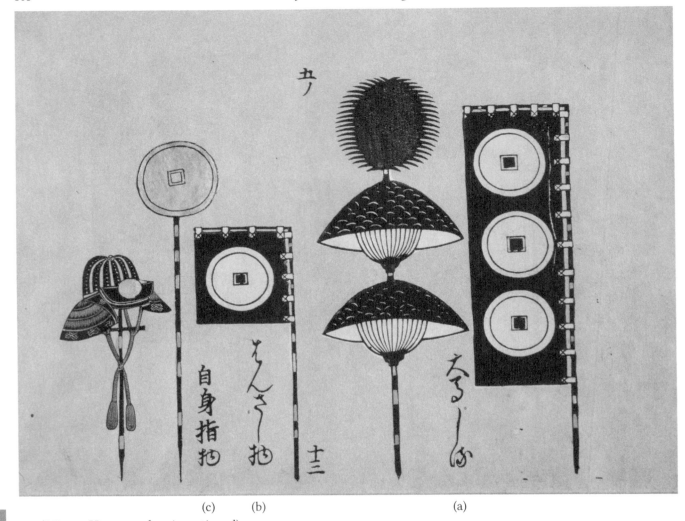

(c)   (b)   (a)

(Mizuno Hyūga-no-kami, continued)

Unlabeled banner

A variant nobori with simpler coin mon, similar to the design on p. 30.

(a) 大多くほ (大馬しる; ō-mumajirushi): great standard
The final 'shi' in "umajirushi" is omitted here.

A mass of feathers and two black umbrellas covered in flat feathers.

(b) そんさし物 (はんさし物; ban-sashimono): guard identifying object

(c) 自身指物 (自身指物; jishin sashimono): personal identifying object
This is a rare caption in full kanji, clarifying the intended kanji for other captions written phonetically. Since Japanese has many homophones and phonetic captions often leave off dakuten to clarify which syllables are voiced, this removes some ambiguity.

A gold-painted wooden representation of the same mon.

Unlabeled helmet

A helmet with a disc helmet crest.

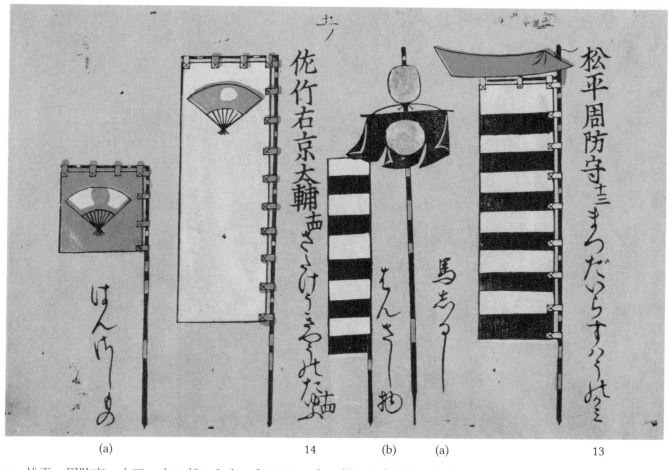

(a)	14	(b)	(a)	13

13. 松平・周防守　十三　まつだいらすハうのかミ (まつだいらすはうのかみ; Matsudaira Suō-no-kami):
"Matsudaira, Provincial Governor of Suō", i.e., Matsudaira Yasushige (松平康重) (1568–1640), who received the title in 1595, or his son Matsudaira Yasuteru (松平康映) (1615–1674), who received it in 1640[25, 松平松井家]

White and black horizontal stripes and a red maneki.

(a) 馬あるく (馬しるし; mumajirushi): battle standard

A black noren with a gold disc below another gold shape, possibly also representing a disc.

(b) そんさく抄 (はんさし物; ban-sashimono): guard identifying object

---

14. 佐竹・右京太輔　十四　さゝけうきやうのたゆふ (さたけうきやうのたゆふ; Satake Ukyō-no-tayufu):
"Satake, Greater Assistant [Director] of Right Capital Administration", i.e., Satake Yoshiaki (佐竹義昭) (1531–1565) or his grandson Satake Yoshinobu (佐竹義宣) (1570–1633)[1, pp. 369–371]
太輔 is read "tayufu" instead of "taifu" here. (See p. 159.)
This section label uses 太 instead of the more common 大 used in the table of contents. This may just be an error.

This white nobori features a mon of a folding fan with black tines and red paper with a white disc. This is an example of a mon in a three-color design. The story behind it is that at the Battle of Yashima, the Taira carried such a fan as a sacred talisman and dared the Genji to shoot at it. Nasu Munetaka took the challenge and hit it in one shot, striking a severe blow to the enemy morale. The Satake family is descended from him, and thus use this mon to recall their ancestor's deed.[24, p. 18]

(a) はんほく物の (はんさしもの; ban-sashimono): guard identifying object

This sashimono reverses the red and white of the nobori. Bleeding or imprecise carving with the red is also visible.

Vol. 5

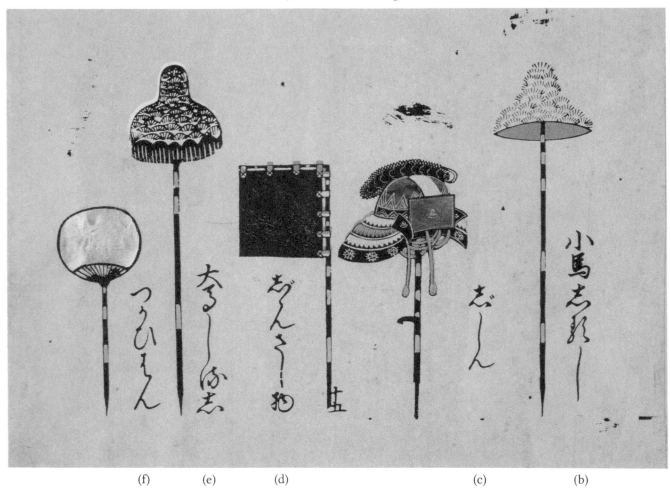

(f)　　(e)　　(d)　　　　　　(c)　　　　(b)

(Satake Ukyō-no-taifu, continued)

(b) 小馬志靫し (小馬しるし; ko-mumajirushi): lesser standard

A hat shape covered with white feathers, similar to those used by Matsudaira Kai-no-kami (see p. 46).[44, p. 2.53] This particular hat shape is known as a *dōjingasa* (唐人笠; literally "Chinese person hat"),[31, p. 105] which could also refer to a helmet with a similar shape.[22, 唐人笠] Compare that used by Asano Aki-no-kami (see p. 128).

(c) 志りん (じしん; jishin): personal [helmet]

A helmet featuring a rectangle helmet crest with what looks like a shell design on the green front piece. Note also the interesting black ridge.

(d) 志ゝんさし物 (じゝんさし物; jishin sashimono): personal identifying object

This is an unusual instance of the kurikaeshi (ゝ) being used after a voiced mora to represent an unvoiced mora.

(e) 大多しはゝ志 (大馬しるし; ō-mumajirushi): great standard

A similar hat shape in black with a fringe of sorts. While here it seems to use flat-laying black feathers, *Shoshō Kisei Zu* identifies it as being made from monkey fur.[44, p. 2.54]

(f) つゝひそん (つかひはん; tsukaiban): messengers

A gold non-folding fan.

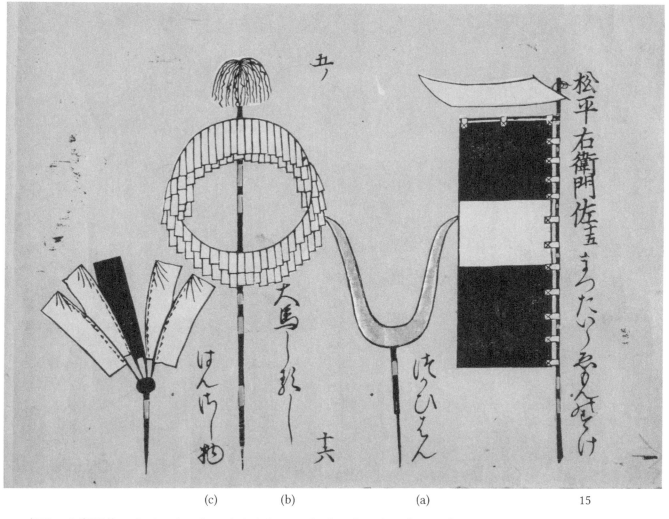

(c)   (b)   (a)   15

15. 㭬平・右衛門佐　十五　まつたい〲ゑ〵んのすけ (まつたいらゑもんのすけ; Matsudaira Emon-no-suke):
"Matsudaira, Assistant [Director] of the Right Gate Guards", i.e., Matsudaira Tadayuki (松平忠之) (1602–1654)[25,
黒田家]

A black nobori with a white horizontal band and a white maneki.

(a) ほうひそん (つかひはん; tsukaiban): messengers

This device imitates the tall horns of a helmet crest.

(b) 大馬〲㹷〲 (大馬しるし; ō-mumajirushi): great standard

This standard is a shidewa, a hoop covered in white paper strips, accompanied by a top-plume. Compare the
shidewa used by Akitsuki Nagato-no-kami (see p. 157).

(c) はんほ〲㹷 (はんさし物; ban-sashimono): guard identifying object

A rare quintuple banner with four white and one black.

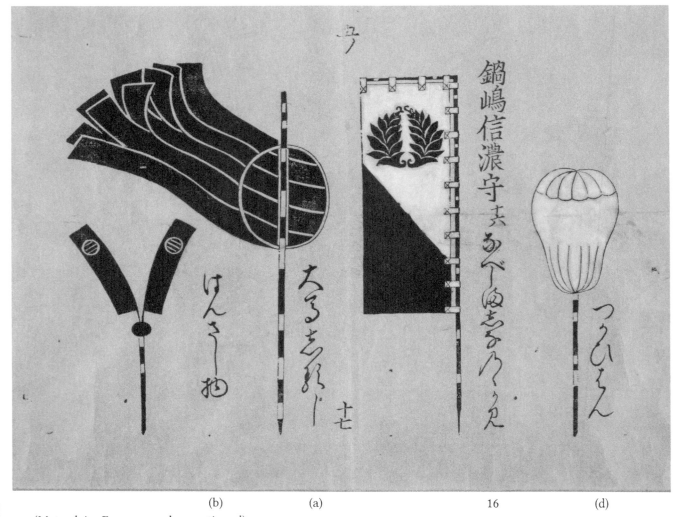

(b)　　　　　　(a)　　　　　　　　16　　　　(d)

(Matsudaira Emon-no-suke, continued)

(d) つゝひそん (つかひはん; tsukaiban): messengers

A cloth bundle with something of a three-dimensional war fan shape.

---

16. 鍋嶋・信濃守　十六　ゐべくぬ志ゐ乃ゝうゑ (なべしましなのゝかみ; Nabeshima Shinano-no-kami): "Nabeshima, Provincial Governor of Shinano", i.e., Nabeshima Katsushige (鍋島勝茂) (1580–1657)[25, 鍋島家]

A black mon of two apricot leaf shapes (see p. 86) over a diagonal division from white to black.

(a) 大多志秋く (大馬しるし; ō-mumajirushi): great standard

A black fukinuki.

(b) はんさくあ (はんさし物; ban-sashimono): guard identifying object

This double banner consists of two black banners each with a three-line rice bowl mon.

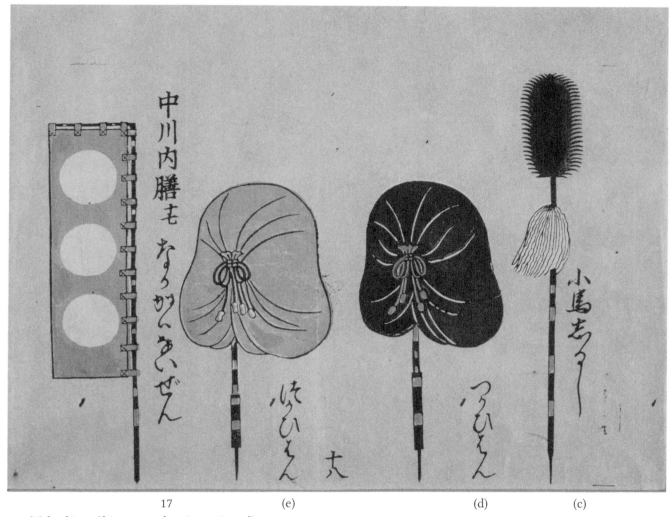

17   (e)   (d)   (c)

(Nabeshima Shinano-no-kami, continued)

(c) 小馬ゑるく (小馬しるし; ko-mumajirushi): lesser standard

A feathered oblong shape and a yak hair plume.

(d) つゝひそん (つかひはん; tsukaiban): messengers

(e) ほゝひそん (つかひはん; tsukaiban): messengers

17. 中川・内膳　十七　なゝかゝハゐいぜん (なかかはないぜん; Nakagawa Naizen):
"Nakagawa, Inner Dining [official]", i.e., Nakagawa Hisamori (中川久盛) (1594–1653)[25, 中川家]

Three white discs on red.

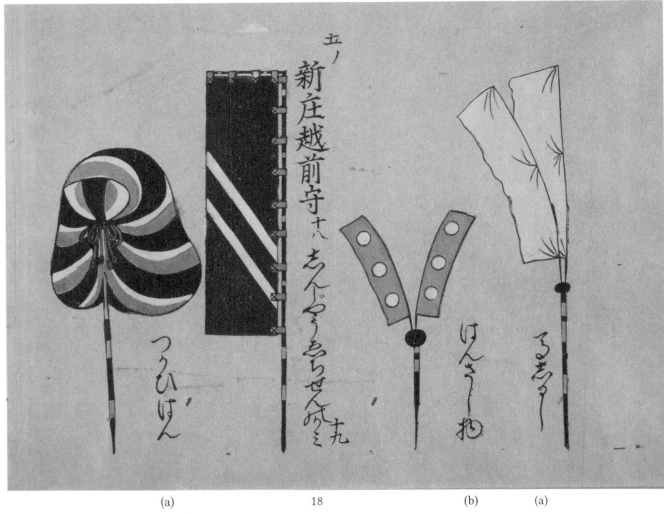

(a)   18   (b)   (a)

(Nakagawa Naizen, continued)

(a) 馬しるし (馬しるし; mumajirushi): battle standard

(b) はんさし物 (はんさし物; ban-sashimono): guard identifying object

---

18. 新庄・越前守　十八　ゑんじやうゑちせんのうミ (しんじやうゑちせんのかみ; Shinjō Echizen-no-kami): "Shinjō, Provincial Governor of Echizen", i.e., Shinjō Naosada (新庄直定) (1562–1618) or his son Shinjō Naoyoshi (新庄直好) (1599–1662)[25, 新庄家]

   Two white diagonal stripes on black.

(a) つゝひはん (つかひはん; tsukaiban): messengers

   A horo with a three-colored design: a swirl pattern in red, white, and black.

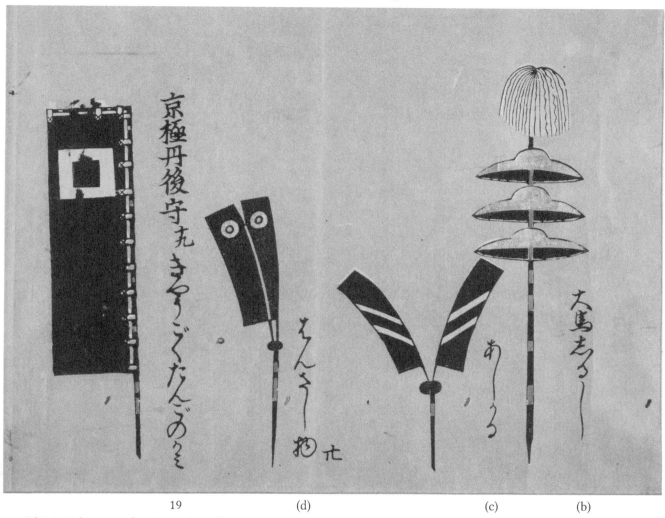

19 (d) (c) (b)

(Shinjō Echizen-no-kami, continued)

(b) 大馬まるし (大馬しるし; ō-mumajirushi): great standard

Three hats and a top-plume of yak hair.[44, p. 1.47]

(c) あしかる (あしかる; ashigaru): foot soldiers

(d) ゑんさし物 (はんさし物; ban-sashimono): guard identifying object

A black double banner each with a gold snake's eye with disc mon.

---

19. 京極・丹後守　十九　きやうごくたんごのゝミ (きやうごくたんごのかみ; Kyōgoku Tango-no-kami):
"Kyōgoku, Provincial Governor of Tango", i.e., Kyōgoku Takatomo (京極高知) (1572–1622) or his son Kyōgoku
Takahiro (京極高広) (1599–1677)[25, 京極家]

A shadowed square mon.

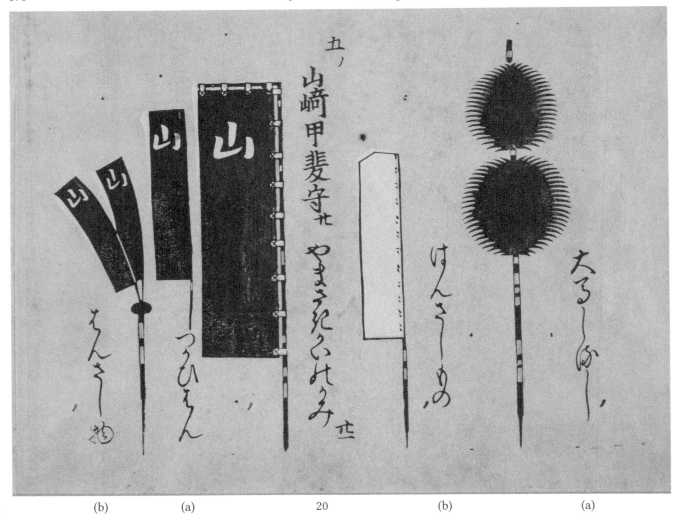

(b)   (a)   20   (b)   (a)

(Kyōgoku Tango-no-kami, continued)

(a) 大馬しるし (大馬しるし; ō-mumajirushi): great standard

    Two feather-covered balls.

(b) はんさしもの (はんさしもの; ban-sashimono): guard identifying
    object

---

20. 山﨑・甲斐守　廿　やまさきかいのかみ
      (やまさきかいのかみ; Yamasaki Kai-no-kami):
      "Yamasaki, Provincial Governor of Kai", i.e., Yamazaki Ieharu
      (山崎家治) (1594–1648)[25, 山崎家]

    A black nobori with the character 山 (yama, meaning
    "mountain"), the first character in the Yamasaki family name.

(a) つかひはん (つかひはん; tsukaiban): messengers

(b) はんさし物 (はんさし物; ban-sashimono): guard identifying
    object

*A kokuin (see p. xxxiv) from Edo Castle featuring
a similar mountain-character mon.*
Photo by Eric Obershaw

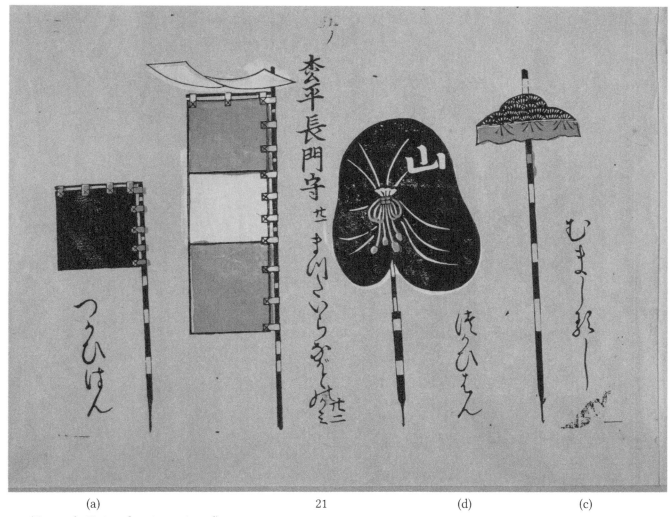

(a)   21   (d)   (c)

(Yamasaki Kai-no-kami, continued)

(c) むまくれく (むましるし; mumajirushi): battle standard

A more ornate umbrella with a flat-laying black feather or monkey fur pattern (see p. 165) and a red cloth hanging from the edge.

(d) ほろひそん (つかひはん; tsukaiban): messengers

21. 杢平・長門守　壮一　まりさいらゐぐとれうミ (まつたいらながとのかみ; Matsudaira Nagato-no-kami): "Matsudaira, Provincial Governor of Nagato", i.e., Matsudaira Hidenari (松平秀就) (1595–1651)[25, 毛利家]

A red nobori with a white horizontal band and a white maneki.

(a) つゝひはん (つかひはん; tsukaiban): messengers

This solid black banner uses red strips of cloth to hold it to the pole.

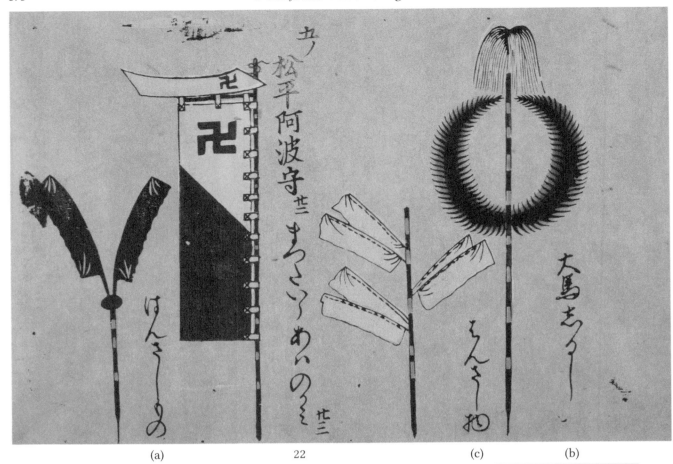

(a)   22   (c)   (b)

(Matsudaira Nagato-no-kami, continued)

(b) 大馬ゐるし (大馬しるし; ō-mumajirushi): great standard

    A yak hair top-plume and a feather-covered helmet crest shape.

(c) そんさし㧱 (はんさし物; ban-sashimono): guard identifying object

    A banner tree of white banners with stitching.

---

22. 松平・阿波守　廿二　まつさいしあハのうミ (まつたいらあはのかみ; Matsudaira Awa-no-kami):

    "Matsudaira, Provincial Governor of Awa", i.e., Matsudaira Yoshishige (松平至鎮) (1586–1620) or his son Matsudaira Tadatsune (松平忠英) (1611–1652)[25, 蜂須賀家]

    A nobori with a black swastika mon and a diagonal division from white to black, accompanied by a white maneki with the same mon. For more on the use of the swastika, see p. 70.

(a) はんさしㆁの (はんさしもの; ban-sashimono): guard identifying object

    The left portion of the black block made accidental contact with the paper before or after printing, resulting in a large smudge that overlays the left portion of this double banner.

The same nobori in "Shoshō Shōki Zu Byōbu", depicting the swastika with different proportions.[45, 23]
Ōsaka Castle Museum Collection

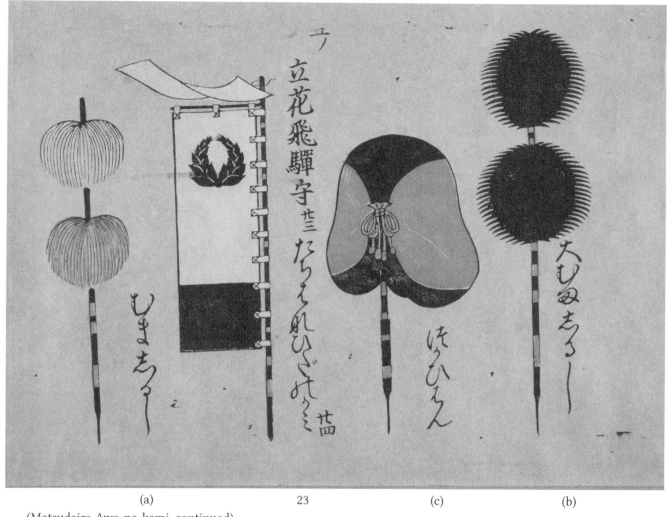

(a)   23   (c)   (b)

(Matsudaira Awa-no-kami, continued)

(b) 大むゐまるし (大むましるし; ō-mumajirushi): great standard

Two feather-covered balls, similar to Arima Hyōbu (see p. 131), Kyōgoku Tango-no-kami (see p. 171), and others.

(c) ほうひそん (つかひはん; tsukaiban): messengers

This red and black horo divides the colors in an interesting and distinctive way.

---

23. 立花・飛驒守　廿三　たちそ𠘨ひざれうミ (たちはなひだのかみ; Tachihana Hida-no-kami):
"Tachihana, Provincial Governor of Hida", i.e., Tachibana Muneshige (立花宗茂) (1569–1642)[25, 立花家]

A black apricot leaf mon (see p. 86) and a horizontal division from white to black.

(a) むまゝるし (むましるし; mumajirushi): battle standard

A white and a red yak hair plume.

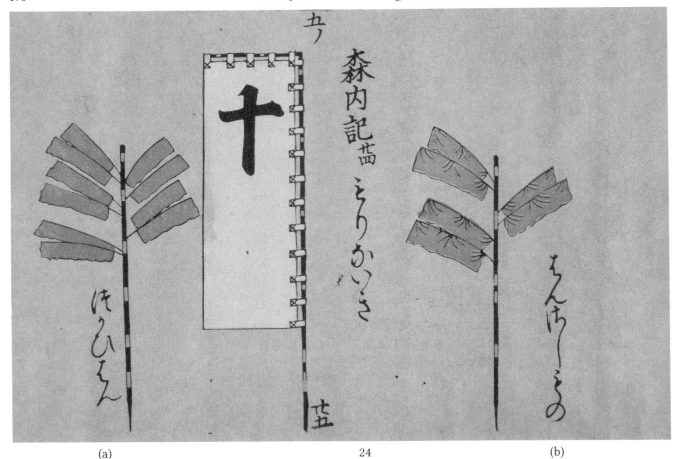

(a)   24   (b)

(Tachihana Hida-no-kami, continued)

(b) てんはしゐの (はんさしもの; ban-sashimono): guard identifying object

A red banner tree.

---

24. 森・内記　廿四　をりゐいき (もりないき; Mori Naiki):
"Mori, Imperial Documents Agency [officer]", i.e., Mori Nagatsugu (森長継)
(1610–1698)[25, 森家]

This cross mon suggests that this samurai was likely a Christian.

(a) ほうひそん (つかひはん; tsukaiban): messengers

A slightly more elaborate red banner tree.

In "Shoshō Shōki Zu Byōbu", Nagat-sugu's mon is a bit closer to a character 十 *(jū, meaning "ten").*[45, 25]
Ōsaka Castle Museum Collection

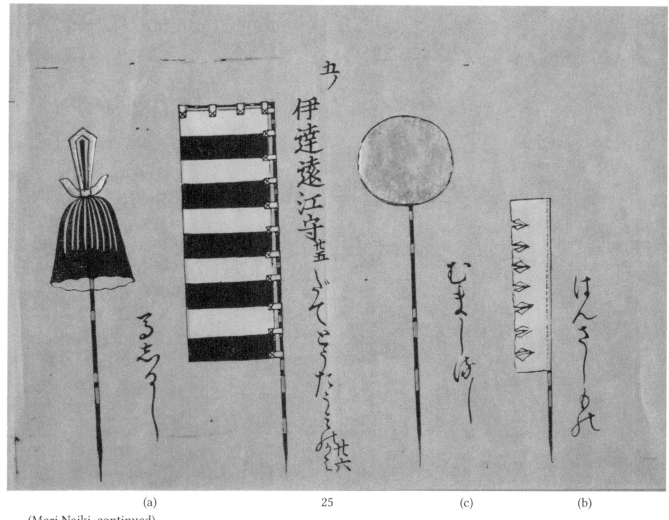

(a)   25   (c)   (b)

(Mori Naiki, continued)

(b) はんさ↓かれ (はんさしもの; ban-sashimono): guard identifying object

A white slashed banner.

(c) むま↓ふ↓ (むましるし; mumajirushi): battle standard

This standard is a round golden ball, similar to a disc mon.

---

25. 伊達・遠江守　廿五　ざてとうたうミれうミ (だてとうたうみのかみ; Date Tōtōmi-no-kami):
"Date, Provincial Governor of Tōtōmi", i.e., Date Hidemune (伊達秀宗) (1591–1658) or his son Date Munetoshi (伊達宗利) (1634–1708)[25, 伊達家]

A nobori of white and black horizontal stripes.

(a) 多志る↓ (馬しるし; mumajirushi): battle standard

This standard features a black "fly trap" and a gold spear head.[53, p. 34]

27   (b)   (a)   26   (b)

(Date Tōtōmi-no-kami, continued)

(b) ぢしんたて物 (じしんたて物; jishin tatemono): personal helmet crest

   This shows a helmet with a crest and a similarly moon-shaped helmet crest device.

---

26. 遠藤・但馬守　廿六　ゑんどうたぢまのうみ (ゑんどうたじまのかみ; Endō Tajima-no-kami):
   "Endō, Provincial Governor of Tajima", i.e., Endō Yoshitaka (遠藤慶隆) (1550–1632) or his heir Endō Yoshitoshi
      (遠藤慶利) (1609–1646)[25, 遠藤家]

   A nobori with a red disc and a diagonal division from white to black.

(a) うまじるし (馬しるし; mumajirushi): battle standard

   A gold non-folding fan.

(b) はんさし物 (はんさし物; ban-sashimono): guard identifying object

   Two gold wooden slats.

---

27. 杦原・伯耆守　廿七　すきそらはうきのうミ (すきはらはうきのかみ; Sugiwara Hōki-no-kami):
   "Sugiwara, Provincial Governor of Hōki", i.e., Sugihara Nagafusa (杉原長房) (1574–1629), who received the title in
      1589, or his son Sugihara Shigenaga (杉原重長) (1616–1644), who received it in 1640[25, 杉原家]

   A nobori with a horizontal division from white to black.

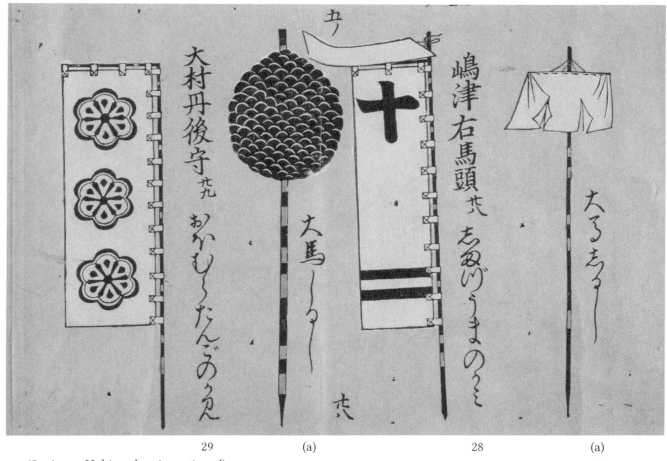

29 (a) 28 (a)

(Sugiwara Hōki-no-kami, continued)

(a) 大弓ゑる〳 (大馬しるし; ō-mumajirushi): great standard

A white noren.

---

28. 嶋津・右馬頭　廿八　ゑゐげうまのゟミ (しまづうまのかみ; Shimazu Uma-no-kami):
"Shimazu, Head of the Right Horse Bureau", i.e., Shimazu Tadanaga (島津忠長) (1551–1610),[1, p. 398] his cousin Shimazu Yukihisa (島津以久) (1550–1610), or Yukihisa's son Shimazu Tadaoki (島津忠興) (1599–1637)[25, 島津家]

A white nobori with a cross mon and two horizontal stripes. This particular mon is somewhere between the standard Christian cross and the Japanese character 十 (jū, meaning "ten"), but it still likely had a Christian connection.

(a) 大馬〳るし (大馬しるし; ō-mumajirushi): great standard

A ball covered in flat black feathers.

---

29. 大村・丹後守　廿九　おゑむ〳たんごのゟ𛀁 (おほむらたんごのかみ; Ōmura Tango-no-kami):
"Ōmura, Provincial Governor of Tango", i.e., Ōmura Sumitada (大村純忠) (1533–1587),[1, p. 192] his son Ōmura Yoshiaki (大村嘉前) (1569–1616), or Yoshiaki's grandson Ōmura Suminobu (大村純信) (1618–1650)

A white nobori with three six-petaled "China flower" (唐花; karahana) mon.[31, p. 26] This design was not based on a particular flower, but based on a fabric pattern imported from China.[6, p. 138] This version, with the thick-then-thin outer outlines, can alternately be identified as a variant of the melon mon (see p.).[19, p. 66] Like the wood sorrel mon (e.g., p. 32), it incorporates stylized sword blades for a more martial design.

(b) (a) 30 (b) (a)

(Ōmura Tango-no-kami, continued)

(a) 大まるほし (大馬しるし; ō-mumajirushi): great standard

> A standard in the shape of a large bell. Large bells were found at Buddhist temples, giving this standard a religious connotation; smaller bells were also used as alarms on the battlefield.[54, p. 29]

(b) はんさしをぜ (はんさしもの; ban-sashimono): guard identifying object

---

30. 土方・丹後守 卅 むぢかさたんごぬっミ (ひぢかたたんごのかみ; Hijikata Tango-no-kami):

"Hijikata, Provincial Governor of Tango", i.e., Hijikata Katsūji (土方雄氏) (1583–1638)[1, p. 650]

> A white nobori with a three-tomoe mon repeated three times. Like other tomoe mon in *O-umajirushi*, e.g. those used by Matsudaira Nakazukasa (see p. 91), these are right-facing tomoe.

(a) むまゑるく (むましるし; mumajirushi): battle standard

> A red noren.

(b) そんほく抄 (はんさし物; ban-sashimono): guard identifying object

Detail from a circa 1615 folding screen showing a painting of a temple bell being carried by a group of begging monks. Tokyo National Museum

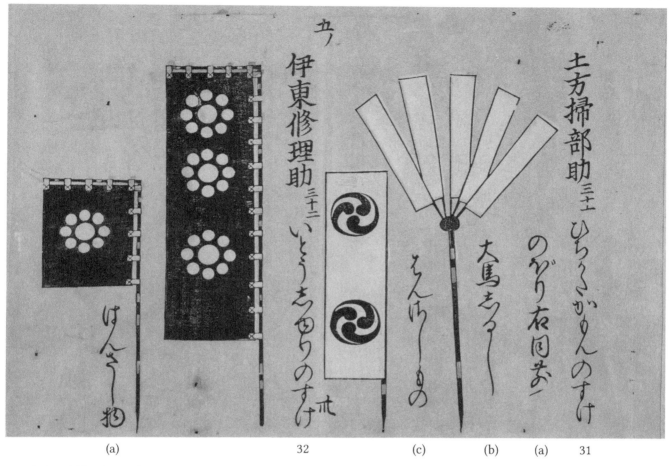

(a)   32   (c)   (b)   (a)   31

31. 土方・掃部助　三十一　ひちかさかゐんのすけ (ひちかたかもんのすけ; Hijikata Kamon-no-suke):
"Hijikata, Assistant [Dir.] of the Bureau of Palace Cleaning", i.e., Hijikata Katsushige (土方雄重) (1592–1628)[25, 土方家]

The numbering used here, 三十一, uses the modern "three tens and one" style, not the 卅一 "thirty and one" used in the table of contents and in page numbering.

(a) のぞり右同あ (のぼり右同支; nobori migi onaji sasae): bears a nobori same as the preceding

While it looks similar to the hiragana 'o', お, the final character in this caption seems to actually be a kuzushiji form of 支, meaning to hold up or support.

This is the only instance in *O-umajirushi* where a samurai is described in the text as bearing the same device as another samurai. Given that the two samurai were brothers, it makes sense that they might share heraldry. Unlike most of volumes 4, 5, and 6, this entry is not in "Shoshō Shōki Zu Byōbu", possibly due to the shared nobori.

(b) 大馬志るし (大馬しるし; ō-mumajirushi): great standard

A white quintuple banner.

(c) そんはしゅの (はんさしもの; ban-sashimono): guard identifying object

32. 伊東・修理助　三十二　いとう志ゆりのすけ (いとうしゅりのすけ; Itō Shūri-no-suke):
"Itō, Assistant [Director] of the Repairing Agency", i.e., Itō Yoshisuke (伊東義祐) (1512–1585)[1, p. 110] or his grandson Itō Sukenori (伊東祐慶) (1589–1636)[1, p. 107]

A nine stars mon.

(a) はんさしゆ物 (はんさし物; ban-sashimono): guard identifying object

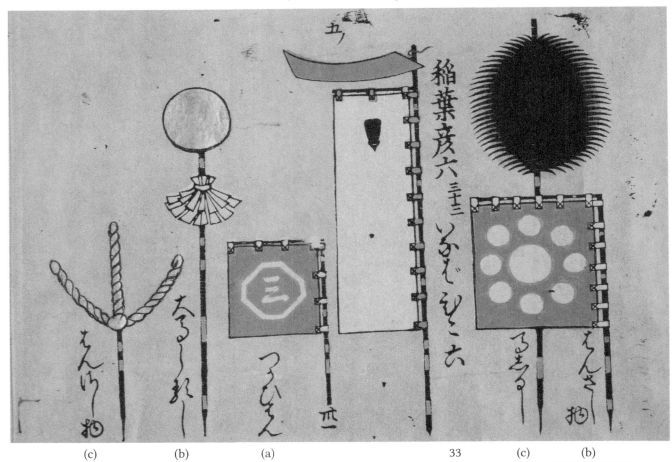

| (c) | (b) | (a) | | 33 | (c) | (b) |

(Itō Shūri-no-suke, continued)

(b) そんさし 物 (はんさし 物; ban-sashimono): guard identifying object

(c) 馬志るし (馬しるし; mumajirushi): battle standard (a large feather-covered ball)

---

33. 稲葉・彧六　三十三　いゐぞゐこ六 (いなばひこ六; Inaba Hikoroku):
    Referring to Inaba Ittetsu (稲葉一鉄) (1515–1588) or his son Inaba Sadamichi
      (稲葉貞通) (1546–1603)[1, pp. 113–114]

    彧六 is a historical variant of 彦六 (which was used in the table of contents).

    This white nobori has a black mon and is accompanied by a red maneki. The mon
    represents a hawk's feather (鷹の羽; taka no hane).[19, p. 51] It's different from the
    more recognizable depiction normally used in mon (see p. xxiii). It somewhat
    resembles single flower petals from *Kenmon Shokamon*.[20, pp. 24–25]

(a) つゝひそん (つかひはん; tsukaiban): messengers

    This uses the same three-in-octagon mon as Inaba Mino-no-kami (see p. 63).

(b) 大馬しるし (大馬しるし; ō-mumajirushi): great standard

    A gold ball and white paper strips, similar to paper strip dashi used, e.g., by Kii
    Dainagon-sama (see p. 12).

(c) そんはし 物 (はんさし 物; ban-sashimono): guard identifying object

    This sashimono is a three-pronged spiral shape similar to the three-pronged
    standard used by Inaba Mino-no-kami (see p. 63).

*The same feather banner, as
shown in "Shoshō Shōki Zu
Byōbu".*[45, 35]
Ōsaka Castle Museum Collection

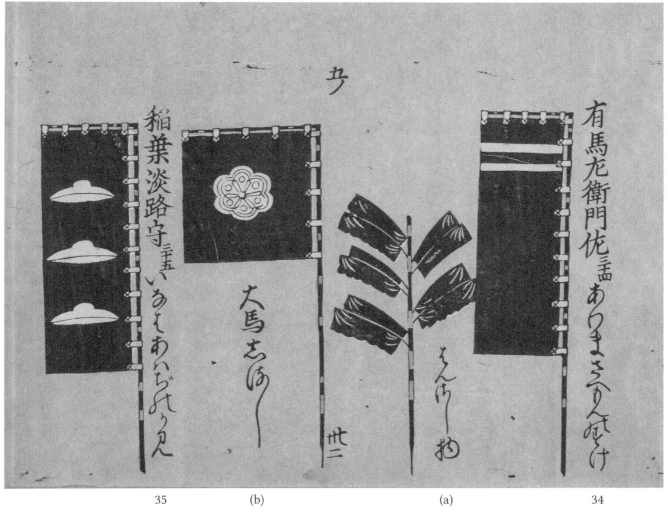

35   (b)   (a)   34

34. 有馬・左衛門佐　三十四　ありまさへ𛀙ん𛀁もけ (ありまさへもんのすけ; Arima Saemon-no-suke):
    "Arima, Assistant [Director] of the Left Gate Guards", i.e., Arima Naozumi (有馬直純) (1586–1641)[25, 有馬丸岡家]
    佐 is a historical variant of 佐 (which was used in the table of contents).

    This section label uses 'he' in "saemon", as opposed to the 'we' used in the table of contents. This suggests that both were pronounced 'e' in the middle of words at this time. See p. xiv for more on these sound changes.

    This black nobori features two white horizontal stripes.

(a) そんほくし物 (はんさし物; ban-sashimono): guard identifying object
    A black banner tree.

(b) 大馬まほくし (大馬しるし; ō-mumajirushi): great standard
    This China flower mon is very similar to the one used by Ōmura Tango-no-kami (see p. 178).

---

35. 稲葉・淡路守　三十五　いな𛀁あハぢ𛀁うゑ (いなはあはぢのかみ; Inaba Awaji-no-kami):
    "Inaba, Provincial Governor of Awaji", i.e., Inaba Norimichi (稲葉紀通) (1603–1648)[25, 稲葉家]

    Three white hat mon on a black background.
        [18, 笠紋]

Vol. 5

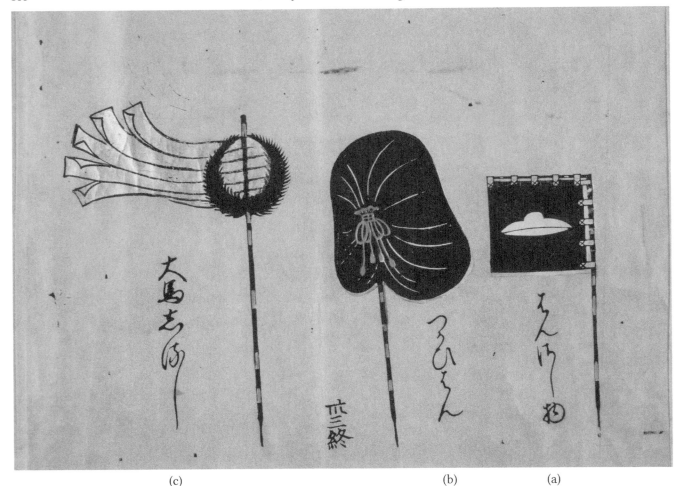

(c)　　　　　　　　　　　　　　　　　　　　　(b)　　　　(a)

(Inaba Awaji-no-kami, continued)

(a) そんはくわ (はんさし物; ban-sashimono): guard identifying object

> This shihō shares the same design as the nobori, using only a single mon.
>
> The general word for this sort of hat in Japanese is kasa (笠), which can also refer to more conical hats. One supposed origin for this mon is given by the Takahashi family. In ancient times, the family had many Shintō priests. Believing that kami, Shintō deities, preferred to alight on high places, they would stand up bamboo poles in order to welcome the kami. The kanji for bamboo is 竹, and the kanji for standing something up is 立. The kanji 笠, meaning hat, happens to consist of two parts deriving from these two kanji. Thus, they adopted this hat mon because of a kanji-based pun on this Shintō practice.

(b) つゝひそん (つかひはん; tsukaiban): messengers

(c) 大馬志はし (大馬しるし; ō-mumajirushi): great standard

> A gold fukinuki fronted with a feather-covered helmet crest shape.

In "Shoshō Shōki Zu Byōbu", the messengers' horo has the hat mon as well.[45, 33]
Ōsaka Castle Museum Collection

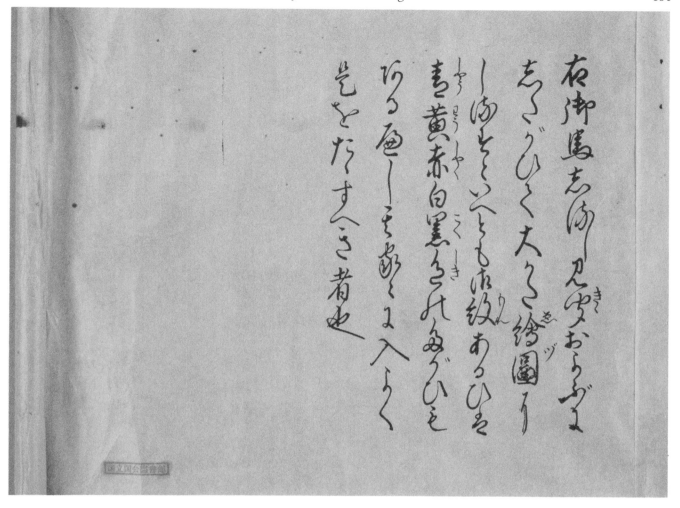

右御馬志流し見へ雯おらずよ
志さうびく大く絵圖し
一海をと次とも木紋あるひを
春黃赤白黑られ糸ぐひを
ける魚しゝ飾くよ入らく
光をたすへき者也

The closing paragraph here is printed with the same block as in the other volumes. This page being added to each volume is the only clear example of intentionally reused blocks in *O-umajirushi*. For translation and discussion, see p. 40.

End Volume 5

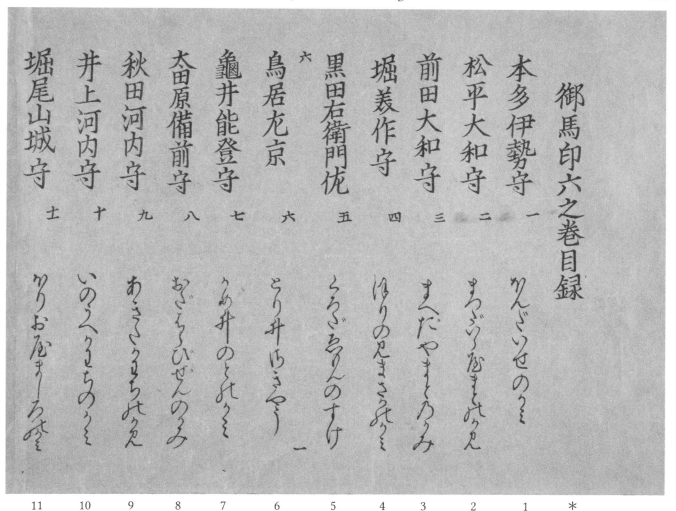

11	10	9	8	7	6	5	4	3	2	1	*

5. 黒田・右衛門佐　五　くろざゑ𛀁んのすけ (くろだゑもんのすけ;
      Kuroda Emon-no-suke (lit. "Kuroda Wemon-no-suke")):
  "Kuroda, Assistant [Director] of the Right Gate Guards", i.e., Matsudaira Tadayuki (松平忠之) (1602–1654)[25, 黒田家]
    Grandson of Kuroda Yoshitaka (entry 3 on p. 76)
    佐 is a historical variant of 佐.

6. 鳥居・左京　六　とり𛀁𛁈きやう (とりゐさきやう; Torii Sakyō (lit. "Toriwi Sakiyau")):
  "Torii, Left Capital Administration [official]", i.e., Torii Tadamasa (鳥居忠政) (1566–1628) or his son Torii Tadatsune
    (鳥居忠恒) (1604–1636)[25, 鳥居家]
    左京 is a historical variant of 左京.

7. 龜井・能登守　七　𛀁め𛀁のと𛀁らミ (かめゐのとのかみ; Kamei Noto-no-kami (lit. "Kamewi Noto-no-kami")):
  "Kamei, Provincial Governor of Noto", i.e., Kamei Koremasa (亀井茲政) (1617–1680)[25, 亀井家]
    龜井 is a historical variant of 亀井.

8. 太田原・備前守　八　おざそ𛁈びぜんの𛀁み (おだはらびぜんのかみ;
      Odawara Bizen-no-kami (lit. "Odahara Bizen-no-kami")):
  "Odawara, Provincial Governor of Bizen", i.e., Ōtawara Harukiyo (大田原晴清) (1567–1631)[25, 大田原家]
    In modern Japanese, 太田原 is pronounced "Ōtawara" and is written 大田原.

9. 秋田・河内守　九　あき𛀁らそち𛀁らゑ (あきたかわちのかみ; Akita Kawachi-no-kami):
  "Akita, Provincial Governor of Kawachi", i.e., Akita Toshisue (秋田俊季) (1598–1649)[25, 秋田家]

10. 井上・河内守　十　いのうへ𛀁らそちの𛀁ミ (いのうへかわちのかみ;
      Inoue Kawachi-no-kami (lit. "Inouhe Kawachi-no-kami")):
  "Inoue, Provincial Governor of Kawachi", i.e., Inoue Masatoshi (井上正利) (1606–1675)[25, 井上家]
    Nephew of Inoue Masashige (entry 31 on p. 191)

    This uses 'i' instead of 'wi' for 井, suggesting that they were pronounced the same at this time. (See p. xiv for more on w-sounds.)

11. 堀尾・山城守　十一　𛀁りお𛀁ま𛁈ろ𛀁らミ (ほりおやましろのかみ; Horio Yamashiro-no-kami):
  "Horio, Provincial Governor of Yamashiro", i.e., Horio Tadaharu (堀尾忠晴) (1599–1633)[1, p. 698]

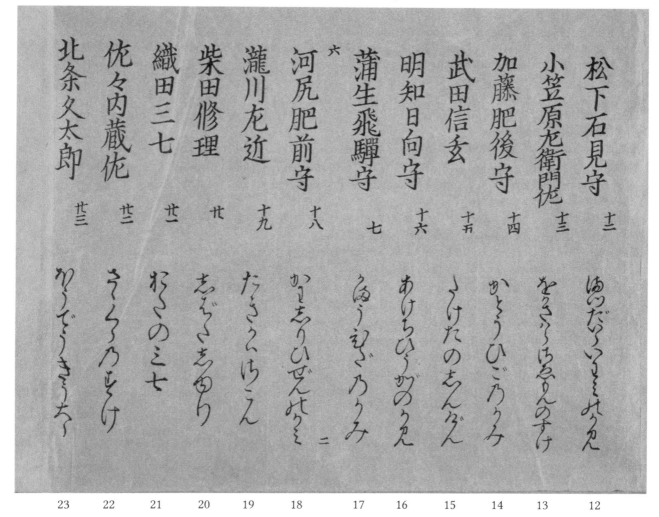

| 23 | 22 | 21 | 20 | 19 | 18 | 17 | 16 | 15 | 14 | 13 | 12 |

12. 松下・石見守　十二　ほつだい〱いてミれうゑ (まつだいらいわみのかみ; Matsudaira Iwami-no-kami):
    "Matsushita, Provincial Governor of Iwami", i.e., Matsushita Shigetsuna (松下重綱) (1579–1627), who received the
    title in 1598, or his son Matsushita Nagatsuna (松下長綱) (1610–1658), who received it in 1636[25, 二代で断絶した大名]

    The pronunciation given here is "Matsudaira"; however, the kanji spell "Matsushita". The correct "Matsushita"
    pronunciation is given in the actual section label.

13. 小笠原・左衛門佐　十三　をゝさハ〱は夭ゐんのすけ (をかさはらさゑもんのすけ;
    Ogasawara Saemon-no-suke (lit. "Wokasahara Sawemon-no-suke")):
    "Ogasawara, Assistant [Director] of the Left Gate Guards", i.e., Ogasawara Nobuyuki (小笠原信之) (1570–1614) or his
    son Ogasawara Masanobu (小笠原政信) (1607–1640)[25, 小笠原勝山家]
    左衛門 is a historical variant of 左衛門, and 佐 is a variant of 佐.

    While the clan name here is written "Okasawara", without the dakuten to make 'ka' into 'ga', the pronunciation
    given in the actual section label includes the dakuten, suggesting that the "Ogasawara" pronunciation is correct.

14. 加藤・肥後守　十四　かとうひごろゝみ (かとうひごのかみ; Katō Higo-no-kami (lit. "Katou Higo-no-kami")):
    "Katō, Provincial Governor of Higo", i.e., Katō Kiyomasa (加藤清正) (1562–1611) or his son Katō Tadahiro (加藤忠広) (1601–1653)[25, 江戸初期国持大名家]

    From a different Katō line than Katō Yasuoki (entry 11 on p. 149) and from Katō Yoshiaki (entry 15 on p. 116). 加藤 is a historical variant of 加藤.

    Katō Kiyomasa was the boyhood friend of Toyotomi Hideyoshi (entry 3 on p. 114) and served him and later the Tokugawa well and loyally. He became one of the most famous warriors in Japanese history. He dispossessed his son, Tadahiro, after suspecting him of plotting against Tokugawa Iemitsu.[53, pp. 48–49]

15. 武田・信玄　十五　さけたのゝんゝん (たけたのしんげん; Taketa no Shingen):
    Referring to Takeda Shingen (武田信玄) (1521–1573)[1, p. 482]

    武田 is a historical variant of 武田, and 信玄 is a variant of 信玄.

16. 明知・日向守　十六　あけちひうがのゝゑ (あけちひうがのかみ;
    Akechi Hyūga-no-kami (lit. "Akechi Hiuga-no-kami")):
    "Akechi, Provincial Governor of Hyūga", i.e., Akechi Mitsuhide (明智光秀) (1528?–1582)[1, p. 22]

17. 蒲生・飛驒守　七　ゝほうむざろゝみ (かまうひだのかみ; Kamō Hida-no-kami (lit. "Kamau Hida-no-kami")):
    "Kamō, Provincial Governor of Hida", i.e., Matsudaira Hideyuki (松平秀行) (1583–1612)[25, 江戸初期国持大名家]

    Father of Matsudaira Tadatomo (entry 10 on p. 77). Married the daughter of Tokugawa Ieyasu (entry 1 on p. 2), and was granted the Matsudaira name in 1607. 飛驒 is a historical variant of 飛驒.

    The 十 (ten) is left off of the number here; it should read 十七 (17).

    The modern pronunciation of "Kamō" is Gamō.

18. 河尻・肥前守　十八　かゝゝりひぜんゝゝゝ (かわしりひぜんのかみ; Kawashiri Hizen-no-kami):
    "Kawashiri, Provincial Governor of Hizen", i.e., Kawajiri Hidetaka (川尻秀隆) (–1582) or his son Kawajiri Hidenaga (川尻秀長) (–1600)[1, p. 265]

19. 瀧川・左近　十九　たきゝゝゝこん (たきかはさこん; Takikawa Sakon (lit. "Takikaha Sakon")):
    "Takikawa, [commander of the] Left Inner [Imperial Guard]", i.e., Takigawa Kazumasu (滝川一益) (1525–1586)[1, p. 476]

    左近 is a historical variant of 左近.

20. 柴田・修理　廿　ゝゝゝゝり (しばたしゆり; Shibata Shūri (lit. "Shibata Shiyuri")):
    "Shibata, Repairing Agency [official]", i.e., Shibata Katsuie (柴田勝家) (–1583)[1, p. 391]

21. 織田・三七　廿一　ゝゝのゝ七 (おたの三七; Ota no Sanshichi):
    Referring to Oda Nobutaka (織田信孝) (1558–1583)[1, p. 216]

    Third son of Oda Nobunaga (entry 1 on p. 114)
    "Sanshichi" was Nobutaka's childhood yobina.

22. 佐々・内蔵佐　廿二　さゝくゝのゝけ (さゝくらのすけ; Sasa Kura-no-suke):
    "Sasa, Assistant [Director] of the Inner Treasury", i.e., Sassa Narimasa (佐々成政) (1539–1588)[1, p. 372]

    佐々 is a historical variant of 佐々, 内蔵 is a variant of 内蔵, and 佐 is a variant of 佐.

    Nowadays, this clan is read "Sassa". Here, since kurikaeshi can imply dakuten, this could be "Sasa" or "Saza".

    This is another instance of a silent kanji. 内蔵 would normally be pronounced "naikura", but it seems in the department name the pronunciation got shortened to just "kura" over time.

23. 北条・久太郎　廿三　ゝうでうきうゝ太ゝ (ほうでうきう太ら; Hōjō Kyūtara (lit. "Houdeu Kiutara")):
    Referring to Hōjō Ujimune (北条氏宗) (1619–1685)[25, 北条家]

    北条 is a historical variant of 北条, and 久太郎 is a variant of 久太郎.

    As with Matsudaira Geki (see p. 115), the pronunciation here does not match the modern reading of 久太郎, Kyūtarō. It uses the same 太 "ta" character.

    The use of the informal given name here is because Ujimune never received a provincial governorship or other formal title.

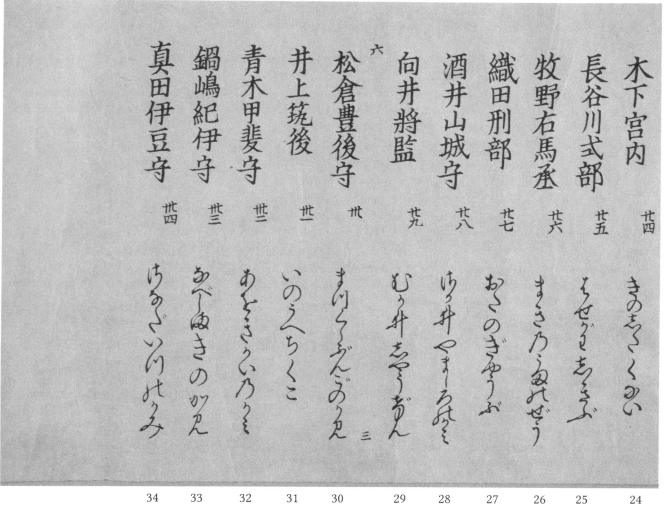

真田伊豆守　鍋嶋紀伊守　青木甲斐守　井上筑後　松倉豊後守　向井將監　酒井山城守　織田刑部　牧野右馬丞　長谷川式部　木下宮内

六　三

卅四　卅三　卅二　卅一　卅　廿九　廿八　廿七　廿六　廿五　廿四

34　33　32　31　30　29　28　27　26　25　24

24. 木下・宮内　廿四　きのまさくゐい (きのしたくない; Kinoshita Kunai):
"Kinoshita, Imperial Household [official]", i.e., Kinoshita Toshifusa (木下利房) (1573–1637)[1, p. 284]
Elder brother of Kinoshita Nobutoshi (entry 8 on p. 149)
宮内 is a historical variant of 宮内.

25. 長谷川・式部　廿五　そせグ〻まきぶ (はせがわしきぶ; Hasegawa Shikibu):
"Hasegawa, Ministry of Ceremonies [official]", i.e., Hasegawa Moritomo (長谷川守知) (1569–1632)[1, p. 628]
式部 is a historical variant of 式部.

26. 牧野・右馬丞　廿六　まき乃うゐせぜう (まきのうまのぜう; Makino Uma-no-jō (lit. "Makino Uma-no-zeu")):
"Makino, Inspector of the Right Stables Bureau", i.e., Makino Yasunari (牧野康成) (1555–1609) or his son Makino
Tadanari (牧野忠成) (1581–1654)[25, 牧野家]
牧野 is a historical variant of 牧野, and 丞 is a variant of 丞.

Inspector (more generally 判官, "jō") was a the third highest rank in the leadership of an office under the Ritsuryō
system, below assistant director (次官; suke) and above secretary (主典; sakan). (The exact title used varied based
on the type of office.) See p. xxi for more information.

27. 織田・刑部　廿七　おさのきゆうぶ (おたのきやうぶ; Ota no Gyōbu (lit. "Ota no Giyaubu")):
    "Ota, Ministry of Justice [official]", i.e., Oda Nobunori (織田信則) (1599–1630)[25, 織田家]
       Nephew of Oda Nobunaga (entry 1 on p. 114)
       織田 is a historical variant of 織田.

28. 酒井・山城守　廿八　ほうᵬやましろᵬうミ (さかゐやましろのかみ;
          Sakai Yamashiro-no-kami (lit. "Sakawi Yamashiro-no-kami")):
    "Sakai, Provincial Governor of Yamashiro", i.e., Sakai Shigezumi (酒井重澄) (1607–1642)[25, 金森家][33, 金森氏]

29. 向井・將監　廿九　むらᵬゐやうぎん (むかゐしやうげん; Mukai Shōgen (lit. "Mukawi Shiyaugen")):
    "Mukai, Commander [of the Imperial Guards]", i.e., Mukai Tadakatsu (向井忠勝) (1582–1641)[22, 向井将監, 向井忠勝]
       將監 is a historical variant of 将監.

30. 松倉・豊後守　卅　まりくゝぶんごのうゑ (まつくらぶんごのかみ; Matsukura Bungo-no-kami):
    "Matsukura, Provincial Governor of Bungo", i.e., Matsukura Shigemasa (松倉重政) (–1630)[1, p. 723]
       松倉 is a historical variant of 松倉.

31. 井上・筑後　卅一　いのうへちくこ (いのうへちくこ; Inoue Chikuko (lit. "Inouhe Chikuko")):
    "Inoue, [Provincial Governor of] Chikugo", i.e., Inoue Masashige (井上政重) (1585–1661)[25, 井上家]
       Uncle of Inoue Masatoshi (entry 10 on p. 187)
       筑後 is a historical variant of 筑後.
       Here again 'i' and not 'wi' is used for 井.

    Although the normal "-no-kami" is omitted, "Chikugo" nevertheless seems to refer to a provincial governorship.

32. 青木・甲斐守　卅二　あをきろいᵬうミ (あをきかいのかみ; Aoki Kai-no-kami (lit. "Awoki Kai-no-kami")):
    "Aoki, Provincial Governor of Kai", i.e., Aoki Shigekane (青木重兼) (1606–1682)[25, 青木家]
       甲斐 is a historical variant of 甲斐.

33. 鍋嶋・紀伊守　卅三　ゐべくはきのかゑ (なべしまきのかみ; Nabeshima Ki-no-kami):
    "Nabeshima, Provincial Governor of Ki", i.e., Nabeshima Motoshige (鍋島元茂) (1602–1654)[25, 鍋島家]
       Son of Nabeshima Katsushige (entry 16 on p. 151)
       鍋嶋 is a historical variant of 鍋島, and 紀伊 is a variant of 紀伊.

    Here 紀伊 is written "Ki" instead of "Kii", two kanji combining into a single mora.

34. 真田・伊豆守　卅四　ほゐざいりᵬうみ (さなだいつのかみ; Sanada Izu-no-kami (lit. "Sanada Itsu-no-kami")):
    "Sanada, Provincial Governor of Izu", i.e., Sanada Nobuyuki (真田信之) (1566–1658)[1, p. 377]
       Father of Sanada Nobuyoshi (entry 22 on p. 5)
       真田 is a historical variant of 真田.

    The province is written "itsu" here, without the dakuten; the actual section label gives the standard "idzu"/"izu" pronunciation.

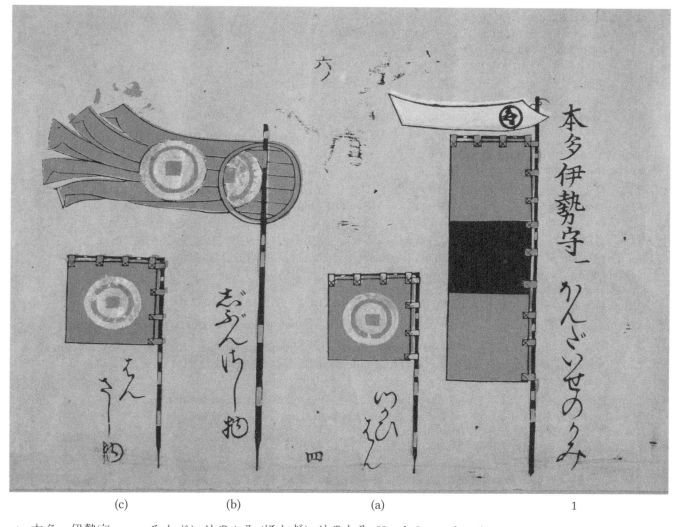

(c)　　　　　(b)　　　　　(a)　　　　　1

1. 本多・伊勢守　一　ゃんざいせのうみ (ほんだいせのかみ; Honda Ise-no-kami):
   "Honda, Provincial Governor of Ise", i.e., Honda Tadatoshi (本多忠利) (1600–1645)[25, 本多飯山家]

   This red nobori features a black horizontal band. The small white nobori features the same standing hollyhock-in-ring mon used by Honda Shimōsa-no-kami (see p. 144).

(a) つうひ　ゃん (つかひ　はん; tsukaiban): messengers

   This red banner features gold mon of a coin, distinguished by the square hole in the middle, in a ring enclosure.

(b) ぎぶんけ↸物 (じぶんさし物; jibun sashimono): personal identifying object

   A fukinuki with the same design.

(c) ゃん　さ↸物 (はん　さし物; ban-sashimono): guard identifying object

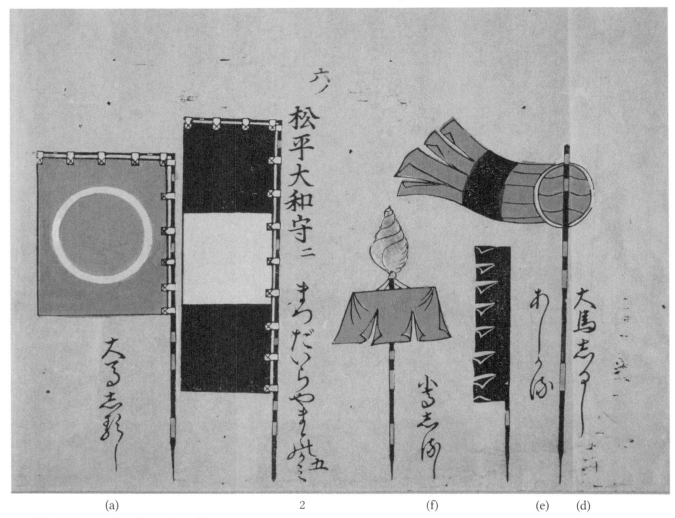

(a)   2   (f)   (e)   (d)

(Honda Ise-no-kami, continued)

(d) 大馬あるし (大馬しるし; ō-mumajirushi): great standard

This fukinuki features the same color scheme as the nobori.

(e) あくろは (あしかる; ashigaru): foot soldiers

A black slashed banner.

(f) 小馬志はく (小馬しるし; ko-mumajirushi): lesser standard

This standard consists of a gold conch shell shape and a red noren. Conch shell trumpets, known as *hora* (法螺), were used for signaling on the battlefield, and were also used as Buddhist ritual implements.[3, p. 275]

---

2. 松平・大和守　二　まつだいらやまとのうミ (まつだいらやまとのかみ; Matsudaira Yamato-no-kami): "Matsudaira, Provincial Governor of Yamato", i.e., Matsudaira Naomoto (松平直基) (1604–1648)[25, 松平川越家]

A black nobori with a white horizontal band.

(a) 大多志釈く (大馬しるし; ō-mumajirushi): great standard

A red banner with a ring mon.

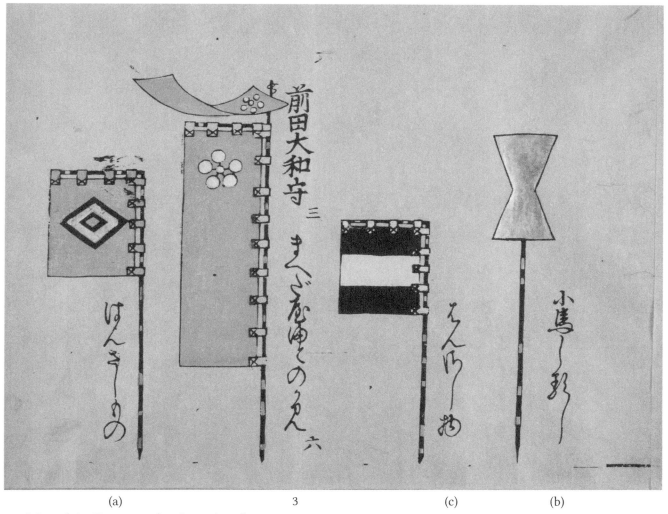

(a) 3 (c) (b)

(Matsudaira Yamato-no-kami, continued)

(b) 小馬〜乳〜 (小馬しるし; ko-mumajirushi): lesser standard

A gold wood standard in the shape of a ryūgo (輪鼓), a type of wooden spinning top that would be rolled along a string attached to two held sticks and used for various juggling-style tricks.[49, p. 294]

(c) そんほ〜物 (はんさし物; ban-sashimono): guard identifying object

3. 前田・大和守　三　まへざゑほとのゔゑ (まへだやまとのかみ; Maeda Yamato-no-kami): "Maeda, Provincial Governor of Yamato", i.e., Maeda Toshitaka (前田利孝) (1594–1637)[25, 前田家]

A variation of the plum bowl motif that shows black connecting lines, making it less abstract than prior instances (e.g., p. 49). This is also an example of a mon used in a three-colored design.

(a) はんさ〜ゃの (はんさしもの; ban-sashimono): guard identifying object

Another three-color design, this one with a sort of doubly-shadowed rhombus mon.

Vol. 6

(a)   4   (b)

(Maeda Yamato-no-kami, continued)

(b) 夢志はく (馬しるし; mumajirushi): battle standard

> A black umbrella with a gold and black hanging cloth border, a bundle of paper strips, and a white yak hair top-plume.

Unlabeled helmet

> A tall catfish tail-style helmet with a disc crest.

---

4. 堀・美作守　四　やりのみまさうせうミ (ほりのみまさかのかみ; Hori no Mimasaka-no-kami): "Hori, Provincial Governor of Mimasaka", i.e., Hori Chikayoshi (堀親良) (1580–1637)[1, p. 700]

> Three black snake's eye with disc mon on a white background.

(a) 自身 (jishin): personal [helmet]

> A gold trapezoid-style helmet crest with two flowers, possibly chrysanthemums, above it.

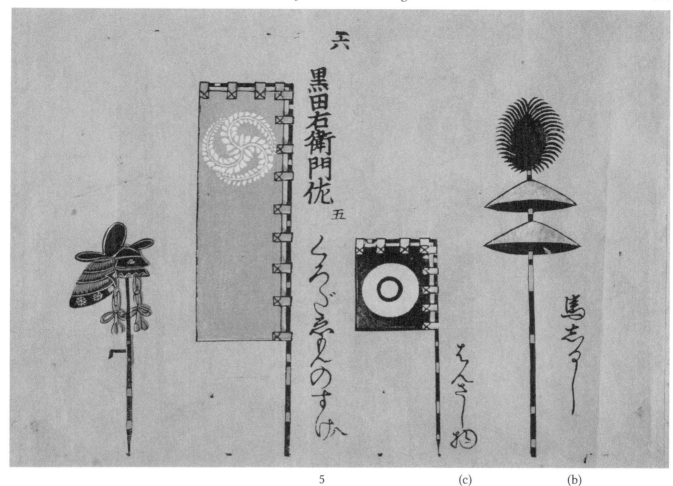

5　　　　　　　　　　(c)　　　　　　　　(b)

(Hori no Mimasaka-no-kami, continued)

(b) 馬志るし (馬しるし; mumajirushi): battle standard

　　Two hats and a feathered top-pole.

(c) そんさし物 (はんさし物; ban-sashimono): guard identifying object

---

5. 黒田・右衛門佐　五　くろざゑもんのすけ (くろだゑもんのすけ;
　　Kuroda Emon-no-suke):

　"Kuroda, Assistant [Director] of the Right Gate Guards", i.e., Matsudaira
　　Tadayuki (松平忠之) (1602–1654)[25, 黒田家]

　This nobori uses the same wisteria tomoe mon as Kuroda Mankichi (see
　p. 83), albeit swirling left instead of the more common right.

Unlabeled helmet

　This helmet has a unique, three-dimensional butterfly-wing-like black
　top crest.

*In "Shoshō Shōki Zu Byōbu", Tadayuki's
nobori has the mon in black and swirling
to the right.*[45, 60]
Ōsaka Castle Museum Collection

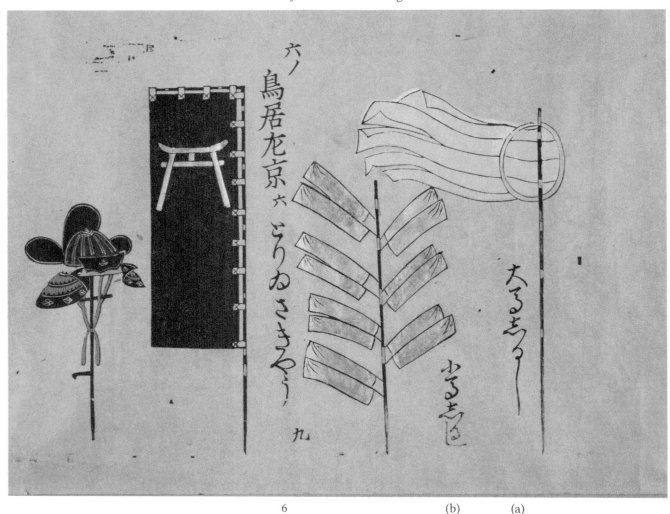

6 (b) (a)

(Kuroda Emon-no-suke, continued)

(a) 大多志る� (大馬しるし; ō-mumajirushi): great standard

A white fukinuki.

(b) 小多志るし (小馬しるし; ko-mumajirushi): lesser standard

A gold banner tree.

---

6. 鳥居・左京　六　とりゐさきやう (とりゐさきやう; Torii Sakyō):
"Torii, Left Capital Administration [official]", i.e., Torii Tadamasa (鳥居忠政) (1566–1628) or his son Torii Tadatsune (鳥居忠恒) (1604–1636)[25, 鳥居家]

A gold shrine gate mon (see p. xxix) on black. Here it is used as a heraldic pun, since the Torii family name is the normal Japanese word for a shrine gate.

Unlabeled helmet

This helmet is very similar to that on the preceding page.

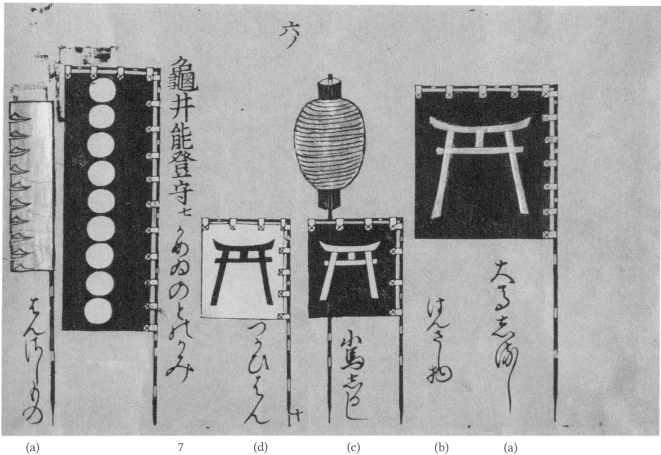

|(a)|7|(d)|(c)|(b)|(a)|

(Torii Sakyō, continued)

(a) 大馬志はし (大馬しるし; ō-mumajirushi): great standard

(b) はんさし物 (はんさし物; ban-sashimono): guard identifying object

(c) 小馬志るし (小馬しるし; ko-mumajirushi): lesser standard

　　A gold paper lantern.

(d) つゝひそん (つかひはん; tsukaiban): messengers

---

7. 龜井・能登守　七　らめゐのとゝらみ (かめゐのとのかみ; Kamei
　　Noto-no-kami):
　"Kamei, Provincial Governor of Noto", i.e., Kamei Koremasa (亀井茲政)
　　(1617–1680)[25, 亀井家]

　It's unclear whether this nobori is intended to have nine disc mon or whether it's
　an unusual arrangement of one "nine stars" mon.

(a) そんほくゝの (はんさしもの; ban-sashimono): guard identifying object

　　A gold slashed banner.

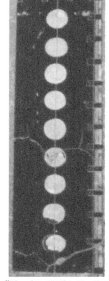

In "Shoshō Shōki Zu Byōbu", Koremasa's nobori is drawn with smaller circles, but the number remains nine.[45, 64]
Ōsaka Castle Museum Collection

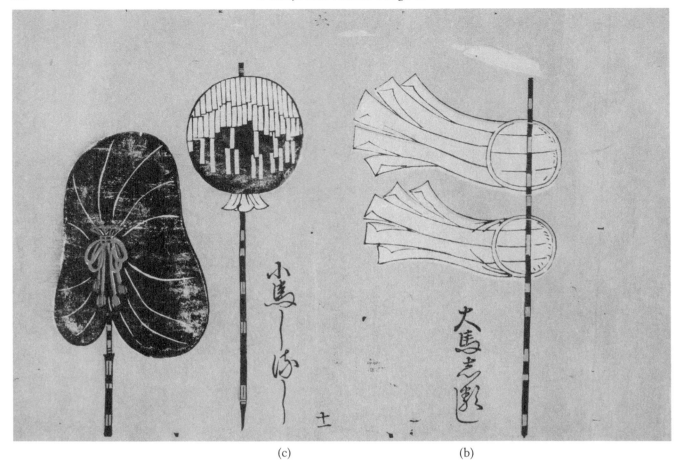

(c)   (b)

(Kamei Noto-no-kami, continued)

(b) 大馬まるし (大馬しるし; ō-mumajirushi): great standard

    A double fukinuki.

(c) 小馬くるし (小馬しるし; ko-mumajirushi): lesser standard

    A black bundle with paper strips on top, similar to the standard used by Mizoguchi Izumo-no-kami (see p. 61).

    Unlabeled horo (canopy)

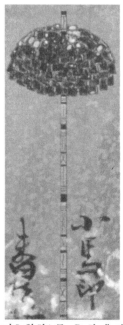

In "Shoshō Shōki Zu Byōbu", this lesser standard is depicted rather differently.[45, 64] *Ōsaka Castle Museum Collection*

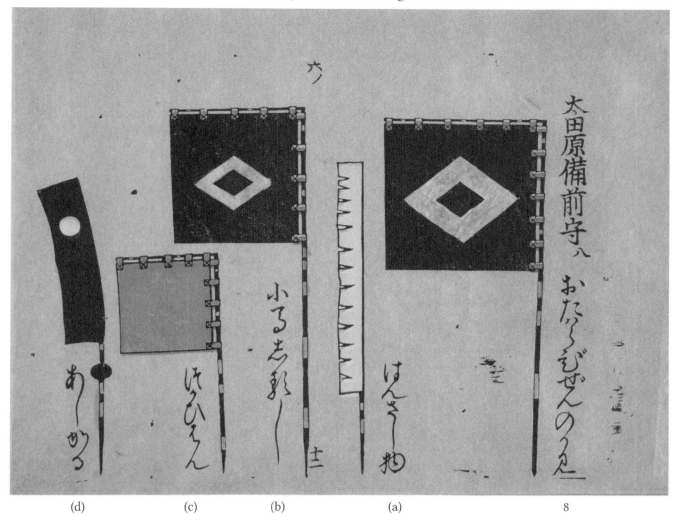

(d)　　　　　(c)　　　　　(b)　　　　　(a)　　　　　8

8. 太田原・備前守　八　おたハらゞぜんのうゑ (おたはらびぜんのかみ; Odawara Bizen-no-kami):
"Odawara, Provincial Governor of Bizen", i.e., Ōtawara Harukiyo (大田原晴清) (1567–1631)[25, 大田原家]

A gold shadowed rhombus mon on black.

(a) はんさゝ抄 (はんさし物; ban-sashimono): guard identifying object

A tall thin white slashed banner.

(b) 小㕮志釈ゝ (小馬しるし; ko-mumajirushi): lesser standard

(c) ほうひそん (つかひはん; tsukaiban): messengers

(d) あゝかる (あしかる; ashigaru): foot soldiers

A black banner with a white disc.

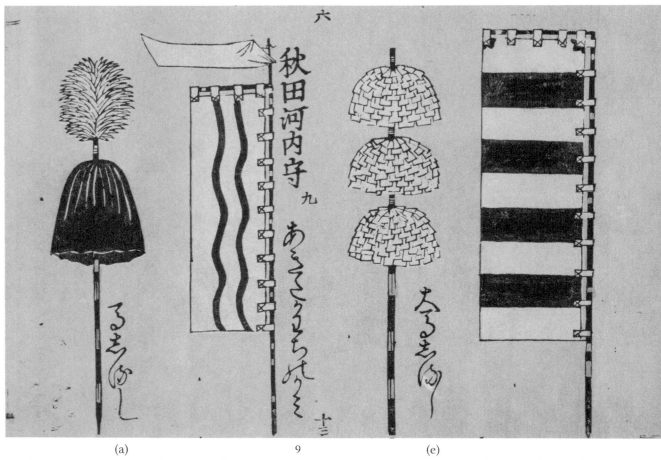

(a)   9   (e)

(Odawara Bizen-no-kami, continued)

Unlabeled banner

A nobori of white and black horizontal stripes, perhaps an alternate primary device.

(e) 大多志はく (大馬しるし; ō-mumajirushi): great standard

Three hemispheres covered in paper strips.

---

9. 秋田・河内守　九　あきさつそちれうミ (あきたかわちのかみ; Akita Kawachi-no-kami):
   "Akita, Provincial Governor of Kawachi", i.e., Akita Toshisue (秋田俊季) (1598–1649)[25, 秋田家]

   A white nobori with two vertical wavy lines, accompanied by a white maneki. Compare the jagged line banner used by Sakai Uta-no-kami (see p. 33).

(a) 多志はし (馬しるし; mumajirushi): battle standard

   A black "fly trap" and a dashi of a tuft of white feathers.

In "Shoshō Shōki Zu Byōbu", Toshisue's nobori is completely different, and the feathers on the standard are black.[45, 66]
Ōsaka Castle Museum Collection

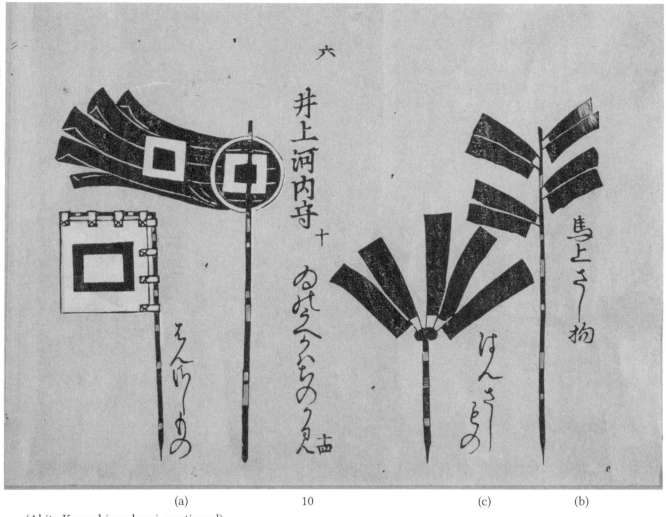

(a)   10   (c)   (b)

(Akita Kawachi-no-kami, continued)

(b) 馬上さゝ物 (馬上さし物; bajō sashimono): horseback sashimono

     A black banner tree.

(c) はんさゝ　ゑの (はんさし　もの; ban-sashimono): guard identifying object

     A black quintuple banner.

---

10. 井上・河内守　十　ゐのうへらハちのゝ见 (ゐのうへかはちのかみ; Inoue Kawachi-no-kami):
"Inoue, Provincial Governor of Kawachi", i.e., Inoue Masatoshi (井上正利) (1606–1675)[25, 井上家]

     This section label uses 'ha' for the 'wa' in Kawachi, instead of the 'wa' used in the table of contents. (See p. xiv for more on the w-sound change.)

     A white shadowed square mon on a black fukinuki.

(a) てんはゝ物の (はんさしもの; ban-sashimono): guard identifying object

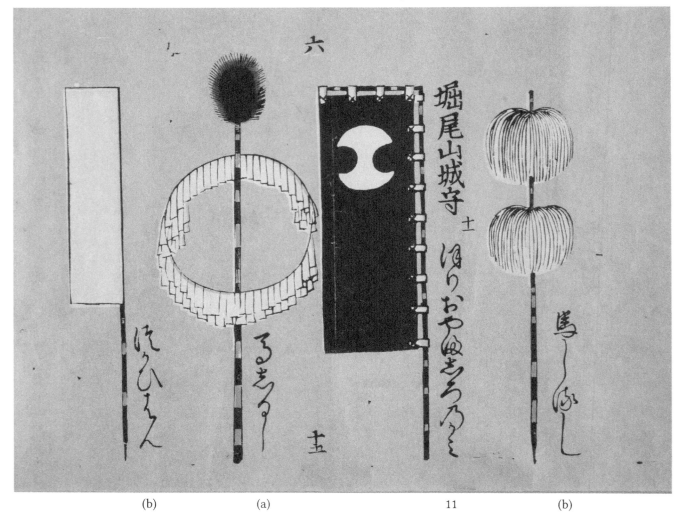

(b)   (a)   11   (b)

(Inoue Kawachi-no-kami, continued)

(b) 馬しるし (馬しるし; mumajirushi): battle standard

 Two ball-shaped yak hair plumes.

---

11. 堀尾・山城守　十一　ほりおやましろのうミ (ほりおやましろのかみ; Horio Yamashiro-no-kami):

 "Horio, Provincial Governor of Yamashiro", i.e., Horio Tadaharu (堀尾忠晴) (1599–1633)[1, p. 698]

 This mon represents a type of weight used by money changers, a fundō (分銅).[49, p. 246] Standard weights were useful to measure amounts of coin quickly and precisely.

(a) 馬しるし (馬しるし; mumajirushi): battle standard

 A shidewa, a hoop covered in white paper strips, accompanied by a black furry top-pole, similar to the standard used by Matsudaira Emon-no-suke (see p. 166).

(b) ほうひそん (つかひはん; tsukaiban): messengers

A gold fundō.
Photo by PHGCOM; used under CC BY-SA 3.0

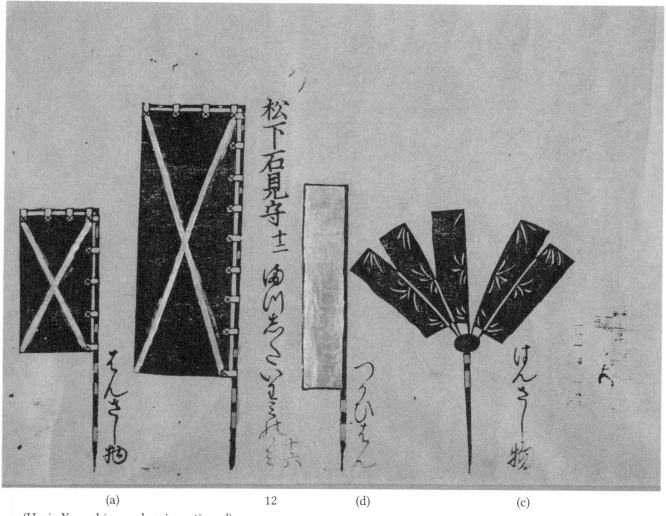

(a)　　　　　　　　　12　　　　　　(d)　　　　　　　　(c)

(Horio Yamashiro-no-kami, continued)

(c) はんさし物 (はんさし物; ban-sashimono): guard identifying object

　　A black quintuple banner.

(d) つゥひそん (つかひはん; tsukaiban): messengers

---

12. 松下・石見守　十二　ほり志さいそミ北ろミ (まつしたいわみのかみ; Matsushita Iwami-no-kami):
　　"Matsushita, Provincial Governor of Iwami", i.e., Matsushita Shigetsuna (松下重綱) (1579–1627), who received the
　　　　title in 1598, or his son Matsushita Nagatsuna (松下長綱) (1610–1658), who received it in 1636[25, 二代で断絶した大名]

　　A gold X shape on black, similar to the X shape used by Niwa no Sakyō (see p. 161).
　　This shape is said to represent the ornamental gables, called *chigi* (千木), on the roof a Shintō shrine.[49, p. 181]

(a) そんさし物 (はんさし物; ban-sashimono): guard identifying object

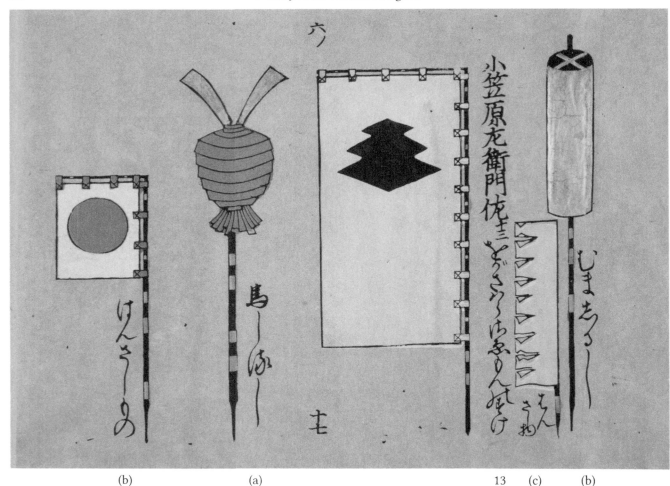

(b)   (a)   13 (c) (b)

(Matsudaira Iwami-no-kami, continued)

(b) むま𛀙る𛀸 (むましるし; mumajirushi): battle standard

> This gold cylinder interestingly has a design similar to the preceding banner on top. It may just represent a support framework for the hollow cylinder. Compare the cylinder used by Matsudaira Shōgen (see p. 82).

(c) そん　さ𛀸𛂆 (はん　さし物; ban-sashimono): guard identifying object

> A white slashed banner.

13. 小笠原・左衛門佐　十三　をゞさハ𛀸はゑ𛂠んのもけ
   (をがさはらさゑもんのすけ; Ogasawara Saemon-no-suke):
  "Ogasawara, Assistant [Director] of the Left Gate Guards", i.e., Ogasawara Nobuyuki (小笠原信之) (1570–1614) or his son Ogasawara Masanobu (小笠原政信) (1607–1640)[25, 小笠原勝山家]

> A black Ogasawara "three stacked rhombuses" mon (see p. 81) on white.

(a) 馬𛀸は𛀸 (馬しるし; mumajirushi): battle standard

> A red paper lantern and two gold wooden slats.

(b) はんさ𛀸𛂠の (はんさしもの; ban-sashimono): guard identifying object

> A red disc on white.

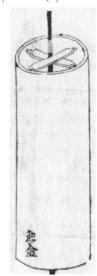

A more detailed version of the same cylinder, from Shoshō Kisei Zu.[44, p. 3.18]

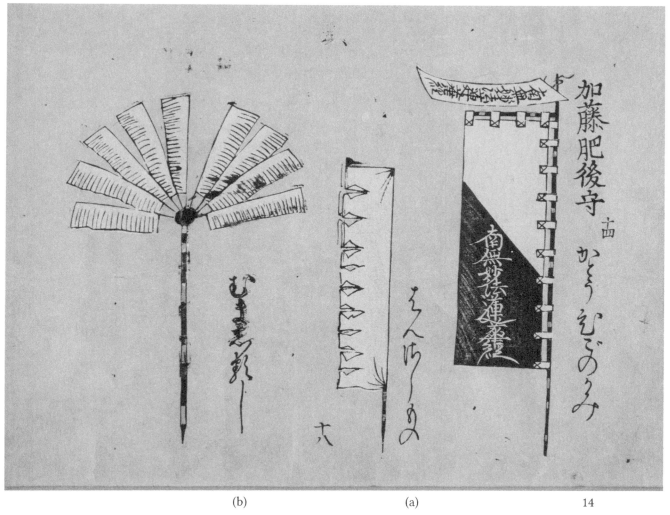

(b)   (a)   14

14. 加藤・肥後守　十四　かとうゐごのゝみ (かとうひごのかみ; Katō Higo-no-kami):
"Katō, Provincial Governor of Higo", i.e., Katō Kiyomasa (加藤清正) (1562–1611) or his son Katō Tadahiro (加藤忠広) (1601–1653)[25, 江戸初期国持ち大名家]

A nobori with a diagonal division from white to black and the mantra 南無妙法蓮華経 ("Glory to the Lotus Sutra"). The accompanying maneki bears the same slogan. This is the same Nichiren mantra used by Hayashi Tanba-no-kami (see p. 110). Kiyomasa was a devotee of the Hokke sect of Nichiren Buddhism.[31, p. 73]

(a) そんはくゆの (はんさしもの; ban-sashimono): guard identifying object

A white slashed banner.

(b) むま志れく (むましるし; mumajirushi): battle standard

An unusual devices made of nine small banners.

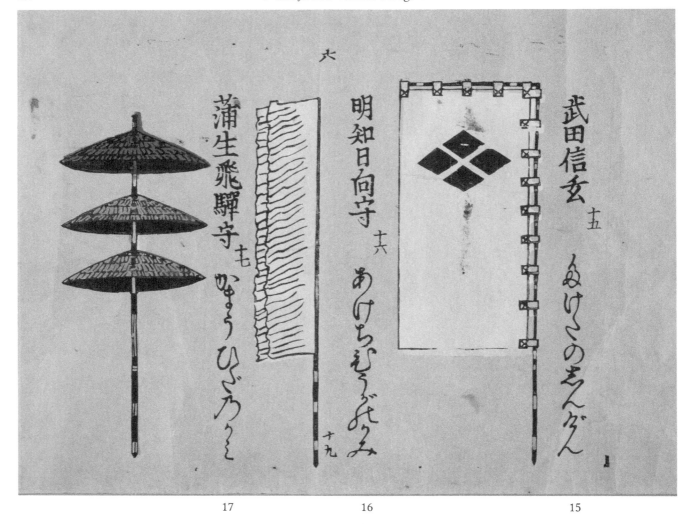

17   16   15

15. 武田・信玄　十五　ゐけさのゑんゞん (たけたのしんげん; Taketa no Shingen):
Referring to Takeda Shingen (武田信玄) (1521–1573)[1, p. 482]

A mon of four rhombuses.

According to legend, this mon dates back to the Takeda ancestor Minamoto no Yoshimitsu. In 1050, during the Former Nine Years War, Yoshimitsu prayed at a Sumiyoshi Shrine for success in battle. In response, the oracle at the shrine announced that the great god of the shrine would give him a suit of armor that had been dedicated to the shrine by Empress Jingū after returning from her invasion of Korea. The armor was called "Tatenashi" (楯無), or "No Shield", meaning that it was so strong no shield was necessary. Up until this point, Yoshimitsu had used a plain white banner, but because the of the rhombus decoration on this armor he and his descendants adopted this rhombus mon.[32, pp. 1193–4]

16. 明知・日向守　十六　あけちゐうがゑろみ (あけちひうがのかみ; Akechi Hyūga-no-kami):
"Akechi, Provincial Governor of Hyūga", i.e., Akechi Mitsuhide (明智光秀) (1528?–1582)[1, p. 22]

A two-layer slashed nobori.

17. 蒲生・飛騨守　十七　かまうひざろうミ (かまうひだのかみ; Kamō Hida-no-kami):
"Kamō, Provincial Governor of Hida", i.e., Matsudaira Hideyuki (松平秀行) (1583–1612)[25, 江戸初期国持ち大名家]

Instead of a nobori, Hideyuki uses a device of three hats.

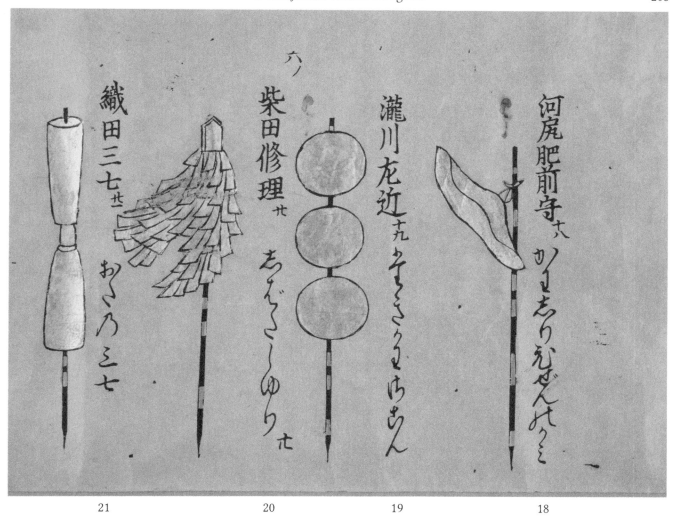

21   20   19   18

---

18. 河尻・肥前守　十八　かゝまりゐぜんのうミ (かわしりひぜんのかみ; Kawashiri Hizen-no-kami):
     "Kawashiri, Provincial Governor of Hizen", i.e., Kawajiri Hidetaka (川尻秀隆) (–1582) or his son Kawajiri Hidenaga (川尻秀長) (–1600)[1, p. 265]
     河尻 is a historical variant of 河尻.

     A gold-painted hanging hat shape with a wavy brim. Compare the standard used by Furuta Hyōbu (see p. 157).

---

19. 瀧川・左近　十九　きゝろそはさん (たきかわさこん; Takikawa Sakon):
     "Takikawa, [commander of the] Left Inner [Imperial Guard]", i.e., Takigawa Kazumasu (滝川一益) (1525–1586)[1, p. 476]

     Three gold balls.

---

20. 柴田・修理　廿　きぞさくゆり (しばたしゆり; Shibata Shūri):
     "Shibata, Repairing Agency [official]", i.e., Shibata Katsuie (柴田勝家) (–1583)[1, p. 391]

     A gold gohei.

---

21. 織田・三七　廿一　おさ乃ミ七 (おたの三七; Ota no Sanshichi):
     Referring to Oda Nobutaka (織田信孝) (1558–1583)[1, p. 216]

     A gold wooden pestle, similar to that used by Inaba Mino-no-kami (see p. 62).

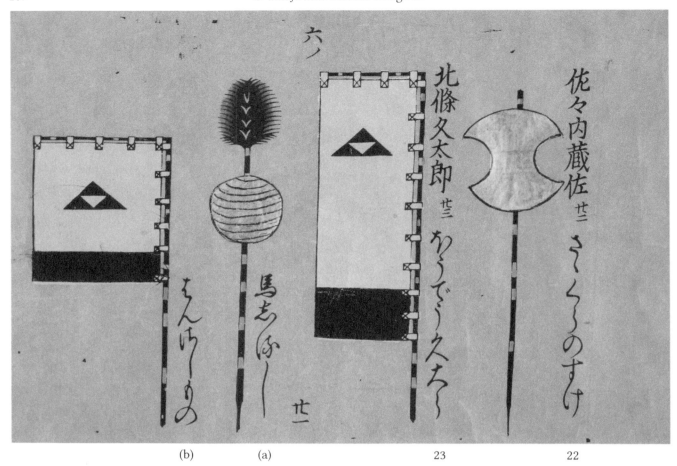

(b)　　　　(a)　　　　　　　　　23　　　　　　　22

22. 佐々・内蔵佐　廿二　さゝくゝのすけ (さゝくらのすけ; Sasa Kura-no-suke):
"Sasa, Assistant [Director] of the Inner Treasury", i.e., Sassa Narimasa (佐々成政) (1539–1588)[1, p. 372]

A gold money changers' weight, the same shape as the mon used by Horio Yamashiro-no-kami (see p. 203).

This is the last entry in the almost-continual run of heraldry in volumes 4, 5, and 6 shared with "Shoshō Shōki Zu Byōbu". The folding screen ends with this series of single-standard samurai, which seems convenient for making sure that the painter would be able to fill the fixed space on the folding screen without having to truncate an entry. There is one later entry outside the run used, Matsukura Bungo-no-kami (see p. 217), potentially due to its relative shortness.

23. 北条・久太郎　廿三　ゔうでう久大ゝ (ほうでう久大ら; Hōjō Kyūtara):
Referring to Hōjō Ujimune (北条氏宗) (1619–1685)[25, 北条家]

This three triangle mon is known as "fish scales" (鱗; uroko). The background has a horizontal division from white to black.

According to legend, Hōjō Tokimasa petitioned the goddess Benten for prosperity for his descendants. After three weeks, she appeared to him, granting his request (with a warning that it would end were they to become unjust rulers) and showing her true form, which was part dragon. She left three scales behind, and this, according to the tale, was the source of the Hōjō mon.[10, p. 141]

(a) 馬ゝほゝ (馬しるし; mumajirushi): battle standard

A gold paper lantern-like shape and a dashi of a tuft of black feathers.

(b) そんほゝゝの (はんさしもの; ban-sashimono): guard identifying object

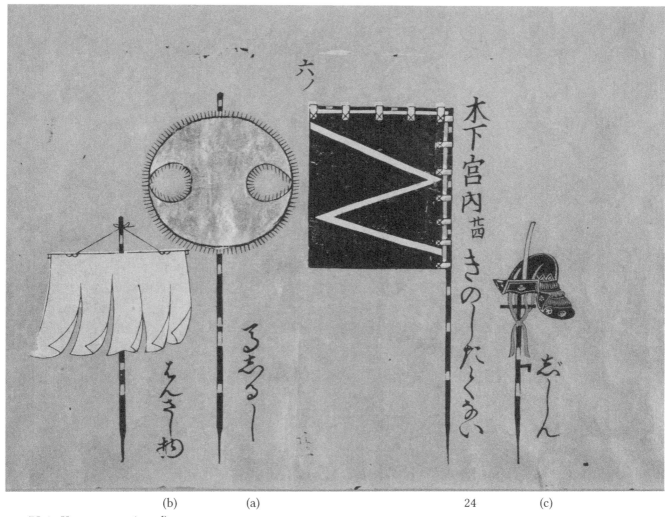

(b)   (a)   24   (c)

(Hōjō Kyūtara, continued)

(c) ぢしん (じしん; jishin): personal [helmet]

This helmet has a helmet crest in the shape of a very tall, thin rectangle.

---

24. 木下・宮内　廿四　きのしたくゐい (きのしたくない; Kinoshita Kunai):
"Kinoshita, Imperial Household [official]", i.e., Kinoshita Toshifusa (木下利房) (1573–1637)[1, p. 284]

This black banner features a jagged line; compare the jagged banners used by Sakai Uta-no-kami (see p. 33) and Niwa no Sakyō (see p. 160).

(a) 馬しるし (馬しるし; mumajirushi): battle standard

This money changers' weight shape has a slightly different shape than the one one the previous page and has a border of fringe.

(b) そんさし物 (はんさし物; ban-sashimono): guard identifying object

A large white noren.

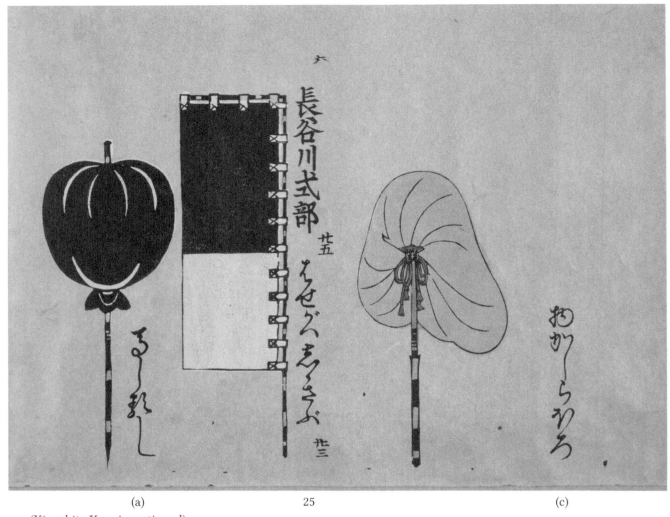

(a)   25   (c)

(Kinoshita Kunai, continued)

(c) 物かしらやろ (物かしらほろ; monogashira horo): foot soldier commander canopy

---

25. 長谷川・式部　廿五　そせぐハまきぶ (はせがはしきぶ; Hasegawa Shikibu):
"Hasegawa, Ministry of Ceremonies [official]", i.e., Hasegawa Moritomo (長谷川守知) (1569–1632)[1, p. 628]

A nobori with a horizontal division from black to white.

(a) 馬しるし (馬しるし; mumajirushi): battle standard

A large black cloth bundle.

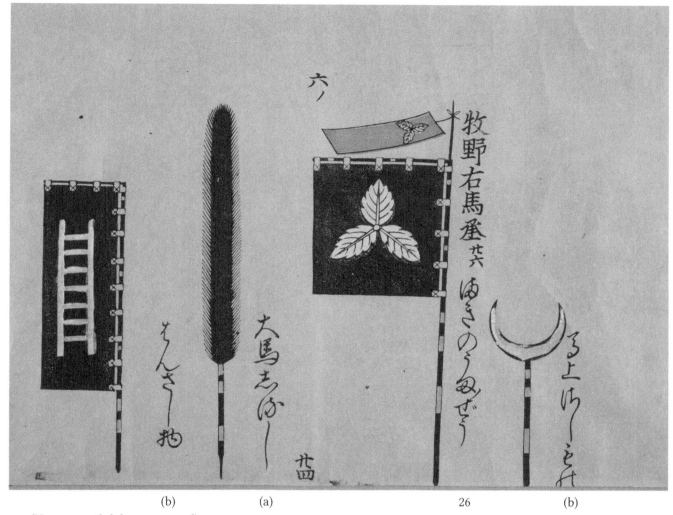

(b)   (a)   26   (b)

(Hasegawa Shikibu, continued)

(b) 多上けくをせ (馬上さしもの; bajō sashimono): horseback sashimono

    A moon-shaped helmet crest.

---

26. 牧野・右馬丞　廿六　ほきのうゐノぜう (まきのうまのぜう; Makino Uma-no-jō):
　　"Makino, Inspector of the Right Stables Bureau", i.e., Makino Yasunari (牧野康成) (1555–1609) or his son Makino Tadanari (牧野忠成) (1581–1654)[25, 牧野家]

    A three oak leaves mon, similar to that used by Matsudaira Tosa-no-kami (see p. 36) but with some stylistic differences. The same mon is used on the maneki.

(a) 大馬志はく (大馬しるし; ō-mumajirushi): great standard

    A feather-covered pole.

(b) そんさく物 (はんさし物; ban-sashimono): guard identifying object

    A gold ladder on a black banner.

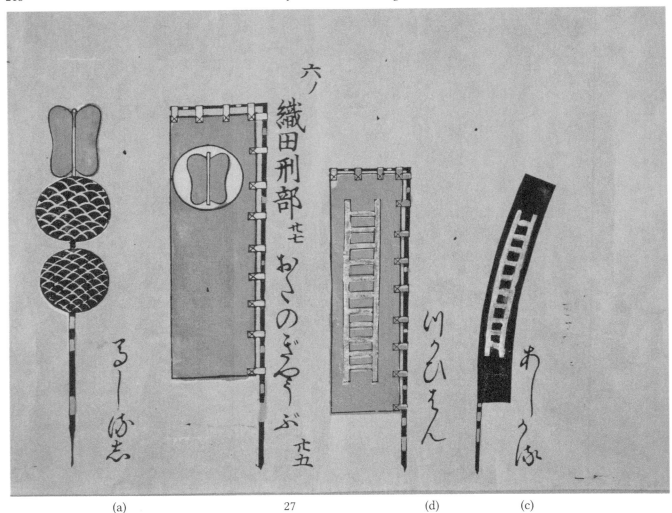

(a)   27   (d)   (c)

(Makino Uma-no-jō, continued)

(c) あしらほ (あしかる; ashigaru): foot soldiers

(d) りらひそん (つかひはん; tsukaiban): messengers

---

27. 織田・刑部　廿七　おさのぎやうぶ (おたのぎやうぶ; Ota no Gyōbu):

"Ota, Ministry of Justice [official]", i.e., Oda Nobunori (織田信則) (1599–1630)[25, 織田家]

A red war fan on a white disc.

(a) 多くほ志 (馬しるし; mumajirushi): battle standard

A similar red war fan above two balls covered in flat black feathers.

A kokuin (see p. xxxiv) from Edo Castle featuring a war fan mon, along with one of three overlapping circles.
Photo by Eric Obershaw

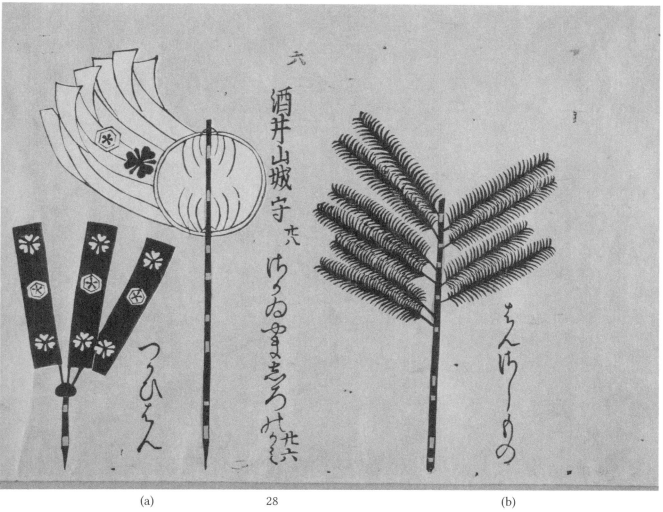

(a) 28 (b)

(Ota no Gyōbu, continued)

(b) そんはくもの (はんさしもの; ban-sashimono): guard identifying object

An interesting device, a tree of feathered poles.

---

28. 酒井・山城守　廿八　はらゐやま志ろ允ろミ (さかゐやましろのかみ; Sakai Yamashiro-no-kami):
"Sakai, Provincial Governor of Yamashiro", i.e., Sakai Shigezumi (酒井重澄) (1607–1642)[25, 金森家][33, 金森氏]

This white fukinuki carries two mon: the Sakai wood sorrel mon (see p. 32) and a mon that seems to be a five-petaled flower of some sort in a hexagon or tortoise shell enclosure. The small size makes it hard to definitively identify the flower. The tortoise shell hexagon was associated with the Izumo Shrine and was often used by devotees.[6, pp. 138–139]

The use of a hexagon enclosure with an interior matching the border color is similar to the ring enclosure used by Matsudaira Tosa-no-kami (see p. 36), though here the flower contrasts.

(a) つゝひそん (つかひはん; tsukaiban): messengers

A triple banner with the same two mon.

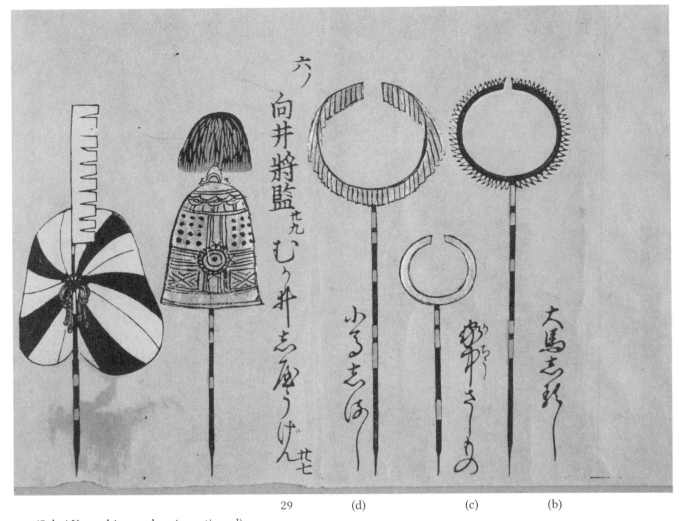

29   (d)   (c)   (b)

(Sakai Yamashiro-no-kami, continued)

(b) 大馬志釈し (大馬しるし; ō-mumajirushi): great standard

> These three identifying objects show the same broken hoop decorated in three different ways: white feathers, gold paint, and gold strips.

(c) 家中さくもの (家中さしもの; kachū sashimono): whole family identifying object

> The kuzushiji kanji here confirm the interpretation of "kachū" as "whole family", eliminating the possibility for homophones.[23, p. 198]

(d) 小马志はし (小馬しるし; ko-mumajirushi): lesser standard

---

29. 向井・將監　廿九　むら升志ゑうげん (むかゐしやうげん; Mukai Shōgen): "Mukai, Commander [of the Imperial Guards]", i.e., Mukai Tadakatsu (向井忠勝) (1582–1641)[22, 向井将監, 向井忠勝]

> A large bell, very similar to that used by Ōmura Tango-no-kami (see p. 179), and a red feather top-plume.

Unlabeled horo (canopy)

> A two-colored horo and a slashed white banner.

Vol. 6

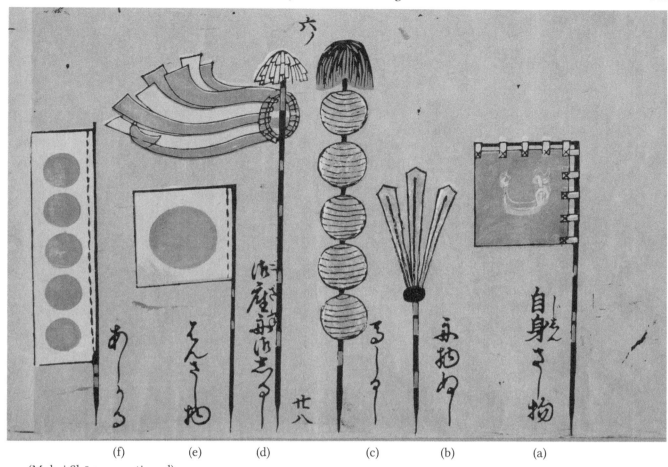

(f)   (e)   (d)   (c)   (b)   (a)

(Mukai Shōgen, continued)

(a) 自身さ〵物 (自身さし物; jishin sashimono): personal identifying object

This purple banner (see p. 72) shows the character む, the first character in the pronunciation of the Mukai family name. It is flipped horizontal, possibly indicating that this is the back of the banner, or possibly a reference to the fact that "muka" (向), the first kanji in "Mukai", can mean "facing" or "opposite".

(b) ふ物ぬ〵 (舟物ぬし; fune mononushi): ship unit leader

Three sword-blade shapes. The two devices on this page are the only examples of ship-related devices in *O-umajirushi*.

(c) 馬〵る〵 (馬しるし; mumajirushi): battle standard

A red top-plume and five gold paper lantern shapes.

(d) 㝵座舟㝵志る〵 (御座舟御しるし; goza-fune o-jirushi): Imperial ship honorable insignia

The furigana assist with the caption, particularly the kuzushiji 座.[23, p. 47]

A red and white fukinuki with a white top-plume of cloth or paper strips.

(e) そんさ〵物 (はんさし物; ban-sashimono): guard identifying object

A red disc on white with visible stitching.

(f) あ〵うる (あしかる; ashigaru): foot soldiers

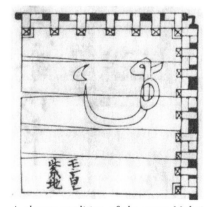

A clearer rendition of the same Mukai mon, from Shoshō Kisei Zu.[44, p. 1.41] *The label indicates a white mon on a purple field.*

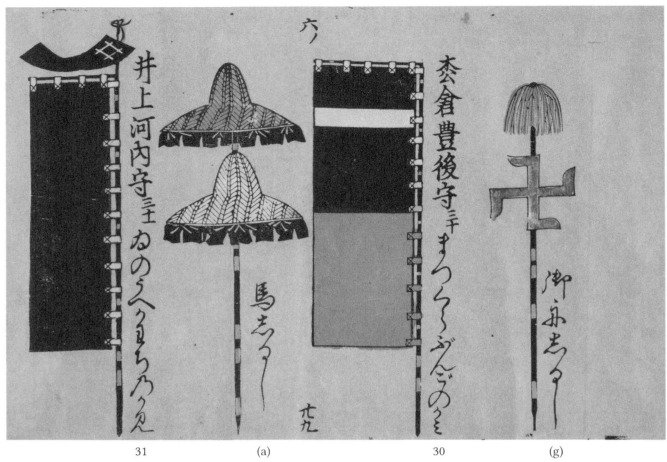

31   (a)   30   (g)

(Mukai Shōgen, continued)

(g) 御舟志る𛀆 (御舟しるし; o-fune jirushi): honorable ship insignia

A silver swastika symbol (see p. 70) and a red top-plume.

30. 松倉・豊後守　三十　まつく𛀆ぶんごのうミ (まつくらぶんごのかみ; Matsukura Bungo-no-kami): "Matsukura, Provincial Governor of Bungo", i.e., Matsukura Shigemasa (松倉重政) (–1630)[1, p. 723]

A nobori with a three-colored design: a horizontal division between black and red and a white horizontal stripe.

(a) 馬志る𛀆 (馬しるし; mumajirushi): battle standard

Two woven hat shapes, in brown and white.

This entry is the only one after the main run in volumes 4, 5, and 6 that's included in "Shoshō Shōki Zu Byōbu". It was probably included because it's the only two-device entry after the main run, which seems to have suited the remaining space. This strengthens the idea that "Shoshō Shōki Zu Byōbu" was directly based on *O-umajirushi* despite the graphical differences. If so, the differences might have been intended as corrections.

31. 井上・河内守　三十一　ゐのうへ𛂞𛁈ち乃うゑ (ゐのうへかわちのかみ; Inoue Kawachi-no-kami):

The table of contents labels this section "Inoue Chikuko", referring to Inoue Masashige. Here, however, it's labeled "Inoue Kawachi-no-kami" ("Inoue, Provincial Governor of Kawachi"), referring to Masashige's nephew, Inoue Masatoshi, who has a section earlier in this volume. This seems to just be an error, with the table of contents likely correct.

A black nobori and a black maneki featuring a well frame mon, reflecting the first character of Inoue (井, i, meaning "well").

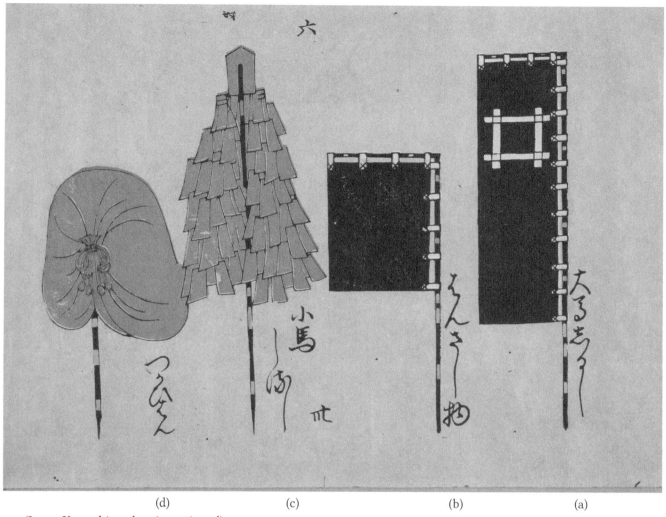

(d)   (c)   (b)   (a)

(Inoue Kawachi-no-kami, continued)

(a) 大享志る〆 (大馬しるし; ō-mumajirushi): great standard

A larger instance of the same well frame mon.

(b) そんさく物 (はんさし物; ban-sashimono): guard identifying object

(c) 小馬 くほく (小馬 しるし; ko-mumajirushi): lesser standard

A large red gohei. (See p. 12.)

(d) つゥひそん (つかひはん; tsukaiban): messengers

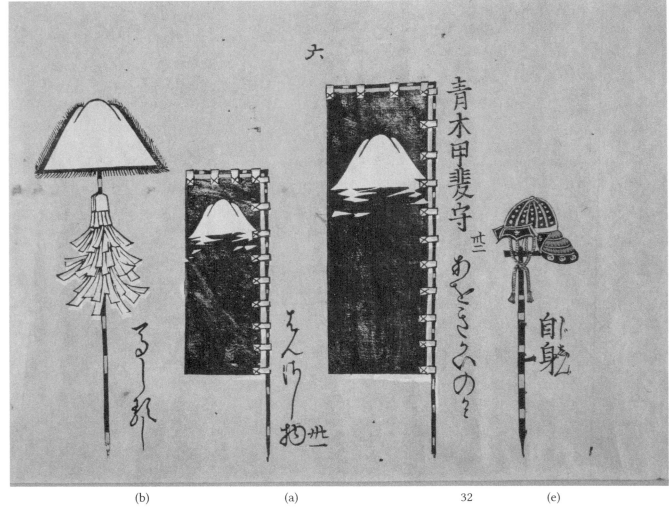

(b)   (a)   32   (e)

(Inoue Kawachi-no-kami, continued)

(e) 自身 (自身; jishin): personal [helmet]

32. 青木・甲斐守　卅二　あをきゝいのうミ (あをきかいのかみ; Aoki Kai-no-kami):
"Aoki, Provincial Governor of Kai", i.e., Aoki Shigekane (青木重兼) (1606–1682)[25, 青木家]

This mon is a depiction of Mount Fuji, known for being the highest mountain in Japan and an active volcano. Mount Fuji has many stories associated with it, and various etymologies suggest that its name means "immortal", "abundant soldiers", "without equal" or "never-ending".

(a) てんはくし物 (はんさし物; ban-sashimono): guard identifying object

(b) 多くれく (馬しるし; mumajirushi): battle standard

Similarly, this standard is a wooden representation of Mount Fuji, with a gohei, a Shintō ritual wand made with strips of paper, hanging below. The mountain has a border of fringe.

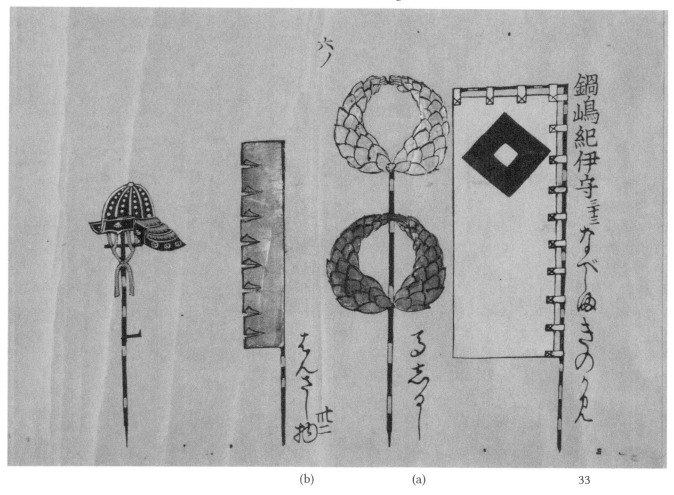

(b)　　　　　　　(a)　　　　　　33

33. 鍋嶋・紀伊守　三十三　なべ⌒ゐきのうゑ (なべしまきのかみ; Nabeshima Ki-no-kami):
"Nabeshima, Provincial Governor of Ki", i.e., Nabeshima Motoshige (鍋島元茂) (1602–1654)[25, 鍋島家]

This mon is a "nail puller", referring to its similarity in shape to the tip of a tool used by carpenters to remove nails, a kuginuki (釘抜き). This was a commonly-used mon among samurai. The idea of generating a large force using a simple tool was compelling, leading to an alternate name "manryoku" (万力), meaning thousandfold power. Another tradition reinterprets the "kugi" (nail) as "kuki" (九城), meaning "nine castles", suggesting that the bearer had much success conquering fortresses.[6, p. 142]

Similar motifs are the rhombus (p. 35) and the square (p. 13).

The (unrelated) Suganuma family uses a mon with a nail puller in a circle. Their mon is based on a story about their ancestor, Suganuma Sadauji. When invading Kakegawa Castle, he came to a closed gate. Undeterred, he tore off the crossbeam with his bare hands, thus serving as a human nail remover.[32, p. 1057]

(a) 馬志るし (馬しるし; mumajirushi): battle standard

This three-dimensional standard seems to depict two wisteria wreaths, one in gold and one in silver. Wisteria was associated with the Fujiwara clan, which ruled Japan in the Heian period (794–1185).

(b) てんさし物 (はんさし物; ban-sashimono): guard identifying object

A slashed banner in grey or silver, an unusual color in *O-umajirushi*.

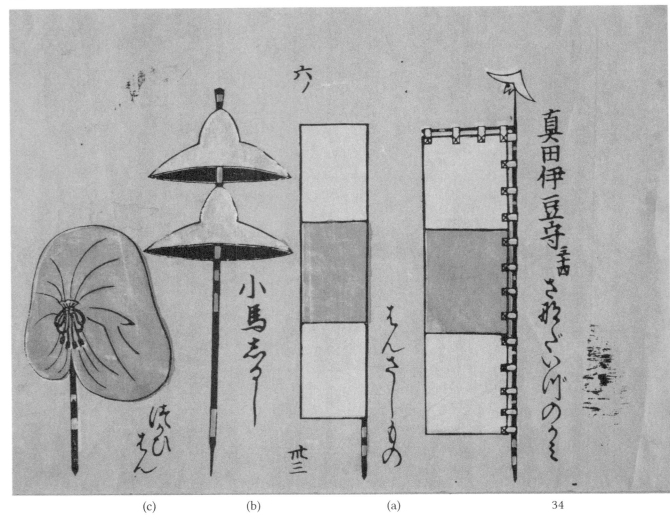

(c)   (b)   (a)   34

34. 真田・伊豆守　三十四　さねださいげのゝミ (さなだいづのかみ; Sanada Izu-no-kami): "Sanada, Provincial Governor of Izu", i.e., Sanada Nobuyuki (真田信之) (1566–1658)[1, p. 377]

This white nobori has a red horizontal band. Accompanying at the top of the pole is a stylized bird shape representing a wild goose (雁金; karigane)[49, p. 117]. The goose symbolized maneuverability.[12, p. 47]

(a) そんさしゝの (はんさしもの; ban-sashimono): guard identifying object

(b) 小馬まるく (小馬しるし; ko-mumajirushi): lesser standard

Two hats on a pole.

(c) ほうひ　そん (つかひ　はん; tsukaiban): messengers

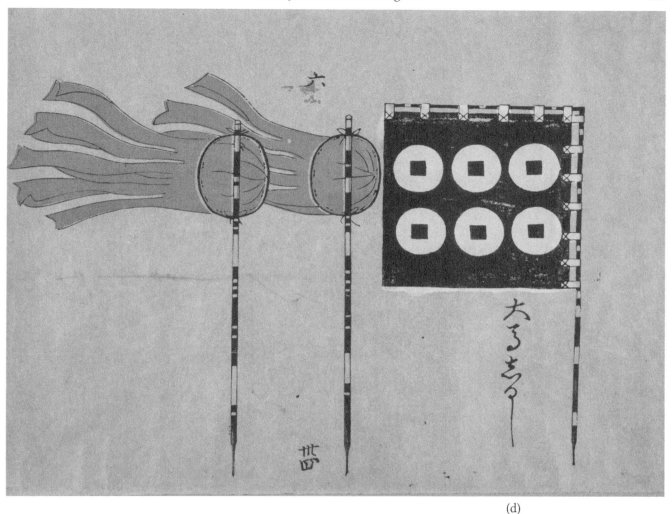

(d)

(Sanada Izu-no-kami, continued)

(d) 大ま志るく (大馬しるし; ō-mumajirushi): great standard

This is another instance of the six coins motif, also used by his son, Sanada Kawachi-no-kami (see p. 30). This depiction uses even simpler depictions of coins.

Unlabeled fukinuki

These fukinuki start the procession of unlabeled fukinuki that end *O-umajirushi*. This is the only instance in *O-umajirushi* of a series of identical devices or of an unlabeled fukinuki. This makes it seem unlikely that these are intended to be part of Sanada Izu-no-kami's section. While Andō Ukyō (see p. 65) used a red fukinuki as his primary device and other samurai used red fukinuki with dashi, it's unclear if there's any connection to a particular individual intended. It may have just been a bright, decorative way to end the work.

A kokuin (see p. xxxiv) from Edo Castle featuring a mon of a single coin using the same simplified design.
Photo by Eric Obershaw

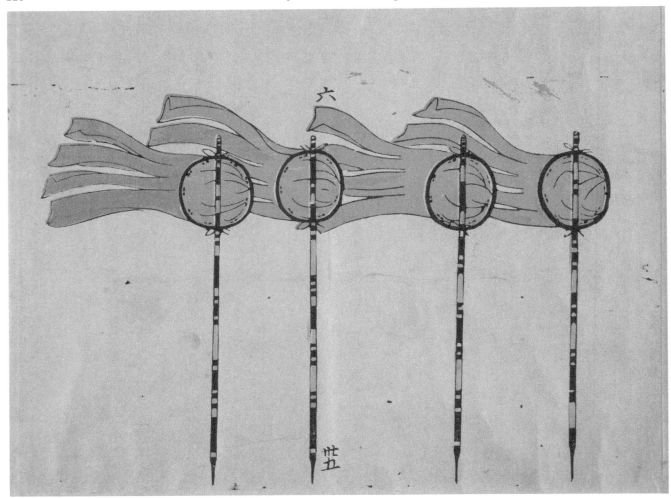

This last color page is repeated twice, with the same block; even the page number is identical. It's unclear if this was intentional to produce a large progression of fukinuki at the end of the final volume, or if it was a mistake. Regardless, this gives us some ability to see how two pages printed with the same blocks might differ, and thus some idea how other copies of *O-umajirushi* might have differed from this one. Note how the colors and registration are different between the two pages.

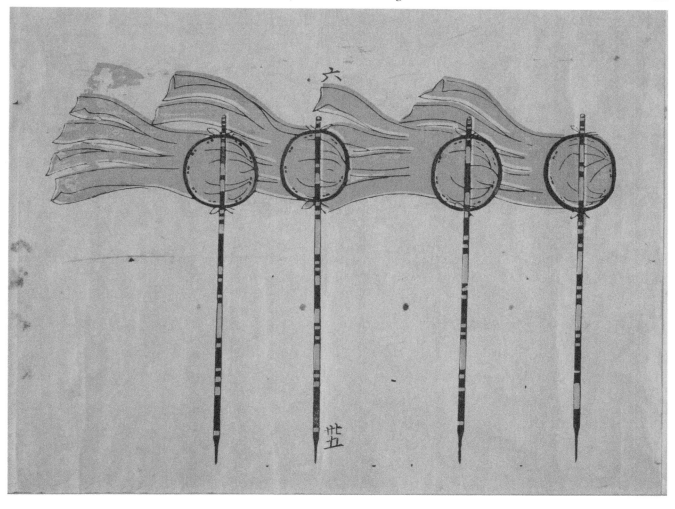

This is the second of the two identical pages. This instance has worse registration, less well-inked blocks, and also extra color in the upper-left where a corner of the red block perhaps briefly touched the paper prematurely.

Vol. 6

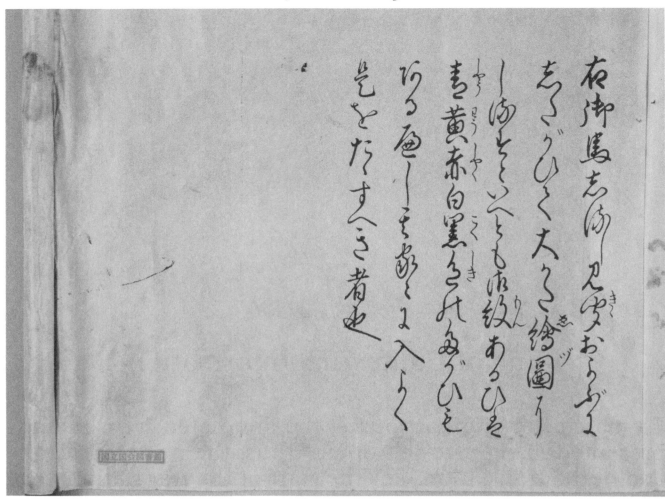

The closing paragraph here is printed with the same block as in the other volumes. This page being added to each volume is the only clear example of intentionally reused blocks in *O-umajirushi.* For translation and discussion, see p. 40.

End Volume 6

Appendix A: Hentaigana: Variant Phonetic Characters

Hentaigana are historical variant hiragana: different ways of writing the same syllable phonetically that convey no semantic difference. Since hiragana developed from simplifications of kanji used for their pronunciations, and many kanji sound the same, there were many different options for which character to use for a given sound, hence many equivalent hentaigana. There was no semantic difference between hentaigana, and they seem to have just been used for variety and as a mark of literacy. They were eventually eliminated by the spelling reform of the early 20th century. Classical Japanese writing used a variety of hentaigana, and *O-umajirushi* is no exception. Here we present each hentaigana used in *O-umajirushi* and its modern equivalent.

Hentaigana	Example Image	Modern Hiragana	Reading	Reference
あ		あ	a	あきつ記ゐグと让ろみ (Akitsuki Nagato-no-kami), p. 157
扰		お	o	扰さのミ七 (Ota no Sanshichi), p. 189
ろ		か	ka	ほろひ　そん (tsukaiban), p. 221
づ		が	ga	そせづハ志きぶ (Hasegawa Shikibu), p. 211
扚		か	ka	扚かくらそろ (monogashira horo), p. 211
がち		が	ga	あけちひうがうのろ尺 (Akechi Hyūga-no-kami), p. 189
記		き	ki	やまさ記ろい让ろみ (Yamasaki Kai-no-kami), p. 171
ぐ		げ	ge	ゐけさの志んゲん (Taketa no Shingen), p. 207
秀		げ	ge	むろ斗志やうぎん (Mukai Shōgen), p. 191
さい		こ	ko	秀きろそ讣さん (Takikawa Sakon), p. 208
ざい		ご	go	ざんげんさゐ (Gongen-sama), p. 2
讣		さ	sa	そん讣く扚 (ban-sashimono), p. 219

Hentaigana	Example Image	Modern Hiragana	Reading	Reference
ば		ざ	za	まき乃でんばう (Makino Denzō), p. 110
し		し	shi	大多志る∫ (ō-mumajirushi), p. 222
じ		じ	ji	自身 (jishin), p. 219
志		し	shi	大多志る∫ (ō-mumajirushi), p. 222
ざ		じ	ji	志∫ん (jishin), p. 210
そ		す	su	をゞさハ∫はゑ𛀙𛀝�そけ (Ogasawara Saemon-no-suke), p. 205
ろ		そ	so	みろくちいつものゝ�€ (Mizoguchi Izumo-no-kami), p. 60
さ		た	ta	おゝのぎやうぶ (Ota no Gyōbu), p. 213
ざ		だ	da	さね𛁈いげのゝ€ (Sanada Izu-no-kami), p. 221
ゐ		た	ta	ゐけさの志んゝ (Taketa no Shingen), p. 207
き		た	ta	きき𛁈そはさん (Takikawa Sakon), p. 208
つ		つ	tsu	つゝひ　そん (tsukaiban), p. 192
づ		づ	zu	𛀙づのひうゞのゝ€ (Mizuno Hyūga-no-kami), p. 162
川		つ	tsu	𛀙ろひそん (tsukaiban), p. 213
𛄚		づ	zu	さね𛁈いげのゝ€ (Sanada Izu-no-kami), p. 221
ほ		つ	tsu	ほろひ　そん (tsukaiban), p. 221
ぼ		づ	zu	まつざい∫ゐろぼろさ (Matsudaira Nakazukasa), p. 77
ほ		つ	tsu	ほろひそん (tsukaiban), p. 203
ほ		つ	tsu	いゐろ𛁈ほのゝ€ (Inagaki Tsu-no-kami), p. 86
く		て	te	志さぐひく (shitagai-te), Afterword, p. 40
る		な	na	きのしたくるい (Kinoshita Kunai), p. 210

Hentaigana	Example Image	Modern Hiragana	Reading	Reference
nec=''		な	na	されざいげのうミ (Sanada Izu-no-kami), p. 221
		な	na	たちそれひざれうミ (Tachihana Hida-no-kami), p. 174
		に	ni	幼々3 (ieie-ni), Afterword, p. 40
		に	ni	絵圖3 (wezu-ni), Afterword, p. 40
		に	ni	ふハのさきやう (Niwa no Sakyō), p. 160
		ね	ne	清藤瀬走るく (goza-fune o-jirushi), p. 216
		の	no	けうゆま走ろれうミ (Sakai Yamashiro-no-kami), p. 214
		の	no	ゐのうへろそち乃う尾 (Inoue Kawachi-no-kami), p. 217
		の	no	はきのうゐノぜう (Makino Uma-no-jō), p. 212
		は	ha	けうひ そん (tsukaiban), p. 221
		ば	ba	志ぞさくゆり (Shibata Shūri), p. 208
		は	ha	あるひゐ (aruhi-wa), Afterword, p. 40
		は	ha	そせグハ志きぶ (Hasegawa Shikibu), p. 211
		ば	ba	さうきバくひざのうみ (Sakakibara Hida-no-kami), p. 80
		ひ	hi	かそ志りむぜんれうミ (Kawashiri Hizen-no-kami), p. 208
		び	bi	おたハくむぜんのう尾 (Odawara Bizen-no-kami), p. 200
		ぶ	bu	ふるさひやうぬ (Furuta Hyōbu), p. 156
		へ	he	けるゑく (aru-beshi), Afterword, p. 40
		べ	be	ひよ乃おりゐ (Hine no Oribe), p. 77
		ほ	ho	物かくらやろ (monogashira horo), p. 211
		ぼ	bo	のぞり右同あ (nobori migi onaji sasae), p. 180

Hentaigana	Example Image	Modern Hiragana	Reading	Reference
か		ほ	ho	御かろ (o-horo), p. 13
ほ		ほ	ho	ほりおやゐ志ろ乃うミ (Horio Yamashiro-no-kami), p. 203
囪		ま	ma	なべくゐきの乃兒 (Nabeshima Ki-no-kami), p. 220
海		ま	ma	ほきのうゐノぜう (Makino Uma-no-jō), p. 212
三		み	mi	さ祀ざいげの乃ミ (Sanada Izu-no-kami), p. 221
兒		み	mi	なべくゐきの乃兒 (Nabeshima Ki-no-kami), p. 220
も		も	mo	そんさくゐの (ban-sashimono), p. 221
毛		も	mo	夛上ほくをれ (bajō sashimono), p. 212
中		や	ya	ほうゐ中ま志ろれうミ (Sakai Yamashiro-no-kami), p. 214
盈		や	ya	むう斗志盈うげん (Mukai Shōgen), p. 215
ゆ		ゆ	yu	志ぞさくゆり (Shibata Shūri), p. 208
四		ゆ	yu	志ぞさ志やり (Shibata Shūri), p. 189
ら		よ	yo	むでうくこう (Hideyoshi-kō), p. 119
く		ら	ra	まつくくぶんごの乃ミ (Matsukura Bungo-no-kami), p. 217
里		り	ri	を里ゐいき (Mori Naiki), p. 152
釟		る	ru	夛く釟く (mumajirushi), p. 219
海		る	ru	小馬 くほく (ko-mumajirushi), p. 218
語		ろ	ro	御ほろひもん 不語 (o-tsukaiban horo), p. 9
毛		わ	wa	ゐのうへろそち乃う兒 (Inoue Kawachi-no-kami), p. 217
升		ゐ	wi	むう斗志盈うげん (Mukai Shōgen), p. 215

Appendix B: Variant Kanji: Alternate Logographic Characters

Many kanji used in *O-umajirushi* are not identical to the forms used today. Some of these are simplified kuzushiji (cursive) forms. Others are minor graphical variations. In some cases, multiple forms of the same character are used in different places in *O-umajirushi*, showing that kanji overall were less standardized than in modern Japan.

Variant Form	Example Image	Modern Form	Reference
中	中	中	あ中さしもの (kachū sashimono), p. 215
丹	丹	丹	土方・丹後守 (Hijikata Tango-no-kami), p. 179
舟	舟	舟	御舟志るし (o-fune jirushi), p. 217
來	來	来	來嶋・出羽守 (Kurushima Dewa-no-kami), p. 160
羽	羽	羽	加藤・出羽守 (Katō Dewa-no-kami), p. 162
美	美	美	堀・美作守 (Hori no Mimasaka-no-kami), p. 195
飛	飛	飛	榊原・飛驒守 (Sakakibara Hida-no-kami), p. 110
馬	馬	馬	大馬志るし (ō-mumajirushi), p. 222
嶋	嶋	島	鍋嶋・紀伊守 (Nabeshima Ki-no-kami), p. 220
同	同	同	のぞり右同お (nobori migi onaji sasae), p. 180
左	左	左	瀧川・左近 (Takikawa Sakon), p. 208
式	式	式	長谷川・式部 (Hasegawa Shikibu), p. 211
尻	尻	尻	河尻・肥前守 (Kawashiri Hizen-no-kami), p. 208

Variant Form	Example Image	Modern Form	Reference
座		座	清座舟御志るく (goza-fune o-jirushi), p. 216
達		達	伊達・遠江守 (Date Tōtōmi-no-kami), p. 176
遠		遠	遠藤・但馬守 (Endō Tajima-no-kami), p. 177
圖		図	絵圖ろ (wezu-ni), Afterword, p. 40
武		武	武田・信玄 (Taketa no Shingen), p. 207
彦		彦	稲葉・彦六 (Inaba Hikoroku), p. 181
越		越	新庄・越前守 (Shinjō Echizen-no-kami), p. 169
三		三	織田・三七 (Ota no Sanshichi), p. 208
戸		戸	戸川・肥後守 (Togawa Higo-no-kami), p. 154
言		言	加賀・中納言 (Kaga no Chūnagon), p. 122
番		番	有馬・玄番 (Arima Genba), p. 115
お		支	のぞり右同お (nobori migi onaji sasae), p. 180
南		南	南部・信濃守 (Nanbu Shinano-no-kami), p. 56
壹		壱	生駒・壹岐守 (Ikoma Iki-no-kami), p. 97
真		真	真田・伊豆守 (Sanada Izu-no-kami), p. 221
倉		倉	板倉・主水 (Itakura Mondo), p. 107
倉		倉	松倉・豊後守 (Matsukura Bungo-no-kami), p. 217
玄		玄	武田・信玄 (Taketa no Shingen), p. 207
髙		高	髙千石ヨリ上ノ　さくの (taka sen-koku yori ue no), p. 127
龜		亀	龜井・能登守 (Kamei Noto-no-kami), p. 198

Variant Form	Example Image	Modern Form	Reference
若	若	若	松平・若狹守 (Matsudaira Wakasa-no-kami), p. 99
藝	藝	芸	淺野・安藝守 (Asano Aki-no-kami), p. 127
菓	菓	葉	稲菓・淡路守 (Inaba Awaji-no-kami), p. 182
藤	藤	藤	加藤・肥後守 (Katō Higo-no-kami), p. 206
藏	藏	蔵	青山・大藏大輔 (Aoyama Ōkura-no-taifu), p. 43
蔵	蔵	蔵	佐々・内蔵佐 (Sasa Kura-no-suke), p. 209
薩	薩	薩	松平・薩摩守 (Matsudaira Satsuma-no-kami), p. 127
宮	宮	宮	木下・宮内 (Kinoshita Kunai), p. 210
㝩	㝩	家	㝩半さくもの (kachū sashimono), p. 215
多	多	多	本多・伊勢守 (Honda Ise-no-kami), p. 192
条	条	条	北条・久太郎 (Hōjō Kyūtara), p. 209
見	見	見	見聞 (mikiki), Afterword, p. 40
承	承	丞	牧野・右馬丞 (Makino Uma-no-jō), p. 212
桒	桒	桑	桒山・左衛門佐 (Kuwayama Saemon-no-suke), p. 154
筑	筑	筑	井上・筑後 (Inoue Chikuko), p. 191
斐	斐	斐	青木・甲斐守 (Aoki Kai-no-kami), p. 219
雲	雲	雲	片桐・出雲守 (Katagiri Izumo-no-kami), p. 158
樂	樂	楽	酒井・雅樂頭 (Sakai Uta-no-kami), p. 32
監	監	監	向井・將監 (Mukai Shōgen), p. 215
監	監	監	松平・將監 (Matsudaira Shōgen), p. 82

Variant Form	Example Image	Modern Form	Reference
次		次	秀次公 (Hidetsugu-kō), p. 121
佀		但	遠藤・但馬守 (Endō Tajima-no-kami), p. 177
佐		佐	佐々・内蔵佐 (Sasa Kura-no-suke), p. 209
佭		使	使ゝん (tsukaiban), p. 94
信		信	武田・信玄 (Taketa no Shingen), p. 207
備		備	阿部・備中守 (Abe no Bitchū-no-kami), p. 135
御		御	御馬印・六之巻・目録 (O-umajirushi Roku-no-maki Mokuroku), Title, p. 186
御		御	御ふ志る〻 (o-fune jirushi), p. 217
御		御	大御馬志る〻 (ō-o-mumajirushi), p. 120
御		御	御ざ舟御志る〻 (goza-fune o-jirushi), p. 216
澤		沢	戸澤・右京 (Tosawa Ukyō), p. 69
淺		浅	淺野・安藝守 (Asano Aki-no-kami), p. 127
溝		溝	溝口・伯耆守 (Mizoguchi Hōki-no-kami), p. 103
濃		濃	鍋嶋・信濃守 (Nabeshima Shinano-no-kami), p. 167
彈		弾	上杉・彈正 (Uesugi Danjō), p. 21
攝		摂	稲垣・攝津守 (Inagaki Tsu-no-kami), p. 86
將		将	向井・將監 (Mukai Shōgen), p. 215
歧		岐	小笠原・壹歧守 (Ogasawara Iki-no-kami), p. 76
﨑		崎	山﨑・甲斐守 (Yamasaki Kai-no-kami), p. 171
幡		幡	本多・因幡守 (Honda Inaba-no-kami), p. 96

Appendices

Variant Form	Example Image	Modern Form	Reference
對	對	対	小出・對馬守 (Koide Tsushima-no-kami), p. 155
狹	狹	狭	松平・若狹守 (Matsudaira Wakasa-no-kami), p. 79
狭	校	狭	松平・若狭守 (Matsudaira Wakasa-no-kami), p. 99
杉	杉	杉	杉原・伯耆守 (Sugiwara Hōki-no-kami), p. 177
杢	杢	松	杢平・右衛門佐 (Matsudaira Emon-no-suke), p. 166
杢	杢	松	杢平・長門守 (Matsudaira Nagato-no-kami), p. 172
榊	榊	榊	榊原・飛驒守 (Sakakibara Hida-no-kami), p. 110
權	權	権	權現様 (Gongen-sama), p. 8
極	極	極	京極・丹後守 (Kyōgoku Tango-no-kami), p. 170
脇	脇	脇	脇坂・淡路守 (Wakisaka Awaji-no-kami), p. 66
扚	扚	物	そんさく扚 (ban-sashimono), p. 220
印	印	印	御馬印・六之巻・目録 (O-umajirushi Roku-no-maki Mokuroku), Title, p. 186
務	務	務	松平・中務 (Matsudaira Nakazukasa), p. 91
郎	郎	郎	北条・久太郎 (Hōjō Kyūtara), p. 209
細	細	細	細川・肥後守 (Hosokawa Higo-no-kami), p. 133
織	織	織	織田・三七 (Ota no Sanshichi), p. 208
織	織	織	織田・刑部 (Ota no Gyōbu), p. 213
紀	紀	紀	鍋嶋・紀伊守 (Nabeshima Ki-no-kami), p. 220
記	記	記	森・内記 (Mori Naiki), p. 175
輕	輕	軽	津輕・越中守 (Tsugaru Etchū-no-kami), p. 70

Variant Form	Example Image	Modern Form	Reference
野	野	野	牧野・右馬丞 (Makino Uma-no-jō), p. 212
駒	駒	駒	生駒・壹岐守 (Ikoma Iki-no-kami), p. 97
驒	驒	驒	蒲生・飛驒守 (Kamō Hida-no-kami), p. 207
鍋	鍋	鍋	鍋嶋・紀伊守 (Nabeshima Ki-no-kami), p. 220

Appendix C: Name Tables

These tables gather the names and titles used in *O-umajirushi* for easier examination. When a name is written more than one way in different parts of *O-umajirushi*, it is given more than one entry.

For each name or title, I give the following pieces of information:

- Reading as given in the translation, including sound changes.
- Literal reading, without sound changes, if different.
- Kanji as given in the text.
- Modern kanji, if different.
- Number of instances of this exact name or title in *O-umajirushi*.
- For titles, the translation. For names, the approximate meaning of the kanji.

For readings, kun (Chinese) readings are in bold, and on (Japanese) readings are in normal font. For jukujikun, special word readings that are not divided into a reading for each kanji, italics are used.

For further information on historical Japanese naming, refer to *Name Construction in Mediæval Japan*,[50] which was instrumental in preparing this appendix.

Titles

Reading	Literal Reading	Original	Modern	#	Translation
A·ki-no-kami		安藝守	安芸守	1	Governor of Aki
A·wa-no-kami		阿波守		1	Governor of Awa
A·wa-no-kami	**A·ha**-no-kami	阿波守		1	Governor of Awa
Awa·ji-no-kami	Awa·dji-no-kami	淡路守		1	Governor of Awaji
Awa·ji-no-kami	Aha·dji-no-kami	淡路守		1	Governor of Awaji
no **Bit·chū**-no-kami	no **Bitsu·chiu**-no-kami	備中守	備中守	1	Governor of Bitchū
Bi·zen no **Sai·shō**	**Bi·zen** no **Sai·shiyau**	備前宰相		1	State Councilor of Bizen
Bi·zen-no-kami		備前守		1	Governor of Bizen
Bun·go-no-kami		豊後守		1	Governor of Bungo
Bu·zen-no-kami		豊前守		1	Governor of Buzen
Chiku·ko		筑後	筑後	1	[Governor of] Chikugo
no **Chū·na·gon**	no **Chiu·na·gon**	中納言	中納言	1	Middle Councilor
Chū·na·gon-sama	**Chiu·na·gon**-sama	中納言様	中納言様	1	Middle Councilor
Dai·na·gon-sama		大納言様	大納言様	2	Major Councilor
Dai·zen		大膳		1	Great Dining [official]
Dan·jō	**Dan·jiyau**	彈正	弾正	1	Imperial Prosecuting and Investigating [official]
De·wa-no-kami	De·ha-no-kami	出羽守	出羽守	3	Governor of Dewa
Echi·go-no-kami	**Wechi·go**-no-kami	越後守	越後守	1	Governor of Echigo
Echi·zen no **Sai·shō**-tono	**Wechi·zen** no **Sai·shiyau**-tono	越前宰相殿	越前宰相殿	1	State Councilor of Echizen

Reading	Literal Reading	Original	Modern	#	Translation
Echi·zen-no-kami	**Wechi·zen**-no-kami	越前守	越前守	2	Governor of Echizen
·**E·mon**-no-suke	·**We·mon**-no-suke	右衛門佗	右衛門佐	1	Assistant [Dir.] of the Right Gate Guards
·**E·mon**-no-suke	·**We·mon**-no-suke	右衛門佐		1	Assistant [Dir.] of the Right Gate Guards
·**E·mon**-no-**tai·fu**	·**We·mon**-no-**tai·fu**	右衛門大夫	右衛門大夫	1	Greater Director of the Right Gate Guards
·**E·mon**-no-**tai·fu**	·**We·mon**-no-**tai·fu**	右衛門大輔	右衛門大輔	1	Greater Assistant [Dir.] of the Right Gate Guards
Et·chū-no-kami	**Wetsu·chiu**-no-kami	越中守	越中守	1	Governor of Etchū
Gen·ba		玄番	玄番	1	Priests and Foreigners Bureau [official]
Gyō·bu	**Giyau·bu**	刑部		1	Ministry of Justice [official]
no **Gyō·bu**	no **Giyau·bu**	刑部		1	Ministry of Justice [official]
Hi·da-no-kami		飛驒守	飛驒守	1	Governor of Hida
Hi·da-no-kami		飛驒守	飛驒守	2	Governor of Hida
Hi·go-no-kami		肥後守		4	Governor of Higo
Hi·zen-no-kami		肥前守		3	Governor of Hizen
Hō·ki-no-kami	**Hau·ki**-no-kami	伯耆守		2	Governor of Hōki
Hyō·bu	**Hiyau·bu**	兵部		2	Ministry of War [official]
Hyū·ga-no-kami	Hiu·ga-no-kami	日向守		3	Governor of Hyūga
I·ki-no-kami		壹歧守	壱岐守	1	Governor of Iki
I·ki-no-kami		壹歧守	壱岐守	1	Governor of Iki
Ina·ba-no-kami		因幡守	因幡守	1	Governor of Inaba
I·se-no-kami		伊勢守		3	Governor of Ise
Iwa·mi-no-kami		石見守		2	Governor of Iwami
I·zu-no-kami	**I·dzu**-no-kami	伊豆守		1	Governor of Izu
I·zu-no-kami	**I·tsu**-no-kami	伊豆守		1	Governor of Izu
·Izumi-no-kami	·Idzumi-no-kami	和泉守		1	Governor of Izumi
I·zumo-no-kami	I·dzumo-no-kami	出雲守	出雲守	3	Governor of Izumo
I·zumo-no-kami	I·tsumo-no-kami	出雲守	出雲守	1	Governor of Izumo
no I·zumo-no-kami	no I·dzumo-no-kami	出雲守	出雲守	1	Governor of Izumo
Ka·ga-no-kami		加賀守		2	Governor of Kaga
Ka·i-no-kami		甲斐守	甲斐守	5	Governor of Kai
no **Ka·mon**-no-kami		掃部頭		1	Head of the Bureau of Palace Cleaning
Ka·mon-no-suke		掃部助		1	Assistant [Dir.] of the Bureau of Palace Cleaning
Kawa·chi-no-kami		河内守		4	Governor of Kawachi
Ken·motsu		監物	監物	1	Goods Oversight [official]
Ki·-no-kami		紀伊守	紀伊守	1	Governor of Ki
-kō	**-kou**	公		4	Noble Lord
Ku·nai		宮内	宮内	2	Imperial Household [official]
·Kura-no-suke		内蔵佗	内蔵佐	1	Assistant [Dir.] of the Inner Treasury

Reading	Literal Reading	Original	Modern	#	Translation
no **Mi·masaka**-no-kami		美作守	美作守	1	Governor of Mimasaka
Min·bu		民部		1	Ministry of Popular Affairs [official]
Mi·no-no-kami		美濃守	美濃守	3	Governor of Mino
Mon·do		主水		1	Water, Ice, and Porridge Office [official]
Mu·tsu-no-kami		陸奥守		1	Governor of Mutsu
Naga·to-no-kami		長門守		3	Governor of Nagato
Nai·ki		内記	内記	1	Imperial Documents Agency [officer]
Nai·zen		内膳		1	Inner Dining [official]
Naka·zukasa	Naka·dzukasa	中務	中務	1	Ministry of the Center [official]
No·to-no-kami		能登守		1	Governor of Noto
O·ki-no-kami		隠岐守	隠岐守	1	Governor of Oki
no Ori·be		織部	織部	1	Weaving Bureau [official]
no Ō·i-no-kami	no Oho·i-no-kami	大炊頭		1	Head of the Bureau of Palace Kitchens
Ō·kura-no-tai·fu	Oho·kura-no-tai·fu	大藏大輔	大蔵大輔	1	Greater Assistant [Dir.] of Finance
Sa·e·mon-no-suke	**Sa·we·mon**-no-suke	左衛門佐	左衛門佐	2	Assistant [Dir.] of the Left Gate Guards
Sa·e·mon-no-suke	**Sa·we·mon**-no-suke	左衛門佐	左衛門佐	1	Assistant [Dir.] of the Left Gate Guards
Sa·kon		左近	左近	1	[commander of the] Left Inner [Imperial Guard]
Sa·kyō	**Sa·kiyau**	左京	左京	1	Left Capital Administration [official]
no **Sa·kyō**	no **Sa·kiyau**	左京	左京	1	Left Capital Administration [official]
Sa·ma		左馬	左馬	1	Left Horses [official]
Sa·ma-no-suke		左馬助	左馬助	1	Assistant [Dir.] of the Left Horses
Sanu·ki-no-kami		讃岐守	讃岐守	1	Governor of Sanuki
Satsu·ma-no-kami		薩摩守	薩摩守	1	Governor of Satsuma
Shiki·bu		式部	式部	1	Ministry of Ceremonies [official]
Shiki·bu-no-**shō·**	**Shiki·bu**-no-**seu·**	式部少輔	式部少輔	1	Lesser Assistant [Dir.] of the Ministry of Ceremonies
Shi·ma-no-kami		志摩守		1	Governor of Shima
Shimo·osa-no-kami	Shimo·wosa-no-kami	下総守		2	Governor of Shimōsa
Shina·no-no-kami		信濃守	信濃守	1	Governor of Shinano
Shina·no-no-kami		信濃守	信濃守	3	Governor of Shinano
Shō·gen	**Shiyau·gen**	將監	将監	2	Commander [of the Imperial Guards]
Shū·ri	**Shiyu·ri**	修理		1	Repairing Agency [official]

Reading	Literal Reading	Original	Modern	#	Translation
Shū·ri-no-suke	**Shiyu·ri**-no-suke	修理助		1	Assistant [Dir.] of the Repairing Agency
Su·ō-no-kami	**Su·hau**-no-kami	周防守		2	Governor of Suō
Taji·ma-no-kami		但馬守	但馬守	1	Governor of Tajima
Tan·ba-no-kami		丹波守	丹波守	2	Governor of Tanba
Tan·go-no-kami		丹後守	丹後守	3	Governor of Tango
no **Tan·go**-no-kami		丹後守	丹後守	1	Governor of Tango
Tonomo		主殿		1	Palace Stores [official]
To·sa-no-kami		土佐守	土佐守	1	Governor of Tosa
Tō·tōmi-no-kami	Towo·taumi-no-kami	遠江守	遠江守	1	Governor of Tōtōmi
Tsu-no-kami		攝津守	摂津守	2	Governor of Tsu
Tsushi·ma-no-kami		對馬守	対馬守	1	Governor of Tsushima
no Tsushi·ma-no-kami		對馬守	対馬守	1	Governor of Tsushima
U·kon-no-**tai·fu**		右近大夫		1	Greater Director of the Right Inner [Imperial Guard]
U·kyō	**U·kiyau**	右京		3	Right Capital Administration [official]
U·kyō-no-**tai·fu**	**U·kiyau**-no-**tai·fu**	右京大輔		1	Greater Assistant [Dir.] of Right Capital Administration
U·ma-no-**jō**	**U·ma**-no-**zeu**	右馬丞	右馬丞	1	Inspector of the Right Stables Bureau
U·ma-no-kami		右馬頭		1	Head of the Right Horse Bureau
Une·me-no-kami		采女正		1	Head of the Imperial Ladies-in-waiting
U·ta-no-kami		雅樂頭	雅楽頭	1	Head of the Bureau of Court Music
Waka·sa-no-kami		若狹守	若狭守	1	Governor of Wakasa
Yama·shiro-no-kami		山城守		3	Governor of Yamashiro
Yamato-no-kami		大和守		3	Governor of Yamato

Surnames

Reading	Literal Reading	Original	Modern	#	Meaning
A·be		阿部		1	corner + part
Ake·chi		明知		1	bright + know
Aki·ta		秋田		1	autumn + rice field
Aki·tsuki		秋月		1	autumn + moon
An·dō	**An·dou**	安藤	安藤	1	quiet + wisteria
Ao·ki	Awo·ki	青木		1	blue/green + tree
Ao·yama	Aho·yama	青山		1	blue/green + mountain
Ari·ma		有馬		3	exist/have + horse
Asa·no		淺野	浅野	2	shallow + plains
Da·te		伊達	伊達	1	that + attain/plural
Do·i		土井		1	earth + a well
En·dō	**Wen·dou**	遠藤	遠藤	1	distant + wisteria
Furu·ta		古田		1	old + rice field
Ha·se·gawa		長谷川		1	chief/long + valley + river
Hayashi		林		1	woods
Hiji·kata	Hidji·kata	土方		2	earth + direction
Hi·ne		日根		1	sun + root
Hitotsu·yanagi		一柳		1	one + willow
Hon·da		本多		3	source/main + many
Hon·da		本田		1	source/main + rice field
Hori		堀		2	moat
Hori·o		堀尾		1	moat + tail/slope
Ho·shina		保科		1	protect + section
Hoso·kawa	Hoso·kaha	細川	細川	1	narrow + river
Hō·jō	**Hou·deu**	北条	北条	1	north + paragraph/line
I·i	**Wi·i**	井伊		1	a well + that
Ike·da		池田		1	pond + rice field
I·koma		生駒		1	life + foal
Ina·ba		稲葉	稲葉	1	rice plant + leaf
Ina·ba		稲葉		2	rice plant + leaf
Ina·gaki		稲垣		1	rice plant + fence
I·no·ue	I·no·uhe	井上		2	a well + above/upper
Ishi·kawa		石川		1	stone + river
Ita·kura		板倉	板倉	1	board + storehouse
Ita·kura		板倉		1	board + storehouse
I·tō	**I·tou**	伊東		1	that + east
Ka·ga		加賀		1	increase + joy
Kame·i	Kame·wi	龜井	亀井	1	tortoise + a well
Kamo·u	Kama·u	蒲生		1	cattail + life
Kana·mori		金森		1	gold + forest
Kata·giri		片桐		1	part of + paulownia
Ka·tō	**Ka·tou**	加藤	加藤	3	increase + wisteria

Reading	Literal Reading	Original	Modern	#	Meaning
Kawa·shiri		河尻		1	river + rear
Ki·i		紀伊	紀伊	1	history + that
Ki·no·shita		木下		2	tree + under/lower
Ko·ide		小出		2	small + exit
Kō·riki	**Kau·riki**	髙力	高力	1	tall + strength
Ku·ki		九鬼		1	nine + oni/demon
Kuro·da		黒田		2	black + rice field
Kuru·shima		來嶋	来島	1	come + island
Kuwa·yama		桒山	桑山	2	mulberry + mountain
Kyō·goku	**Kiyau·goku**	京極	京極	2	capital + extremely
Mae·da	Mahe·da	前田		1	ahead + rice field
Maki·no		牧野	牧野	2	pasture + plains
Matsu·daira		杢平	松平	5	pine + peace/flat
Matsu·daira		杢平	松平	2	pine + peace/flat
Matsu·daira		松平		17	pine + peace/flat
Matsu·daira	Matsu·taira	松平		3	pine + peace/flat
Matsu·kura		松倉	松倉	1	pine + storehouse
Matsu·ra		松浦		1	pine + inlet
Matsu·shita		松下		1	pine + under/lower
Mi·to		水戸	水戸	1	water + door
Mizo·guchi		溝口	溝口	2	ditch + mouth
Mizu·no	Midzu·no	水野	水野	1	water + plains
Mizu·no·ya	Midzu·no·ya	水谷		1	water + valley
Mori		森		1	forest
Mo·ri		毛利		2	hair + advantage/profit
Muka·i	Muka·wi	向井		1	facing + a well
Nabe·shima		鍋嶋	鍋島	2	pot + island
Naga·i	Naga·wi	永井		1	eternity + a well
Naga·i		永井		1	eternity + a well
Nai·tō	**Nai·tou**	内藤	内藤	2	inside + wisteria
Naka·gawa		中川		1	middle + river
Nan·bu		南部	南部	1	south + part
Ni·wa	Ni·ha	丹羽	丹羽	1	vermillion + feather
O·da·wara	O·da·hara	太田原		1	plump + rice field + field
O·gasa·wara	Wo·kasa·hara	小笠原		2	small + bamboo hat + field
O·gasa·wara	Wo·gasa·hara	小笠原		1	small + bamboo hat + field
O·gasa·wara	O·kasa·hara	小笠原		1	small + bamboo hat + field
Oka·be	Woka·be	岡部		1	hill + part
Oku·daira		奥平		1	interior + peace/flat
O·ta		織田	織田	3	weave + rice field
O·wari	O·hari	尾張		1	tail/slope + lengthen
Ō·ku·bo	**Oho·ku·bo**	大久保		1	big + long time + protect
Ō·mura	Oho·mura	大村		1	big + village
Saka·i		酒井		1	alcohol + a well

Reading	Literal Reading	Original	Modern	#	Meaning
Saka·i	Saka·wi	酒井		4	alcohol + a well
Sakaki·bara		榊原	榊原	1	sakaki tree + field
Sana·da		真田	真田	2	true/reality + rice field
Sa·sa		佐々	佐々	1	assist + (repetition mark)
Sa·take		佐竹		1	assist + bamboo
Sen·goku		仙石		1	hermit + stone
Shiba·ta		柴田		1	brushwood + rice field
Shima·zu	Shima·tsu	嶋津	島津	1	island + harbor
Shin·jō	**Shin·jiyau**	新庄		1	new + manor
Sō	**Sou**	宗		1	sect
Sugi·wara	Sugi·hara	杉原	杉原	1	cedar + field
Tachi·hana		立花		1	stand + flower
Take·ta		武田	武田	1	martial + rice field
Taki·kawa	Taki·kaha	瀧川		1	waterfall + river
Tera·zawa	Tera·zaha	寺澤	寺沢	1	temple + swamp
To·da		戸田	戸田	1	door + rice field
To·gawa		戸川	戸川	1	door + river
Tori·i	Tori·wi	鳥居		1	bird + reside
To·sawa	To·saha	戸澤	戸沢	1	door + swamp
Tō·dō	**Tou·dou**	藤堂	藤堂	1	wisteria + hall
Tsuchi·ya		土屋		1	earth + roof/shop
Tsu·garu		津輕	津軽	1	harbor + light/minor
Ue·sugi		上杉		1	above/upper + cedar
Waki·saka		脇坂	脇坂	1	side + slope
Yama·saki		山﨑	山崎	1	mountain + cape

Nanori (Formal Given Names)

Reading	Literal Reading	Original	Modern	#	Meaning
Hide·tsugu		秀次	秀次	1	excel + next
Hide·yoshi		秀吉		1	excel + good fortune
Kyū·ta·ra	**Kiu·ta·ra**	久太郎	久太郎	1	long time + plump + son
Masa·mune		まさむね	政宗	1	government + sect
Nobu·naga		信長	信長	1	faith/trust + chief/long
Nobu·tada		信忠	信忠	1	faith/trust + loyalty
Shin·ta·ra		新太郎	新太郎	1	new + plump + son

Yobina/Tsūshō (Informal Given Names)

Reading	Literal Reading	Original	Modern	#	Meaning
Ge·ki		外記	外記	1	outside + chronicle
Hiko·**roku**		彦六		1	young scholar + six
Man·kichi		万吉		1	10,000 + good fortune
no **Sa·mon**		左門	左門	1	left + gate
no **San·shichi**		三七		1	three + seven

Personal Hōmyō (Buddhist Names)

Reading	Literal Reading	Original	Modern	#	Meaning
Den·zō	**Den·zau**	傳蔵	傳蔵	1	propagate + storehouse
no **Shin·gen**		信玄	信玄	1	faith/trust + mysterious

Posthumous Hōmyō (Buddhist Names)

Reading	Literal Reading	Original	Modern	#	Meaning
Gon·gen-sama		權現様	権現様	1	incarnation of a buddha in a kami + honorific
Tai·toku·in-sama	**Tai·toku·win**-sama	台徳院様		1	pedestal + virtue + institution + honorific

Bibliography

[1] Abe Takeshi (阿部猛) and Nishimura Keiko (西村圭子). *Sengoku Jinmei Jiten (*戦国人名事典; *"Sengoku Personal Name Encyclopedia"*). Shin Jinbutsu Ōraisha (新人物往来社), 1987.

[2] Amimoto Mitsuyoshi (網本光悦). *Ichi kara shiritai! Kamon to Myōji: Karaa Han* (イチから知りたい！家紋と名字：カラー版; *"I want to understand from scratch! Family Crests and Surnames: Color Edition"*). Seitōs a(西東社), 2014.

[3] *Art of the Samurai: Japanese Arms and Armor, 1156–1868*. The Metropolitan Museum of Art, 2009.

[4] "Buke no Kamon no Yurai o Saguru (武家の家紋の由来を探る; 'Search for the Origins of Samurai Family Crests')". http://www2.harimaya.com/sengoku/bukemon.html.

[5] "Denshi Kuzushiji Jiten Dētabēsu (電子くずし字字典データベース; "Electronic Broken Character Dictionary Database")". http://clioz39.hi.u-tokyo.ac.jp/ships/ZClient/W34/.

A searchable database of examples of Japanese characters from various historical Japanese documents, with citations. Excellent resource for deciphering historical hentaigana and kuzushiji.

[6] Dower, John. *The Elements of Japanese Design: A Handbook of Family Crests, Heraldry & Symbolism*. Weatherhill, 2005.

In addition to a large number of mon, organized by motif, Dower provides notes about each motif, discussing its history and symbolism. While some notes are lighter on facts than others, this is one of the most useful books on mon available in English for those interested in historical perspective. Its introduction also provides general historical context.

[7] *Edo Bakufu Yakushoku Bukan Hennen Shūsei (*江戸幕府役職武鑑編年集成; *"Edo Shōgunate Managerial Position Books of Heraldry Compilation by Year Aggregation"*). Vol. 1. Tōyō Shorin (東洋書林), 1996.

[8] *Edo Bungaku 25: Tokushū: Tashoku-zuri no Rekishi to Haikai Ichimai-zuri (*江戸文学 25：特集：多色摺の歴史と俳諧一枚摺; *"Edo Literature 25: Feature: The History of Many-Colored Prints and Haikai Single-Sheet Prints"*). Ed. Kira Sueo (雲英末雄). Perikan-sha (ぺりかん社), 2002.

[9] *Family Crests of Japan*. Stone Bridge Press, 2007.

[10] Griffis, William Elliot. *Japan: in History, Folk-Lore and Art*. The Riverside Press, 1892.

[11] Habu Michihide (羽生道英). *Tokugawa Iemitsu: Eimei, Buyū no Sandai Shōgun (*徳川家光：英明・武勇の三代将軍; *"Tokugawa Iemitsu: Third-generation Shōgun of Intelligence and Bravery"*). PHP Kenkyūjo (PHP研究所), 1999.

[12] Hawley, W. M. and Kei Kaneda Chappelear (金田景). *Mon: the Japanese Family Crest*. W. M. Hawley, 1994.

[13] Hearn, Lafcadio. *The Romance of the Milky Way, and Other Studies & Stories*. Houghton Mifflin, 1905.

[14] "Ippongi Shinbun (一本気新聞; 'One-Track Mind Newspaper')". http://www.ippongi.com/.

[15] Izumi Seiji (和泉清司). *Edo Bakufu Daikangashira Monjo Shūsei (*江戸幕府代官頭文書集成; *"Edo Shōgunate Chief Magestrate Document Aggregation"*). Bunken Shuppan (文献出版), 1999.

[16] *Japanese Emblems and Designs*. Ed. Walter Amstutz. Dover Publications, 1994.

[17] *Kamon no Subete ga Wakaru Hon: Mite Tanoshii Yonde Manaberu* (家紋のすべてがわかる本：見て楽しい読んで学べる; *"All is Understood about Crests Book: Fun to See Read and Learn"*). Ed. Takasawa Hitoshi (高沢等). PHP Kenkyūjo (PHP研究所), 2012.

[18] "Kamon no Yurai (家紋の由来; 'The Origins of Family Crests')". http://www.harimaya.com/o_kamon1/yurai/a_yurai/yurai.html.

[19] Katō Tetsuo (加藤鐵雄). *Sengoku Bushō "Hata Sashimono" Taikan* (戦国武将「旗指物」大鑑; *"Sengoku Military Commanders 'Flags and Banners' Encyclopedia"*). Sairyūsha (彩流社), 2010.

[20] *Kenmon Shokamon* (見聞諸家紋; *"Various Observed Family Crests"*). http://dl.ndl.go.jp/info:ndljp/pid/2533035 1467–1470.

This is a scan by the National Diet Library Digital Collections of an 1809 copy of *Kenmon Shokamon*; this copy is listed by the later alternate title *Higashiyama-dono Monchō* (東山殿紋帳, "Higashiyama-dono Crest Register"), referring to Ashikaga Yoshimasa, shōgun when *Kenmon Shokamon* was originally published. It has annotations in red presumably added at some point after the original *Kenmon Shokamon*.

[21] Komori, N. "Rekishiteki Kanatsukai Kyōshitsu (歴史的仮名遣い教室; 'Historical Kana Orthography Classroom')". http://www5a.biglobe.ne.jp/accent/kana/.

[22] "Kotobank (コトバンク)". https://kotobank.jp/.

[23] *Kuzushiji Kaidoku Jiten* (くずし字解読辞典; *"Cursive Deciphering Dictionary"*). Ed. Kodama Kōta (児玉 幸多). Tōkyōdō Shuppan (東京堂出版), 1993.

[24] McClatchie, Thomas R. H. "Japanese Heraldry". *Transactions of the Asiatic Society of Japan*. Volume V, Number I 187? pp. 1–23.

[25] Mizuno Hyūga-no-kami (水野日向守). "Edo Jidai Daimyō Sōran (江戸時代大名総覧; 'Edo Period Daimyō Guide')". http://homepage3.nifty.com/hyuuga/daimyou/daimyou.htm.

A collection of tables of geneaological information compiled from *Kansei Chōshū Shoka Fu* (寛政重修諸家譜; "Kansei [Era] Revised Various Families' Genealogy"), a manuscript published around 1800.

[26] Morimoto Shigeru (森本繁). *Konishi Yukinaga* (小西行長). Gakken, 2010.

[27] Munsterberg, Hugo. *The Japanese Print: A Historical Guide*. Weatherhill, 1982.

[28] "Nihon Kirishitan Monogatari (日本キリシタン物語; 'The Story of the Japanese Christians')". http://www.pauline.or.jp/kirishitanstory/.

[29] *Nihon Kokugo Daijiten: Dai Nihan* (日本国語大辞典　第二版; *"Japan National Language Great Dictionary: Second Edition"*). Shōgakkan (小学館), 2000–2002.

[30] *Nihon Monshō Daizukan: Rekishi to Kurashi no Naka no Minshō 5000* (日本紋章大図鑑―歴史と暮らしの中の紋章5000; *"Japanese Crest Big Illustrated Encyclopedia: 5000 Crests amon? their History and Circumstances"*). Also known as *A Pictorial Book of Japanese Heraldry: The Mon*. Hyakunensha, 1978.

[31] Nobunaga Ohno (大野信長). *Sengoku Bushō 100: Kamon, Hata, Umajirushi FILE* (戦国武将100：家紋・旗・馬印FILE; *"100 Sengoku Military Commanders: Family Crests, Banners, and Battle Standards File"*). Gakken, 2009.

[32] Numata Raisuke (沼田頼輔). *Nihon Monshōgaku* (日本紋章学; *"Japan Heraldry"*). http://kindai.ndl.go.jp/info:ndljp/pid/980775?__lang=en Meiji Shoin (明治書院), 1926.

[33] Nekhet. "Kakei Risuto (家系リスト; 'Family Lineage List')".
http://reichsarchiv.jp/%E5%AE%B6%E7%B3%BB%E3%83%AA%E3%82%B9%E3%83%88.

[34] Obershaw, Eric. "Jcastle: Guide to Japanese Castles". http://www.jcastle.info/.

[35] *O-umajirushi (御馬印)*. Second edition. http://cudl.lib.cam.ac.uk/view/PR-FJ-00970 Cambridge University
Library, 1656.

[36] "O-umajirushi Rokkan (御馬印　6 巻; 'O-umajirushi Six Volumes')". *National Diet Library Digital Collections.*
http://dl.ndl.go.jp/info:ndljp/pid/1288484?__lang=en 1624–1644.

A complete scan of a copy of *O-umajirushi* with some basic contextual information.

[37] Sakuraki, Shin'ichi, Helen Wang and Peter Kornicki. "Catalogue of the Japanese Coin Collection (pre-Meiji) at the
British Museum".
http://www.britishmuseum.org/pdf/Catalogue%20of%20the%20Japanese%20Coin%20Collection.pdf
The British Museum, 2010.

[38] Salter, Rebecca. *Japanese Woodblock Printing*. University of Hawaii Press, 2001.

[39] Satow, Ernest. "On the Early History of Printing in Japan". *Transactions of the Asiatic Society of Japan*. Volume X
1881. pp. 48–83.

[40] Seal, F. W. and C. E. West. "Sengoku Biographical Dictionary".
http://www.samurai-archives.com/dictionary/index.html 2003.

[41] "Shinmon". *Encyclopedia of Shinto*. http://k-amc.kokugakuin.ac.jp/DM/dbTop.do?class_name=col_eos.

[42] Shirane, Haruo. *Classical Japanese: A Grammar*. Columbia University Press, 2005.

[43] Shirane, Haruo. *Classical Japanese Reader and Essential Dictionary*. Columbia University Press, 2007.

[44] *Shoshō Kisei Zu (諸将旗旌図; "Various Commanders' Flag and Banner Illustrations")*.
http://www.library.yonezawa.yamagata.jp/dg/AA170.html 1637.

[45] "Shoshō Shōki Zu Byōbu (諸将旌旗図屏風; 'Various Commanders' Flag and Banner Illustrations Folding Screen')".
Ōsaka Castle Museum Collection, 1632.

The numbering used in these citations is based on the numbering used in the copy available at
http://kyotobenrido.com/shopdetail/000000000825/.

[46] Stone, George Cameron. *A Glossary of the Construction, Decoration and Use of Arms and Armor in All Countries and in
All Times*. Dover Publications, 1999.

[47] Strange, M.J.S., Edward F. *Japanese Illustration: A History of the Arts of Wood-cutting and Colour Printing in Japan*.
George Bell and Sons, 1904.

[48] Takahashi Ken'ichi (高橋賢一). *Hata Sashimono (旗指物; "Banners and Sashimono")*. Shin Jinbutsu Ōraisha
(新人物往来社), 1996.

[49] Takasawa Hitoshi (高澤等). *Kamon no Jiten (家紋の事典; "Family Crest Encyclopedia")*. Ed. Chikano Shigeru
(千鹿野茂). Tōkyōdō Shuppan (東京堂出版), 2008.

[50] Throndardottir, Solveig. *Name Construction in Mediæval Japan: Revised Edition*. Potboiler Press, 2004.

[51] Totman, Conrad. *Japan before Perry: A Short History*. University of California Press, 2008.

[52] Turnbull, Stephen. *Samurai Heraldry*. Osprey Publishing, 2002.

[53] Turnbull, Stephen. *The Samurai Sourcebook*. Cassell & Co, 2000.

Appendices

[54] Turnbull, Stephen. *War in Japan 1467–1615*. Osprey Publishing, 2002.

[55] Yamashita Masaya (山下昌也). *Ieyasu no Kashindan: Tenka o Totta Sengoku Saikyō Gundan* (家康の家臣団：天下を取った戦国最強軍団; *"Ieyasu's Group of Retainers: the Strongest Sengoku Army Corps that Took the Whole Country"*). Gakken M Bunko, 2011.

[56] Yoshida, Kogorō. *Tanrokubon: Rare Books of Seventeenth-Century Japan*. Kodansha International Ltd., 1984.

Further Reading

In English

Samurai Heraldry,[52] by Stephen Turnbull, is the best overview of pre-Edo Japanese heraldry available in English. His *The Samurai Sourcebook*,[53] is a good English source for heraldry used by particular notable individuals from the Sengoku period to the dawn of the Edo period, as well as other information such as major battles individuals participated in.

For explanations of mon specifically, John Dower's *The Elements of Japanese Design: A Handbook of Family Crests, Heraldry & Symbolism*[6] is a good English source which talks about history and associations for various motifs.

In Japanese

Two Japanese sources on the heraldry of this time stand out as accessible for using extensive pictures and a straightforward organization: *Sengoku Bushō 100: Kamon, Hata, Umajirushi FILE* (戦国武将100：家紋・旗・馬印FILE; *"100 Sengoku Military Commanders: Family Crests, Banners, and Battle Standards File"*)[31] by Nobunaga Ohno (大野信長) and *Sengoku Bushō "Hata Sashimono" Taikan* (戦国武将「旗指物」大鑑; *"Sengoku Military Commanders 'Flags and Banners' Encyclopedia"*)[19] by Katō Tetsuo (加藤鐵雄).

There are many sources on mon available in Japanese; my favorite was *Kamon no Jiten* (家紋の事典; *"Family Crest Encyclopedia"*)[49] by Takasawa Hitoshi (高澤等), which has good historical context and other supplemental information on various motifs.

For a look at the history of color woodblock printing, *Edo Bungaku 25: Tokushū: Tashoku-zuri no Rekishi to Haikai Ichimai-zuri* (江戸文学 25：特集：多色摺の歴史と俳諧一枚摺; *"Edo Literature 25: Feature: The History of Many-Colored Prints and Haikai Single-Sheet Prints"*),[8] edited by Kira Sueo (雲英末雄), is an excellent source.

Included Images

p. ii Utagawa Yoshikazu
Kawanakajima no kassen
Japanese, 1857
Woodcut, color
35.2 x 24.1 cm (left panel), 35.4 x 24 cm (right panel)
Library of Congress Prints and Photographs Division
FP 2 - JPD, no. 734 a, b (A size) [P&P]

p. iv *Sekigahara Kassen Byōbu*
Japanese, 1854
The Town of Sekigahara Archive of History and Cultural Anthropology
`http://commons.wikimedia.org/wiki/File:Sekigaharascreen.jpg`

Sekigahara Kassen Byōbu
Japanese, late Edo era (19th century)
The City of Gifu Museum of History
`http://commons.wikimedia.org/wiki/File:Sekigahara_Kassen_By%C5%8Dbu-zu_%28Gifu_History_Museum%29.jpg`

p. vii *Shoshō Kisei Zu* (諸将旗旌図)
Japanese, Edo Period, 17th century
Six-panel folding screen: colors on paper
117.8 x 288.5 cm (46⅜ x 113⅜ in.)
Ōsaka Castle Museum Collection

p. viii *Meireki 4 Bukan* (明暦四年武鑑; Meireki Shi-nen Bukan)
Japanese, 1658
Kokugakuin University
`http://k-aiser.kokugakuin.ac.jp/digital/diglib/meireki/mag1/pages/page001.html`

p. ix Yoshida Mitsuyoshi
Shinpen Jinkoki (新編塵劫記 3巻)
National Diet Library, Japan
`http://dl.ndl.go.jp/info:ndljp/pid/3511858/73?__lang=en`

p. xii *Mukujoko-kyo; Vimala-nirbhasea-sutra* Japanese, 764–770
Blockprint in Japanese on paper inside a wooden 3-storey pagoda
Each scroll 45 x 6 cm
The Schøyen Collection, Oslo and London
MS 2489
`http://www.schoyencollection.com/pre-gutenberg-printing/21-2-printing-paper/ms-2489`

p. xiii After Ryūshū Shūtaku
Fudō Myōō and Two Attendants
Japanese, Nanbokuchō period (1336–92)
One of a triptych of hanging scrolls; hand-colored woodblock print on paper
Image: 102.3 x 35.6 cm (40¼ x 14 in.)
The Metropolitan Museum of Art, New York
The Harry G. C. Packard Collection of Asian Art, Gift of Harry G. C. Packard, and Purchase, Fletcher, Rogers
Harris Brisbane Dick, and Louis V. Bell Funds, Joseph Pulitzer Bequest, and The Annenberg Fund Inc. Gift, 1975
1975.268.27
www.metmuseum.org

Printer's woodblock
Japanese, ca. 1730
Wood
27 x 13.7 cm (10⅝ x 5⅜ in.)
The Metropolitan Museum of Art, New York
Rogers Fund, 1918, 18.78
www.metmuseum.org

p. xvii *Sashimono (personal flag)*
Japanese, Azuchi-Momoyama period, 17th century
Dyed silk
73.0 x 156.0 cm
Tokyo National Museum
F-20138-4
http://www.emuseum.jp/detail/100509/004/000

Tosa Mitsunobu
Detail from *Legends about the origin of Kiyomizu-dera Temple, emaki, scroll 1*
Japanese, Muromachi period, 1517
Color on paper
33.9 x 2250.5 cm
Tokyo National Museum
A-43
http://www.emuseum.jp/detail/101303

p. xviii Yukinoshita Sadaiyé (active 17th century)
Detail from *Armor (Gusoku)*
Japanese, 17th century
Iron, lacquer, silk, gilt copper
H. 174.0 cm (68½ in.)
The Metropolitan Museum of Art, New York
Rogers Fund, 1904, 04.4.9a–l
www.metmuseum.org

School: Kutsuwanaoshi School, Japanese
Tsuba with design of paulownia crest Japanese, Momoyama–Edo period, early to mid-17th century
Main material: iron; decorative technique: forging and engraving
Overall: 9.6 x 9.1 x 0.4 cm (3¾ x 3⁹⁄₁₆ x ³⁄₁₆ in.)
Museum of Fine Arts, Boston
Special Chinese and Japanese Fund, 13.2162
www.mfa.org

Mounting for a sword of the tachi type with decoration of crests
Japanese, Edo period, 17th century
Silk, leather, gold
Tsunagi (wooden blade): Honaki wood (Magnolia Obovata)
Overall: 109.5 x 15.5 cm (43⅛ x 6⅛ in.)
Museum of Fine Arts, Boston
Charles Goddard Weld Collection, 11.5097b
www.mfa.org

p. xix *Helmet (Hoshi Kabuto)*
Japanese, 14th century
Iron, lacquer, leather, silk, copper-gold alloy (shakudō)
26.7 x 43.8 cm (10½ x 17¼ in.); Wt. 3120 g (6 lb. 3 oz.)
The Metropolitan Museum of Art, New York
Gift of Bashford Dean, 1914, 14.100.44
www.metmuseum.org

Photograph by Vassil
Harikake kabuto
Japanese, early Edo Period, 17th century
Photographed at Ann and Gabriel Barbier-Mueller Museum
Licensed under CC0 via Wikimedia Commons
https://commons.wikimedia.org/wiki/File:MAP_Expo_Oitaragainari_kawari_kabuto_XVII_02_01_2012.jpg

Helmet (Suji-kabuto Akoda-nari)
Japanese, late 15th–16th century
Iron, lacquer, copper, gold, silk
The Metropolitan Museum of Art, New York
Rogers Fund, 1913, 13.112.10
www.metmuseum.org

p. xxiii *Sasa Rindo*
Licensed under CC BY-SA 3.0 via Wikimedia Commons
http://commons.wikimedia.org/wiki/File:Sasa_Rindo.svg

Mukai
Japanese crest chigai Takanoha
Licensed under CC BY-SA 3.0 via Wikimedia Commons
http://commons.wikimedia.org/wiki/File:Japanese_crest_chigai_Takanoha.svg

p. xxvi Mukai
Japanese Crest Karahana
Licensed under CC BY-SA 3.0 via Wikimedia Commons
http://commons.wikimedia.org/wiki/File:Japanese_Crest_Karahana.svg

Detail from the "Yadorigi" chapter of the *Illustrated Handscroll of the Tale of Genji*
Japanese, late Heian period
Tokugawa Art Museum
http://commons.wikimedia.org/wiki/File:Genji_Emaki_Yadorigi3.JPG

Kanō Yoshinobu
Detail from *Battle Scenes of Genji and Heishi at Yashima*
Japanese, 17th century
Paper, gold, color
154.5 x 351 cm
Kobe City Museum
https://www.google.com/culturalinstitute/asset-viewer/battle-scenes-of-genji-and-heishi
-at-yashima/cwHHb1m8QVdiWg

p. xxvii Hidanokami Korehisa
Detail from *Illustrated story of The Late Three Years War, scroll 1*
Japanese, Nanbokuchō period, 1347
Color on paper
45.7 x 1957.4 cm
Tokyo National Museum
A-11187

p. xxix Mukai
Japanese Crest Ume
Licensed under CC BY-SA 3.0 via Wikimedia Commons
http://commons.wikimedia.org/wiki/File:Japanese_Crest_Ume.svg

p. xxx Detail from *Illustrated Tale of the Heiji Civil War: Scroll of the Imperial Visit to Rokuhara*
Japanese, Kamakura period, 13th century
Color on paper
42.2 x 952.9 cm
Tokyo National Museum
Donated by Matsudaira Naoaki, A-9976

Artist Unknown, Japanese
Avenue of Crested Curtains, from Vol. 8 of Soga monogatari (The Tale of the Soga Brothers)
Japanese, Edo period, 1663 (Kanbun 3)
Woodblock print (sumizuri-e); ink on paper
One page; 22.5 x 16.3 cm (8⅞ x 6⁷⁄₁₆ in.)
Museum of Fine Arts, Boston
Gift of Mrs. Jared K. Morse in memory of Charles J. Morse, 53.2765
www.mfa.org

p. xxxi Hishikawa Moronobu (菱川師宣)
Detail from *A Visit to the Yoshiwara*
Japanese, late 1680s
Ink, color, and gold on paper
21¼ x 693 in.
John C. Weber collection
http://scrolls.uchicago.edu/scroll/visit-yoshiwara

Detail from *The area in and around the Kyoto city (Funaki version)*
Japanese, Edo period/17th century, circa 1615
Color on gold-leafed paper
162.7 x 342.4 cm each
Tokyo National Museum
A-11168
http://www.emuseum.jp/detail/100318

Attributed to Kano Takanobu (1571–1618)
Scenes in and around the Capital (rakuchū-rakugai zu)
Japanese, Momoyama period (1573–1615)
Pair of six-panel folding screens; ink, color, and gold on gilded paper
Each, 81.3 x 265.4 cm (32 in. x 8 ft. 8½ in.)
Fukuoka City Museum

Ciphers
Kawara Museum (91)
Photographed at the Kawara Museum
Licensed under CC BY-SA 3.0 via Wikimedia Commons
http://commons.wikimedia.org/wiki/File:Kawara_Museum_(91).JPG

xxxii *Fragment of Bugaku costume*
Japanese, Heian or Kamakura period, 12th or 13th century
Silk, patterned gauze, embroidered with silk
Overall: 21.6 x 26cm (8½ x 10¼in.)
Museum of Fine Arts, Boston
Gift of Yamanaka & Co., 35.1964
www.mfa.org

Portrait of a Warrior
Japanese, Momoyama period, late 16th century
Hanging scroll; ink and color on silk
Image: 121.4 x 85.2 cm (47¹³⁄₁₆ x 33⁹⁄₁₆ in.)
The Metropolitan Museum of Art, New York
Purchase, 2003 Benefit Fund, 2004, 2004.309
www.metmuseum.org

Surcoat (Jinbaori)
Japanese, 17th century
Silk, felt, metallic thread, wood, lacquer
97.3 x 63.3 cm (38⅜ x 25 in.)
The Metropolitan Museum of Art, New York
Purchase, Charles and Ellen Baber Gift, 2006, 2006.95
www.metmuseum.org

Appendices

p. xxxiii Tosa Mitsunobu
Detail from *Legends about the origin of Kiyomizu-dera Temple, emaki, scroll 1*
Japanese, Muromachi period, 1517
Color on paper
33.9 x 2250.5 cm
Tokyo National Museum
A-43
http://www.emuseum.jp/detail/101303

Toyokuni Utagawa I
Rokō Segawa IV as Tomoe-gozen
Japanese, 1800
Ukiyo-e print
http://commons.wikimedia.org/wiki/File:Rok%C5%8D_Segawa_VI_as_Tomoe-gozen.jpg

Portrait of Naoe Kanetsugu
Japanese, 16th century
Public Domain via Wikimedia Commons
Yonezawa City Uesuki Museum
http://commons.wikimedia.org/wiki/File:Naoe_Kanetsugu02.jpg

Torii Kiyonobu (1664–1729)
Dekishima Hanya Seated on a Cherry Tree
Japanese, Edo period, ca. 1700–05
Polychrome woodblock print; ink and color on paper
55.9 x 32.4 cm (22 x 12¾ in.)
The Metropolitan Museum of Art, New York
The Francis Lathrop Collection, Purchase, Frederick C. Hewitt Fund, 1911, JP649
www.metmuseum.org

p. xxxvi *Clothing tray (midarebako) with decoration of shells, autumn grasses and crests*
Japanese, Momoyama period, end of the 16th century
Kodai-ji ware. Wood; lacquer with gold, silver maki-e decoration
56.6 x 53.3 x 7.7 cm (22⁵⁄₁₆ x 21 x 3¹⁄₁₆ in.)
Museum of Fine Arts, Boston
Keith McLeod Fund, 1998.58
www.mfa.org

Stationery Box in Kōdaiji style
Japanese, Momoyama period (1573–1615), early 17th century
Gold- and silver-foil inlay, gold maki-e, on lacquered wood
21 x 15.6 cm (8¼ x 17¹⁵⁄₁₆ in.)
The Metropolitan Museum of Art, New York
Purchase, Lila Acheson Wallace Gift, 1987, 1987.82a, b
www.metmuseum.org

Kōami School
Portable Writing Cabinet with Tokugawa Family Crests, Chrysanthemums, and Foliage Scrolls
Japanese, Edo period (1615–1868), late 17th century
Lacquered wood with gold and silver takamaki-e, hiramaki-e, and applied gold foil on nashiji ground
22.9 x 21.6 x 37.1 cm (9 x 8½ x 14⅝ in.)
The Metropolitan Museum of Art, New York
Bequest of Stephen Whitney Phoenix, 1881, 81.1.133a–h
www.metmuseum.org

Dish with Design of Rafts, Oars, Caps, and Tokugawa Family Crest of Hollyhocks
Japanese, Edo period (1615–1868), end of the 17th century
Porcelain with underglaze blue (Hirado ware)
Diameter 20.3 cm (8 in.)
The Metropolitan Museum of Art, New York
Gift of Charles Stewart Smith, 1893, 93.3.461
www.metmuseum.org

xxxvii *Raiban (Abbot's seat) with gentian flower roundel design*
Japanese, Kamakura period, 13th century
Maki-e lacquer
Tokyo National Museum
http://commons.wikimedia.org/wiki/File:Raiban_(Abbot%27s_seat),_Kamakura_period,_13th_century,_gentian_flower_roundel_design_in_maki-e_lacquer_-_Tokyo_National_Museum_-_DSC05111.JPG

Quiver (ebira)
Japanese, Early Edo period, 17th century
Bamboo, leather, lacquer, fur, horn, snakeskin
Ann and Gabriel Barbier-Mueller Collection

Attributed to Tosa Mitsumochi (active 1525–ca. 1559)
Detail from *Red and White Poppies*
Japanese, Momoyama (1573–1615)–Edo (1615–1868) period, early 17th century
Six-panel folding screen; ink and color on gilt paper
167.0 x 374.7 cm (65¾ x 147½ in.)
The Metropolitan Museum of Art, New York
H. O. Havemeyer Collection, Gift of Mrs. Dunbar W. Bostwick, John C. Wilmerding, J. Watson Webb Jr., Harry H. Webb, and Samuel B. Webb, 1962, 62.36.1
www.metmuseum.org

xxviii Kano school
Kanô Namban-ji
Japanese, circa 1600
Public Domain via Wikimedia Commons
http://commons.wikimedia.org/wiki/File:Kan%C3%B4_Namban-ji.jpg

p. 20 Detail from *Armor of the* Tachidō *Type*
Japanese, Early Edo period, 17th century
Iron, gold, lacing, bear fur, silver, wood, leather, horsehair
Ann and Gabriel Barbier-Mueller Collection

Appendices

p. 46 Samuraiantiqueworld
Antique Japanese tusurumaki, a woven holder for a bow string
Licensed under CC BY 3.0 via Wikimedia Commons
`http://commons.wikimedia.org/wiki/File:Tsurumaki_string_holder_3.JPG`

p. 179 Detail from *The area in and around the Kyoto city (Funaki-version)*
Japanese, Edo period/17th century, circa 1615
Color on gold-leafed paper
162.7 x 342.4 cm each
Tokyo National Museum
A-11168
`http://www.emuseum.jp/detail/100318`

p. 203 PHGCOM
Kobundō, "Fixed" Tei mark (定), Ishime (石目) emblem.
Photographed at Japan Currency Museum
Licensed under Creative Commons Attribution-Share Alike 3.0 via Wikimedia Commons
`https://commons.wikimedia.org/wiki/File:Kobundo_4.jpg`

Glossary

ashigaru (足軽): foot soldiers, generally peasants hired or conscripted by samurai leaders. Ashigaru were commonly armed with pole arms, bows, swords, and (after the arrival of the Portuguese) guns.

ban (番): a guard, a member of an elite samurai guard unit

ban-sashimono (番指物): a banner or other device worn on the back by samurai in a *ban* (guard) division.

bukan (武鑑): a book of samurai mon, many of which were published in the Edo period (1603–1868)

chitsuki bata (乳付旗; "loop-attached banner"): a banner attached with loops to both a vertical pole and a horizontal top crosspiece

daimon (大紋; "great mon"): a large-sleeved kimono with enormous mon on the sleeves

daimyō (大名, literally "great name"): hereditary feudal lords who ruled particular territories.

dakuten (濁点): marks (゛) added to a hiragana or katakana character indicating that the syllable should be voiced. In classical Japanese works, dakuten were treated as optional and not always included even for voiced characters.

dashi (出し): a small non-banner object attached like a maneki

fukinuki (吹貫): a large hollow streamer formed of strips of cloth attached to a ring

furigana (振り仮名): small hiragana placed alongside or above kanji to indicate their pronunciation. Furigana are generally used for obscure words that may be unfamiliar, words that may be ambiguous, and in material aimed at children.

gezami (下座見): officials responsible for identifying the heraldry of visiting or passing daimyō and ensuring they were treated with the proper respect

gohei (御幣): a Shintō ritual wand hung with paper strips.

gunbai (軍配): a rigid, non-folding war fan used for signaling, to block arrows, and as a sun shade

han (藩): a geographic domain over which a given daimyō had control. Domains had boundaries unrelated to province boundaries and were ranked according to surveyed rice production.

haguma (白熊): undyed or white yak hair, used for plumes on standards and to imitate hair and moustaches on helmets. The kanji literally mean "white bear".

hentaigana (変体仮名; "alternate characters"): archaic hiragana used for phonetic spelling before the script reform in 1900. They have different origins and shapes than the modern hiragana, but each has the same pronunciation as a modern hiragana and conveys no semantic difference.

hiragana (ひらがな or 平仮名): one alphabet of Japanese syllabic characters, used to write verb endings and some native Japanese words

hishi (菱; "water chestnut"): a rhombus design used in mon, either alone or in stacks of three. See, e.g., the mon used by Matsudaira Emon-no-taifu (see p. 53).

hiōgi (桧扇; "cypress fan"): a folding fan made of distinct wood slats not connected by silk or paper

horo (母衣): a sort of cloak or canopy worn on the back and designed to inflate when the wearer is riding a horse, used for identification and to protect against arrows. They were worn by messengers, bodyguards, and other elite samurai.[52, p. 30]

jibun (自分): "oneself", identifying a device that would identify the daimyō personally, either worn by him or carried by a personal assistant that would keep close

jinbaori (陣羽織): a long sleeveless coat worn over armor before battles

jishin (自身): "oneself", effectively a synonym for *jibun*. Often used in the text of *O-umajirushi* to indicate a daimyō's personal helmet.

jōmon (定紋): a primary or formal mon; the mon a family or individual uses most frequently or regularly.

kachū (家中): "whole family", referring to a device that would be used by a daimyō's family members

kachishu (徒士衆, also read kachishū): humble samurai who served as bodyguards on foot. The kanji literally mean "junior samurai multitude".

kaemon (替紋): a substitute or alternative mon; any mon other than a family or individual's primary jomon.

kage (陰; "shadowed"): describes a mon that's drawn hollow, with an outline rather than filled in.

kamon (家紋): mon associated with a particular family

kana (仮名): Japanese phonetic characters, comprised of the hiragana and katakana alphabets

kanji (漢字): logographic characters imported from China

kataginu (肩衣): a formal sleeveless jacket generally worn with a formal kimono and hakama (pleated trousers)

katakana (カタカナ): one alphabet of Japanese syllabic characters, used in modern Japanese for foreign loanwords and for emphasis. In *O-umajirushi*, katakana is only used for particles (words similar to English prepositions).

kirisaki (切裂, "slashed thing"): a banner with parallel slashes dividing it into streamers

ko-umajirushi (小馬印): lesser standard, the less prestigious or prominent standard for a daimyō who used two standards.

koku (石): a measure of rice representing the amount that would feed one person for a year (about 280 liters). Rice was used to measure income and wealth in feudal Japan, and the various domains were measured by their rice production.

kokuin (刻印; "carved mark"): symbols, usually mon or mon-derived, carved into quarried stone blocks identifying the owner or source

koshisashi (腰指し): an identifying object attached by a cord to a pole, which was worn stuck in the back of the obi of mounted samurai. The kanji literally mean "lower-back identifying [thing]".

kuginuki (釘抜き): a "nail puller", a tool used to remove nails from wood. Describes a geometric mon of a shadowed (hollow) square standing on a corner. See, e.g., the mon used by Nabeshima Ki-no-kami (see p. 220).

kuzushiji (崩し字): cursive (literally "broken") characters

maneki (招き): a small nagare hata attached at the end of the pole of a larger banner

mon (紋): Japanese heraldic crests, similar to Western coats of arms, that identify particular families and institutions.

monchō (紋帳): a book of mon of merchants, actors, or prostitutes, similar to a bukan except in which people it covered

monogashira (物頭): a samurai who commanded a group of ashigaru (foot soldiers). A monogashira could also be called an ashigaru-taishō (足軽大将) or an ashigaru-gashira (足軽頭).

mora: a "short" or "Japanese" syllable represented in Japanese by a single kana or a kana followed by a small 'ya', 'yu', or 'yo'. In Japanese, a mora is called an *on* (音). A Japanese mora is represented in English by a consonant followed by a vowel, a consonant followed by 'y' followed by a vowel, a vowel not preceded by a consonant, a syllabic 'n', or a doubled consonant (glottal stop). A "long vowel" is two morae. For example, "kaemon" is four morae: "ka-e-mo-n", and "Kyūan" is also four morae: "Kyu-u-a-n".

mumajirushi (馬印): the pre-sound-change spelling of "umajirushi"

nagare hata (流れ旗; "flowing banner"): a loose banner attached only to a top crosspiece

nanori (名乗): a formal given name used by samurai and the court nobility.[50, p. 421]

nobori (幟): a tall identifying banner attached to a vertical pole and a top horizontal crosspiece

noren (暖簾): a banner or curtain with vertical slashes

nuikurumi bata (縫いくるみ旗; "sewn and covered banner"): a banner with its vertical pole and horizontal top crosspiece sewn into its edge. This style is less common than the "chitsuki bata" method of attaching the banner to its poles with small strips.

o-umajirushi (御馬印): "honorable battle standards"; "umajirushi" with an honorific prefix

oni (鬼): a type of Japanese monster or demon that features heavily in Japanese folklore, depicted as gigantic humanoid ogre-like creatures with brightly-colored skin.

ryakuji (略字, "abbreviated characters"): a simplified form of a kanji that uses fewer strokes, used in kuzushiji (cursive) writing

saihai (采配): a commander's baton with a tassel made of leather or paper strips or yak hair, used for signaling

sakite (先手): the vanguard or front lines of an army

sashimono (指物, "identifying thing" or 差物, "raised thing"): a banner or other identifying object on a pole that was attached to the back of armor, often used to indicate a samurai's daimyō or unit affiliation.

shaguma (赤熊): red or black dyed yak hair, used in a similar way to *haguma*. The kanji literally mean "red bear", though the term is still used for yak hair dyed black.

shidegasa (四手笠): a standard in the shape of a conical hat with Shintō paper strips hanging from its edge

shidewa (四手輪): a hoop hung with paper strips in a similar way to a *shidegasa*

shihō (四方): a square banner

shihan (四半): a banner half again as tall as it is wide

suhama (洲浜 or 州浜): an abstract geometric design, somewhat resembling a collection of three circles, that supposedly represents a wavy sandbar projecting out into the ocean. Used, for example, by Hine no Oribe (see p. 84).

taifu (大夫 or 大輔): Two different titles in the Ritsuryō system. 大夫 means "greater director", and is the director (長官, kami) title used for the head of an agency (職; shiki), a division above a bureau. 大輔 means "greater assistant" and is a assistant director (次官, suke) title (one level lower) for a ministry (省; shō), which is the division above an agency.

tanzaku etsuru (短冊柄絃): a device resembling a tree with strips of poetry paper tied to its branches

tatemono (立物; "standing thing"): a metal crest, often in the shape of horns, attached to the front of a helmet. Also can be pronounced "datemono".

tentsuki (天衝): a two-pronged helmet crest with a shape similar to a sasumata (刺股), a weapon used to trap criminals non-lethally

tetsubō (鉄棒): a long, thin, wood or iron club with metal studs or spikes.

tomoe (巴): a comma-shaped design associated with Hachiman, Shintō god of archery and war. Variously identified as a whirlpool, an ancient Japanese comma-shaped jewel such as the jewel in the imperial regalia, or with a type of leader wrist guard used by archers.[6, pp. 145-146]

tsukaiban (使番): a battlefield messenger; this was a position given to distinguished samurai.[52, p. 30]

tsūshō (通称): an informal given name for common use, often reflecting birth order[50, p. 425]

tō-uchiwa (唐団扇): another name for a gunbai war fan

uchiwa (団扇): a rigid, non-folding fan, generally approximately round in shape

umajirushi (馬印): the battle standard used by a daimyō. Literally meaning "horse insignia", this could be an ordinary rectangular banner or a more elaborate object on a pole, and was generally carried alongside the daimyō.

ō-umajirushi (大馬印): great standard, the more prestigious or prominent standard for a daimyō who used two standards. Using two standards was a statement of power or societal position, implying that the daimyō commanded a large enough body of troops that multiple standards were necessary. Later in the Edo period the practice of using two standards would be formally restricted to daimyō of a certain income.[53, p. 23]

Periods of Japanese History

The periods of Japanese history are generally based on the effective rulership of Japan, with the exception of the Sengoku period, below.

Nara (710–794): Imperial rule from the capital in modern-day Nara

Heian (794–1185): Rule by the Fujiwara nobility from the capital in modern-day Kyōto

Kamakura (1185–1333): Rule by the Kamakura shōgunate

Kenmu Restoration (1333–1336): Imperial rule under Emperor Go-Daigo

Muromachi (1336–1573): Rule by the Ashikaga shōgunate

Azuchi-Momoyama (1573–1603): Effective rule by Oda Nobunaga (entry 1 on p. 114) and his successor Toyotomi Hideyoshi (entry 3 on p. 114)

Edo (1603–1868): Rule by the Tokugawa shōgunate from their capital in modern-day Tōkyō

The **Sengoku** period is defined by the weakening of Japan's official central government as various samurai factions battled for control over various parts of Japan. Its exact boundaries are a matter of debate; it overlaps both the Muromachi and Azuchi-Momoyama periods, and is sometimes viewed as continuing into the early Edo period. I treat it as starting with the Ōnin War in 1467 and ending with the unification of Japan by Toyotomi Hideyoshi (entry 3 on p. 114) in 1590.

Index

Appendices

Appendices

Appendices

Appendices

CPSIA information can be obtained at www.ICGtesting.com
Printed in the USA
BVOW10s2008180215

388382BV00001B/1/P